The Reluctant Minister

Memoirs by

David W. Torrance

British Library Cataloguing in Publication Data:
a catalogue record for this publication
is available from the British Library

ISBN 978-1-871828-87-0

Typeset in 10.5pt Minion Pro at Haddington, Scotland

Printing and cover design by
West Port Print and Design, St Andrews

Contents

The panels on the cover, from left to right:, represent:

country of China	open Bible
the army	burning bush (Church of Scotland)
Seaside Missions	beehive

You can hear the voice of David Torrance in these pages – his self-deprecating style and his amused smile. David was born into a family who have truly remarkable missionary credentials. Born in China one of six children, he grew up in an atmosphere of scholarship and selfless commitment in the service of the church and of the Lord.

After school and war service, he tells the story of ministry in a variety of parishes, a new town, a city housing scheme, and a rural parish in the Borders. His firm biblical teaching has strengthened people's faith, and his listening ear and his widely-acquired wisdom have won him a high reputation.

This is a book well worth reading, because David has had such a comprehensive connection with parish and scholars and missionaries, and with so many of the major events of his lifetime. Here are the details of an amazing life, and insights into the relevance of the church and the gospel through more than 90 years.

The Very Revd Dr John Miller

I count it a privilege to commend this autobiographical account of the life and service of one of the Church of Scotland's most distinguished ministers. It is a work rich in human interest, redolent of the grace of God, and completely honest in describing both the author's struggles with a sense of call to the ministry, and the highs and lows of subsequent pastoral experience.

His reflections on ministry are of great value. One does not need to agree with every view expressed to recognize in this book the frank and absorbing story of a Christ-centred, people-loving minister, for whom no conceivable calling is more satisfying and fulfilling. To us all, especially those in or contemplating the ordained ministry of the church, it brings illumination, encouragement and challenge, in equal measure. I pray that it will receive a wide readership.

The Rt Revd Dr Angus Morrison

Foreword

In writing my memoirs I never anticipated, nor yet intended, that anyone other than my family should read them. The fact that they are published now and made available to others is due entirely to the persuasive powers of my valued friend, the Revd Jock Stein, whom I have known, along with Margaret, for many years. Jock, while still a student at New College, took part in a mission to my parish in Livingston. Some years later, when working with Home Mission, he led a further mission to my parish in Aberdeen. Our involvement in ministry has brought us together many times. Jock has given considerable encouragement in the writing of these reflections. Having read them, he edited them, and was adamant that others would enjoy and be encouraged by them also.

The title, *The Reluctant Minister*, reflects the struggle which I had over some years in accepting God's call for me to become a minister. I was converted to Christ as a boy aged five at my mother's knee. Christ and the Gospel, prayer and the Word of God, always meant a lot to me. I read the Bible and prayed even through the years when I resisted God's call to ministry. I was for a long time in a somewhat strange position, not unlike that of many others. I wanted Christ and his help, yet was afraid to commit myself unconditionally into his hands, because I was afraid of what God was asking. I knew that God was calling me to be a minister of the Gospel, but nothing attracted me to the ministry. I argued that I had no gifts for that calling. My resistance to God's call, as I have recorded in my memoirs, lasted until shortly after the end of World War II. When I finally surrendered to God's call, the miracle took place. Suddenly to my utter astonishment the call to ministry became very attractive. I was astonished to discover that now I wanted to become a minister! All my previous reluctance vanished.

Over the years I have greatly enjoyed the ministry. I have not found ministry easy. I believe however that there is no calling more satisfying and spiritually fulfilling. I am deeply grateful that God lovingly overcame all my earlier resistance and called me to serve him as a minister and servant of the Gospel.

I sincerely thank Jock Stein for his editing, his encouragement and friendship. This book is published with the prayer that it may encourage others in the Lord's work.

North Berwick, April 2015

Dates

The youngest of six children, I was born to missionary parents in China in 1924, 22nd June. My father's name was Thomas Torrance and my mother was Annie Elizabeth Sharpe.

My siblings were Mary (born 1912, 10th May), Tom (born 1913, 30th August), Grace (born 1915, 7th January), Margaret (born 1917, 30th September), and James (born 1923, 3rd February).

My father was born in 1871, 12th March and in 1896 at the age of 24 arrived in China to be a missionary with the China Inland Mission (CIM). In 1910, he travelled back to the UK, then returned to China to work with the American Bible Society in 1911. It was in China that he met my mother.

She was born in 1883 23rd October and had travelled to China in 1907, also at the age of 24, to be a missionary with the CIM. They met in Sichuan, married in 1911 when my father returned to China. My mother then resigned from the CIM. The first four children were born and then in 1920, the family travelled to Shanghai and on to Scotland for a furlough. They returned to China in 1921.

In 1927, the six children and our parents left China to travel to Scotland. Once the family were settled in Scotland, my father returned to China for seven years until his retirement in 1935.

Note

Some names in the book have been changed to protect the identity of the people concerned.

Chapter 1

Early Days

"Praise the Lord, O my soul; all my inmost being, praise his holy name". "Sing to the Lord, for he has done (and will do) marvellous things". These words of Psalm 103, and 98, which my father loved, encourage us to praise the Lord for his love, his salvation and all the blessings which he showers so continually upon us. They express my gratitude to God for the privilege of being born into a happy Christian home and for the blessings of God which have surrounded my life.

I was born to devoutly Christian parents, for which my siblings and I have always been profoundly thankful to God. Our parents prayed for each of us before we were born, dedicating each one to the Lord to be set aside for the furtherance of the Gospel. As a result each of us has grown up with a strong faith in the Lord and have never doubted Him. Largely as a result of their prayers, their teaching and example, all three of their sons entered the ministry and all three daughters married ministers. Two of their daughters, Grace and Margaret, together with their husbands served for several years as missionaries in Central Africa; in Malawi and Northern Rhodesia (Zambia). Mary's husband, Dr Ronnie S. Wallace, served first as a parish minister in Scotland then as a professor of theology at Columbia Theological Seminary in Decatur, Georgia, U.S.A.

Both my parents, following their conversion, individually answered the call to go as missionaries to China.

Father

My father came from farming stock. He was born in Muirhead Farm, Harthill, Lanarkshire. My grandfather was a dairy farmer. He earned his livelihood travelling around Harthill selling milk, butter and cheese, both of which were made on the farm. Father was the eldest in a family of two sons and three daughters.

The family worshipped in the Kirk of Shotts, a church which many years before had witnessed the greatest spiritual revival which Scotland ever experienced and which in subsequent years led to revivals in other parts of Scotland.

Father was converted in his late teen years, through a neighbouring Free Church minister, Mr Shaw. With his conversion he felt the call to the ministry and to the mission field. Unlike two cousins, Dr David Torrance who went as a missionary doctor to Tiberias, Israel and the Revd John Torrance who went as a missionary to India, my father's family belonged to what was known as the 'Auld Kirk', or Established Kirk, the Church of Scotland. His cousins were Free Kirk.

At that time, our Scottish Foreign Missions all belonged to the Free Kirk. The Auld Kirk had none. This immediately caused my father a dilemma. Although he was converted through a Free Church minister whom he respected and loved, it was too big a thing in those days to cross from the Auld Kirk to the Free Kirk. At the same time my grandfather, despite being a religious man with his own theological library, said to my father that if he went into the ministry of the Auld Kirk at home, he would pay for his way through college, but if he went to the mission field, he would not give him a penny!

My father, convinced that he was called both to the ministry and to the mission field, was therefore dependent on grants and scholarships. Accordingly he studied at Hulme Cliff Methodist College in Derbyshire and (as then named) Livingstone College, London. He was much attached to his parents and later on they did help him financially. He kept his allegiance to the Church of Scotland.

Having been inspired by the work of David Livingstone in Africa, Father first thought to go to Africa with the London Missionary Society (LMS). However the door closed and at 24 years of age he went to China with the China Inland Mission (CIM). He left Scotland in 1895 and arrived in January 1896. After language study near Shanghai he was stationed in Chengdu in the interior Province of Sichuan. He soon gained a remarkable grasp of the language and customs of China, working both in the city and in the outlying district. He served the mission for 15 years after which certain difficulties arose which led him to resign from the CIM and return to Scotland, but not before he was asked to consider taking over the work of the American Bible Society as Superintendent for West China.

When he was in Scotland he attended the famous World Missionary Conference in Edinburgh in 1910. During the conference he was officially offered and accepted the post of Superintendent of the American Bible Society for West China, based in Chengdu. After his return to China he was fully exonerated in regard to the difficulties that had arisen and the Mission apologised for certain false and slanderous accusations which had been made. He, thereafter, along with my mother, had very happy relations with the CIM.

Later he was also made Superintendent of the British and Foreign Bible Society for West China, although continuing to be Superintendent of the American Bible Society, from which he drew his salary and later his pension. Both Societies were based in Chengdu. The American Bible Society also had an office in Chungking for which Father was also responsible. Father was extremely happy in his new work. Clearly his transfer to the American Bible Society was the hand of God. On the first of August 1911, he married my mother, who until then was a single CIM missionary based in Kwan Shien, which was some thirty miles, or a day and half journey travelling on foot, to the west of Chengdu, at the foot of the mountains which bordered Tibet. Mother, although very happy to join my father in his new work, found it quite a wrench to leave the CIM.

In China marriages took place before the British Consul. Thereafter the couple proceeded to a church service. The British Consul told her that whereas she had duly signed the required forms prior to the church service, her husband had signed the required forms the day before! Hence, Mother used to joke throughout their marriage, saying that my father was married to her the day before she was married to him!

If Father was required to do or write something he always endeavoured to do it right away. Procrastination or delay was not in his nature. I often teased him after he returned to Scotland, as when he required to make a journey by train he would book a seat on the train a few days before. On the day of travel, however, he always arrived too early at the station, so often he caught the train before, and because he had not reserved a seat, had to stand!

In his new post Father was his own master and had the freedom to be the pioneer missionary that he was. He worked tirelessly preaching and, with his Chinese colporteur helpers, distributing Bibles and portions of Scripture. He wrote many of his own Gospel tracts and never, as my mother used to say, lost an opportunity to preach the Gospel.

Pandas and Other Interests

My father had a great interest in history, as the Tribute on the next page indicates. He had permission from the authorities to open and explore many of the ancient tombs, and he helped to establish the Museum of West China in Chengdu. He also introduced Western bulls to the mountain people.

From his frequent trips to remote areas he brought back stories of 'unusual bears'. Others were interested in such animals, such as Hugo Weingold who obtained a panda cub in 1916. However my father had seen them and written of them in letters before that. In 1916 he had been in those areas for twenty years. Of course, no Westerner 'discovered' giant pandas, the local peoples knew about them!

The following letter by John Hykes, Agent Secretary for China of the American Bible Society, was treasured by the family (the same thoughts were reflected on his final exit and farewell from China):

Tribute to the Rev. Thomas Torrance, 1920

Dear Mr. Torrance,

I, on the eve of your departure for Scotland on a well earned furlough, wish to assure you of my unqualified satisfaction with the manner in which you conducted the work of Szechuen Sub Agency. During the nine years this field has been under your supervision your personal sales have amounted to 243,677 books and those of your native staff to 908,873 – total of 1,153,490. Such a result in circulating the Scriptures could only be achieved by regular, persistent, unremitting hard work. Your devotion and zeal have commanded my admiration and I often felt worried over your prodigal expenditure of strength and energy. In your work you have been a man of one aim, to distribute the Word of God as widely as possible among the people of Western Szechuen. By this I do not mean that your object has been merely to sell large numbers of books, but to make the purchasers wise unto salvation by explaining to them God's message of salvation through Jesus Christ. I thank God that you never missed an opportunity of preaching to the low and high and that you have always been an evangelist. I know that your efficient help in evangelistic services of many different denominations in Szechuen has been blessed by God and greatly appreciated by missionaries. It does not surprise me that I have frequently had from Szechuen missionaries the highest possible commendation of your character and your work. Recently one said to me "Everybody, both Chinese and Foreigners, in Szechuen love Mr. Torrance".

Your pure life, your high sense of honour and your loyalty to the right have commanded my highest admiration ever since I had the pleasure of knowing you. Your relations to the Chinese have been ideal. You inspired them by example and influenced them by love. I am aware of your friendly relations with officials from governor down, and how they sought your counsel and advice. In the good influence you exercised over them, I am sure you served the cause of Christian missions.

I am very pleased that you have been able to devote some of your holiday vacations and leisure time in investigating the cave burial places dating back over 3,000 years; and this to throw light on an ancient people and civilisation. I am sure that both the home management as well as myself are proud of our "missionary antiquary" as you are dubbed in a late number of the Record.

I wish you and Mrs Torrance and the four lovely children a very happy visit in the home country. I cannot think of any greater pleasure than having you associated with me in work until I am ready to put off the harness.

Yours very sincerely

John R. Hykes, Agency Secretary

In the years that followed he and his helpers distributed many millions of Bibles and portions of Scripture, and over one million in his last year. It was said of him when he retired in 1935 that no one had done more to further the Gospel in West China.

Return to Scotland

Because I left China when I was three years old I do not remember life in China. My earliest memories are of London Zoo which we visited before travelling north to Scotland. The family by then included six children, and we returned to Scotland in 1927. Because of considerable unrest in China, it was thought too dangerous for the family to return to China, so the family remained in Scotland and Father returned to China alone. It was a very difficult decision for my parents who loved each other and a difficult decision for my mother who had felt such a strong call to China. Father would be absent from the family for seven years. He had opened up work in the mountains among the Quiang people and felt that his work must continue. Mother felt that a continuance of her missionary calling was to ensure that the family grew up to love and serve the Lord.

Father finally returned to Scotland in 1935. Aged 64 he was still very active and preached fairly regularly in various churches as well as serving in a number of locums, particularly during the war, sometimes for two years at a time.

Until the end of his life he was a passionate evangelist. He carried Gospel tracts in his pockets and where possible never lost an opportunity to witness to Christ. He could be surprisingly frank and to the point, both in preaching and in personal conversation with others. Yet he had a kindly, gentle, winsome manner and I was never aware of anyone ever being annoyed or upset by what he said. He often preached for me in my first parish. My elders told me that he would say to them, when talking before a church service, "I hope none of you gentlemen indulge in the disgusting habit of smoking", knowing that probably all of them did! However in expressing his own abhorrence of smoking he would say it in a loving way with a sense of humour, so that none were offended. They were very fond of him.

Over the years he influenced a remarkable number of people or was a means of their conversion. One well known minister of the Church of Scotland was converted through my father. One Sunday evening after preaching Father arrived home and put on his slippers. He then, to my astonishment, pulled a tobacco pipe out of his pocket. I said, "Dad you have started smoking!" When he pulled out six pipes and two tobacco pouches, I said in my astonishment, "Dad you have stolen them!" He explained that the minister in whose parish he was preaching told him that he could not give up the habit of smoking. My father in his direct way said, "Let us kneel down and ask God to deliver you and fill you by his Spirit". In rising from his knees Dad said, "Now give me your pipe and tobacco". That was this minister's conversion to Christ. Quite often he would call and visit my father. He said one day to me during a meal that his great regret in the ministry was that he did not meet my father years earlier.

Father had a deep influence on us all. From him, as from mother, we felt that to be a Christian was to witness to Christ and evangelise.

Mother

My mother also was converted in her teen years and with her conversion felt the call to mission and evangelism. Soon she felt the call to Overseas Mission and to China. She studied at Redcliffe College, Chelsea and then in the CIM Mission's Training Home at Grove Park, London. Like Father she was 24 years old when, in 1907, she arrived in China. After language study, again near Shanghai, she was stationed in Kwan Shien, thirty miles west of Chengdu at the foot of the mountains bordering Tibet. She married Father four years later. They had three daughters and three sons, Mary, Tom, Grace, Margaret, James and myself. The family came back to Scotland in 1927.

Whereas Mary, my oldest sister was born in Shanghai, my two other sisters, two brothers and myself were born in Chengdu, in the Province of Szechuan. Despite her family commitments with six children, mother was asked to lead weekly Bible studies for some thirty nurses in the Canadian School, and teach in the Canadian girls' school and a men's college. She taught Bible, grammar, history and literature.

The family left China in 1927 at a time of deep political unrest. Shortly prior to our return to Scotland, a Canadian missionary doctor had been killed in the near-by missionary hospital; a lady missionary friend of my mother's who was staying with us at the time was beheaded in the street very near our house (the intended victim was my mother); and a large and dangerous riot had taken place outside our house when the ring leaders were agitating for the deaths of all Christians and foreigners.

My parents felt that China and particularly the area where we lived was too dangerous for the family to return to China, whereon my father returned to China alone and served another seven years in China.

Father had opened up Christian work and established several churches among the Quiang people, a minority people group of about 300,000 who lived in the mountains to the west of Chengdu. He believed, I think rightly, that they are of Semitic origin. Father was fluent in Mandarin

Chinese and also I understand, one of very few westerners who spoke the Quiang dialect or language. For many years he had worked as the sole white missionary among these Quiang and believed that his work among them was not finished, hence the difficult decision to go back alone.

Father's returning to China alone was a very big and a sacrificial decision for both my parents to take. Father felt the loneliness of the situation, which he mentioned in his letters. He wrote home each week and also wrote individually to us as children. Mother made sure that we each wrote to him each week; we were always mindful of him, so that despite the vast distance between us, he never seemed to be far away. In our daily prayers as a family we always prayed for him and his work. When Father finally returned in the spring of 1935 the whole family went down to the then Caledonian railway station in Edinburgh to meet him. It was a joyful re-union.

For two or possibly three years the family lived in Bellshill near Glasgow, where I commenced school, and then moved to Edinburgh, on Father's recommendations, and stayed in a flat at 25 Warrender Park Road, on the South side of Edinburgh. I think I was six at the time.

Prayer was all Important to my Parents and in our Home

They always emphasised that the Christian life involved a personal relationship with a living Lord. Mother often spoke of the person of the Lord Jesus as someone who was living and alive, someone whom we can meet and know personally and who wanted day by day to speak to us and calls us to obey him. The Christian faith is not just something to be understood intellectually. It is something living and alive and something which the youngest child can relate to and something which relates to our everyday living. For this personal emphasis I have always been deeply grateful to my parents.

My parents also stressed the importance of the Bible as God's Word and the importance of listening to and knowing God's Word. Father to the end of his life could recite the whole book of Psalms and also the Epistle to the Romans. He encouraged us to learn many of the Psalms although none of us managed to memorise them as he did.

The Christian faith affected and controlled the way that we lived as a family. Every day Mother gathered together the family for a reading from God's Word and prayer. The various needs and interests of the members of the family, together with the needs and interests of the wider church were laid before the Lord. We always prayed for Father when he was in China and for his work in China. In addition Mother prayed individually with us before going to bed. Later after his return to Scotland Father as well as Mother led us in family worship.

As a result, like my brothers and sisters, I have never doubted the presence of the Lord. God was always very real and prayer has always been a basic part of my life. As a boy of 4 or 5 years, I remember lying in bed on a summer evening. I did not feel sleepy and for a long time watched a fly buzzing around on the top pane of the window. Again and again it would fly down to the bar in the middle of the window and fly up again. As a child I wanted it out of fun to play on the lower pane but it would not. Therefore I closed my eyes and asked God to put it on the lower window so that it could play there. I opened my eyes and the fly was on the lower window. I remember laughing. I knew it was all a piece of nonsense, but I had a wonderful feeling that God was near. He loved me, was prepared to come down to my level, to listen to and answer my childish prayers. That simple, childish incident meant a lot to me, deepening my awareness of God and the value of prayer. God was always very real to me.

Not only as a family, but also individually, we experienced many answers to prayer. As a family we were each aware and thankful to God for sparing Father's life after he had gone back to China alone and when some communists went in search of Father to kill him. Mother at the time went to a prayer meeting in the local church. Some 27 people were present. When the leader asked whom they should pray for, Mother explained that her husband was a missionary in West China and she felt that he was much in need of prayer at that time. Although those present did not know my father, we were new to the area, several prayed for Father. When Mother wrote and told Father how they had prayed for him he asked for the day and time of that prayer meeting. It so happened that he was in the mountains in the home of a Quiang Christian. The communist soldiers who wished to kill him searched every home in that village except the home in which he was in. They passed the door on the same day and at the same time as the prayer meeting in Bellshill. God answered prayer. Such answers were treasured in the family, long remembered and confirmed our faith in God.

We knew that God had answered prayer many times for the family in China and that without answered prayer the family would never have survived in China.

I was five years old when I gave my life to the Lord and asked that my name be written in the Lamb's book of Life. James did likewise when he was six.

Our parents were concerned that we should each have a thorough knowledge of God's Word. On my sixth birthday my mother showed me a calendar, and told me that there were seven days in a week and fifty two weeks in a year. She said if I read three chapters of the Bible every day and five on Sundays, I would read the whole Bible in a year. It is a custom which the whole family was encouraged to do. Although at six I did not manage to read the recommended chapters every day, I did read the whole Bible before leaving Primary School. I continue to read the Bible every year and have done so for very many years, although in retirement I have been reading the Bible three and sometimes four times, each year. Mother also encouraged me and the others of the family always to pray each time we opened the Bible before reading. We were encouraged to ask the Lord to speak personally to us. She said, which I never forget, that when we grew up we would find that many people would deny that the Bible was God's Word or would say many wrong things about it and deny its inspiration, but if we heard God speaking to us through the Bible and through the passage which we were reading, then we would know that the Bible is God's Word and we would never doubt it. I, and I think the others of the family, were never given any theory about Scripture or its inspiration. We were simply told that it was God's Word and that God spoke to us through it. If we were prepared to listen we would hear him. I have always been grateful for what Mother said and have never doubted God or that the Bible is God's Word.

Primary School

With our moving to Edinburgh, James and I went to James Gillespie's Primary School in Marchmont Road. It was a short distance from our house. It was a good school and we were very happy there, although school discipline was much stricter in those days than it is today. I confess that I was strapped in Primary 1 in Bellshill and last received the strap in form 5 in Secondary School at Blairgowrie! It was not that I was ever really naughty, but I found it hard to concentrate on work at school, enjoyed life, had lots of fun and was rather mischievous.

In my final year at Primary School, in Primary 7, some eleven of us out of approximately twenty five (or possibly more) children gained a scholarship which was open to all Edinburgh schools. Our teacher, Miss Marshall was immensely proud of us and marched us round to stand in front of every class. It was quite an achievement and a great tribute to the teaching which we received. I received an Intermediate scholarship. My brother James had the previous year gained a slightly better award. Our parents used these scholarships to send us to the Royal High School, which was a fee-paying school. The year in which I commenced attending the Royal High school was 1936. Without scholarships our parents could not have afforded to send us there. In our coming to Edinburgh both Grace and Margaret, who were much older and still at school, attended Boroughmuir High School, which academically was and is an excellent school.

My brother James was just over 15 months older than me and in the class immediately ahead of me. We were close friends and knew one another well. James always told me that as regards behaviour he was a 'saint' at school. I doubted it but for a long time was unable to disprove it. I could not make the claim because unfortunately for me in Primary School James had witnessed my being punished with the belt. However, when I went up to High School where we had different teachers according to the various subjects taught, when I said in one class room that my name was Torrance, the teacher immediately said, "Have you a brother in 2A"? When I replied in the affirmative, he immediately asked, "Are you as wild as your brother?" The same question was asked with the same rejoinder in the next class. I thereon went home with great glee to announce what two different teachers had said and that James was not the saint at school which he claimed to be. Some time later I received further proof when James came home with two or three purple bruises on his face and no collar on his shirt. It had been torn off in a fight with a very much older boy and bully who had taken the ball with which James and his class-mates were playing. James, who was always to the fore, tackled the boy but came off worst in the fight.

The Royal High, which was not a large school, had three streams, A, B and C. The A Division, which had the brighter pupils studied Classics which meant learning Latin, along with French, History and Mathematics, from Form 1 and starting Greek in Form 2. Science we dropped at the end of third year, but we continued with Mathematics and History. Pupils in B and C Divisions studied the Science subjects, hopefully to Higher level.

Because I commenced high school with a bursary, I, as was James, was placed in the A Division and remained within it all my time in High School. However, looking back, I have to confess that I largely dreamed my way through most of my early years at High School. I found it hard to take lessons seriously and had a poor academic career. I enjoyed life too much to be overly troubled about studies. In some of my classes I came bottom in the class and had to sit in the front seat, under the strict eye and discipline of the teacher. As a result, I had in the next term done well and been allowed to sit at the back of the class, only to descend to the bottom when no longer working under the strict eye of the teacher! I remember my form master Norman Dixon saying in my third year, "Torrance, I do not understand you. At times I think that you should be at the top of the class and you are at the bottom!" It is a tribute to my various teachers and their commitment to teaching and the welfare of their pupils, for which I am deeply grateful, that I finally passed my senior exams at school and was accepted as a student at university,

As a boy, I played a lot of sport or simply played with friends. On many a Saturday James and I cycled over to Liberton to play with Donald Fleming, whose parents had been missionaries in China. Donald was also a pupil at the Royal High School although he was slightly older. His mother had died and his father was in a nursing home so Donald stayed with his aunt in Kirk Brae, Liberton. She was always kind to us and often invited James and myself to join them for tea. Together we roamed the countryside or played along Blackford Glen. Donald bought an old motor bike which we used to drive up and down the road to Blackford Quarry. Both James and I kept pigeons. Donald also started, so that from time to time we swapped pigeons. Donald however did not follow our interest in keeping bees.

Bee Keeping

Mother was very fond of nature and in walks would draw our attention to the wild flowers, trees and birds. With our frequent playing in the woods at North Berwick, while staying in the caravan on Bass Rock Farm, we became interested in the wild bumble bees. Sometimes we explored a bumble bee's nest, which is a very beautiful thing. Bumble bees do not make wax like the honey bees but store their honey in little sacks about the size of a beech nut. The sacks are rather papery and made of chewed leaves. I remember our gently enlarging the hole into a bumble bee's nest under the roots of a tree, grabbing a handful of little honey sacks and then running away! The honey tastes the same as that of the honey bees. If we were stung in the process it helped us to think that we had earned the honey and not stolen it from the bees!

The father of one of the boys with whom we played in the woods had a swarm of honey bees in an orange box. We would lift the box and look at the bees. I do not remember our being stung in the process, why I do not know. With our interest and enthusiasm in regard to bees, our sister Grace, who was teaching, kindly gave us £3 which enabled us to buy a WBC hive with bees from a farmer, Mr Middleton, in East Lothian. She also gave us seven shillings and sixpence which paid for James to attend a ten week course on bee keeping at the college. James came home and taught me.

I was thirteen when I started bee keeping. It was a hobby which I much enjoyed and continued with for over 50 years. We kept the bees in the garden in Edinburgh at 12 Chalmers Crescent. In our early days, in catching swarms and looking after the bees we often did things which later I discovered were wrong and unhelpful. We learned the hard way but enjoyed it.

When I stayed with Tom in Alyth, Saul Thompson, an elder and farmer, bought five empty bee hives at a market. He gave two to his son Gordon and kindly gave me three. The very next day when I came home from school I discovered to my delight that a swarm of bees had moved into one of the hives. Thereafter I set about building bee hives. Tom kindly provided money for me to buy the necessary combs and bee appliances, so that very soon I had twelve bee hives.

With raspberry bushes in the field over the wall and next to the garden, and a lack of spraying of the raspberry bushes, which in later years was so disastrous to bees, it was almost impossible not to have a goodly supply of honey. So began our selling of honey to make pocket money.

My bee protection clothing in those days was very inadequate so that I frequently got stung. Sometimes, having discovered that, at a meal time, we had no honey on the table, I rushed out and hastily took off some honey from one of the hives, without troubling to put on a hat and veil or use smoke. Several times I was stung on the face and, with the swelling, an eye closed. My cure on those days was to jump on my bicycle and go for a long run. I found that the cold air soon reduced the swelling and enabled me to see.

High School

With our many and happy ploys, I often dreamed through classes at school about them, instead of concentrating on what was being taught. Inevitably, in my early years at high school, I did not do so well as I should have done, had I been able to concentrate on school work.

In my school years, I never asked for, nor received, help from my parents in regard to homework or school lessons, although they liked it if and when I did well, which was not often. At the end of my third year, I came bottom of class 3A. The Form teacher wrote in my Report Card, for which I required a parent's signature, that I played far too much sport. I gave it to my father, without my saying anything. He read it, signed it, looked at me very sorrowfully but never said a word.

Because of my parents' attitude, I never felt as do many children, to be under any pressure to do well at school, for which I am deeply grateful. They had faith in the Lord that in the end all would be well and I would go on to university. Their one great concern was that I, and each of us, grow up as men and women who love the Lord and live good profitable Christian lives. That for them was what mattered. Their concern was our spiritual, not academic development.

Evacuation

By the summer of 1939 it was clear that war with Germany was imminent. The government was recommending and making plans for children in the major cities to be evacuated to places in the country, away hopefully from air attacks and bombing. My eldest sister Mary and her husband Ronnie Wallace were staying in the Manse of Crosshill, Ayrshire, where he was minister. Crosshill is a lovely country parish in south Ayrshire. Mother immediately planned for James and me to stay with Mary and Ronnie, who also agreed to welcome Ronnie's brother George's young family, although they did not stay for more than a few months. James and I attended Maybole Academy. I was now in my fourth year of high school and James in his fifth.

The Royal High School along with the Merchant Schools of Edinburgh had, and continue to have an excellent academic and sporting record. We found things to be very different in Maybole. Academically it was a good school but the ethos was very different; there was not the same emphasis on sport and many, perhaps most pupils, were not motivated to go on to further education. The Manse at Crosshill had a large garden and we much enjoyed country life. We often played with the children in a local farm, doing many things which we could not do in the city.

My brother Tom was inducted as parish minister of the parish of Alyth in Perthshire in the spring of 1940. Tom was then unmarried and my mother immediately felt that I should leave Crosshill and stay with Tom and keep him company. James continued to stay in Crosshill, and continued attending Maybole Academy, where he passed his Higher Examinations and became school sports' champion. After staying in Alyth with Tom and myself, over the summer, in October 1940 James returned to stay with my parents in Edinburgh and commenced studies at Edinburgh University.

Alyth

For me, the decision to stay in Alyth with Tom was a very happy one. Tom and I seemed to get along very well together. He was over 11 years older than me, and I came to know him much better. I enjoyed his company and I believe he enjoyed mine. We always had a very happy relationship. When he was free we often played chess together and sometimes went trout fishing together. Tom had a housekeeper, Mrs Edwards, who cooked and cleaned the house.

My parents, and Mother particularly, although not overly concerned about my school work, continued to be concerned about our Christian understanding and education. In addition to daily prayers and their regular teaching of Scripture they encouraged us in our reading of Christian books and theology. We were encouraged to read Bunyan's *Pilgrim's Progress*, Martin Luther's commentary *Epistle to the Galatians*, Robert Bruce on *The Mystery of the Lord's Supper* and Samuel Rutherford's *Letters*, all of which were among my mother's favourites. At Alyth, I read Martin Luther's *Bondage of the Will*, and was introduced to Calvin's *Institutes*.

Both Father and Mother played a big part in our Christian upbringing. Father, as a minister and evangelist, with his wide knowledge of Scripture and grasp of Scottish theology, always held before us the importance for Christians to actively witness to Christ. Mother's influence was different but complementary. Tom often referred to Mother as the theologian of the family. She was the one who first introduced Tom to Karl Barth giving him Barth's book on the creeds, *Credo*. She possessed through her knowledge of Scripture, remarkable spiritual insight. I owe much of my early understanding of Scripture to her. At Alyth I was able to discuss theology and what I read with Tom and learned much from him.

Blairgowrie High School

After Easter, 1940, I enrolled at Blairgowrie High School. It was over five miles distant and I normally cycled to school, having been given my brother-in-law, Bobby Walker's bicycle when he went to Africa. I was now in my third term of the 4th year at high school. I dropped the study of French (which I later regretted) but continued studying English, Latin, Greek, History and Mathematics. Gradually I came to concentrate better on my school work, although without the more disciplined approach of the Royal High School and no organised sport, to which I was accustomed, I got into various mischievous scrapes and found myself being called into the head master's room on a fairly regular basis! He did not punish me but lectured me! I passed my Higher Examinations in my fifth year. Because, however, I wanted to pursue Latin and Greek at University and did not, despite the pass, achieve a sufficiently high mark, for my sixth year at school I returned to Edinburgh and to the Royal High School in September 1941.

The Royal High School emphasised the teaching of the classics, Latin and Greek, which I found helpful. After gaining higher marks in Latin and Greek and in anticipation of entering university, I sat an open scholarship examination for those seeking to enter the ministry. Father was retired and my parents did not have sufficient money to pay for my university fees. Candidates sitting the exam could choose four subjects in which to be examined. I chose Latin, Greek, English and I think Mathematics, but it may have been History, I do not remember. For both Latin and Greek there were several books that were prescribed. In the weeks leading up to the examination I worked extremely hard. Five of us sat the exam and to our surprise all five of us were awarded a scholarship! Possibly being war time, there had been a lack of candidates and money had accumulated. The other candidates were Ian Pitt Watson (who became a professor of Practical Theology), Alex Cheyne (who became a professor of Church History), Bill Macdonald (who became a moderator of the General Assembly, having gained a first class honours in Classics) and Bobby Henderson (who was a neighbouring minister in Melrose when I was minister in Earlston, and gained, I think, a first class honours in History). We were not told who had come first in the examination or how we compared to one another.

My obtaining the scholarship was a great blessing financially. I applied and was awarded along with it, a Carnegie Scholarship.

Potato Rogueing

In 1940 when James and I were at Alyth, a farmer, Saul Thomson suggested that James and I take a two week course at the Agricultural College in Edinburgh in order to qualify as potato roguers. Saul Thompson was a very fine elder of the Barony Church of which Tom was a minister. Saul Thompson and his partner Willie Muir were the largest seed potato merchants in Scotland, supplying both Scotland and England. After attending lectures for two weeks, we were required to sit an examination covering over sixty varieties of potato and the various diseases to which potatoes can be subject. After passing successfully we were given an agricultural certificate qualifying us to work as potato roguers. In those days, if students gained over 70 per cent in their examination, they could apply to the Agricultural Board to be employed as a potato inspector. Both James and I gained over 70 per cent but in loyalty to Saul Thompson who had recommended us to the college we worked as roguers for him. We started at seven in the morning and worked, with a break for lunch, until five in the afternoon. Occasionally, under pressure we worked from 6pm to 9pm but found that physically tiring. We calculated that each day we walked about eleven or twelve miles up and down the drills between the potatoes.

We enjoyed the work. We were out in the fresh air in all weathers in lovely country. We also felt and enjoyed the challenge. Our skill as roguers was being tested. After we had rogued a field the field was inspected and the potatoes classified Stock Seed, A, B or H. In those days, between

Stock seed and Class A, there was £2 per ton of potatoes difference. There was £1 per ton difference between class A and class B and £1 difference between class B and class H. Only on one occasion did a field which we rogued fail to win the desired class certificate. The inspectors were young and although the farmer was content and told us not to worry, we felt that our reputation was at stake and urged the farmer to appeal. As a result the senior inspector and a colleague examined the field, upgraded the classification, commended the roguers and advised the farmer not to lose them. His recommendation greatly helped us. When at the end of the season James told Saul Thompson that we were not coming back the following year but were applying to be inspectors, he asked what an inspector was paid. We informed him that as roguers we were paid £1 per day but an inspector was paid £2 per day. He promptly offered to pay us £2 per day. On the ground that inspectors generally only worked for three weeks but we as roguers were able to work for six, we agreed to continue working as roguers.

For a six day week we each received £6 and more if we worked overtime. In our second year we received £12 per week and more if we worked in the evening. In 1941 and 1942 that was a considerable wage! Along with our academic scholarships, we were able to finance our academic education and contribute to our expenses at home, living with our parents.

Over the years, in three separate churches, I have recommended to my young people who were studying at university and seeking summer jobs, to apply for potato rogueing. I was unsuccessful and did not persuade anyone apart from my own family! Grace, David and Ruth each rogued potatoes in the summer. Students I think were not attracted to working in the open air in all weathers.

Fishing etc

Living with Tom at Alyth I enjoyed tremendous freedom. I soon met and came to know some of the young people who belonged to the church of which Tom was minister. James Lindsay was a farmer, an elder in the church and had a large family of one daughter and six sons. Tom and I were often in their house and some of their sons were fairly near to my own age. They taught me to shoot rabbits and hares. Today, I do not enjoy killing animals for sport, but being young I enjoyed it then.

Saul Thompson, who was an elder and farmer had two sons, Gordon and David. Gordon was apt to be a 'harem scarem'. He was about my age and often we went out together after rabbits or other game.

I became particularly friendly with Harry Williams. His father was an elder and gardener. He attended to the Manse garden and taught me how to tend and prune fruit trees, which I appreciated. Harry had an older sister and a younger brother. His sister became a nurse and he and his brother both became doctors. Harry and his brother taught me how to 'guddle' trout, that is catching trout with one's hands. Both were expert – I would have four while they would have twelve. Harry and I often cooled off on a hot day in some of the pools of the Alyth burn.

I first fished with a rod on the river Girvan, in Ayrshire, and remember catching one trout. On that occasion I met the village poacher who showed me how to catch trout using only a landing net. That is illegal and today I would not do it, but as a boy occasionally when I was not catching fish with the rod, I used the landing net successfully.

It was at Alyth that I really learned the art of bait fishing. One very wet evening, Saul Thompson and the former minister of Alyth, another Mr Thompson, who with his wife was staying with Saul and his wife at the time, took me with them up to the head of Glen Isla beyond the Tulchan Lodge. It was a wet evening and rained continually but the minister taught me where to find trout and how to catch them. Under his guidance I caught six that evening and after that went fishing many times on my own. On occasion I arose at five o'clock on a Saturday morning and cycled up Glen Isla and fished in the burn that flows out of a Loch. I fished the pools below Reekie Lynn and good stretches of the river up Glen Isla and some times stretches of the river in Strathmore, near Meigle. A favourite place where I often fished was Tully Murdoch, a hill burn which flowed into the Alyth Burn. When I left the army in September 1946, James and I fished one Friday at Tully Murdoch. We started at 11 o'clock and fished on to 7.00pm. We fell into a keen competition, whereon I caught 60 trout and James 67! I believe the day when that is possible has long gone.

Poles and Italians

At the end of the street on which the manse was situated there was a wooden Scout hut. That had been commandeered by the army because a contingent of Polish soldiers were stationed in Alyth. A group of Polish doctors, who were Jewish, some of whom were highly trained and skilled, were billeted there. Some six or seven of them often visited us in the manse and I used to play chess with some of them, who impressed me by their knowledge of Greek.

Anti-Semitism had for generations been endemic in Poland, hence Hitler located some of his worst death camps for killing Jews in Poland. As a result, the Jewish Polish doctors who came to the manse were privates. They were not commissioned and not permitted to practice medicine in the Polish army. They were compelled to do many of the more menial tasks in the army, such as peeling potatoes, washing dishes and sweeping floors. They told us that the only person who was permitted to practice medicine in the Polish unit in Alyth was a vet!

That was my first encounter with anti-Semitism. I was astounded as a boy to discover that a Polish soldier in Alyth could only be attended to by a vet and not by a Polish doctor, who was skilled, because he was a Jew. Those who came to the manse were very keen that Tom should help them and recommend that they be transferred to the British Army where they would be accepted as doctors. I do not know the outcome of these recommendations.

Between Alyth and Meigle which was less than three miles south of Alyth was a prisoner of war camp. I think many of the prisoners were Italians. I often saw them being conveyed up Glen Isla where they helped to cut down trees. I used to wonder at what seemed to be a fairly relaxed oversight of these prisoners, and tended to think that the Italians, in particular, appreciated being out of the war.

Bombing Raids

In Alyth we escaped the bombings which took place first in part of Edinburgh and then in Clydeside. Because of the heavy defences in the Forth Valley quite a number of German planes came north to Dundee, flew along Strathmore and then down to Glasgow. Only on one occasion do I remember bombs being dropped a little way outside of Alyth, I think in response to a car's lights. However, we often watched them on their way to Glasgow and Clydeside. At night we saw the search lights, and quite often a plane being caught in the beams of the search lights. On such occasions we could see the tracer shells that were fired.

At that time, and because of the bombing, my sister Mary with her child, David, came to stay at Alyth. Having moved from Crosshill, her husband Ronnie Wallace now had a parish in Shawlands, Glasgow.

In the summer of 1940, Tom, James, I and some three others camped up at the head of Glen Isla, in the Cannes, some four or five miles north of the Tulchan Lodge. After about 12 days, because of the commencement of deer shooting, we were asked to move further down Glen Isla. After spending a long day on the hills, we packed our tents and trudged down the four or five miles to the Tulchan Lodge and pitched our tents in Glen Brichty. It was midnight before we were finally settled. Having forgotten about the war and the need for complete blackout, we had a large fire burning. We had just made a large pot of tea before turning in. Suddenly we heard a German bomber coming up the Glen toward us. Clearly it had seen our camp fire. It was flying low and making toward us. We immediately threw our tea on the fire to dampen the flames, and crouched round holding a blanket to conceal the hot embers. The plane flew directly overhead and a few moments later released its load of six bombs. Mercifully they landed a few hundred yards away on the other side of a hill and did no damage, apart from blowing six holes in the hillside. We were afraid to light any more fires!

In Alyth however there was always strict attention to fire-watching in the centre of the village. Although a boy, I regularly took my turn at fire-watching. A telephone and fire-bucket were provided. An air-raid alarm would be sent when enemy planes crossing our shores threatened to come near. If we received such a warning we were required to pass it on and take the prescribed action in case of fire, as a result of bombing. Thankfully we never were bombed.

Return to Edinburgh

Although I came back to Edinburgh in time to recommence studying at the Royal High School, in the autumn of 1941, both James and I returned to Alyth for the summer, until university commenced in October. We both joined the armed forces. I enlisted in the army in December 1942 and James joined the RAF early in 1943 and in the same year Tom went off to serve with the Church of Scotland Canteen service and acted as an army chaplain first in North Africa and then in Italy.

In Alyth I enjoyed Tom's companionship and learned much from him. I loved Glen Isla, the hills and the country around Alyth. I enjoyed fishing and bee-keeping, and many happy times with friends.

No one could have had a happier childhood. I belonged to and grew up in a very loving, happy Christian family. I never ever heard my parents argue, quarrel or raise their voices. They could be strict but did not administer corporal punishment. Mother's form of punishment was to send a child to his/her room and ask him/her to meditate and ask "What is God thinking?" They were always kind and loving. Once in China when Tom had misbehaved, Father uncharacteristically told Tom to go and bring a stick. Tom went away and came back with a straw! This became a family joke. I never remember any quarrels or arguments among my siblings. We were a united family always supportive of one another. On the very rare occasion when I disagreed with James, the disagreement was over in minutes. We were always the closest of friends.

With the Psalmist I can truly say: "Lord, you have assigned me my portion and my cup; you have made my lot secure; the boundary lines have fallen for me in pleasant places; surely I have a delightful inheritance" (Psalm 16:5,6). Praise the Lord!

Chapter 2

Military Service: 1942-1946

According to my military papers I served in the army in the Royal Scots from 24th Dec. 1942 to 24th Feb. 1944, and in the Royal Signals from 25th Feb. 1944 to 2nd Sept. 1946. For the first eight months I was a soldier in the Territorial Army. Prior to that I served in the JTC (Army Junior Training Corp) in my sixth year in the Royal High School in Edinburgh and in the STC (Army Senior Training Corp, formerly Officer Training Corps or OTC) on my enrolment as a student in Edinburgh University. As I was born on the 22nd of June, 1924 I expected to be called into national service in the summer of 1942 when I turned 18. As that did not happen I commenced studies at university.

Army Selection Board

During the war, courses were run in the universities to train people for the specialised branches of the armed forces. These courses lasted six months. Having already commenced university study, I was included in one of these courses. Along with a few others I was asked if I would like to join the Army Intelligence Service and learn Japanese. Perhaps foolishly I declined. Thereon I was called to meet before an Army Selection Board. Their concern was to direct students into the branches of the armed forces where special skills were required. Latin and Greek, which I was studying, were, of course, of no use to the military. I was told that at that time there was considerable need for people in signal communication and I was assigned to the Royal Corp of Signals. I was advised to study such subjects as electronics, which to me sounded horrific. It is not advisable to commence military service by arguing with the commanding officer or the chairman of a Military Board, but I did! I said no matter what the need of the army was, I wished to join the infantry. The chairman of the Board, a colonel or brigadier, unaccustomed to anyone objecting to the Board's direction, or command, promptly over-ruled my objections and said, "Signals! Dismiss!" To my surprise, the adjutant, a captain in the Royal Scots asked, "Could we make one exception?" Thereon, and again to my surprise, the chairman said, "Agreed! One exception! Infantry! Dismiss".

Looking back I think that anyone in wartime who has the opportunity to enter some other branch of the army as I did but volunteers for the infantry is crazy! I was young and, at the time, I was much relieved to have my wishes granted. I joined the Royal Scots. This entailed a medical examination, taking the oath of loyalty to king and country and receiving my first day's pay, two shillings (10p). I was given, not a conscription number but a regimental number normally given to regular soldiers, namely 3067344. As such I became in army records, a volunteer.

Territorial Army

Having been granted permission to study at university for the next six months, with the original intention that I would enter a specialised branch of the army, I was enlisted as a member of the Territorial Army. I did not think about it at the time but in so far as I had enlisted in infantry and not in one of the specialised branches of the armed services I should not, I believe, have been allowed to continue my studies at University. However an exception had been made in my case. The consequences of that exception were not carried through. Hence, having enlisted in the Royal Scots, an infantry regiment, I simply continued my study of Latin and Greek. The six months that were allotted ended for me after the middle of June. My degree exams took place at the end of the first week in June. I passed them successfully and therefore completed my first year at university before going off on full time military service.

Having enlisted in the army I was required, while at university, to do military service every Friday so that I could not attend any university classes that day. My classes, in Latin and Greek, were not arranged to suit my military responsibilities, as I assume would have been the case if I had been preparing for one of the specialised branches of the army.

Military duties occupied most Sunday afternoons and often several weekends. As far as I remember they also occupied each Tuesday evening and, on many occasions, lasted all Tuesday night until the following morning. I always returned in time to attend morning classes at university on a Wednesday morning.

Battle exercises were generally very strenuous. On one occasion when running with a mortar gun in addition to my rifle and pack I strained a muscle in my leg. Doctors advised that I should temporarily cease military service. Not wishing to do that, I temporarily became attached to the Royal Signals, which I quite enjoyed.

A Mock Battle

In May, for the Victoria holiday weekend, my unit was involved in a mock battle with the Polish Tank Corps. It lasted from Friday morning until Wednesday morning. We spent our first night in the Lammermuir Hills above the village of Garvald in East Lothian. I had by then slept many nights in the open air without a tent or other covering. Hitherto, I had been able to choose to sleep under a tree, despite the discomfort of the tree roots, as a protection against dew or rain. It was the first time that I spent the night camped without any cover on the side of a hill. We were each issued with one blanket. Our army rain capes were designed so that they could be used as a ground sheet. Two soldiers could choose to button their capes together to form a small bivouac or sleep separately. I chose to sleep separately and used my cape as a ground sheet. After rolling myself in the blanket, I went to sleep. I awoke at five o'clock in the morning feeling cold and discovered that in the night I had rolled some twenty or thirty feet down the hill and had left my blanket and groundsheet behind! Thereafter I always carried a length of light rope. As dusk came on, I tied both blanket and cape around me so that if I rolled, everything rolled together! It is not something which, I believe, would have been permitted, if observed. A soldier is meant to be ready and prepared to rise at short notice.

We were engaged in a mock battle against a Polish Tank Corps. From Garvald we crossed over the hills to Longformacus and camped beside a small burn or stream. From there, we walked, in one day, approximately 30 miles. We crossed over the hills to the village of Lauder, and from there over Soutra Hill to the village of Humbie. Each company in crossing the hills followed the map reference that it was given. This meant that one company would follow the route of a valley between the hills while the next company climbed over the hill. In B Company, the one which I was in, we climbed up and over probably the highest hill on our route. Endeavouring to keep a strict line of defence, we were required to climb keeping abreast of each other.

On that climb, in addition to my field pack and rifle, I was carrying a 28lb. radio. With the additional weight, I was in climbing the hill, a little behind the rest of the line but not more than 15 or 20 paces. The officer in charge of our company was a captain from the Gordon Highlanders. He swore at me all the way up telling me to keep abreast of the line. On reaching the top we immediately saw some Polish tanks, some five or six hundred yards away coming toward us, over the moor. We flung ourselves flat in peat hags (lower lying dips) for cover, while our mortars opened fire with blank ammunition.

The captain, who seemed to me fairly highly strung and excitable, remained standing on the skyline as he ordered me to send a radio message to the Artillery Battery to provide covering fire. A Company on our left, having encountered the tanks before we did, was already on the air asking for artillery help. I told our captain that I could not radio at present, explaining that A Company was on the air. I would do so as soon as possible. To attempt to interrupt the communication of another party before they were finished, would create a radio jam when no one could speak or be heard. It was strictly forbidden to attempt to break into another's radio communication and thereby make all radio communication impossible. The captain, unable to grasp the situation, kept swearing and cursing me, telling me to interrupt A Company and speak to Artillery. Suddenly the Umpire appeared and told the captain that he was 'dead' because he was standing on the skyline and, unlike the rest of us, had not taken cover. As I had not appreciated his swearing and lack of understanding, I confess I burst out laughing, which was not very gracious of me. I learned later that the poor chap was, later on in the war, killed in Germany.

In some exercises in the army we sometimes were on the move for three days without any provision for sleep. Being in the open air in such circumstances I have literally slept standing on my feet, while leaning against a haystack, or slept in the midst of taking a radio message. On this occasion we were given little food. In the morning at Longformacus we were given two level spoons of rice crispies and one level spoon of milk. I do not recall that we were officially given any other sustenance until we had walked thirty miles to the village of Humbie, which we reached that evening. When we reached the main road leading to Lauder we walked in customary military practice, with each section of about nine men walking on opposite sides of the road, and about 30 yards apart. Progress was slow as aeroplanes kept diving low overhead and we had to keep flinging ourselves into the ditch at the side of the road.

When we entered Lauder town square and were passing a baker's shop, we were greeted with the strong and to hungry soldiers overpowering, smell of new bread. Each soldier had the same thought and looked to the soldier in the rear, hoping that he might slip off and supplement our rations. The sergeant major leading our section clearly had the same thought. He halted us and said that he would give us two minutes. All that was available in the shop were large apple tarts. We had scarcely each purchased one, when we were called to action as tanks had been observed coming down the road from the north. My platoon was called to take up its position at the north end of the town. Looking behind me, I was amused to see soldiers running with a rifle in one hand and an apple tart in the other! We were not allowed to enter any homes. However as the soldiers took up positions in various doorways, kindly housewives appeared offering cups of tea. These were readily accepted and as the soldiers drank the tea they asked the housewives to stand on the road and tell them when the tanks appeared!

Our visit in Lauder did not have a happy ending. A friend, Bill MacDonald, who was in the artillery told me what happened. They had five and twenty five pounder guns. As they reached Lauder Town House, suddenly tanks appeared at the far end of the square. Without thinking, they fired. Their shells were blanks but, sadly, the blast blew out the windows of the near-by houses. We were glad to leave Lauder. Bill entered the Church of Scotland ministry after the war.

We camped at Humbie and arrived home on Wednesday morning in time for me to sit a term exam in Roman History. I received 30 marks out of 80. It was the only examination in which I failed at university. Under the circumstances I had done no work for it. However, I worked hard on Roman History over the next two to three weeks and passed the subject in the degree exam in June along with Latin and Greek, so completing successfully my first academic year at university.

Full Time Army Service

To my surprise I did not receive a regular army posting until the beginning of September. We were however kept occupied first with a military camp in the Border hills near Stobo, where I discovered how rugged some of the Border hills can be. This was followed by a military exercise with the 52nd Scottish Division in Aberdeenshire and Inverness-shire. The 52nd Division was a Scottish Lowland Division trained and equipped for mountain warfare. They trained in the Cairngorm Mountains. The $7/9^{th}$ Battalion of the Royal Scots, to which my unit in the Territorial Army was attached, served in the 52nd Division.

Then I received, along with over 30 other students from different universities, a regular posting to Worcester and for six weeks was attached to the Lancashire Regiment. It was the first time that I had encountered the Lancashire accent, which I did not always find easy to follow. It was also the first time that I had seen such lush growth among the trees and plants in the countryside. Worcestershire I found to be a lovely county.

Each soldier is required to wear at all times a disk around his neck recording his name and religion. I was much amused when a student from Liverpool University announced that he was an atheist. This was greeted with strong opposition from our company sergeant. He said, "I am having no atheist in my company! You are Church of England!" So, in army records, that was what he was!

Royal Scots

Six weeks later, I was posted back to Scotland to the Royal Scots Depot at Dreghorn on the edge of Edinburgh. We trained on the Pentland Hills and sometimes on the Moorfoot Hills.

Because of the desire for a high standard of physical fitness we had each day, when not on field exercises, one hour of physical training. Sometimes this included a four mile cross-country run. I was never a fast sprinter like my brother James who was sports champion at school. Cross-country running I enjoyed. I never excelled but generally came in fifth or sixth out of one hundred men.

We were required to be able to march 25 miles in a day, to cover ten miles in two hours equipped with field pack and rifle and two miles similarly clad in 17 minutes. I accomplished the ten miles in one hour thirty nine minutes and was second in my unit. I was able to accomplish two miles in fourteen minutes. The two mile course ended with a jump over an artificial pond about 9 or 10 feet long, 6 feet wide and 3 feet deep with water. Determined not to get wet, I simply flung myself across it in an ungainly bound. It was remarkable the number of men who reached the pond, hesitated, jumped and fell into the water!

During the course a few of us were marked out as possible candidates for a commission. We were made leaders of different sections so that our qualities of leadership could be tested. We underwent extra physical tests, which seemed to tax us to the limit and also were put through a driving school, driving 15 cwt Bedford trucks. This was a course I much appreciated.

At the end of our course I and the other selected candidates attended a three day Officer Selection Course, when we were tested for our individual qualities as soldiers and our ability to work together in a team. A commission in infantry normally involved three months in a Pre-OCTU (Officer Cadet Training Unit) course and six weeks in an OCTU course. Having passed the Selection Course I received word that I would be sent to a Pre-OCTU course in mountain infantry stationed at Loch Maree in Ross-shire. A commission in mountain infantry would I think have inevitably meant joining the 52nd Division. It was, to my knowledge, the only mountain infantry Division in the British army.

I had enjoyed battle courses, assault courses, the hard physical exercises and the training that we had undergone. Toward the end of our training we were taught a certain amount of unarmed combat which I also enjoyed. I enjoyed wrestling and boxing at school and I boxed in the army (although today it is a sport that I hate). However, we were also taught and given a considerable amount of bayonet practice. We were informed that each bayonet has a blood groove to draw the maximum amount of blood from the opponent. We practised using sacks stuffed with straw and were told that to fight successfully with a bayonet we must develop a passionate hatred for the enemy. This, to use a Scot's word, scunnered me. I came to hate it. I felt that it is one thing to kill a person at a distance of one or two hundred yards. It is something different to look a person in the eye and seek to kill him with a bayonet. I felt that I just could not do it. Consequently I began to regret that I had volunteered for infantry.

While I was waiting to be posted to Loch Maree, because of my hatred for the possibility of fighting with a bayonet, I asked my parents to pray that I might be transferred to another branch of the army. Two or three days later another soldier and I were suddenly, without consultation, transferred from infantry and posted to the Royal Corps of Signals in Catterick in England. From the human point of view it was customary during the war to transfer a soldier, or soldiers from one unit to another depending on the needs of the army at the time. Previously, when I had appeared before a Military Board at university I was told that the need at that time was for Signal Communication. From the spiritual point of view I felt that my transfer was a remarkable answer to prayer. I felt relieved although I missed the Royal Scots and have continued to have considerable affection for the regiment. I missed the sound of the bagpipes.

The Royal Signal Corps

Being transferred to Signals meant that Officer training was postponed or cancelled. I was required to undergo another period of training. Once again I, along with a few others, was selected for possible commissioning. As a junior NCO (Non Commissioned Officer) I was again given charge over a section of soldiers and tested for leadership qualities. I was also taught how to project the voice and drill a squad of soldiers on the far end of the parade ground.

As a Section leader I developed at this time a rather bad habit. When the bell sounded in the morning, I leapt out of bed and roused the boys. When all were up ready to wash and breakfast, I jumped back into bed for another five or ten minutes sleep! On one dreadful occasion I overslept and awoke as the boys were going on parade. I leapt up and dressed but missed my place on parade. There are three sections in a platoon and three platoons in a company. I was leader of number one section of number one platoon and would normally, following our platoon sergeant, be first on parade. On this occasion I went on parade following behind the third platoon. As opportunity arose, I slipped forward until finally I took my place at the front of the parade. I well remember the look of astonishment on the face of the platoon sergeant when he turned and saw me. Surprisingly, no one ever mentioned the matter and I was never disciplined.

At the end of the course I was called before our commanding officer to receive my assessment in regard to my going forward for officer selection. He complimented me as a soldier and commended me on my leadership qualities. I thanked him but before I could salute and depart, he looked at me and with a flicker of a smile said, "You like to take life easy!" I was most abashed. Clearly he must have heard about my early morning habits. Yet, neither he nor anyone else mentioned it. I had actually, after that dreadful day when I slept in, begun to reform.

With others I again attended a three-day Officer Selection Course. We were asked to write down our choice of the Corps or regiment in which we wished to be commissioned. My first choice was Signals, with which I was now familiar. My second choice was the Reconnaissance Corps. Every army in wartime needs patrols to penetrate behind the enemy lines to secure important information. It was a dangerous job but seemed to offer excitement. My third choice was mechanised infantry.

At the end of the course, I was called before the commanding officer. From what he said I had done well and seemed to have come first in the selection course, which I found gratifying. He said regretfully however, that at that particular time all men between 19 and 30 years of age could only be commissioned in infantry. He said that if I agreed to return to infantry the recommendation that I would receive was such that I would by-pass Pre-OCTU training, go straight to OCTU and be commissioned within six weeks. Naturally the receiving of an Army Commission was tempting. However, because of my continued dislike and horror at the possibility of fighting and killing a person with a bayonet, I declined.

Postings to 79th Division and 115 Assault Brigade

I was then posted to the 79th Division in Norfolk and informed that we would be going to Burma in the war against the Japanese. My time there was brief and spent largely on one military exercise after another, yet not on a Saturday. Happily I found my brother James stationed only a few miles away; James was in the RAF and stationed with No 2 Bomber Command; he served in radar with ground crew. James was able to get a pass giving him leave of absence from his unit over Friday night and all day Saturday. I was able to acquire a day pass for all day Saturday, but not one overnight. Consequently James came over to where I was. When he intimated that he was my brother he was duly smuggled in to our camp and given bed and breakfast! We then spent a glorious day sailing together on the Norfolk Broads. We did this on at least two and possibly three occasions. After that I was suddenly, without warning or consultation, posted to 115 Assault Brigade.

I knew of no one else who was so selected or who left 79th Division. Why I was selected to join a special assault force I do not know. I wondered if it was because of my infantry background.

115 Assault Brigade, stationed on the South Coast near Plymouth, was a highly trained, highly equipped assault force trained in beach landing. Attached to the Brigade (which was British Army) was a fleet of small landing craft, LCMs (Landing Craft Mechanic) and LCTs, (Landing Craft Tank), together with escort vessels including a destroyer, belonging to the American Navy. The LCMs were for transporting infantry and LCMs for transporting vehicles, armoured and otherwise.

The Brigade also had a number of Ducks, which were armoured vehicles able to float and travel through water.

Instead of going to Burma, I was now told that we would be going to the Channel Islands. The Channel Islands were the only part of Britain captured by Germany. The plan was first to capture Guernsey, leave one battalion to hold the island, and then capture Jersey. The battalion to which I was attached was due to engage in the double assault of both Guernsey and Jersey. Our military exercises were always in preparation for this assault.

Our entire time seemed to be spent training on the moors, rock climbing on the cliffs of Devon and Cornwall, sometimes on the beach learning how to use explosives, and learning to get on and off boats. Speed on disembarking was all-important because of the likelihood of being required to do so under enemy fire. I was attached to a LCT, which could hold 150 vehicles, below deck and above. My position was on deck. For speed in disembarking, each vehicle was required to reverse on to a boat. Because the boats were flat-bottomed, they were able to come partly on to the shore. We embarked on the beach.

Looking back in later years, I can only describe some of the obstacles in the assault course which we did as 'hair-raising'. For example, when we were encouraged to cross a bay some forty or fifty feet above rocks, on a single rope with field pack and rifle. On crossing the bay, in order to leave the rope that we were on, we were required to catch another rope, in order to swing oneself over the top of the far cliff landing five or six feet back from the edge. The cliffs were pretty precipitous. Although we were encouraged to tackle all the obstacles we were not compelled to tackle some of them because of the danger involved. One slip meant death. Out of fifty men generally not more than six would tackle the whole course. I was one of the six and always tackled everything. I felt fit. I enjoyed the challenge, the thrill and the sense of danger. We were as a Brigade on 'stand by', waiting for word to go into action, which could come at any time. In tackling these obstacles, I always had before me the fact that the following week I might be required to do something similar under enemy fire. I preferred to learn how to do it when there was no enemy fire.

Mercifully we were never required to try and capture the Channel Islands. After the war I learned that because they were the only part of Britain occupied by German troops, under Hitler's orders they were the most heavily defended place in Europe. We did not know that at that time, or were certainly never told. In Guernsey and, I think, Jersey the Germans had tunnelled from one side of the island to the other and as such were able to transport their guns, ammunition and soldiers from one side of the island to the other secure from our guns. If we had attempted to capture the islands our casualties would have been extremely high. Having landed in Normandy the Allies by-passed the Channel Islands, which were not liberated until the end of the war.

One Sunday morning our Commanding Officer announced that he had just received a telegram from the War Office saying that the operation to capture the Channel Islands was cancelled. The Brigade would be scrapped as a fighting unit and would be replaced by men of graded health who would be used to hold territory captured from Germany. He said that, beginning with the youngest soldiers, we would be sent to the Far East, for the war against Japan. At 20 years of age I was one of the youngest. To prove the authenticity of that decision six soldiers, myself included, were sent off the following Thursday.

For a long time I thought that someone at the War Office must be drunk to scrap a special, highly trained Assault Brigade at that stage in the war. At the end of the war, in India, I met some of the soldiers from my unit in 115 Brigade. They had been sent to India for the expected final assault on Japan. They told me what had happened. Six of us having left on the Thursday, five more were posted out on the following Monday. The Brigade was then sent to France, not for beach landings but for river crossings. They were used, for example in the crossing of the River Meuse. With their training and the kind of equipment which they had, it was their task to help create pontoon bridges and punch a hole in the enemy lines in order to allow the rest of the Allied army through. It was a dangerous task when no doubt they sustained heavy casualties.

Clearly, the intimation concerning the scrapping of the Brigade as a fighting force, which appeared to be confirmed by the posting out of eleven men, was an Intelligence exercise to try and mislead German Intelligence, concerning British military plans. Such exercises, or lies, were common in the war.

The day following the intimation that I would be posted to the Far East our Sergeant Major, who seemed kindly disposed toward me asked if I was willing for him to substitute another soldier in my place. Although I appreciated his good will toward me, I immediately said "No" on the ground that if that soldier, having gone in my place was killed, I could never live with my own conscience. As it happened, my refusal meant that I escaped the fighting in France and Germany.

Transit Station

The six of us were sent to Darlington for a brief period. There we were re-equipped with tropical equipment and joined a unit of approx. 550 men which was assembled to take part in the war against Japan.

Before going abroad and in transferring from one unit to another I was three times on my arrival in a new unit given a form asking about the school or type of school in which I was educated. In these days it was considered important if one had attended a Private School. It seemed to help toward promotion in the army. I objected to the issue of privilege because of one's education. I therefore declined to fill in this form. After signing my name I wrote diagonally across the page in large letters "Scot"! I was never challenged, and never asked to fill in the paper properly.

Voyage to India

We sailed in December from Greenock on the Clyde, on the Strath Naver, a P & O passenger liner converted and armed as a troop carrier. We joined a convoy of some twenty ships. The Strath Naver was I believe a ship of 27,000 tons. Some 5,000 troops were on board. On either side of us were other troop ships and we were escorted by corvettes, long sleek military boats able to travel at considerable speed. We sailed round the north of Ireland and out into the north Atlantic and then south well clear of Europe.

We hit a storm. The sailors said that it was not a bad storm but I had never before seen such mountainous waves. When the troop-ships on either side plunged we could see their propellers in the air and about one third way down the keel. Then we could see a third way down the keel from the prow of the ship. I was mercifully never sick, as were a large number of others, although I did not feel like eating much for two days.

As the storm ceased there was an enemy submarine warning. Being the largest ship in the convoy, the Commodore was on the Strath Naver. Two of the corvettes escorting the convoy were called alongside and the Commodore spoke to them over a loud speaker. The two corvettes sped off at speed. I watched them disappearing over the horizon. I do not know what happened but we received no further warning of enemy ships or submarines.

When we were abreast of Gibraltar, the convoy split up and the Strath Naver raced singly, on its own, at top speed through the Straits and through the rest of the Mediterranean towards Port Said and the Suez Canal. At Aden we rejoined a convoy under escort and sailed for Bombay.

Our travel from the UK to India took a month. On the ship I was asked if I would allow my name to go forward for a commission, I presumed this time in Signals. I was glad to be asked. However, a commission in Signals normally meant almost five months training. I felt that I had so far spent a long time in training or moving from one unit to another and I did not wish to spend the rest of the war in a training camp. I do not regard myself as a brave man, but I felt that I would like to play a small but active part in helping to win the war. I therefore declined. I was then posted to a Training Division!

India

To my knowledge, most of my unit simply crossed India and joined the war in Burma. A few of us were held back and sent to other units – I do not know why. Two of us, Ken Slater and myself, were sent first for about two weeks to Agra and then to the 14th Indian Division, although not to the same Brigade. It was a jungle Division, which gave Indian troops experience of the jungle and trained them in jungle warfare. Indian troops came to us trained, spent three months further training in jungle warfare and went on to Burma.

During our brief stay in Agra, the unit which I was with was challenged by the local Indian cricket team to a match. At a hasty trial game among ourselves, I was chosen to be a bowler. In my school days I had bowled regularly. The ground was hard and the balls consequently were fast. The Indians did not like my bowling. I took six wickets and we knocked out the India team for only 52 runs! I do not remember the number of our runs. To everyone's surprise we won decisively.

At Agra, Ken and I also managed to visit the world-famous Taj Mahal and Agra Fort, both of which were fascinating.

14th Indian Division

Our duties entailed maintaining all communications 24 hours a day, 7 days a week. We were located in hilly, forested country in the Central Provinces, in the postal district of Chindwara, a fairly large village with a variety of shops. It was the area where Rudyard Kipling based his jungle stories about Mowgli. In every direction as far as the eye could see there were rolling hills and trees, with little native population. In places, the trees thinned out and there were open spaces with grass. It was in such a place that we were camped.

There were three Brigades camped at Singhori, Gangiwara and Tuniabund. The Brigades, as the crow flies, were between two and four miles apart. Because of the nature of the terrain, the travelling distance through jungle and by path and dust roads was twice that far. I was stationed at Kulbhera which was the Divisional Head Quarters. There were various Indian battalions camped nearby, making us almost like another Brigade. The General and his Chief of Staff occupied three thatched huts about two or three hundred yards from our Signals' Office tent. It was the centre for the Division's internal and external communications. In Kulberha we were some four miles from the village of Chindwara.

Every Indian Division, during the war, had a sprinkling of British officers and NCOs and at least one entirely British unit. We had in the Brigade at Gangiwara an artillery Battery of probably some 400 or 500 British gunners. In the signals unit there were, I think, eight of us who were British. The Indians who served with us in Signals were there for experience and training.

One of the first things I did when I joined the Division was to ask an Indian helper to scrub all my webbing equipment, in order to wash off the blanco (the standard cleaning agent for equipment), so loved by the British army. I always found blanco kept the hands and fingernails dirty and I never liked it. It was not used in the Indian Army or at least not in my Division.

I then, in my concern for personal comfort, bought in the bazaar in Chindwara, two white cotton curtains. I had hoped to buy sheets but because I could not find any, I bought curtains, which served the purpose just as well. Sleeping under an army blanket in the heat I found intolerable.

Chindwara was shortly afterwards, and for the next nine months, out of bounds to all army personnel, first because of an outbreak of smallpox, then cholera, followed by Typhus, Cholera again and then plague. One epidemic followed the other in close succession. I used to wonder how, with so much disease, anyone survived.

We were all vaccinated against small-pox before leaving the UK or on our immediate arrival in India. We were vaccinated again when around Easter time there was a small outbreak of small-pox within the division. We were inoculated against cholera every three months, because the inoculation against cholera did not last long. A soldier was only inoculated against plague if he happened to be in contact with a rat, dead or alive, or required for military purposes to visit the Indian bazaar, or be in contact with local village folk.

About two miles from our camp and in another direction from Chindwara there was a small very primitive jungle village. Our *dhobi wallah* (the man who washed our clothes) came from that village. Fairly near to the village was some open ground, which the army sometimes used. One day some 56 corpses of people from the village who had died from cholera, were lying there. The village was within the area used by the army. The next day our *dhobi wallah* told us with great excitement and much gesticulation what had happened that morning. When he awoke he found that the village was surrounded by soldiers. Every man, woman and child was brought out and made to pass down between two rows of soldiers. At the end, a needle was stuck into the arm of each person. Probably none of the inhabitants of the village could read or write, and to my knowledge were not consulted or asked whether or not they wished to be inoculated. Regardless of what their wishes might have been, all of them were inoculated against cholera. There were no reporters in those days to announce to the world that the army had 'broken the human rights' of these humble village folk! Their action halted the outbreak of cholera and I think it was the right thing to have done in the circumstances.

Life in a Jungle Division

This was totally different from the life in any other unit in which I had served. In my first night, alone in my tent, I had scarcely got into bed when a pack of jackals opened up nearby. The howling of jackals is similar to the howling of wolves although higher pitched. When one pack opened up, immediately five or six other packs would open up all around, often very near. For two or three minutes the air would be rent with their cries, before once again the air was quiet. That is what happened that night. Suddenly I heard the patter of feet and the swish of grass outside as jackals rushed past my tent. Being new to it all and not knowing what to expect, I simply pulled the blanket over my ears! We rarely saw jackals because of the long grass. They were shy creatures and we soon became very accustomed to their cries.

On my first night on duty I was the only one who spoke English. English and Urdu were the two national languages in India. Some 200 different languages and dialects are spoken in India. Urdu is a mixture of languages but primarily composed of Hindi and Marathi. In order to join the Indian Civil Service or the army, an Indian was required to speak one or other national language.

The Indians with whom I was on duty during my first night only spoke Urdu. I felt the pressure to immediately start to learn the language. I was never proficient in Urdu but I managed to acquire a working knowledge of the language, which was a great help when visiting an Indian bazaar or when travelling.

Although the other British soldiers with me accepted our situation, none of them really seemed to enjoy living in the jungle. I very much enjoyed it. I was glad, despite the simplicity of our life, to be away from civilisation, to be in the midst of God's creation and to be living in fairly wild country. I enjoyed the beauty, the variety and wildness. I also enjoyed being trusted to get on with what we were required to do without being constantly supervised.

I never, however, came to terms with snakes, scorpions and crocodiles! I hated them. They reminded me of the story in Genesis and the fall! Scorpion spiders were fairly numerous. We quickly learned to avoid them. When entering a tent they could travel fast and made us jump out of their road. On the other hand, lizards, which were about a foot long and common, we welcomed because of their ability to catch and eat mosquitoes. I personally never saw a tiger, although others occasionally saw them. Neither did I see elephants although they were not far away. I presumed that the presence of so many troops caused them to avoid us. I certainly saw deer and literally hundreds of monkeys of various kinds. One particular variety of monkey, which I thought handsome, was tall, thin, had a long tail and was grey with a black stripe. On one occasion I saw a baby one about ten or twelve paces away. I had a sudden desire to acquire a baby monkey as a pet. As soon as I moved, however, its mother dropped down from a tree, grabbed it and leapt up another tree. It would have been dangerous to try and catch it with the mother nearby.

Again, on one occasion, having said good night to another soldier before entering our respective tents, I had just time to light my lamp, when I heard a loud shout saying, "There is an animal in my tent". When I rushed out, I could see a fairly large animal at the edge of the circle of light. When I shouted, it fled. What it was we did not know. It seemed too large to be a jackal, apart from which jackals generally roamed in packs. It might have been a wolf although, despite Rudyard Kipling's jungle stories, we were not aware of wolves in the area. Quite possibly it was a black leopard. A black leopard (which the lads wrongly called a black panther) for months prowled through one of the camps and despite the setting of guards, was never shot.

We had one amusing occasion. Two of us were playing chess one night in one of the tents, when suddenly we heard the sound of heavy feet. We leapt up seizing whatever weapon we could lay our hands on. We had no rifles with us. As we crouched waiting for whatever it was to appear, suddenly to our astonishment a donkey trotted by! Where it came from and where it was going and how long it would survive alone in the jungle, we did not know. We were some miles away from any Indian village.

The trees in our area were broad leafed and when close together formed a thick canopy overhead. They were probably not more than forty to fifty feet tall although there were exceptions. They were certainly not tall like the ones which I saw in Bengal and which grew in Burma, where there was a higher rainfall. On one occasion when walking through thick forest with another soldier, we startled a troop of four or five hundred monkeys, with one immense creature like a small gorilla, who I imagine was their leader. As far as possible when off duty, we only walked through thick forest in the heat of the day between 11am and 3pm when larger animals were sleeping.

Life was very simple. We had very few books. We had to create our own means of recreation. Between Kulberha and Tuniabund there was, at a distance of about a mile from our camp, a good sized river. Quite often some of us enjoyed swimming in it. On the other side of our camp there was another river. I only once swam in it, before I learned about the crocodiles.

For meals we ate, for fourteen months, what was called K Rations. These were small boxes of food labelled, 'Breakfast', 'Lunch' and, I think, 'Supper' or 'Evening Meal'. Each box was filled with dry, compressed food, which contained the right balance of vitamins. The food was not cooked or heated. Our K Rations were supplemented with corn beef, which was served up in every conceivable form, plus mangos. Mango trees grew wild with us and were plentiful, as was tea. In one of the army camps near us there was a small Indian canteen where we were able to buy limes, and sometimes hard boiled eggs and occasionally an odd tin of fruit to add variety to our diet, which otherwise never changed.

Living in tents we were conscious of the weather. The winter climate was marvellous with a temperature of around 70°F in November and December. The temperature rose fairly rapidly reaching 90° in February, when for two or three weeks we had a little monsoon. This involved about one hour of rain each day for about three weeks. During this period we frequently experienced quite violent wind storms and whirlwinds, or 'dust devils'. I saw the tents of an entire battalion flattened in seconds. Once, one ripped the fly covering of my tent, despite its being heavy canvas, from end to end, as if it had been cut with a sharp knife.

By the month of May the temperature rose to above 100° and in June before the monsoon broke, to 117°. I enjoyed the heat. Often when sleeping outside of the tent because of the heat and under the stars, I was grateful to be in India as I thought of our soldiers in Europe suffering both cold and rain. Mosquito nets were necessary and we were glad to have them because of the many insects and mosquitoes. In the monsoon period they seemed to emerge in vast numbers.

In the Division we were not allowed to wear a shirt during the day. It was considered to be healthier and helped us to avoid suffering from heat rash, a nasty irritation of the skin. We wore shorts, bush hats, boots and gaiters. At night we were required, from about 6pm onward to wear shirts and long trousers because of mosquitoes. As a result of not wearing shirts, we became extraordinarily brown and became darker than some Indians. I was told that my back was no longer brown but black. We had no sun cream and wore no protection against the sun, yet became remarkably accustomed to it. We were not told about the danger of skin cancer, which was probably not known at that time.

Although we were issued with army sandals we were not allowed to walk through grass with them and we did not wish to do so. In the monsoon the grass grew to four or five feet tall. During the dry season it dried and withered and the stalks became quite sharp and could draw blood. In the army we called the grass 'spear grass' (probably it was elephant grass). Walking through such grass could be painful. At the same time in our area, there were a variety of snakes including black mambas. They were small black snakes rather like a large shoelace. Their bite was desperately dangerous and generally fatal. We were glad of the protection of army boots and gaiters.

Indian Soldiers

I was deeply grateful to have been called to serve with Indian troops. We had Hindu, Muslim, Sikh and Madras battalions, which included men from South India and also Ghurkhas.

The Indian army was a volunteer army. The Indian soldiers were extremely loyal. We could never have won the war in Burma without them. Flung together as we were in a jungle division, there developed a remarkable spirit of comradeship and trust between British and Indian soldiers. We relied on each other, helped each other and made many friends. I often said to Indian soldiers, "I am sure you would rather serve under Indian officers and NCOs." They always replied, "No! We prefer to serve under the British. We are treated better and more fairly."

Within the different battalions, Indian soldiers were always made to serve, if not under British, then under officers and NCOs of the same ethnic origin and religious persuasion. We had many Dalits (in the Hindu caste system, 'untouchables') serving in the army. It would have been impossible to ask other Indian soldiers to serve under them. Many of the Dalits were Christians and no doubt because they had attended

Christian schools, tended to be among the more educated among the Indian soldiers. Likewise Muslims were not asked to serve under Hindus nor Hindus under Muslims. In regard to Ghurkhas, I am not sure whether it mattered whether those over them were Hindu or Buddhist, so long as, if not British, they were Ghurkhas. Under British command they all served happily together, although they would not have done otherwise.

We had one Ghurkha battalion in the division. They were magnificent soldiers. We lost them over an unhappy incident. One night a Ghurkha soldier became separated from his patrol and walked down the street of a primitive jungle village. Although he explained to the headman that he was a soldier and had lost his way, another villager threw an axe, which killed him. The dead soldier's comrades, I think without killing anyone, raked the village with machine gun fire. The general ordered a court martial whereon the entire battalion of some six hundred men, mutinied. It was a difficult issue when in the battalion, there were probably not more than 12 British officers and NCO's and possibly less. It was promptly solved by announcing that the battalion was needed in Assam. The battalion left knowing that they were being disciplined and yet left happily and with dignity being told that they were needed in Assam. Such was British diplomacy!

Although I enjoyed life in the Division, and enjoyed serving both with my fellow British and Indian soldiers, I occasionally became restless. Once again I was in a training unit and not actively engaged in the war. I had above all, a great longing to go to China, the land of my birth. I volunteered for China several times but to no avail. We did not have many troops in China, beside which, to send one soldier out of the Division meant there was need to draft another one in. The army was not interested in that kind of exercise. It was only later on, I think after the end of the war in Europe, that two or three other British soldiers joined us in our unit.

The end of the war in Europe, in May 1945, did not really affect us. The war in Burma overshadowed everything which we did, and so far as we were concerned, nothing changed. Our only celebration was to walk four miles and listen to a speech by the officer second in command of our division. He simply said that the boys in Europe had done a grand job and told us to make sure that we did our duty when our time came!

Shortly after the end of the war in Europe a message came into the Division enquiring whether anyone was interested in China and asking for volunteers. Surprisingly we were not told anything about the nature of the enquiry and in my eagerness to go to China, I did not enquire. I immediately volunteered. Apart from being asked about the nature of my interest and my background I was told nothing. The other soldiers told me that I was mad to volunteer, as I did not know what I was letting myself in for. I replied that in my concern to go to China I did not care what was being asked. I think that in my enthusiasm I would have been happy to have parachuted into China if that was the only way in which I could get there.

Military Intelligence

I presume enquiries were made concerning me and recommendations obtained, for shortly afterwards I was asked to report to a military unit in Delhi. When I arrived I discovered that I had been transferred from Signals to the Army Intelligence Corps and was due to learn Chinese in India. If I had been asked to learn Chinese in China I would have happily agreed – I had no desire to learn Chinese in India! Soldiers already on the course tried to encourage me saying that while learning Chinese one was given the rank of Sergeant and on finishing the course was automatically commissioned. To agree to study Chinese, I had to agree that I would stay in the army for the next two years. That in itself did not seem to be a problem. The war was not over and I expected to be in the army for at least another two years.

What was I to do? Agreeing to study Chinese in India did not guarantee that I would go to China, where we had few troops. I was desperate to go there and being stuck for many months in India, with no guarantee of ever going to China, did not seem to me at the time the best way to achieve my goal! My problem therefore was how to escape from Army Intelligence to which I now belonged! I was interviewed by various British and Chinese officers. I did not like to confess that my sole aim in volunteering was to go to China. I therefore tried to persuade them that as I had always been a combatant soldier, I would better serve the cause of the war effort if I continued to be a combatant soldier rather than a member of Army Intelligence! To my relief I was successful in my persuasion. They agreed to release me from Army Intelligence and I was asked what I would like to do. Not knowing what better to answer, I replied that I would prefer to return to the 14th Indian Division, but not immediately! I thought that I might as well have a holiday when I had the chance. They happily agreed and accepted my suggested date of return, which was in about ten days time.

Did I make a foolish decision? I have sometimes wondered. I had twice been offered the opportunity of joining Military Intelligence. On the second occasion I had actually been transferred to Intelligence. Today and looking back, I feel that serving as an officer in Army Intelligence is something that I would have much enjoyed. The knowledge of another language is always valuable. I would love to be able to speak and understand Chinese or Japanese. However, I was young and the decision I made reflected the way that I felt then. At the time I was more interested in seeing China and the world and in quest of adventure, than in any form of serious language study.

Holiday in Delhi

I moved from the comfortable quarters of the Intelligence Unit where I was billeted to the greater comforts of the Wavell Military Hostel in New Delhi. There I enjoyed better food and comfort than I had enjoyed since joining the army.

I had a marvellous few days exploring both New and Old Delhi. British soldiers were not actually permitted, for health reasons, to enter the walled city of Old Delhi. I rode through it in a *tonga* (a horse drawn taxi cab). I found the old city fascinating. Seeing it made me feel that time had stood still. It looked as if life in the city had not changed for centuries. I felt that I was stepping 1,000 years back in history. I was saddened by the desperate poverty and poor dwelling houses in which the people lived. I was also horrified by the piles of sewage and the smell. It had to be seen and smelled to be believed. In one street a black pile of sewage about fifteen or twenty feet high almost covered the width of the street. There was just room for the *tonga* to circumvent it. I did not descend from the *tonga*.

I found New Delhi in contrast an attractive city, not unlike many in the West, before I returned on the agreed date to the simple, humble life of living in a jungle division.

The End of the War

The war against Japan ended suddenly in August, following the dropping of two atomic bombs. We were surprised at the sudden end but as soldiers, breathed a sigh of relief. The war seemed to have dragged on for so long.

I have over the years listened to many discussions in Church circles, chiefly from pacifists, about how wrong it was to drop atomic bombs. I have on various occasions read the military reports and analysis of the war against Japan. As such, I have always felt that the dropping of the bombs was right and saved many lives both Allied and Japanese. According to military estimates, to have continued using conventional weapons and for the Allies to have landed in Japan, would have cost around three million lives. The dropping of the two bombs cost just under three hundred thousand lives (I do not know the number of those injured and affected by radiation). The dropping of the bombs and the bringing of the war to an end, however wrong, was, in my opinion, the lesser of two evils.

For the best part of the next six months, however, we continued what we were doing. Little changed. The East continued to be in turmoil. In Malaya, guerrilla fighting against the communists began breaking out and later developed into war. Following the Japanese surrender, heavy fighting broke out in Indonesia. The Indonesians, having seized the artillery and armour which the Japanese laid down, fought the Dutch for independence. That fighting continued for quite some time.

Our only celebration was again to walk four miles to where the artillery guns of the Division had been banked in two rows. This time there was no speech either to thank us or tell us to do our duty. Instead, we had to sit for two hours as each gun kept firing. Sitting by a gun and listening to it firing without earplugs is extremely unpleasant. To listen to an entire battery for two hours is agony. We sat with our hands clapped over our ears waiting for it all to stop. We did not think much of our victory celebration! Sadly, one of the guns near to where I was sitting jammed. Although there is a particular procedure to follow when a gun jammed, often gunners risk ramming the shell with a pole down the front muzzle. Two sergeants proceeded to do this and the shell suddenly exploded. One sergeant lost two arms and the other one arm. It seemed extremely sad for two soldiers to come through the war and in a victory celebration to be so wounded and maimed.

The ending of the war against Japan did however bring about great changes in India, although these changes did not immediately affect us in the army. The Government had promised to give India independence, which the Indians had long wanted. With it came the programme to divide India from Pakistan. Burma also was clamouring for independence, with various ethnic groups not in harmony.

In India, Muslim and Hindu riots started to arise with considerable loss of life. With them came the feeling that the Indian army, which had been so loyal and had done such a magnificent job during the war, could no longer be relied on to quell sectarian riots. It was feared that in a Muslim-Hindu riot, Muslim soldiers would likely side with Muslims and Hindu soldiers would likely side with Hindus. With the decision to disarm the Indian soldiers in our Division, I and another British soldier were ordered to take a truck and collect the rifles from all the Indian soldiers belonging to the Royal Corps of Signals in the Brigade in Tuniabund. On this occasion we were not permitted to take an Indian driver, which was unusual. The soldiers cheerfully brought their rifles and stacked them in an immense pile, although they probably knew the reason why they were surrendering their weapons. We then asked them to load them on to the truck. Because of the rough jungle terrain, with no roads for a considerable part of the way and the need to cross a river, there was every possibility that some of the weapons, on a bumpy journey, might drop off an overloaded truck. To try and prevent this happening my colleague drove and I, amid much laughter and good humour on the part of the Indians, climbed up on top of the rifles. They waved us off with all the laughter, banter and unsolicited advice characteristic of other armies. The political changes that were beginning did not alter the loyalty of the Indian army or their good will toward the British. If any of them had objected to our removing their rifles we could have done nothing about it.

Holiday Leave in Kashmir

In September Ken Slater, who was stationed in Singhori, and I went on a month's leave to Kashmir. I was tempted to spend our leave in another jungle area and observe wild life and tigers from the back of an elephant; but because we were already living in the jungle we felt that it would be a greater change to spend our leave in the mountains of the Himalayas. We enjoyed a superb leave. For the first 8 days or so we stayed in Srinigar, horse riding and water skiing on the Dal Lake. Ken had done a considerable amount of horse riding back in the UK. I was a novice but enjoyed the experience. For the next fortnight and more we stayed in the village of Gulmarg, a village 7,000 feet above sea level, on the slopes of Mount Apharwat. We travelled from Srinigar to the foot of Mount Apharwat by bus. We had to walk, or travel on horseback, the next four miles up through the forest. Gulmarg, a small village with a bazaar was situated on a fairly extensive plateau just above the tree line, with Apharwat at 13,500 feet towering above it.

We travelled, I on a Kashmiri pony and Ken on a marvellous tall horse. The Kashmiri ponies were small, sturdy and sure footed but I was keen to hire a much larger animal. The Indian from whom I hired the pony told me that he had a horse, so I asked him to bring it. On reaching Gulmarg I waited near the bazaar while Ken went on to the bungalow where we would be staying. It was about three quarters of a mile distant. Fairly soon I heard the clatter of horse's hooves and saw its owner galloping toward me. At first glance, with its mouth open it looked a formidable animal. It seemed to be the replica of the horses which the Scots Greys rode at the beginning of the war, before they were mechanised and became a tank corps. I felt sure that it was either an ex-army horse or the offspring of an army horse. My knees trembled when I first saw it and I was tempted to tell the owner to take it away! However, pride prevented me and made me show a brave face and made me determined to ride it. No sooner had I mounted it than it was off. I was unable to control it and it entered a yard full of other horses. The owner of the yard yelled and flung up his arms whereon the horse turned. Mercifully it took the road up to our bungalow. It was a long gentle slope. We went up at a very fast gallop. I can still feel the thrill of that ride. I was not an experienced rider and had no control of the horse. I leaned over its neck and clung on. There was a ditch on either side of the road and the whole way up I kept wondering which ditch I would land in. However I did not fall off.

When the horse reached the top of the hill, Ken who had walked his horse at a leisurely pace, was just dismounting. Thankfully my horse halted beside his and I was able to slip off it. Ken looked at me and said, "David, I never knew that you could ride a horse like that!" I wickedly never told him that I had had no intention of riding a horse like that! It was a powerful, spirited horse, with a mind of its own. I came to love it and kept it for the rest of our holiday. Unlike Ken's horse, it often did not wish to go more than a fast trot, until Ken raced his horse up behind. When its nose touched the hindquarters of my horse, then, its ears would go back and off it would go with tremendous speed. It seemed as if it could go like the wind. Once we turned for home it was always different. On our homeward journey we often crossed a polo ground. As we did so, with little or no prompting, it would cross it at a very fast gallop. I always enjoyed the thrill.

The bungalow, owned by white business people, was extremely comfortable. We were waited on by Indian servants, all of whom expected and were, duly tipped at the end of our holiday. Sitting up in bed I had a magnificent view of the snow capped peaks of Nanga Parbat, all over 26,000 feet. Other Himalayan mountains reaching to Afghanistan could also be seen.

Each day we collected a packed lunch and roamed the area on horseback, exploring several of the valleys and steep mountain passes around. On one occasion we climbed Mount Apharwat. At around 10,000 feet we climbed on foot. After reaching about 12,000 feet we climbed through an area where the air was very thin. We had been warned about it. It was something which neither of us had ever previously experienced. We had repeatedly to stop, gasping for breath. On reaching the top and walking along the ridge the air was fresh and completely different. The view from the top was magnificent. In the dry clear air we could see range after range of snowy mountains up to 150 miles away, in Tibet and Afghanistan.

The journey back to Srinigar and then back down the long winding mountain road to Lahore was memorable and sometimes dangerous.

Smallpox

About ten days after arriving back to my unit, one night when on duty I ran a temperature and did not feel well. I reported to an Indian doctor in the morning. When he told me to report to the hospital I was immediately concerned. We were supplied with Mepacrin to combat malaria and were required to take one or two tablets each day. On leave in the hills (and outside the malarial region) I had not taken any Mepacrin, nor any since. I knew that in hospital by testing both my urine and blood they would discover that I had disobeyed orders in not taking the prescribed daily dose, so whether sick or not, I would be disciplined. Therefore, before another soldier drove me to hospital I swallowed 12 tablets of Mepacrin! I knew that that amount was sometimes given in acute cases of malaria.

Being in the jungle, the hospital consisted of a number of large thatched roofed huts. I was admitted to a ward with all white patients suffering mostly from malaria. That night my temperature was taken at intervals and I gave several blood tests. The immediate reaction of the doctor was that I had malaria suppressed by Mepacrin! After he received the results of my blood tests he said that there were no signs of malaria and began to think that it might be jungle fever or typhus. He explained to me that the typhus in India was different from that in North Africa. One is spread by lice and the other by mosquitoes. I do not remember which is which. He kept asking if I had any spots on my body. On the third or fourth day I showed him red spots which had begun to appear and he immediately diagnosed smallpox. With that announcement something short of panic arose. I was highly infectious with a disease that was generally fatal and had been in a general ward with other patients for a few days. Everyone in the ward, possibly in the whole hospital and those in my unit had to be immediately vaccinated. I was transported and isolated in another hut.

The doctor came to see me shortly after my arrival in isolation. He told me how prevalent the disease was and that in the Arakan in Burma that it was so common among the coolies that they simply vaccinated them and they walked around with it. He warned me to expect another steep rise in my temperature. He told me that that was the period of greatest danger, when most people with the disease die, and that the last person they had with smallpox was now pushing up daisies! He told me however that they would look after me.

I was not worried by what he said. I was simply amused by his bedside manner and what as a doctor he said to a very ill patient!

He also questioned me about my recent movements concerned to find out where I contracted the disease. According to the time taken for the disease to develop once infection has taken place, it seemed that I became infected on the train between Lahore and Delhi, on my way back from leave.

I cannot remember whether he visited me again. He would be concerned not to carry infection from me to other patients. I was prescribed some form of oral medication and medication to treat the spots on my body, which cause irritation. Small-pox produces red blood spots, which are flat, and can cover the face, hands and body. When someone has recovered from small-pox they are generally marked by numerous dimples. My spots were not too numerous and over the years the dimples have disappeared.

That first night in isolation I had a very high temperature. When the temperature subsided, I could not eat for a number of days and became incredibly weak, scarcely able to raise myself up in bed.

The hut in which I was isolated had three separate rooms, with a concrete floor. I was in a room at one end. The room in the middle was empty. Two soldiers from the Royal Medical Corps were billeted in the room at the far end. Their task was to keep an eye on me. Beyond taking my temperature and bringing me meals on a tray, they were not permitted to stay and chat. For most of the time I remained alone in isolation.

The nurse of the ward in which I was first admitted called some days after my admission to the isolation ward, and gave me, to my great appreciation, two books. One was by a doctor in the Oxford Group who had written about faith healing. The other was *The Psychoanalysis of Every Day Life,* by Sigmund Freud. Apart from these the only other two books which I had were my Bible and a Penguin paperback of songs written possibly for the first war.

The one other visitor I occasionally had was that of a sister from an Indian ward. Her husband had been killed in the Northwest Frontier of India and she herself had had black-pox. Black-pox is a severe form of smallpox. The spots instead of protruding above the skin form under the skin and are dark or black in colour. It is rare for someone who has black-pox to survive. She told me that for some days she had a temperature of 105°F, but miraculously survived. After having smallpox or black-pox the body develops an immunity making it impossible to contract the disease again. Because of her immunity she occasionally came for a brief chat.

After telling the male orderlies for a number of days to take away the food which they brought, because I was unable to eat, one day the orderly simply laid down the food beside my bed. He told me that I must eat it and departed. It took me two hours to eat that first meal because of my physical weakness. My jaws had difficulty in functioning. Thereafter I gradually gained strength. When I was able, I began to walk out on to the veranda in my pyjamas.

Until I had completely recovered I remained in isolation. It helped me to understand and sympathise with lepers! I never however felt lonely, despite having no one to talk to most days. I remained remarkably cheerful. Even when I was gravely ill, I had never doubted that I would recover.

I enjoyed having my Bible. I read and pondered over the two books which the nurse had given me and spent many a long hour amusing myself by imagining conversations and incidents in daily life and trying to interpret them from the standpoint of Freud. It occupied my mind although I did not agree with Freud. I felt that he was fundamentally wrong in his analysis and position.

After I was able to walk out on to the veranda, a soldier from my unit who had been admitted to hospital with a poisoned hand, came to visit me. He had to stand about twenty yards away and shout. He gave me news of all that had happened since the announcement of my contracting smallpox. He confirmed that everyone had been vaccinated. When the doctor learned that he shared a tent with me and had actually used my bed with my sheets, because I had given him permission, the doctor was alarmed. In his concern the doctor vaccinated him again. Then in his anxiety and in his unwillingness to wait and see whether the other vaccinations had taken, the doctor vaccinated him a third time! The lad laughed over it. Neither he nor anyone else contracted smallpox at that time. In addition to giving me the news he very kindly used to come and throw bananas across to me, which I appreciated.

At last the day came when my time in isolation was over. The sister who had had black-pox came to inform me and to give me my instructions. She told me that next door they had placed a large aluminium bath with warm water containing a strong disinfectant. I was to drop my pyjamas on the floor on entering and submerge every part of my body and head in the water. A towel lay on the other side of the bath. After using it, I was drop it on the floor and leave it there. I was then to cross to the other side of the room where they had laid out a set of new clothes. Thereafter everything, which I owned and everything, which I had touched, including my bed had all to be burned. When it came to my Bible I asked if that also must be burnt. It was the only item which I was allowed to keep and which survived the flames. I returned to the general ward and soon after returned to my unit. It was not long before I fully regained all my strength and was back in the medically top category of A1.

Before going into hospital I occasionally corresponded with Mr Williamson, a Church of Scotland minister and senior chaplain to British army troops in India. I had first met him on the boat when travelling to India. He had kindly sent to me on loan, two books. One was *The Christian*

Experience of Forgiveness by H.R. Macintosh. The other was possibly *The Person of Jesus Christ*, also by H.R. Macintosh, but I do not remember. On my return from hospital I wrote to him, told him that I had had smallpox and apologised that I was unable to return his two books because they had been burned along with the rest of my possessions. I did not hear from him again, nor did he offer to loan me any more books!

Christmas 1945

A little different from previous Christmases spent in the army! The boys bought a pig for our coming Christmas celebrations, but the medical officer for health reasons would not allow us to eat it. We therefore bought a chicken. Because pressures had become a little easier, two of the lads drove a truck ninety miles south to the city of Nagpur and returned with 700 bottles of beer and 15 bottles of spirits. Although we were a small British unit. They drank it all in just under a week! I was the only one who did not drink. Alcohol had not been available while the war was on and for them it was their first taste of alcohol for a long period. I had never seen nor imagined a group of men consuming so much. On Christmas morning and for a good part of the day I was the only one on my feet. The rest were in their beds with sore heads. I greeted them saying, "What a way to spend Christmas!" I had to do the entire work of our section on Christmas day. It was quite an insight into human nature.

Disbanding of the Division

Toward the end of January we were told that the Division would disband. When the news came out, the Indians very generously and kindly treated the British in our Signals unit, by way of farewell, to an enormous Indian feast. I found it agony to eat so much but it would have been gravely discourteous not to eat all that was laid before us. After that, I ate nothing until the evening of the next day! It was a generous gesture on the part of the Indians, and was an indication of the warm relationships which we enjoyed.

As the Division began to wind down I was the first in our unit to volunteer to leave and was told to report to Mhow, a long established army base. I arrived at six o'clock in the morning. After I had washed and breakfasted I reported at 7 o'clock to the administrative office and volunteered to be sent anywhere east of India. Having volunteered several times and been unsuccessful in my attempts to be sent to China, I broadened my horizons. A unit had been sent to Indonesia the day before. I had missed it by a day. I went back in the afternoon to enquire if any posting had come through and went back each day for a fortnight with the same request.

No doubt it was unwise and foolish to volunteer to be sent east of India. Heavy fighting was taking place in Indonesia. With their ethnic differences both Burma and Malaya were restless and deeply troubled. Guerrilla fighting had arisen in Malaya and sometime later gave way to full scale war. At the time, my knowledge of these situations was limited although I knew something about them. I wanted to see as much of the world as possible at the expense of the army and having been stuck for a long period in a training division I wanted some sort of action and adventure.

Bill McDonald had, as a captain in artillery, served for a period in the 14th Indian Division. He was transferred to the 25th Indian Division serving in Indonesia. He told me after the war that Britain had two Indian divisions in Indonesia. They suffered heavy casualties and Bill said that he and his colonel were the only two officers left in his unit. The unit, which I missed by a day, was apparently the last which Britain sent to Indonesia. Britain was afraid to send further reinforcements fearing that in our supporting of the Dutch, the troops we had there already would be massacred.

Britain was faced with a dilemma. Britain and Holland, to which Indonesia at that time belonged, operated quite different colonial policies. The Dutch, in their interpretation about the cursing of Ham in Genesis 9:25 believed that they were the white masters and coloured people were servants. As white masters they were accustomed to appropriate the wealth of Indonesia. They did not seek to build up an Indonesian Civil Service nor wish to allow the Indonesian people to rule themselves. Britain on the other hand, had built up an excellent Civil Service in India and had promised India independence. How could Britain keep the good will of India and assure them of our sincerity in promising them independence and yet continue to help the Dutch in their colonial policy? Although Holland was our ally in the war, Britain declined to help the Dutch further in Indonesia. At that, the Dutch brought down a Dutch Armoured Division to Singapore in order to support their battles against the Indonesians. Thereupon to the fury of the Dutch, and it was a fury which lasted against the British for a long time, the British navy blockaded the Dutch Division in Singapore and would not allow them to cross to Indonesia!

Bengal

At the end of the fortnight, having daily presented my request to the man in charge of postings, he said, "I do not care where you go! You are leaving here with the next posting that goes out of here!" Two days later I was posted to a station in Bengal about ten miles north of Calcutta and a little way off the road to Barakpore. We were billeted in huts around a small lake in the midst of a forest of giant palm trees. We were not a large unit.

Calcutta, even in those days, was a very large city. Chowringi, the main street and those nearby, in the centre of the city were lined with large shops not unlike a western city. A few streets away everything was different. To me walking through them seemed, like entering the walled city of Old Delphi, and to be stepping back in history 1,000 years. People were desperately poor and housing totally inadequate. Little seemed to have changed over the centuries.

In Calcutta there was a large and very fine open-air swimming pool. When off duty, and with little else to occupy us, we spent several hours there. There were other British army units stationed at Barakpore and near Dumdum, although I do not think that they were large. We used to hitch a ride into the city on one of our own army trucks or on the trucks belonging to these other army units.

I played football in the army, when opportunity arose and whenever duties permitted both in Bengal and when I was with the division in Chindwara. Some of the lads were very skilled in the game and with much patience some tried to teach me how to kick a football, which is so different from kicking a rugby ball, with which I was more familiar. I never really acquired the skill. However I showed sufficient promise to be selected to play in various matches between different army units. On several occasions, in the excitement of the game, when I should have scored a goal I forgot all that I had been taught and in rugby style kicked the ball over the bar! I was invariably but good naturedly booed! These teams were composed of both British and Indian soldiers. I was always amazed how far some Sikhs playing with bare feet could kick a ball.

There were about fifty men in our unit, but possibly less. We were responsible for military communications throughout Bengal and beyond. We also had the responsibility of helping to keep the peace in Calcutta. We were not asked to produce patrols and I do not know whether other units were asked. We were simply asked to help when a riot occurred.

In the two years following the end of the war and leading up to the granting of independence and the partition of India and Pakistan into two separate nations, the country was seething with unrest. Muslim and Hindu riots were breaking out all over the country with great loss of life. The anger of these rioting mobs was not, primarily at least, directed against us, although on occasion it could be. For a short time things would remain quiet and for most of my time they were quiet and then suddenly without warning, or without warning to us, a riot would break out. In a riot, when, presumably because one side thought that the army was supporting the other side, bricks and stones would sometimes be hurled. On these occasions rioters thought nothing of overturning an army truck and setting it on fire. Our orders were always to fire over peoples' heads. We were not allowed to hurt anyone. It was not an easy situation and often dangerous. I personally did not know of any soldier being killed. Some were certainly injured and required hospital treatment. I never felt comfortable walking through the streets of Calcutta. In a civil population it was impossible to know who was friend or foe and when bricks or stones might be thrown. I used to think that it was easier during the war. At least we knew that the Japanese were the enemy.

As the soldier in my unit who had served longest in India, I was offered a month's leave in the middle of June. I mentioned that I already had had leave the previous September. Because that was within another unit it was discounted. I was therefore delighted and planned to go to Darjeeling. From there, there was a road which led to Tibet. I was informed that it crossed a mountain pass over 14,000 feet above sea level, which sounded exciting. My father as a pioneer missionary had worked with mountain tribes on the border of China and Tibet. Having been unsuccessful in my attempts to persuade the army to send me to China, my ambition now was to try to visit and explore something of Tibet. I planned to hire a mule in Darjeeling to help in my travels. This time I would be going alone. No one else in my unit was offered leave at that time. I was looking forward immensely to seeing and exploring what would be for me, new places.

I had arranged to leave Calcutta on a Friday early in the afternoon and travel by train to Darjeeling. On the Wednesday that same week, I suddenly received word that I was being granted home leave. Because of the long journey between India and Scotland and the time required for travel, I was being offered two months leave of absence, leaving on the Friday morning two-day's hence, the same day on which I had arranged to go on leave! I was stunned! The possibility of going home at that time had never occurred to me. I was desperate to see Darjeeling and to try and visit Tibet. I looked forward immensely to doing so. I came to my senses when a soldier seeing my consternation at the news said, "You don't want to go home!" When I accepted the offer of home leave, I somehow knew, with profound regret, that I would never again see Darjeeling or visit Tibet.

Muslim/Hindu Riots

I left Calcutta on the Friday morning, in June 1946, for the start of the long journey home to Scotland. About two days after I left, there occurred in Calcutta the largest riot that had occurred for some time. Five thousand people were killed, hacked to death by axes, knives or beaten by clubs. The lads teased me about it and said that I had it all thought out and planned to be absent when the riot occurred! I asked them what they did about it. For comparatively few soldiers to face a rioting crowd that must have been well over fifty thousand, with the knowledge that they can do little or nothing about it, is daunting and very dangerous. They replied that I knew the order that we could only fire over peoples' heads, so they stayed indoors and then went and helped pick up the dead bodies of five thousand men, women, children and babies. A most gruesome thing to do! I do not think that under the circumstances they could have done anything else.

I have often reflected on that riot and on the many other riots that took place. What should the army have done? Even in company with neighbouring British army units, military numbers called to face such riots would be small. It is extremely difficult and dangerous to confront large frenzied mobs, fighting and hacking each other to death. What should Britain have done in the face of these riots? During the months and years following the end of the war and leading up to the granting of Independence and the partition of India and Pakistan, approx. two million people were killed, several million became displaced and several millions more became refugees. Was it right to stand aside and allow it to happen? The order only to fire over peoples' heads came from people in command at the top. I do not imagine that it was just a military decision. The politicians must have been involved.

Until the granting of Independence, however, Britain was primarily responsible for law and order. By failing to keep law and order, does Britain not bear some responsibility in there being so many deaths? Was Britain not in some way guilty and do we in Britain not all share that guilt? I have often thought about it and felt troubled.

It would have taken considerable force to quell some of those riots. It would have involved bloodshed. People would have been killed, but not two million! Britain was tired of war. Soldiers were weary. The British had no heart to be heavily involved where British lives were not, primarily, at risk. At the time, we almost certainly had too few British soldiers in India to be effective in maintaining peace. We could no longer rely on the Indian army because of doubt over whether Indian soldiers would be neutral in quelling sectarian riots. Yet there were British soldiers elsewhere and other Commonwealth divisions at Britain's disposal. I do not know the answer to these questions, which, as I have said, have often troubled me.

The figure of two million deaths and the number of displaced people and refugees was never to my knowledge ever intimated in Britain or ever made public. I have never heard these figures mentioned in any documentary programme and I have never heard or seen any real record of those troubled years. I have never seen, heard or read about the British army in India during those years, and the difficulties which soldiers faced. Two different friends who served in Army Intelligence for many years confirmed that they had seen the figure of two million deaths in military records. If the war in Burma has often been called the 'forgotten war', then those troubled years in India leading to Independence and Partition, are the forgotten years in British history. A curtain of silence seems to have been drawn over them.

My limited experience of that period in India has always made me feel very sympathetic toward our troops who were in Northern Ireland. Soldiers are not trained to deal with civil unrest. It is very easy for armchair critics, whom I have heard voicing their opinions in the General Assembly of the Church, to criticise the actions of our soldiers. It is quite different to be in a situation where one is called to make an instant decision and act immediately. I have also often wondered whether Christian pacifists would approve of the pacifist position that the army in India was compelled to adopt, in the face of such incredible bloodshed. Would they feel no sense of responsibility or guilt?

Arrival Home

I arrived home to a great welcome from my parents and family. Both brothers had been released from the services, Tom from chaplaincy work in Italy and James from the RAF. Shortly after arriving home I received word from Edinburgh University that they had reserved a place for me commencing in October of that year. Two or three months earlier, while I was in India my father had sent me a small cutting, of only four or five lines, from the Scotsman newspaper intimating that the university would apply for the early release of promising students. I doubted whether I was a promising student but nonetheless wrote to the secretary saying that I had seen the intimation in the Scotsman and asked that "when they were perusing the lists in quest of promising students they would give my name due consideration". I assumed that after such a request they must have concluded that I was a promising student!

I called and spoke to the secretary, or assistant secretary of the university. She happened to be a lady who studied at university with my older sisters and knew who I was. I explained that although I was grateful to be offered a place in the university in October I would at that time be back in India. On her recommendation, the university wrote to the War Office asking that I be held in the UK until the results of my nomination for release was known. I thereon received a telegram from the War Office asking that I remain in UK until further notice. I was finally released on Sept. 3rd 1946.

Chapter 3

Call and Preparation for Ministry: Prior to 1946

My time in the army was spiritually a turning point in my life. I struggled against God's call to the ministry for a long time and only accepted his call when I was in the army in India, after the war was over.

My varied experiences of army life, meeting people from all walks of life and in different situations, taught me and prepared me in a way which nothing else could, for the work of ministry and evangelism. I am deeply grateful to God.

I was five years old when at my mother's knee I prayed and committed my life to the Lord. I grew up in a loving and godly home where every day we met as a family for worship, listened to the Word of God read by one of our parents and prayed. As a family we witnessed many answers to prayer. I never ever doubted the Christian faith. I was taught to read the Bible and to worship regularly in church. I read the entire Bible through while still in Primary School. The Christian Faith always meant an enormous amount to me.

In the army I always carried a Bible in my battle dress pocket or in my ammunition pouch when it was empty, along with a small separate copy of the Psalms. In the army, if there was no compulsory church parade and I was off duty I always went to church. I met with fellow Christian soldiers for Bible study, prayer, and fellowship when I could. At home growing up and in the army there were several times I felt the near presence of God and was deeply conscious of his love. Nonetheless, when I heard God calling me for the ministry, for years I resisted.

Resistance

My resistance to God's call was all the more inexcusable in that in every unit in which I served in the army, although my fellow soldiers knew that I was a Christian, I was never criticised for my faith. No one ever adversely commented or joked about my faith or about my going to church. It was always the reverse. Because of my faith I often seemed to be accorded a certain respect. I was well received in every unit in which I served, often with consideration and kindness. I made friends in every unit in which I served. I often felt, undeservedly, that I was regarded not simply with a sense of respect but even envy because of my faith.

Prior to my going overseas a Jewish soldier said that watching me he was amazed. He said, "The army has never coarsened your life. You never swear". I wasn't guilty of grumbling or complaining. He said, "Before enlisting in the army,

I was like that. I never swore or behaved the way that I do now. It is the effect that the army has had on my life, but it has not had that effect on your life. You amaze me!" I could detect not just respect but a touch of envy.

In those days the country was more religious. During the war there was a more serious outlook. Life was uncertain. No one knew what lay ahead. That no doubt influenced the way in which I was treated.

In India serving with a small British unit in the 14th Indian Division, although I was the only one who went to church, no one every joked or criticised me about my Christian faith. Often, when I was off duty and about to set off for church, one of the lads would voluntarily offer the information that a truck happened to be available and it would save the four-mile walk to church.

When I did not drink, as did the others during Christmas week 1945, no one criticised. Because of my abstinence and conduct I even seemed to acquire a new respect and was commended!

In India although I played in various football matches against other army units, I never played on a Sunday. Yet no one ever commented, criticised or tried to persuade me otherwise. They seemed cheerfully to accept that a Christian would not play on a Sunday. They always kept my place for me on the team when we played on other days.

The welcome, the friendships which I enjoyed, the respect that I received from my fellow soldiers, the lack of any criticism concerning my Christian faith is a strong rebuke to my prolonged resistance to God's call to ministry.

Reasons for my Resistance

My father was a minister. He had served as a missionary in China for 40 years. He was above all to the end of his days an evangelist. Mother also had served as a missionary and was a deeply spiritual woman. I loved both of my parents. I loved and respected my father. From him and also from my mother, I always felt that the call to ministry was the call to evangelise. I was afraid to evangelise, to challenge people with the Gospel and seek to persuade them to give their lives to Christ.

What I read in Acts chapter 2, about the apostles and their preaching in the open air deeply troubled me. When the apostles after receiving the Holy Spirit preached in the open air people mocked! I did not want to be mocked! I was afraid of being mocked! I did not want to preach in the open air yet always, when I heard God calling me to be a minister I felt that he was calling me to preach in the open air and to be an evangelist.

For a long time I resisted God's call to the ministry. Although I believed the Gospel, although I wanted the Lord and loved him, I was afraid to let go and truly surrender to him my life. I was afraid of what he would ask of me. I was afraid about what others might say and think of me, if I was a minister. I was more concerned to receive the approval of men than the approval of God! In my resistance to God's call, like Moses I tried to make many excuses. I endeavoured to raise various objections.

God Breaks Down my Resistance, Answers my Objections

1 I tried to argue that people outside the church do not really want to hear the Gospel.

When on a military exercise on the moors in the North of England I had occasion to share a tent with three others. Although I liked them and we got on well they were not Christians. One particularly swore a lot. At night we simply slept on the ground in our boots and in our trench coats for warmth. We were permitted to remove our field packs. I used mine as a pillow. On our first night together, when I thought the others were asleep I pulled out my Bible and started to read. Suddenly a voice said, "Dave, is that a Bible that you are reading?" When I replied in the affirmative he said, "Why not read to us all what you're reading there!" So I was compelled to read to them all and they listened in silence. In that incident, I knew in a powerful way that God was answering my objection and abolishing my excuse. Some people at least did want to hear the Gospel!

While in that same unit I used to meet with a group of 12 or 15 others for Bible study, prayer and Christian fellowship. They came from different units. One evening one of them invited me to go a walk with him because he wanted to tell me about his receiving the Holy Spirit. He told me that he was a Pentecostal. I had never before heard of the Pentecostal Church. It was new to me. He described how on one occasion the Holy Spirit had come upon him in a remarkable way. I told him that I had received the Holy Spirit when I was converted. He said that what he was talking about was something different and something special which happened only after conversion. I was puzzled and a little sceptical. When later I went into the NAAFI (Navy, Army, Air Force Institute) canteen, several soldiers told me that the sergeant major was after my blood! He had come to the canteen and asked for the orderly sergeant and was on the war-path because I was not there! Although a junior NCO I was required to take my turn in the duties of 'Orderly Sergeant'. It had been my turn to be on duty in the canteen that evening, to ensure that all was well, which it always was. Each morning a DRO (Daily Routine Orders) notice was put up on the notice board, stating our respective duties and the programme for the day. We were obliged to read it every morning. Although normally very diligent on such matters I had failed to read the notice that morning and was unaware that it was my turn to be on duty that evening. My immediate reaction was to think if that soldier was really full of the Holy Spirit why was he not able to tell me that I should have been on duty!

The sergeant major was a regular soldier and strong disciplinarian. However, although I was careful to keep out of his way for the next few days, surprisingly he never asked for me or reprimanded me. I then began humorously to wonder if perhaps there was something special about the working of the Holy Spirit! On a more serious note, my conversation with the other soldier and what he said made me think more deeply about the Holy Spirit. God in his own way was speaking to me and challenging me.

2 I next, like Moses when God first called him, argued I was not fluent. I was not able to speak about Christ. I had no gift of speech.

When I was with 115 Assault Brigade, I attended when possible a Methodist church in a country village a little over two miles from our camp. When I returned on my first Sunday evening, I hunted for a post box to post a letter to my parents; I asked another soldier, an engineer, if he knew where I could find one. Very kindly he showed me where it was. He was about my own age. His studies at university had also been interrupted by military service. He asked me what I had been doing. I told him that I had gone to church but we did not talk about it. At his invitation I joined him for a cup of tea in the canteen. Before saying good night, having discovered that we were both free the following Saturday afternoon we agreed to meet and go sailing together. As we were pulling in the boat he said, "Last Sunday when I met you, you said that you had gone to church, are you going tomorrow?" When I said I was, he asked if he could go with me. This happened for the next three weeks. We went to church on the Sunday and went sailing on the Saturday afternoon. On our third occasion together, when walking back after the service, he said, "Dave you are a Christian." I said, "Yes". He said, "You have never talked to me about Christ".

What he said hit me hard. I knew once again that the Lord was answering my arguments and excuses, saying, "Yes, you can speak! You must! I am calling you to speak! I am calling you to be a minister!" The shock of the other lad's request and knowing that God was speaking to me, brought perspiration to my brow. I stammered, "Where do I begin?" He said, "You will have to begin at the beginning. I know nothing about the Christian faith". I doubt whether ever before he had attended church. He was one of those remarkable people who, when you spoke about the Gospel, simply accepted what was said and believed. He did not have a Bible so I gave him mine. I required to write home and ask my parents to send to me another Bible. I still had however my copy of the Psalms.

No doubt our being in a Special Assault Brigade and, being on 'stand by' and awaiting orders to go into action, opened his mind to the Gospel. Nonetheless God spoke to me powerfully through this encounter.

I still however, endeavoured to resist God's call to ministry, and continued to insist that I had no gifts for ministry. My continued resistance to God's call took away much of the joy that I should have had over the lad's conversion. I kept arguing that in spite of everything and despite his conversion, people outside the church did not really want the Gospel and would simply mock. Acts 2:15 still kept coming into my mind and troubling me. I was far more concerned about what other people might think than about what God thinks. I also still tried to argue that I had no gifts for ministry. I was unable to speak effectively about Christ.

About that time I remember sitting and looking out to sea. I was reflecting on our commission to attack and capture the Channel Islands. We all were aware that some time earlier a Canadian Assault Force like 115 Brigade although smaller had been ordered to attack Dieppe on the French coast. Although they brought back valuable information for the Allies they had sustained very heavy casualties and the raid was generally believed, at the time, to have been a failure. We hoped that our attack on the Channel Islands would be successful, but every soldier knew, without talking about it, that we also could sustain many casualties and many could be killed. I was not disturbed. I do not remember feeling afraid. All that troubled me was the question of the ministry. I remember saying to myself that I hoped that I would be killed because if I came back God would put me in the ministry! How mad and sinful I must have been!

In saying what I did I had a deep inner feeling that, come what may, God was determined to bring me back because he was determined to make me a minister! That fact depressed me and hung as a black cloud over me until the end of the war.

God's Grace

The journey by boat to India lasted a month. On the boat, I met for fellowship with a group of other Christians, whom I had not known previously. One in particular helped me in his sharing of his experiences. He had been on the beach at Dunkirk for seven days waiting and hoping to be picked up and rescued. He prayed and said to God that if God answered his prayer he would give his life to the Lord. After being rescued and for approximately two years, he did nothing. At last God broke through his resistance and he surrendered his life to the Lord. There was that in his story with which I could empathise. The faith of the other Christian soldiers and my conversations with them were a help to me.

On several evenings I stood on deck looking up at the stars or watching the waves of the sea. On these occasions, God seemed very, very near. I was very aware of his presence. I thought of my parents. The knowledge that they would be praying for me and for my brothers, I found very strengthening.

I wanted the Lord. I believed in him and yet still I was afraid to fully surrender my life and accept his call to ministry.

God Acts Regardless of Me

On board ship I met Ken Slater, another signaller in my unit. He was a little older than me and had studied four years at university before enlisting in the army. He was a strong humanist and spoke as many did of, "a marvellous, brave new world after the war". We had many vigorous discussions about his humanism and agnosticism. Despite everything I liked him and we became friends. Both of us were withdrawn from our unit and instead of going to Burma were posted to Agra and then to the 14th Indian Division. We were not sent to the same Brigade. Ken was stationed in Singhori and I in Kulberha.

In Agra we shared a tent together. One evening I was lying on my bed in the tent. It was dark and I was enjoying listening to the noise of countless insects. The tropics at night are always noisy. Suddenly Ken entered the tent. He looked at me and said, "This is a wonderful world" (or something to that effect). In the light of our many discussions concerning his humanism, I felt that he was taking a swipe at me. I was annoyed. He had disturbed my enjoyment of the evening. I said, "Shut up and sit down! You know that you are talking nonsense. It is not a wonderful world. That is why there is a war and why you and I are here as soldiers". He sat down and after a short silence said, "I would like to become a Christian". That stunned me. I had been rude to him. I had told him to shut up! I had told him that he was talking nonsense. In all our discussions he had never once hinted that he was weakening in his humanism or had any desire to become a Christian. Now he was saying that he would like to become one!

I felt deeply rebuked by God and humbled and felt that God was saying loud and clear, "David, I will use you regardless of what you say or do and regardless of your many excuses! I am calling you to be a minister!"

I endeavoured to explain to Ken how to receive Christ, his forgiveness and salvation. I held out my Bible toward him and said that if I were to give him this book as a gift, all he could do was, not to buy it, but simply to accept it as a gift. I tried to explain that God has given Christ to be our Saviour. We are asked simply to receive him as a gift from God. We prayed and Ken asked Christ to come into his life. He thereon asked if he could keep my Bible as a gift and as a reminder that he had received Christ as a gift from God. I gave it to him and wrote and asked my parents to send me another one. Later, we would go on holiday together to Kashmir.

God's Amazing Grace

When I was ill with smallpox and in isolation, when my temperature went up very high the second time I had a remarkable night spiritually. Having mentioned it to a Christian friend who was a medical consultant, he asked me whether I was delirious. Perhaps medically I was, I do not know. I was filled with an incredible spirit of praise, thanksgiving and joy, which lasted all night. I was alone but had an amazing awareness of the love and near presence of God. To me it was like what some people have called 'a baptism of the Holy Spirit'. I had never before had such an experience, nor yet since. In the days that followed, although feeling very weak and, for a time, unable to eat, I was amazingly upheld. Throughout my entire period of isolation, although hours and days passed when there was no one to talk to, I never felt lonely. I never felt depressed. I was aware that the majority of people who fall ill with smallpox die from the disease. Yet I never doubted that I would recover and be restored to health. I was very conscious of the hand of God and of his presence and was grateful.

God Overcomes my Resistance

After my return to my unit and I had fully recovered, I began to think about what I would do after being released from the army It was November and the war was over. I heard God saying again, "The ministry!" This time, despite all that had happened and my experience of the grace of God, I said with determination, "No! I will be a medical missionary and give my life in helping the poor." I did not want to be a doctor but I felt that I would willingly do anything rather than be a minister. I was prepared to try and compromise with God. I had seen plenty of poor people in India. I felt that I would happily spend my life helping them. However excellent the work of a medical missionary is, it was not what God was calling me to do. For the next three days my life was in turmoil. I felt completely torn apart. I do not know what other soldiers thought. I think that they must have noticed it. After returning from hospital I had a tent to myself. Toward the end of the third day as I approached my tent and entered, I knew that God was in that tent. I did not see him but I felt as if physically I could touch him. God said, "The ministry!" Again, I said, "No!" This time I felt that God caught me by the scruff of the neck. I heard him say, "All right, you will never again have peace of mind or any joy." In a state of utter frustration, I knelt on the bare ground and said, "All right Lord, I will be a minister and it is your look-out!" It was the most disgruntled prayer that I ever prayed. I said to the Lord, "It is your look-out" because I still felt and argued that I had no gifts for ministry and like Moses was not eloquent and was slow of speech (Exodus 4:10).

Immediately, a miraculous change took place. The dark cloud, which had hung over me for so long, because of my resistance to accepting the call to the ministry, suddenly lifted. I was filled with a marvellous peace and joy. What astonished me most was, that having before said in my folly that I would rather die in the war than be a minister, the ministry now suddenly seemed to me very attractive. To my utter astonishment I now found myself wanting to be a minister and to share the Gospel with others. Although that was long ago, I can still feel the peace and joy of the days that followed and my continued astonishment over my changed attitude to the ministry.

Acceptance of God's Call Tested

The reality and sincerity of my acceptance of the call to the ministry was soon tested. The Division chaplain, an Anglican, told me that there was a sergeant, Miller Scott, in the artillery battery in Gangiwara, who planned to enter the ministry of the Church of Scotland after his discharge from the army. He had graduated with an MA degree. I had told the chaplain that I hoped and planned to become a minister. The chaplain asked if Miller and I would organise and run Church of Scotland services in Gangiwara. The chaplain knew nothing of my spiritual struggle before accepting God's call. I did not tell him. I happily, and without hesitation, accepted the challenge.

So began my first humble attempts in ministry as I preached to fellow soldiers, in a tent set aside for the purpose. Miller and I decided that we would take it in turns either to lead the services or to preach. On our first Sunday the entire Battery came to church. When Miller explained that this was not a compulsory church parade, the majority turned and left. Thirty or forty mostly Scots remained. I have no recollection of the theme of my sermons or what I said, or yet what Miller said. I had only my Bible to help me and a book of daily readings, *My Utmost for His Highest*, by Oswald Chambers. When the thirty or forty Scots kept coming to the services, I was tempted to think that, insofar as I was concerned, they did not come because of the preaching but because of their loyalty to fellow Scots! I can only imagine that my first and early sermons were poor stuff! However I believe that God honoured our humble efforts. The experience helped me.

In the Division (as previously mentioned) we were not permitted to wear a shirt during the day, only shorts and bush hat. We were allowed to carry a shirt to church, to put it on before the service, but take it off as we left the church. In our services in Gangiwara I chose to wear a shirt. Miller chose to lead the services and preach without a shirt. Years later, when speaking to him during a meeting of the General Assembly, I teased him and said that he was probably the only minister of the Church of Scotland who had preached without a shirt!

Preparation for Pastoral Ministry

Christmas week of 1945 was for me a preparation for ministry and particularly for the pastoral side of ministry. I knew each man in my unit. We had lived, worked, shared together over many months. We had lived in complete harmony. We had helped each other. I had experienced consideration and even acts of kindness from each one of them. I liked each of them. I had been brought up in a sheltered home and had never been exposed to the company of men who drank and could drink heavily, when the opportunity and temptation arose. That week, living, sharing in the mess tent, speaking to them, sharing in their games and competitions as they drank, when I did not, went a long way toward delivering me from the fear and hesitation of speaking to such men, on the streets or in pubs, in later evangelism.

To my surprise, although I did not drink, I acquired a new respect from the others. A sergeant who I thought might in civil life become an alcoholic, and who that week drank the most, in seeking to compliment me said that never before had he met a Christian who would speak or join in their competitions, when they were drinking. The respect that they awarded me was not simply that I had to carry through their military duties on that occasion! That week also helped to open my eyes and to create in me a far greater concern about the curse of alcohol and the devastating effect it can have on so many otherwise good and kindly people.

We had two British signallers in the Brigade at Gangiwara. Around that time a vacancy occurred by one leaving for home. That same sergeant said that I would not be sent to Gangiwara and therefore promoted, although I was next in line for promotion, because I did not drink. I think that in his way he meant it kindly because of the need in Gangiwara to share the same mess tent with other soldiers who drank. I was not disturbed.

Prayer Prior to Leaving the Army

I was discharged from the army on the second of September 1946.

War and the killing of another human being is desperately wicked. I had never killed someone else. I had however, served in combat units and thereby helped others to kill. I had been part of the war effort. I felt

I needed to pray and ask and receive God's forgiveness for my part in the war effort. As I prayed for forgiveness I was aware that if it had been possible to turn the clock back, I would have done the same thing again. I felt that Britain in going to war in 1939 had chosen the lesser of the two evils which confronted the nation. Nonetheless the lesser evil was still wrong and we all needed God's forgiveness.

Other Reflections

Many other thoughts swept through my mind and have continued to do so from time to time over the years.

Why was I alive? It is a question that many like myself asked at the end of the war. Why was I alive, when so many very fine Christians were killed and many whom I personally knew and many of the boys I had known at school and had played with and grown up with, were killed?

Why as a combatant soldier had I never been called actively to engage in the war? Why on every occasion when serving in a combat unit was I suddenly, without consultation and without any given reason, transferred to another unit, when by remaining in that unit I would have gone into action?

If I had been commissioned in mountain infantry after training at Loch Maree, I would most likely have been posted to the 52nd Mountain Division and gone with them to Holland and Germany.

If I had remained in the 79th Division I would have gone with them to Burma.

If I had remained in 115 Special Assault Brigade I would have gone with them to France.

If I had remained in the unit with which I had gone to India, I would have gone with them to Burma.

If my wishes in answer to my repeated volunteering request had been answered I would almost certainly have been involved in the war in Indonesia or in the conflict in Malaya.

Why did I miss by one day, in my arrival at Mhow, the last posting to Indonesia?

Why did I miss, by approximately two days, the largest and most violent of the riots that took place during the time when I was attached to the unit in Bengal?

Why did I miss the gruesome task of helping pick up 5,000 dead bodies?

I have no answer to any of these questions. I felt that the unseen hand of God had somehow rested on me, controlling and over-ruling my entire army career.

In my youth, like many other young men, I tended often to be motivated by the spirit of adventure and tended to think little of risk or danger. With advancing years I have become more cautious and like to think that I have become wiser. I have long been grateful that God overruled my youthful aspirations.

On leaving the army I felt humbled and deeply grateful to God for watching over me and not giving up on me for resisting for so long his call to ministry. I felt deeply grateful to God for not only calling but, I felt in the end, compelling me, to accept the call to enter the ministry.

I also felt thankful to God for good health, which I continue to enjoy. Medically, the army placed people in four categories, A, B, C and D. Each category was subdivided into four smaller categories. Categories A1 to C3 were conscripted into the forces. The others were not. Each person, as far as possible was assigned to a unit suitable to their medical category. Apart from one illness I was always in category A1 and in that category was discharged. I was thankful for that.

I had matured through my army experience. I felt and knew that I was no longer a boy but a man. Experiencing the rough and tumble of army life had taught me many things, which I would otherwise never have learned. I have always regarded it as a vital and important part of my preparation for ministry and for evangelism. It gave me greater courage and confidence in sharing the Gospel with people from different walks of life.

Decisions Taken

I have certainly pondered over some of my decisions. Was I right to turn down the opportunity to serve in Military Intelligence? As I have said, looking back, I know that that is something I could have greatly enjoyed.

On the human level, I have sometimes regretted not being commissioned. Yet, I have felt that for the purposes of ministry and evangelism, it was right that I was not. I feel that I learned more and was better equipped through serving in the ranks, than I would have been if I had been commissioned. Several times, in the years immediately following the war, when engaged in evangelistic missions, when I spoke to working men on the street or in pubs, they tended at first to dismiss what I wished to say, by suggesting that I had been an officer in the army and therefore did not understand their position. When I said that I had served in the ranks their attitudes always changed. They became more friendly and it was easier to share with them the Gospel.

Was I foolish to volunteer to serve in the Infantry, or in the Reconnaissance Corps (which I did at an Officer Selection School) or to volunteer to serve anywhere east of India? In growing older, my outlook on many issues has changed and (as I have said) I have become more cautious.

Civil Life

I left the army ready to throw myself into studies at university and New College in preparation for the ministry. I was also ready and wanting to throw myself into active evangelism.

I found it an immense privilege, and it was an immense help to me, to meet, through the university Christian Union and through New College, with other ex-service students, whose faith had been strengthened during the war and who shared the same enthusiasm for evangelism. We formed lasting friendships.

My premonitions about preaching in the open-air did in fact materialise! After accepting God's call, and shortly after resuming my studies at university I went the following Easter on my first evangelistic mission with D.P. Thomson. At the very start of that mission, without any forewarning, I was called to preach in the open air! I was given no time to think or prepare! What I for so long had dreaded actually happened! It helped to lay aside my fears.

To help in open air preaching, as a student at New College, another student Malcolm Ritchie, who was a little older than me, each Sunday evening one summer collected two chairs from the rooms of the Christian Union. We carried them down to the Mound, off Princess Street, where like Hyde Corner in London, there were several open air meetings and people spoke on a variety of subjects. Standing on our chairs Malcolm and I preached the gospel, challenging people to believe in Christ. We were regularly interrupted by hecklers and had to learn to think on our feet and give a ready response. It was good training. I have since preached many times in the open-air and witnessed people converted. On that first occasion and since I have pondered and laughed over my earlier fears. God has a kindly sense of humour.

My Parents' Prayers

My parents had six children. Before each was born they prayed and dedicated each one to the Lord. I did not know that I and my brothers had been dedicated to be ministers of the Gospel, until after I had accepted the call to the ministry. In order to be sure that I, for example, did not enter the ministry under family pressure but entered because I was called by God, my mother on various occasions, and despite wanting me to be a minister, asked whether I wanted to be a doctor. My parents were concerned that if I, or my brothers, entered the ministry it was a clear call from God.

I am very grateful for my parents' prayers and for their dedication of each of us to the ministry and the Lord's work. I have often wondered if that is partly why I never really seemed to have had much option in the matter. I felt that God compelled me to be a minister. My two brothers also entered the ministry and my three sisters married ministers. Two of my sisters with their husbands went to the mission field.

My wife and I likewise dedicated our three children to the Lord before they were born. It has been a great joy to us that they each love the Lord. My son is a minister of the Church of Scotland.

Further Note

Despite the fact that in the 14th Indian Division there were comparatively few British soldiers, four of us, although not serving in the same unit or Brigade, entered the ministry of the Church of Scotland: Miller Scott, Bill McDonald, Jim Frazer and myself.

The only other person whom I have met who served in that Division was a Pakistani. I met him when he was a patient in a hospital, in the Scottish Borders. I was at the time hospital chaplain. When I first met him he was in the patients' sitting room dressed in the white robes of a Muslim. When I approached him he at once said defensively, "I am a Muslim". Thinking by his fairly pale complexion that he was from somewhere in the Middle East, I asked if he was an Arab. He said no, he was from Pakistan but had been in Scotland for thirty years. I asked him what he did before coming to Scotland and to my surprise he said he had been in the Indian Army. When I expressed to him my astonishment he said that he had been in the Indian army but transferred to the Pakistan army after partition. Chancing a long shot I asked whether in the Indian army he had come across the 14th Indian Division. This time he was surprised and said that he had served in the 14th Indian Division. I asked him in which Brigade he had served and then I told him that I had served in the same Division and same Brigade.

That changed everything. The following week when visiting his ward, with doctors, nurses and other patients present, and while I was still entering through the door, he noticed me. Immediately he leapt to his feet, saluted and flung both arms around me in the middle of the floor. He embraced me like a long lost brother and asked me to come and sit with him. He told me that he prayed for me and asked that I should pray for him. Here we were, a Muslim, dressed in the white robes of a Muslim and I a Christian minister wearing a clerical collar. All barriers of religion and race were set aside. For him our meeting recalled his youth. For me it brought back happy memories of the warm friendships and the feeling of mutual loyalty, of the one to the other, which as British and Indians we enjoyed, when serving together in the Indian army.

Chapter 4

University: 1942-1943, 1946-1953 and other Academic Work

I matriculated at Edinburgh University in October 1942, at the age of 18 and enrolled in the Arts Faculty. It was a great and pleasant change from school. Because I joined the university Senior Training Corps I studied only two subjects, Latin and Greek. Shortly afterwards I enlisted and became a member of the Territorial Army. This involved training all day on Fridays, every Sunday afternoon and every Tuesday afternoon or evening, and on several occasions all Tuesday night and several weekends. I inevitably missed all Friday lectures. Under the circumstance I would have found it difficult to have studied a third subject.

Arts Faculty

I worked hard at my studies and passed the degree examinations in both subjects. I did not however to my regret gain a merit or honours certificate, which I felt that I deserved in Greek. I gained an average of 75 marks in my examinations over two terms and normally Beta plus plus in all my textual translation exercises. 65 and over was the qualifying mark for a first class certificate in examinations and Beta plus plus was regarded as qualifying for a First Class Certificate. I do not think I ever dropped below Beta plus plus. However I had missed a lot of classes and I presume that was the reason for my not receiving an honours certificate. In addition to my missing lectures each Friday I also deliberately missed several other lectures in Greek from Professor Calder. He was a great authority on Greek tombstones and lectured on these for a full term. Many of these inscriptions were fragmentary and I could not muster any enthusiasm over them, in addition to which I found Professor Calder's manner of lecturing sepulchral! I would love to have done Inter-Honours Greek on my return to university after the war but, because I did not gain an honours certificate I would have required to ask for a special concession to do so, explaining the circumstances under which I was placed in my first year. I chose not to do so.

On my return to university in October 1946, I continued in the Arts Faculty and studied for an honours degree in Philosophy. We were not permitted to study philosophy in first year, on the ground that its study required more maturity. Accordingly an honours course in Philosophy generally commenced in one's second year and lasted four years. It was a five year course altogether.

The course embraced Logic and Metaphysics, Moral Philosophy and one year in Psychology. With my interest in history, I also studied European History for a year. In Logic and Metaphysics I had Prof. A.D. Ritchie. Early in his career he had been a marine biologist. His interest and study in the principles of scientific method led him into philosophy. Through his influence, scientific method has remained for me a lasting interest. In Moral Philosophy I studied under Prof. John Macmurray, who had been much influenced by the Jewish philosopher Martin Buber, who wrote the book, *I-Thou*. His teaching introduced me to Jewish thought over against classical Roman and Greek thought – a helpful preparation for studying theology.

I worked hard, gaining five academic awards and scholarships in the Arts Faculty, including two medals in the study of philosophy, a junior medal in Moral Philosophy and senior medal in Logic and Metaphysics. On graduating the way opened for me to become a Philosophy lecturer assisting Mr Duncan, who now had a post in Canada. However, no matter how much I enjoyed philosophy I knew that God was calling me into the ministry. At the same time I began to feel that the academic world, and in particular philosophy, in which I had become immersed was an unreal world. I wanted to be in touch with ordinary people and their thinking.

Faculty of Divinity

After graduating with an MA degree I entered New College in 1950 to study for a Bachelor of Divinity (BD). I had the privilege of studying under Prof. J. S. Stewart and Prof. William Manson, both in New Testament. James Stewart more than any other professor linked together the theological understanding and the spiritual pastoral application of the New Testament. He was a dear saint and later Moderator of the General Assembly of the Church of Scotland. Manson, a biblical and conservative scholar, introduced us in depth to the theology of the New Testament. I still remember with appreciation his lectures on the Epistle to the Romans.

In Dogmatics I had G.T. Thomson, a brilliant linguist. In the First World War he served in the Middle East as an Arabic interpreter for General Allenby. Originally liberal in theology he changed under the influence of Karl Barth and translated Barth's *Church Dogmatics* vol. 1 part 1. By the time I studied under him he had embraced High Calvinism and believed in 'double predestination'. The text book which he asked us to read was Heppe's *Reformed Dogmatics* – a good discipline, though an indigestible way to learn theology! It introduced to us a long list of High Calvinist theologians. GT introduced each new one succintly in an unforgettable and unorthodox way. One student in my class humorously asked who was Karl Barth. The unforgettable reply was, "A very great man who suffers from verbal diarrhoea!"

I studied Divinity under Professor John Baillie (also a former Moderator of our General Assembly). He was a devout churchman whose book on Prayers has been translated into a number of different languages. Theologically he was liberal and never to my mind was able fully to reconcile his personal faith and his theology. However, I learned much from him. We were required to read one of his own publications, *The Philosophy of Religion.* For Church History I studied under Professor James Burleigh and also my brother Tom, who taught Church History at New College from 1950-52. I also studied Systematic Theology under Tom for one term in my third year.

For Old Testament Language, Literature and Theology I had Professor Norman Porteous, who was conservative and Professor Oliver Rankin. The latter was an outstanding Hebrew scholar, an able teacher but an extreme liberal in theology. In his class examinations I felt that he was incapable of understanding or accepting any theological position other than his own and so in answering his examination questions, I did not state my own position. I simply said that according to this or that position, this is what is believed. It was quite a discipline. To my astonishment he gave me in one examination, what is normally unheard of, full marks in Old Testament theology – despite the fact that I believed none of it!

Later, when I went to Basle I felt that I had to slough off all that I had learned from Professor Rankin and begin again in my understanding of Old Testament theology. In this I was, and continue to be, greatly helped by Karl Barth. Throughout my ministry and particularly when engaged with writing a sermon I frequently read Barth's exegesis of an Old or New Testament passage. His exegeses are published in small print in his *Church Dogmatics* and I generally found them to be excellent. Sadly some people in their reading of Barth are tempted to omit reading the small print.

For my BD degree I specialised in Systematic Theology and in particular in Christology. I also studied the Philosophy of Religion. I was not really interested in the latter. However the text books prescribed by Professor Baillie for the final exams, included such books as David Hume's *Dialogue of Natural Religion* and Immanuel Kant's *The Third Critique.* Because I had already read, and was familiar with, some of the books prescribed when studying philosophy, by taking the Philosophy of Religion as my second subject, it was easier for me to concentrate on Systematic Theology and Christology, which was my prime interest.

Van Reebeck Celebrations in South Africa, 1952

In my second year at New College, special centenary celebrations were held in South Africa commemorating the setting up of the Dutch colony in South Africa. The Dutch Reformed Church to which Van Reebeck belonged believed, with their interpretation of the cursing of Ham in Genesis chapter 9 verse 25, that the coloured peoples of the world should serve the white people. This was the theology that lay behind Apartheid, whereby the white population was separated from the black and government was in the hands of the whites.

The South African Government issued invitations for white people of other countries and churches to share in their celebrations. The Archbishop of Canterbury declined the invitation. White Anderson, minister of the collegiate charge of St Cuthbert's Church, Edinburgh and Moderator of the General Assembly, accepted the invitation to represent the Church of Scotland in the celebrations in South Africa.

My brother-in-law, Kenneth MacKenzie and his wife (my sister Margaret) were home from Africa on furlough and staying in our house with my parents. They were missionaries in Central Africa. Kenneth was deeply disturbed that our Moderator had accepted the invitation, thereby, in his opinion, compromising and undermining the witness of our missionaries to the African. He discussed the issue with me. My parents were missionaries in China. I grew up in a family who believed that people of all nations are one in Christ Jesus. I was also strongly influenced by my experience in the army in India when I served with Indian troops in an Indian Jungle Division, in which there were comparatively few British soldiers. We British and Indians were thrown together and regarded each other with great respect. The Indian soldiers were extremely loyal and many friendships developed.

I abhorred the doctrine of Apartheid. I requested a meeting of all students in New College, undergraduates and post-graduates, to debate the issue. Almost the entire student population of the college attended. With Kenneth's help I drew up six resolutions, calling on the Moderator to recall his acceptance of the invitation to South Africa, stressing the importance of the Church's witness to the Africans, stressing that we are all one and equal in Christ, and rejecting the doctrine of Apartheid. I delivered a fairly long speech, thanking them for coming, explaining the issues before the Church, and seeking their support. In my year there was a very fine student from South Africa, Robert Robertson. When I put my proposals to the meeting he opposed me although later he became an outspoken and courageous opponent of Apartheid.

The meeting by an overwhelming majority accepted each of my six proposals. Only six students led by Robertson opposed.

We agreed to send all six proposals to the other three theological colleges of Glasgow, St Andrews and Aberdeen. Kenneth and I also sent the six proposals to quite a number of ministers whom we thought would be sympathetic, asking them to raise the issue in their Presbytery. The response was encouraging. I think the other three theological colleges were unanimous in their support, as were many Presbyteries. It was intimated in the public media that the Moderator, because of the strength of opposition to the Church of Scotland being represented at the Van Reebeck celebrations, had altered his decision and declined the invitation to go to South Africa. The other three theological colleges had simply adopted and forwarded the six resolutions agreed by the students of New College. Likewise several, if not all the Presbyteries who discussed the issues, accepted and forwarded the same six resolutions. I was therefore daunted but pleased to read in the Newspaper, that when the Moderator was interviewed in regard to the withdrawal of his acceptance to attend the celebrations, he said that the opposition had arisen from a single source in New College. I was grateful that he did not mention my name. I was comforted however when Professor John Baillie, the Principal of New College and Professor Burleigh said that they were proud that the opposition to the visit of the Moderator had come from within New College and were proud that the students of New College had manifested such an interest in the Church's mission to the world and the issues confronting South Africa.

Academic Awards

In New College I was awarded approximately 10 prizes and scholarships. I was, like my two brothers, Tom and James, Dux of New College, awarded the First Cunningham Fellowship and the Glover Kidd and Maxton scholarship to enable me, if I so desired, to engage in post graduate studies for three years. Because I could not hold both scholarships I surrendered the First Cunningham Fellowship and it was given to Mike Campbell. In the end I accepted the Glover, Kidd and Maxton Scholarship for only two years, declining it for the third year, because I felt that God was calling me to evangelism and the pastoral ministry.

In those days to determine who should be Dux of college and receive the First Cunningham Fellowship, the procedure seemed to me then and now rather quaint. I do not know if today they follow the same procedure. The marks of every term exam in all three years were counted up. The one with the highest marks was acclaimed Dux. I beat Michael Campbell who was second by approximately 160 marks. Mary Lusk (later Mrs

Mary Levison) came third. However, Tom told me that my brother James beat me by one mark and I beat Tom by half a mark! We three brothers were each in turn Dux and came very close together in our marks! I was personally pleased to have beaten Tom by half a mark – although what was half a mark over three years? Nonetheless it gave me moderate satisfaction, although in the years ahead both Tom and James went far ahead of me academically.

Although I was awarded the First Cunningham Fellowship, following my final exams I received the second prize. Mary Lusk was awarded the first prize. Tom told me confidentially that I had actually beaten Mary Lusk but the external examiner in marking my papers had chosen to deduct four marks from each of my papers because of my bad writing, something of which he never previously had heard. The penalty for bad writing however did not affect my receiving an honours BD with Distinction (in 1953). Tom confidentially showed me a sample of my writing and that of Mary Lusk. Contrasting the two sets of handwriting I sympathised with the external examiner! I never mentioned that to Mary Lusk or any other student.

With my prize money I bought a clerical frock coat which I used on wedding occasions when I was a parish minister and used at the weddings of my daughter Grace and my son David. With money from my scholarship I bought a scooter motor bike which I used to travel to Basle. Mike Campbell, who chose to pursue post graduate studies in Germany kindly agreed to accompany me to Basle, before travelling on to Germany. He later came to study in Basle for the summer semester.

It was an eventful journey. My bike had a structural fault in that the two condensers on the magneto fly wheel were placed too close together. As a result when the lights were switched on at night, the condenser affecting the engine blew, cutting out the engine. It took me some time to discover the problem. In Paris, when about to travel down the Champs Elysée, the engine cut out. It was early evening and shops and business were closed. Not knowing what else to do, I sat on the pavement and dismantled and temporalily repaired my engine. We spent the night in Paris. The following evening before arriving in Basle the engine again cut out and I completed the journey being towed by Mike Campbell on his motor bike. Despite its problems, the motor bike enabled me to explore Basle and the surrounding countryside in addition to travelling to Geneva and seeing something of the Swiss Alps. On my return to Scotland the bike again broke down north of London. This time I put the bike on a train and returned by train to Edinburgh. I sold the bike back to the motor bike firm who sold it to me, explaining the problem.

Basle, Switzerland

I benefited from and enjoyed my studies in Basle under Professors Karl Barth and Oscar Cullman. Both had a deep influence on me, particularly Barth. Their teaching and writings have guided me since in all my biblical and theological studies. Barth was undoubtedly the greatest Reformed theologian since John Calvin, and I owe much to him.

In Basle and under Karl Barth I was engaged in doctoral studies planning to write a thesis and hoping to gain a DTheol (Doctor of Theology) degree. I met personally with Barth, I think in his home, shortly after my arrival. He agreed that the subject of my study should be, *The Doctrine of the Church and Sacraments in the Writing of John Knox and the Influence upon him of his Contemporaries, Bucer, John Alasko and John Calvin.*

I stayed, as did my brothers Tom and James before me, in the Alumneum, a theological residence attached to the University. I and an Irish student, Francis Boyd were the only two British residents. There were four American students, one Italian, one French and a German speaker from Alsace Lorraine and the others German and Swiss. Prof. Cullmann and his sister Fraulein Cullman were unmarried and acted as house father and mother. Prof. Cullman always dined with the students but not Fraulein Cullman. We were a happy community.

I soon discovered that my brother Tom was held in high respect. Prof. Cullman later wrote urging him to succeed Barth on the latter's retirement. However, Tom told me before I went that as a student, staying in the Alumneum, he incurred the displeasure of the establishment. He had etched on the back of a wardrobe door a Scottish thistle with its Latin motto!

Now, there is a difference between reading German and hearing it spoken. I had taught myself German but on arrival, I found that it took some days before I could readily understand what was spoken in German. Hence, in my first few days a Swiss student used to speak to me in Latin. I think on my second day, I suddenly heard a loud shout, "Herr Torrance *venite* (come here)". When I entered the room next door, he swung open his wardrobe door and asked in Latin, "Is this your brother?" There I saw on the back of the door a large Scottish thistle about eighteen or twenty inches in height and underneath the Latin words, *Nemo me impune lacessit* (No one injures me with impunity). It was done with considerable artistic skill using a hot poker. Underneath in small letters was the name of my brother, Tom Torrance. Tom had left his mark! What he did was I think unheard of in Switzerland or in Germany.

The only two languages permitted in the Alumneum were French and German. The German students did not appear to know French so we never communicated in French. I never had a good knowledge of German, and did not always find it easy to communicate only in German. To the laughter of the others, on several occasions, I made many amusing mistakes.

One afternoon I took a German student on my motor bike in order together to explore some stalactite caves. At the evening meal the Swiss student, sitting next to me, asked where I had been. The German words for 'cave' and 'hell' are and sound, similar. When I mistakenly said that I had gone to hell, there was a shout of laughter. He asked if it was very hot, I replied no it was cold. When he asked was it very dry I replied no it was wet, with water dripping from the roof. He replied that is impossible because it is very hot and dry! The entire room, including Professor Cullman, understood my mistake, shared in the laughter and although understanding what I hoped to say, declined to enlighten me about my mistake. I was compelled to retire to my room and consult a German dictionary to discover what all the laughter was about.

On another occasion, at meal time I and the student sitting next to me were discussing skiing, as I planned to ski over the winter vacation. I told him in conversation that my brother Tom enjoyed skiing but that on one occasion when jumping came down on a rock and broke his coccyx. Not knowing the German word for coccyx, I chanced the German word for tail! It is a word we sometimes use in English for that part of the back bone. It is never used in that connection in German! There was an immediate shout of laughter that was soon taken up by the other students. Professor Cullman at the top of the table asked what was the joke and was told that my brother Tom had a tail (an animal tail), which he broke when skiing.

Barth's classes were divided between 'Learners' and 'Hearers'. 'Learners' who numbered about 12, sat with Barth around the top table. 'Hearers' who numbered over 100 formed the rest of the class. With my limited knowledge of German I chose to attend classes as a 'Hearer'. I did not have the courage of some of my American friends who sat with Barth around the top table as 'Learners'. In addition to learning to speak German some of them had also started for the first time to learn Greek and Latin. Barth did not think that one was educated in theology unless one could read Greek and Latin. I was amused that often they came to me asking me to help them translate their Greek or Latin, but I admired their courage and readiness to attend classes as 'Learners', who could at short notice be asked to answer a question.

I worked hard and read a lot. I attended in German Barth's lectures on Christology, which are published in volume 4 part 2, of his *Church Dogmatics*. I also attended a small tutorial of approximately six students, which was conducted in English. We studied volume 1 part 1, of the

Church Dogmatics. It was Barth's custom to ask each student in turn to summarise in their own words approximately 50 pages of the *Dogmatics.* This we were required to read to the rest of the class as a basis for discussion. I was grateful for this discipline. We soon discovered whether Barth felt that we understood what he was saying. I have long felt that other theological tutors should develop the same practice.

Barth, unlike many other professors in Europe, did not live on a pedestal. He was an approachable kindly man. In his pastoral concern he used regularly to preach to people in prison. He had a rich sense of humour, unafraid to tell a joke against himself. He said that one day an American student came to him proposing to study for a thesis on 'Nothingness'. He had initially gone to Holland but the Dutch professor with whom he conferred suggested that it would be better for him to study in Basle under Karl Barth. When Barth asked him why he came (presumably because Barth believed that God created the world out of nothing), according to Barth, the reply was, "I wanted to come to the fountain of nothingness"! Barth thought this was a great joke.

Although he was always very approachable we tended to live in awe of him. I certainly never argued with him as did one of the Greek Orthodox students in the English Tutorial class. One day Barth said to us, "My friend here thinks that I am not saying enough about God the Holy Spirit. I believe that I am called to direct the Church to Jesus Christ. I believe that it is for the next generation to develop the doctrine of the Holy Spirit." After the tutorial he took the student by the arm and the class for a coffee.

Each day I read a chapter of the Bible in Hebrew, a chapter in Greek and a chapter in Latin. In the Alumneum, there was a short daily act of worship. We were required to take turns in leading worship. I therefore found it helpful in taking my turn, to have become familiar with the Bible in German, particularly when it came to leading in prayer. I regret that I have not continued to read the Bible in Hebrew and German. Without using one's knowledge of a language, one soon forgets it.

Professor Cullmann and his Sister

Fraulein Cullman, despite my lack of fluent German, frequently, almost regularly, came into my room for a chat. She seemed in some way to favour me. She complimented me to others claiming that I had a greater grasp of the German language than I had. Like her brother, she spoke very clear 'High German' (Barth was a native Swiss and spoke with a guttural accent) but tended to speak fairly fast making it not always easy for me. She was quite a character and I often quietly and mischievously teased her. She always wanted to know everything about what I did and why. I think in curiosity she sometimes would often enter and explore my room in my absence. On returning from the Christmas vacation, I opened my Christmas cards. I thought it a pity to immediately discard all of them. The walls of my room were bare, so I kept four with attractive pictures and pinned them on the wall. Fraulein Cullman was immediately interested. Why had I kept these four and who were they from. She pointed to each one in turn and was able to say, having previously read them, who had sent them. She pointed to the fourth, and asked specifically who was the sender. It happened to have come from Mary Lusk, a former class mate in New College, who was studying in Germany. I kept it because of its attractive appearance. I knew that in German (at least in my time) that it was the custom always to address a fellow student either as Mr or Miss and never by their Christian name. It was not the custom to use the word 'friend' unless the person was particularly intimate and it was not the custom to use the word 'girl friend' unless one was engaged to be married or nearly so. I mischievously replied that Mary Lusk was simply one of my girl friends!

On another occasion Fraulein Cullman came into my room in a state of shock. In the summer semester a Korean professor came to stay in the Alumneum. When Fraulein Cullman was walking with her sister in the garden of the Alumneum, she met the Korean professor who in greeting her asked, "How old are you?" Taken aback and much startled by his request, she replied "what do you think?" She was shocked and mortified when he replied "70"! She was probably at the time in her late fifties. She came into my room to unburden herself. I listened with interest and endeavoured to express sympathy concerning the assessment of her age.

I mischievously and wickedly did not say to her at the time, what I said two days later. She was still in shock and speaking about the incident, so I said that the Korean professor by suggesting that she was 70 was intending a high compliment. I explained that in China, a customary greeting was to ask a person when introduced, "How old are you?" The customary response was, "What do you think?" If the person asking the initial question wished out of respect to honour the person they always replied with a figure well in advance of the obvious age of the other person. I told Fraulein Cullman that probably there was the same custom in Korea. The fact that she had made, albeit in shock, the customary response, "What do you think?" had evoked an answer intended to be an expression of honour and respect.

I was not the only one to tease Fraulein Cullman. Shirley Guthrie, an American student and later professor of Systematic Theology in Columbia Theological Seminary, told me that he found a dead pigeon in the garden. When the Cullmans were both out he crept up the stairs to her bedroom and laid the dead pigeon on her bed. Listening to her shrieks when she discovered the bird, Shirley rushed upstairs to comfort and reassure her, saying that the window being open the bird must have flown into the room and died on her bed!

In the Alumneum Italian girls were employed to do all the cooking and cleaning. We were not meant to speak to them. To my brother James and myself, they seemed to be treated as if they belonged to a lower class, almost like slaves. I did not appreciate the way that they were treated, and with Shirley Guthrie I often spoke to them when the Cullmans were not present. In return they used to come into our rooms surreptitiously and collect and iron our washing. They also would often bring us the remains of a fruit salad. They felt it important always to enter our rooms and depart unobserved, with the empty dishes.

Prof. Cullman, as my brother Tom once said, was the most innocent egoist that he had ever met. At least three times in conversation he asked if I had read his book on 'Peter'. I had read several of his other publications but had not read this book. I always felt that he would have been deeply hurt by my confessing that I had not read it, when he clearly felt that it was one of his best publications. Hence each time I answered his question by saying that I greatly enjoyed his book on 'Time'! Thereon we launched into a discussion on 'Time' and some of the issues he had raised and I escaped having to confess that I had not read the book of which he was so proud.

Occasionally, when some of the other students, Swiss and German, were not around, Prof. Cullman invited me to join him for coffee and cream cakes in a cafe. He seemed very partial to cream cakes and I could not afford them. When the other students had departed on vacation and while we were still in the Alumneum, he on occasion invited Shirley Guthrie and me to join him and his sister for a meal upstairs in his flat. I found them to be a kind couple.

The Pull of Scotland

As the year advanced I became, despite my enjoyment of study, increasingly restless, wondering whether I was called to an academic career or to the parish ministry. I felt pulled in two directions. A theology which was not centred on Christ was to me, to use a phrase from my brother Tom, a 'paper theology'. The theology of both Oscar Cullman and Karl Barth was certainly centred on Christ. I greatly appreciated them both and learned much from both of them. Likewise a theology which did not relate practically to the faith of the ordinary person did not attract me. Despite my enjoyment of study, as my year in Basle advanced, I increasingly felt that the academic world was an unreal world. I wanted to be in touch and to minister to people in real life.

I had greatly enjoyed and spiritually benefited from my experience as a student assistant minister in parish ministry and in evangelism. At the same time, the way that God had spoken to me when I was in the army, the clear call to personal evangelism, weighed heavily with me. I wanted to do what God wanted. I had initially registered and made plans in pursuit of a doctorate, planning to study for three years. However the more I prayed seeking God's will for my life the more confused I became.

I returned home for the summer, having chosen my room in the Alumneum for the ensuing year, a warmer room than the one I had had. Two days before my planned return to Basle in October 1954, in my continued confusion, I knelt and prayed. I told God that in these days post Pentecost, I ought to be able to discern his will for my life through the Holy Spirit. I told the Lord that I was sorry that I was incapable of knowing his will, so told the Lord that I would toss a penny. It was up to the Lord to ensure that the penny landed in the way that he wanted, because I would abide by what ever happened. I tossed a penny and according to my agreement, the indication was that I should remain in Scotland. I was at first somewhat shaken but within half an hour was certain that God was calling me to stay in Scotland. I still did not know whether God was calling me to an academic career or to the parish ministry. In the meantime, therefore, until God made his will clearer, I transferred my doctoral studies to Edinburgh.

I am not proud of the way that I made this decision and do not recommend it as an example for others to follow.

It was arranged that I study for a PhD under Professors Jim McEwen and Jake Burleigh. Prof. Burleigh wisely suggested that the subject of my proposed thesis was too wide. I must narrow the focus of my studies and concentrate on John Knox. I felt that his advice was wise. Bucer had written no less than 70 books and manuscripts, all of which were in Latin. At that time none had been translated into English. The original subject for my proposed thesis was suggested by my brother Tom, himself a hard worker able to read Latin fluently. The thought of not seeking to plough through Bucer in Latin was a relief and comforting. My knowledge of Latin was never as good as that of Tom's.

Following my return from Basle, I was soon able to buy a complete set of Barth's *Church Dogmatics.* I have many times, with particular interest and when preaching, read his exegesis of biblical passages, which are published in small print. I was fortunate to able to purchase my copies of the *Church*

Dogmatics very cheaply on the grounds that every volume I think with one exception has a printing fault which, in reading, I never notice.

At the beginning of January 1955 I submitted to Prof. McEwen a preliminary outline of 40 pages of my thesis. A few days later I received a telephone call from D.P. Thompson asking that I join him in evangelism, working full time for 'Tell Scotland' (see chapter 6). I accepted, believing that this was God's call and as a result I never resumed work on my projected thesis.

I have always enjoyed and taken an interest in Biblical Theology, although assured that I was called to the pastoral ministry. Subsequently, from time to time, there have been occasions when I received a request to lecture in the academic world.

About three years after my ordination and induction as minister of Livingston parish, Tom said he had been invited to go to America and would be absent from New College for three months. He invited Dr R.S. Wallace, who later taught theology in Decatur, USA, and myself to lecture to his classes. We agreed. I lectured to a first year class of some 25 or 30 students, who I believe were all preparing to be ministers. All were graduates. Because I wanted to know who was in the class I sent round a sheet of paper and asked each student to write down his name and his degree(s). When I read the paper I was daunted by seeing that one student, Paul Re'emi had six degrees including a DLitt (Doctor of Literature) which is the highest degree awarded in the UK. He did not have a degree in theology, so I wondered if there was something that he did not know and which I might be able to teach him! However he turned out to be a quiet, humble and lovely man. Tom had just written a book on the Catechisms[1] officially authorised by the Church of Scotland since the Reformation. He asked that that should be the subject of my lectures. I enjoyed the experience, finding it challenging and yet daunting.

Shortly afterwards, Tom invited me with the agreement of the Faculty, to join him as a lecturer in theology at New College. I declined in favour of continuing in parish ministry. My brother James was appointed and went on later to become Professor of Theology and Divinity at Aberdeen University.

Likewise when two ministers in New Zealand wrote and asked if I would agree to their putting my name forward for a chair in theology in Knox College, in Dunedin, New Zealand, I declined. I felt sure that God wanted me to remain in the parish ministry in Scotland.

1 T.F. Torrance, *The School of Faith,* James Clarke, London 1959.

Shortly after that Tom asked that I should join with him in editing a new translation of Calvin's twelve commentaries on the New Testament. To this I agreed. A number of translators were appointed. The arrangement was that I receive each new translation, edit it, and, as I thought best, approve or alter the suggested translation. The work lasted over a number of years. Some translators were more diligent and worked faster than others. The ones whom I found gave me most difficulty, surprisingly held an honours degree in Latin and Greek! I often retranslated many passages, even several pages when the translator had expressed difficulty in translating or when I felt that the translator had not grasped Calvin's thought. Finally I passed everything over to Tom with my recommendations. Tom had the final say. We worked happily and well together.

Twelve years after my ordination and induction as minister of the Parish of Livingston, St Andrew's University advertised for a reader to teach Theology and Mission. I was encouraged by my former teacher, Professor J.S Stewart to apply for the post which I did. I was not accepted, possibly not considered. I had been too long in the parish ministry, and too long out of the academic world. Also, apart from my co-editing Calvin's Commentaries from Latin to English, I had not published any work.

The only occasions when I seriously wondered whether God wanted me to continue in parish ministry in Scotland, arose when I was approached and invited, without my seeking, to teach theology in Africa, first in Nigeria, then in South Africa and then in Botswana (at that time called Bechuanaland). On all three occasions I agreed along with my wife. In the case of Nigeria, when I was minister in Livingston, we were interviewed and underwent the necessary medical examinations, but the door closed as it did in the call to South Africa and Botswana.

In the case of Botswana, I was suddenly approached one morning by the United Free Church, when I was minister of a church in Aberdeen and asked if I would initiate the theological training of ministers in that country. Formerly ministers in Botswana had all been trained either in South Africa or Southern Rhodesia (now Zimbabwe). That door was now closed. None hitherto had been trained in Botswana. Would I go, initiate theological education in Botswana and work with an African who hopefully would take over the work after five years? I said that I was not prepared to leave the Church of Scotland. However after consulting the secretary and members of the Overseas Council of the Church of Scotland, they welcomed the proposal to make a joint appointment on behalf of both the Church of Scotland and the UF Church.

My wife was excited. Before our marriage she had worked as a missionary doctor under the United Free Church in a hospital in

Molepolole in Botswana. She knew the local African language, loved the Africans and wanted us to go. I was accordingly interviewed for the position both by representatives of the UF Church and the Church of Scotland who readily supported our going. Once again, after all was agreed the door closed. Dick Sales, a missionary in South Africa who had taught theology for twenty years in the college at Alice (to which I also had been invited a few years before only to have the door closed), was at the time, as I understand, in Botswana. Like several other missionaries, he had lost his visa to continue working in South Africa, on the ground that he had been caught having a meal with an African. In the dreadful days of Apartheid, eating, drinking and socialising with Africans was expressly forbidden. Expatriates caught so doing lost their visas. It was natural and I think right that Dick Sales was appointed to initiate theological education in Botswana. So the door closed again. I was astonished at the repeated closing of the door when without my asking, the invitation was given to teach theology in Africa. I found it a helpful test as to whether I and my wife would surrender all to Christ and do whatever he asked.

A year later after that door closed, I was again invited to go to Botswana and initiate theological education by extension. This time I said, "No!" When I had assented the previous year, the agreement was that I and the family would stay in Molepolole where there was a school geared to the University of Durham. Consequently the children could stay at home until they were ready to go to university. This later invitation entailed our staying 200 miles north of Molepolole, so that the children would require to go to a boarding school in South Africa and probably learn Afrikaans. I was unwilling to be parted from the children. I wanted along with my wife to be responsible for their upbringing in the Christian faith. At the same time, this second appointment meant a willingness to travel the length and breadth of Botswana which was twice the size of France. I told the UF Church who had again approached me to go to Botswana, that they needed to appoint a younger, unmarried man.

In declining this second invitation, my wife and I felt that God wanted us to remain in parish ministry in Scotland. However great my inadequacies and failures in the ministry have been, I am certain that God called me not to an academic but a parish ministry.

I have greatly enjoyed and felt fulfilled in the work of the parish ministry. Since my retiurement, I have also appreciated being invited to speak at various meetings and conferences, especially theological conferences. I am grateful when despite my inadequacies, failings and humble efforts, God has graciously chosen to bless what I have endeavoured to do for him.

Chapter 5

Ministry and Evangelism: 1942-1953

In commencing studies at the University of Edinburgh in 1942, following in the steps of my brother James and older siblings, I joined the Christian Union. I enjoyed meeting with other Christian students and sharing with them in Christian fellowship and Bible studies. Through the Christian Union both James and I, like our older siblings, made many friends. We all learned from one another.

In those early days students from the CU held services in some of the wards of Edinburgh Royal Infirmary. I shared in these and for the first time in my experience spoke at a Christian service. Because of military commitments I could not attend these ward services each week, but did so as often as I was able. They were welcomed by the patients and it greatly helped those of us who took part.

My next experience in leading worship and preaching was in the army in India after the end of the war, when another soldier, Miller Scott and I were asked by our Anglican chaplain to take Church of Scotland services in the Brigade at Gangiwara, where some five or six hundred British gunners were stationed. We both agreed to conduct services. I found the services helpful and a good preparation for the years ahead.

Evangelism

Having finally, while in the army, accepted God's call to the ministry, I recommenced my university studies with great enthusiasm and, along with them, threw myself into evangelism. Having struggled against the call to the ministry for so long, and having found great peace and joy, after accepting God's call, I wanted to do all that I could to forward God's work. Like many others of my generation, who had come through the war when so many others and close friends had been killed, I felt that my life had been spared by God for a purpose. In the years following the end of the war there was in our universities and throughout the country a great burst of evangelism, which continued for about ten or twelve years. Through these years there were missions all across Scotland. These missions run by different churches and different denominations were brought together under 'Tell Scotland', an umbrella movement under which these various missions took place. The Church of Scotland continued to expand its membership, peaking in 1956, with a membership of about one and a quarter million. At University the majority of students were older and more mature than those later who entered university straight after school. Many students had had dangerous and dramatic experiences. Whereas some lost what faith they had during the war, others came to faith in Christ or had their faith strengthened.

My brother James told me that in his class of approximately 25 or 26 students in New College in 1948 or 1949, Professor Stalker, of Glasgow, was once invited to give a couple of lectures. Professor Stalker was a liberal theologian. When he proceeded to make light of, or deny, some of the New Testament miracles, suddenly the entire class hissed him. Stalker was startled, closed his lecture notes and walked out. As James said, Stalker did not appreciate that every last student in that class had come through the war. Some had been prisoners of war. Others had had remarkable experiences. They had encountered God and were not prepared to come back from the war and be told that there were no such things as miracles. These students were sure of their faith and many of them and others throughout the universities threw themselves into evangelism seeking to share with others the Christian faith. I have always felt that it was an immense privilege to be at university at that time, to discuss with these mature students issues of the faith and, with them, share in many evangelistic campaigns.

My First Participation in Mission

I engaged in my first evangelistic campaign in Newburgh, Fife, during the Easter vacation in 1947. It took place under the leadership of the Revd D.P. Thomson. I travelled north with Jimmy Barr who had been converted at an SU week-end conference, which I had attended, in the previous autumn. Jimmy Barr had been a Fleet Air Arm pilot during the war. We arrived on a dull coldish March day. We were invited to warm ourselves with others of the team, in front of the fire in the church hall where the mission was centred. I remember looking forward to lunch. Before that happened however one of the team, Willie Young, who later became a missionary and bishop in the Church of North India, tapped me on the shoulder and asked if I would help, along with another team member, Nelson Gray in carrying some equipment.

As we were walking down the street, I asked what it was that I was carrying and where we were going. I was informed that I was carrying an open-air pulpit and that we were going to a lunch hour open-air service outside the gates of a local factory. I asked who would be speaking and was told that I was! That is what happened! Approximately 40 men joined our open-air meeting. Willie opened the meeting by announcing that a new member of the team had come all the way from Edinburgh that day in order to speak to them! I had no time to collect my thoughts – I do not remember what I said. I did my best and the men listened. In this I felt very much the hand of God. In the army I had for long resisted the call to the ministry on the ground that if I accepted the call, God would call me to preach in the open air. I had thought of the apostles preaching in the open air on the first day of Pentecost and how many in the listening crowd had mocked them and said that they were drunk. That horrified me. I had no desire to preach in the open air and be mocked. Yet here, on my first mission and on the first day, I was catapulted into preaching in the open air! Under God, that first experience helped me overcome the fear of preaching in the open air and in the years that followed I regularly and often preached in various missions, in the open air.

I learned much from D.P. Thomson in my first experience of mission. I was startled on one occasion with his direct challenge to a large gathering of young people to give themselves to Christ, wondering how much they really understood. Some 28 boys of approximately 14 years of age responded to the challenge. Each of us on the team were assigned two or three boys to counsel. I later discovered that at least two of those boys later entered the ministry, one in the Congregational Church and the other Alistair Morton, in the ministry of the Church of Scotland. I met Alistair some years later when he was home on furlough from Africa and we recalled that mission with D.P. Thomson.

Two Other Events from that Mission

Bob Gordon. In the church hall in Newburgh I slept on the floor next to Alistair Gordon who was studying to become an agricultural missionary. Alistair had a brother Bob who was a close friend of my brother-in-law Kenneth Mackenzie. He was a medical student and committed Christian who hoped to become a missionary. Although medical students were exempt from military service during the war until they completed their studies and were qualified doctors, Bob volunteered for the army. He served with the 51st Highland Division in North Africa but was killed in Normandy. The truck in which he was travelling was blown up by a land mine. Bob was badly wounded and died three days later. As a captain he asked his sergeant to write a short letter home to his uncle and aunt. His parents had died when he and his brother Alistair were boys and his uncle and aunt had brought them up. In that letter he said that he was not afraid to die. He knew that he was going to be with the Lord. That letter and his death led directly to his brother Alistair's conversion. Until then Alistair had been a somewhat wild lad. I was glad to meet Alistair. The memory of Bob's death and his letter home stayed with me. They came to mind for many years at every funeral which I conducted as a minister.

A Christian from Nagaland. The other event concerned a student from Nagaland in North East India, although I have forgotten his name. He was the first Naga to go to university and the first to come to Europe. He took his first degree at a University in India and had come for further study in Scotland. The Indian government had offered him the post of governor-general of Nagaland, a country or district which the Indian government found hard to control. The Nagai had been war-like head hunters. He declined the offer believing that his mission under God was to translate the Bible into his native language.

During the mission he told us his story which was a remarkable one. His father, the son of a tribal chief, had crossed over the hills for seventy miles with a war party and attacked a village where there were Methodist Christians. Remarkably, during the course of that raid his father became a Christian. On his return, the elders, because of his Christian faith, rejected him from their village. For three weeks he lived alone in the jungle surviving by eating berries and any food that he could find. During those three weeks his grandfather was killed by a bear. His grandmother, bereft of her husband, persuaded the elders of the village to search for her son and bring him back. Following his return to the village another person was converted. Without a Bible or any other Christian contact the two men crossed over the hills to the village that earlier they had raided. Once they had committed to memory one of the Gospels they returned home and taught others in their village. Later they returned across the hills in order to memorise another book of the Bible which in turn they taught to others. Gradually the church among the Nagai grew and became established, through the Holy Spirit and without any Western missionary help. Today I understand there are very many Christian churches in the land and the people have become deeply influenced by the Gospel.

During the mission in Newburgh, DP (as D.P. Thomson was affectionately known) invited a different member of the team to lead evening prayers. When it was the turn of the one from Nagaland, he intimated that his reading was from the Epistle to the Romans. I could not help noticing that whereas he held the Bible open before him, he did not actually read it. He quoted it, a longish passage, from memory!

Summer Missions

In July 1947, I went on my first CSSM (Children's Special Service Mission) seaside mission to Ely in Fife. It was led by a friend Malcolm Ritchie who had served as a captain in the Royal Artillery Regiment in Italy. Malcolm became a minister in the Church of Scotland. Although I had attended seaside missions as a boy in North Berwick, prior to World War II, it was a valuable introduction to the leadership of a beach mission.

For several years my brother James led student summer missions to various towns in Scotland: Dunfermline and Rosyth, Perth, Kilmarnock and Motherwell. The teams taking part were fairly large. Students came from Christian Unions in the four Scottish Universities of Edinburgh, Glasgow, St Andrews and Aberdeen. Before agreeing to go on mission to a certain town, we first asked for approval from the local presbytery and the agreement by the local ministers that all the churches in that town participate. We also asked for a civic reception on the part of the town council so that our activities were well known in advance. Today people, when told, find it surprising that our requests both to the local presbyteries and the various town councils were always granted, an indication of the remarkable secular change that has come about, both in the church and in society.

Later in 1947, I took part in an IVF (Inter-Varsity Fellowship) evangelistic mission in Dunfermline and Rosyth, in Fife. In Dunfermline James was assisted by Brian Thomson, who also had served in the army and later became a minister of the Church of Scotland.[1] I was asked to lead a parallel mission in Rosyth. This I found quite a challenge. The two teams slept and ate in the same church halls in Dunfermline. We shared together in Bible study each day and then divided as we concentrated on our two missions. We did a lot of street work, speaking to people on the streets, inviting them to our meetings and challenging them with the Gospel of Christ. Each night we held an evangelistic service in a church, in both locations. The mission was for a fortnight and two or three of us took it in turn each night to preach. We did our best to challenge people to commit their lives to Christ. I do not now have a copy of the sermons which I preached but remember choosing for that and later missions, such texts as "Lot . . . pitched his tents near Sodom" (Genesis 13:12) and "You have been weighed on the scales and found wanting" (Daniel 5:27). "Jesus said, 'Come, follow me, and I will make you fishers of men'" (Mark 1:17). "Jesus said, 'Zacchaeus, come down immediately. I must stay at your house today'" (Luke 19:5). These were passages which gave a serious challenge. Despite our inexperience, attendances at our nightly services were always encouraging. It was always a great joy and a strengthening of our faith to see people converted and lives change.

I learned much through these missions. I felt that my experiences, sharing in the rough and tumble of army life and meeting all kinds of

1 Sadly, Brian Thomson died while still comparatively young with cancer.

people, helped me immensely in speaking to people about Christ and also in preaching as I tried to proclaim the Gospel in ways that the ordinary person would understand. On several occasion I met working men who at first were ready to turn away: when they discovered that in the army I had served in the ranks and had not been commissioned, they stayed and were prepared to listen to what I said.

When my brother James graduated from New College and moved on to post graduate studies in Basle, I was invited to succeed him in leading these summer missions. Because of time, and because the work in organising and leading these missions was so great, I declined. James was succeeded by Bruce Kendrick who led a mission to Edinburgh. Bruce had been converted during service as a paratrooper in the army.

Evangelistic Activities in University

Our activities were not limited to participating in organised missions. Throughout my time at university I took an active part in the programme of the Christian Union, the Edinburgh branch of the IVF. There were meetings every week. We also met regularly for Bible study and prayer and held various mission breakfasts. The CU in Edinburgh was one of the larger gatherings in the UK. We had about 200 members and some 220 students met weekly, comparing well with those who attended such meetings in Oxford (OICCU) and Cambridge (CICCU). Unlike some of the other Christian Unions in other universities where often science and medical students predominated, we had in Edinburgh a good number of theological and prospective theological students as well as those from the faculties of Arts and Medicine. As a result, I think we probably had many more serious theological discussions than those which took place in other universities. We learned from each other as well as from our professors.

As members of the CU we were always active in discussing issues of the faith with other non-Christian student friends, and we invited them to meetings of the Christian Union. Debates with fellow students often continued over lengthy periods as we shared the same university lectures.

Edinburgh CU always organised at least one retreat during each autumn term. During the Easter vacation, together with CUs from the other four Scottish Universities, we took part in a three or four day retreat, sometimes in St Andrews and more often in the Youth Hostel at Balloch, Loch Lomond. During these retreats we witnessed many conversions. I mention four.

1 ***James Barr***. Jimmy, as he was known, was studying Latin and Greek and gained a First Class Honours degree. His father the Revd Allan

Barr was a professor in the UF College. Jimmy came to the first autumn conference, which I attended. My brother James was instrumental in his coming to receive Christ as Saviour. Jimmy spoke to me on the night of his conversion and as far as I can recall, we spoke about the nature of commitment to Christ and I prayed with him. A few months later, we travelled together to the mission in Newburgh under D.P. Thomson, and which I have already mentioned. Jimmy had a brilliant academic career and became a well known professor in Old Testament studies, lecturing in Edinburgh, Manchester and the USA.

*2 **George Morris.*** Commencing in the year 1946 there was a strong group of Christian medical students. They witnessed various conversions among other students in their year. They told me of one particular student, George Morris, for whose conversion they were particularly praying. I agreed to join them in prayer. George was invited and agreed to come to the Easter conference which that year was held in St Andrews. Following the conference he came to my house to tell me his story. He had grown up in a non-Christian home. He had seen active service in the army during the war and had come through safely. Now that the war was over he felt in need of some kind of Christian faith. He responded to a Roman Catholic invitation in the university and for a year attended a class on the Christian faith run by the Roman Catholic Church.

At the end of the year, instead of joining the Catholic Church he thought that he would look around and discover what other churches had to offer. During this period while walking up George the Fourth Bridge, a street in central Edinburgh, he saw in the window of a Christian book shop a book entitled *Salvation by Grace alone*. He did not go in and buy the book but was deeply impressed by the title. After being taught by the RC Church about 'penance' and the necessary contribution of good works in order to receive salvation, he at once believed in terms of the title of that book that we are saved solely by the grace of God. With that conviction he came to the conference at St Andrews. At the end of the conference, the speaker conducted a communion service. He invited all who loved the Lord and all who wanted to love the Lord to share in the communion service. George told me that whereas he knew that he did not love the Lord, he nonetheless felt that he wanted to love the Lord. Hence he took communion. He told me that when he took the bread in his hands and more particularly when he took the cup he suddenly knew with certainty that Christ Jesus had died for him and forgiven him. He was converted in participating in the sacrament of Holy Communion. I found the story of his conversion a moving confirmation of John Calvin's teaching, over against that of Zwingli, who taught that the sacrament is for those who already have faith. For Calvin, the sacrament is for those who have faith and for those who sincerely want it. George and his wife Margaret became medical missionaries in South Yemen until sadly Margaret's health broke down. They continued as friends of my wife and myself for many years.

*3 **Murdo.*** Murdo was another person whose conversion took place at an Easter conference. He was a mature student about ten years older than myself. When I first met Murdo during my Arts course he was an ardent and aggressive communist. The Christian faith and indeed any religion was anathema to him. Learning that I was a Christian and planning to study for the ministry he frequently confronted me with his atheistic views, anathematizing my faith. At times I found his presence embarrassing. The honours philosophy class was small. There were about six of us. Each week we met with members of staff, our lecturers and tutors, for lunch in a nearby restaurant. On several occasions having entered the same restaurant and seeing me he would come over uninvited. Having introduced himself as a friend of David's (which he was not), he sat down with us and proceeded to try and convert us students and staff to his views on communism!

One year after praying and asking the Lord whom I should invite to our Easter conference, I felt the Lord saying, "Invite Murdo". I was horrified. I thought "Surely not Lord. I have endured a lot of verbal abuse from Murdo. If I invite him to a Christian conference, this will occasion a lot more abuse!" However the more I prayed about it, the clearer it became that I must invite Murdo. I did not look forward to doing so, but felt the Lord saying that I must. I remember entering what we called 'the Old Quad' and seeing Murdo standing on the steps outside the university library. With some trepidation I went across and told him that the Christian Union was participating in a Christian conference that Easter at Loch Lomond and I invited him to come. To my astonishment he took my invitation seriously and said that he would like to come and discover what Christians had to say. It was the first time that he had spoken to me in this way without mocking my Christian Faith.

I felt rebuked of the Lord for my lack of faith. Murdo came to the conference. I chose to share a room with him. One night he went through an emotional crisis and professed conversion. He told me his story. For seven years he had been a committed member of the communist party and taken part in their underground activities. To become a member of the communist party it was necessary to renounce all religions. He told me however that as a child his parents had taken him on holiday to Nairn. One day he wandered along the beach toward a seaside service taking place on the sands. The only thing that he could remember about that service, were the words spoken by the minister who said that "God is love". Those words had burned themselves into his mind and soul. All through his years as a member of the communist party when he was required to renounce allegiance to any and all religions, he could not get rid of the words "God is Love".

In the providence of God, the speaker at that Easter conference was the Revd Jimmy Duncan, a missionary in Kalimpong, North India. He was the same minister who many years before had spoken at a seaside mission in Nairn, the one which Murdo had visited as a boy of five and who had said the words "God is love", which had burned themselves into Murdo's soul. Murdo discovered God speaking to him at the conference and that was his conversion. Murdo, however, had quite a long way to go before being able to settle down. On returning from the conference he went in to his party headquarters and announced that he had become a Christian. He tried to hold on to the Christian faith and also his commitment to communism and this precipitated a psychological breakdown. When I last met him, he still maintained that he had become a Christian.

4 George. I was studying philosophy at the time when I first met George who was studying for an honours MA degree in another subject. He was an able student who had been dux of his school before studying at university. He told me that he planned to study for the ministry but wished to study theology in Glasgow on the ground that it was more liberal than the other three colleges of Edinburgh, St Andrews and Aberdeen. What he said troubled me and I found myself praying for him. The more I prayed for him the more I felt compelled to pray for him. For two weeks I made a point of speaking to him every day and sharing with him a coffee or a meal. Then I asked him to read from the New Testament 1 John chapter one. He told me that after reading that chapter he could no longer pray, which puzzled me. After further prayer I telephoned and reminded him that, in his own words, he could not pray after reading that chapter. I told him that it was because he was a sinner and would not acknowledge and confess his sin to God. In fact because he would not acknowledge or confess his sin I suggested that there was little point in his praying because he would not get through to God.

In mentioning sin, I did not have in my mind any thought about the nature of his sin. Homosexuality did not enter my mind. For the next few days he avoided me and I felt that sadly we had parted company. Then he telephoned me. He asked who had been speaking to me about him. I assured him that no one had and I had not mentioned him to a single soul. He asked then why had I said what I did. I told him that I had been praying for him and had felt that God wanted me to say what I did. He asked if he could talk to me at my house. When he came he told me that sadly he had mixed with the wrong company at university, with people who were practising homosexuals, and asked if I would pray with him. I said that I would only pray with him if he was prepared to acknowledge that what he had being doing was wrong and was prepared to ask God for forgiveness. He agreed, we knelt in prayer and both of us prayed. When he looked at me after prayer his face was glowing. He said that he felt that the faith which he had as a boy had returned to him. It was perhaps a simple and straightforward case. George was the first person that I pastorally counselled who was tempted toward homosexual activity or had a homosexual orientation.

Although there is no genetic reason for a person having a homosexual orientation there is a biological cause along with some other eight or nine other causes which psychologists have identified. Some after much prayer and counselling are helped and undergo re-orientation, others do not and cannot be blamed. They need our love and support. Even so, homosexual practice according to Scripture is wrong.

University Missions

Over and above our weekly evangelistic meetings and our annual summer missions to other parts of Scotland, we had the occasional mission to the university. At first, the initiative and responsibility for planning a university mission lay with the students. After the appointment of a university chaplain, missions were arranged by the chaplain. When responsibility lay with the students, we would invite a well known speaker and arrange a number of special meetings. On one occasion we invited D.T. Niles from Ceylon (Sri Lanka).

Publicity fell largely on students of the CU. In addition to displaying posters and inviting friends and fellow students, we would at the beginning of a lecture ask the professor or lecturer for permission to announce the mission programme to his class and invite members of the class to the mission meetings. I confess to having to muster my courage to do this. However, to my knowledge permission was always given and the intimations were always well received. No one ever objected, interrupted or heckled. These were during the years immediately following the war. I wonder if today, when the church is in some quarters facing a militant atheism and scepticism, whether students announcing such evangelistic missions would receive the same permission or be so courteously received.

Edinburgh CU

For the year 1947-48, I was elected president and chairman of the Christian Union. My brother James had preceded me. I had entered into my honours years in philosophy, so that my time required to be disciplined. However I much enjoyed the experience. It helped me to know a large number of students from different faculties as well as strengthening my faith and deepening my commitment to evangelism.

Shortly after becoming president I recommended that we change one of the clauses of our aims and basis. The CU committee supported the change. I did not like the phrase "the infallible and inspired Word of God", and altered it to read, "The Bible is the Word of God". It was simpler and more biblical.

To my surprise however, on a Sunday afternoon two or three weeks later I was invited to meet in the premises of the Edinburgh Medical Missionary Society (EMMS) in George Square, with Douglas Johnson, founder and secretary of IVF, from London, and about fifteen largely or entirely English students. I was challenged about why I wished to lower the evangelical flag and seek to accommodate the SCM (the Student Christian Movement). I told them that I was in no way seeking to lower the evangelical flag and had never thought of, or consulted with members of the SCM in my alteration of the CU aims and basis. I told them that I was seeking to be thoroughly biblical because only if we were truly biblical could we helpfully proceed in evangelism. I said the 'Word of God' was God, the Son of God. It was wrong to talk of the inspired Word of God just as it is wrong to say that Jesus is the inspired Son of God. He was and is God. I was quite happy to say with St. Paul that all Scripture was given by inspiration (2 Timothy 3:16), only that was a rather long statement for printing in our invitation programmes. It was simpler just to say that "the Bible is the Word of God".

I had to assure them that I truly accepted and believed all Scripture as inspired of God. I added that I was happy to say if they wished that I also believed the covers! I was challenged about my missing out the word 'infallible'. I said that the Bible is a human word written by men under the inspiration of God and is an infallible witness to the Word that is God. But that is not the way that the word 'infallible' was being used in the statement of faith. I told them that it was wrong to try and impose upon scripture a misplaced human logic. If we were going to advance the Kingdom of God we had to be careful always to present the gospel in a correct, biblical and theological way. I declined to alter my correction of the aims and basis of the Edinburgh CU. I think Douglas

Johnson was reluctant to accept what I said but was unable to argue against it.

IVF Student Executive Committee for UK

On the completion of my presidency of the Edinburgh CU, I was invited for the next two years to be the male student Scottish representative of IVF, along with Lilian Campbell[2] from Glasgow, and become a member of the UK Student Executive Committee, planning for student conferences and special activities in the UK. With this appointment I felt that Douglas Johnson must have approved of me for quite clearly he had recommended my appointment. In those days there were two students, a man and a woman, appointed to represent Scotland on the central committee along with the IVF Scottish Secretary, who at that time was the Revd Albert Rainsbury, an Irishman.

At my first meeting of the central committee, I was not happy in that before we could commence, once again each of us had to sign the aims and basis of the IVF which each of us had signed when appointed to our local meeting. I pointed out my theological and biblical objection to the wording of the statement that we were required to sign, namely that "the Bible is the inspired, infallible Word of God". I stated the same objections which I had stated in Edinburgh and said that I signed on the understanding that the Bible is the Word of God and that all scripture was given by inspiration. They graciously accepted what I said. In those days, English students and even theological students were hesitant to try and argue with Scottish students theologically. I was told to my dismay that evangelical dioceses in England would grant scholarships to prospective students for the ministry only if they refused to study theology! The fear was that if they studied theology they would become liberal. Hence they had to take their degree in Church history or in a subject which would not persuade them in a liberal direction! Happily, things have changed since those days.

At that first meeting of the central committee, I intimated that we in Scotland had agreed to open our annual Easter Conference for Christians and non-Christians. I had earlier been challenged by Oliver Barclay, the Assistant General Secretary of IVF. He was surprised and at first critical to discover that we had invited many non-Christians to our Easter Conference at Loch Lomond, although I believe that he was won over in his thinking by witnessing some of the many conversions which took place. I insisted

2 Lilian Campbell, a journalist and solicitor, married Bill Carmichael in 1955. Bill was a conservationist in the Colonial Forest Service in Tanganyika. Later he entered the ministry of the Church of Scotland and was minister in Restalrig, Edinburgh. He died in 2000.

that our policy in inviting non-Christians was right, on the ground that the Word of God rightly preached will edify the saint and convert the sinner!

Previously all such IVF Easter conferences had been held as conventions to strengthen and build up the faith of believers. I was much encouraged when, after my recommendation and the discussion that followed, it was agreed that henceforth all their conferences would be open to both Christians and non-Christians. My conviction that this was the right biblical and evangelical position had been greatly strengthened by the conversions to Christ which we in Scotland had witnessed.

There was another occasion when meeting with the central committee left me deeply disturbed. We received a report of an all-university mission which had taken place in Oxford. The University chaplain at that time was the Revd Howard Guinness. Howard was a well known evangelical who had helped to establish the IVF in the USA. I had previously heard him speaking. Howard announced his desire to conduct an all-university mission. OICCU (which represented IVF in Oxford) immediately offered their support. When the SCM in Oxford also offered to support the mission OICCU was persuaded (possibly by Douglas Johnson) to withdraw their support for the mission. Howard carried on with the mission with the support of SCM and others. The central committee, when I was present, agreed unanimously to accept the recommendation that because Howard Guinness had in their opinion, compromised his evangelical witness by working with the SCM he should never again be invited to be a speaker at an IVF conference. I was appalled and disturbed. I could not bring myself to speak or would have been tempted to hit them or burst into tears because of what I felt to be their unchristian attitude. I hastened to my room in order to be alone. I felt that any prospective minister in the Church of Scotland could easily find himself in a similar position to that of Howard Guinness.

The problem of co-operation with SCM and with those with whom we may not fully agree evangelically arose some three years later and split apart the Edinburgh Christian Union. I was near the end of my final year in New College: Reid, the chaplain to Edinburgh University planned an all university mission the following year. Both Edinburgh SU and SCM agreed to support him in the planning and conduct of the mission. In preparation for the mission members of CU and SCM were meeting weekly for prayer. Mark Wilson,[3] a student in Glasgow, was at that time the IVF Scottish student representative. Quite unexpectedly Mark appeared at the beginning of one of our weekly meetings and asked

3 Mark Wilson became a minister of the Church of Scotland and he and his wife served very ably and well for a long time as missionaries in North India.

to speak. He had been sent by Douglas Johnson and his colleagues to instruct us to cease forthwith our joint prayer meetings with SCM. If we did not we would be disaffiliated from IVF.

The meeting erupted! The committee with the support of the majority refused to comply. The result was that the Edinburgh CU was disaffiliated. The Christian Union split, which was very sad. The majority continued as the CU. A smaller group continued as IVF. I moved on to further studies in Basle so was not further involved. It was a very unhappy episode. Having spoken critically at the meeting of IVF's action, what I said was reported back to Douglas Johnson and the leaders of IVF. For a long while I think that I was regarded with suspicion, although Dr Oliver Barclay spoke to me a year later in London and was very anxious for reconciliation. I was certainly never invited to be a guest speaker at an IVF conference. However, in the years ahead, after the two evangelical groups in Edinburgh came together I was invited to speak to the Edinburgh CU and as a minister in Aberdeen was invited to speak several times to the CU in Aberdeen and invited to lead a series of talks on the prophet Micah.

I discussed the issue of co-operation between IVF and SCM with my father, and the two groups praying together. He immediately asked me to read Philippians chapter 1, particularly verses 15-18. Paul said, "Some preach Christ out of envy and rivalry", others "do so in love . . . But what does it matter? The important thing is that in every way, whether from false motives or true, Christ is preached. And because of this I rejoice." Father's concern was that as Christians we are called to preach Christ, to make him known in whatever way and to endeavour to advance the Kingdom of God. We are all imperfect. With some people we may be ninety per cent in agreement in their interpretation of the Gospel, with them we can travel together for ninety per cent of the way. With others we may be only ten per cent in agreement, therefore we can travel together for ten per cent of the way. As sinful and imperfect human creatures we will never agree one hundred per cent with anyone. This however should never hinder us as Christians from seeking to work together with everyone, whenever possible. I found my father's advice very helpful then and subsequently over the years.

Friendships and Camping Holidays

Chiefly through the Christian Union I came to meet and in some cases became close friends with quite a number of fellow students from different university faculties. We met at CU meetings, Bible studies, missionary meetings and in the course of various walks which were organised and took place in the Pentland Hills.

Also, five or six of us used to go camping together for ten or possibly 14 days each summer. In addition to my brother James there was Geoff Irvine (who became a doctor and missionary in Africa) and Malcolm Bolton (who became a teacher). On occasion Bruce Kenrick (who became a minister and missionary in India), Bill McDonald (later Moderator of the General Assembly) and Bobby Wright (who became an agricultural lecturer). Apart from Malcolm Bolton, who cycled, we hitch-hiked (often on fish lorries) to our various destinations. We generally camped in the West Highlands, first in Skye, then Wester Ross, in Achiltibuie (where we were able to stay together in a croft belonging to a man called Max de Hamel, who was a second cousin of Winston Churchill), the Gairloch and Lochinver and also in Arran. We had many happy days together tramping and climbing over the hills or swimming in the sea.

On one occasion we camped in the hills at the foot of the Sma' Glen in Perthshire. On this occasion, apart from James and myself there was Bruce Kenrick, Bruce Paton (who became a doctor) and Bob Buchanan (who became a doctor and for a period worked in Malawi in Africa). On this occasion Bruce Kenrick had deliberately asked John Paton to join us in order to help him in his Christian faith. After our walking over the hills, in the evenings we closed the day with Bible discussion and prayers.

In our camping in those days we had none of the light weight tents and camping equipment, which are so common today. After the war we bought ex-army crawl-in tents which were remarkably heavy compared to modern tents. James and I also bought sleeping ground sheets or bags, the upper part which was made from ex-parachute silk. As a result in our many travels and in the many miles that we walked we carried remarkably heavy loads but we were young and fit.

On these camps we enjoyed many biblical and theological discussions, continuing to learn from and help one another.

New College 1950-1953

Throughout the three years I was a student at New College, I combined my studies with a student assistantship in a local parish church. Although my motive in securing student assistantships was not financial, nonetheless the money which I received was welcome. Along with others whose studies at university had been interrupted I received on my return to university an ex-service scholarship, which as far as I can recall, amounted to £137 per annum for five years. It was in those days a large sum. It paid for my university expenses, books and contributed towards my living expenses etc. As ex-servicemen we were among the affluent at university. Because however an honours MA in philosophy lasted five years, my ex-service scholarship finished at the end of my first year in New College.

I had two further years to complete before graduating with a BD degree. The money received as a student assistant was therefore both welcome and necessary. The usual amount paid to a student assistant was £120 per annum. Both Broughton Place Church in Edinburgh and St Mary's Haddington, to which I was attached, had large congregations and were the best paid of the student assistantships. Broughton Place Church paid £200 and St Mary's Haddington £250. Haddington however was some 17 miles from Edinburgh so that I paid approx. £50 for travel and meals in the course of my assistantship. Through the kindness of Professor Porteous I was also given a church scholarship which covered my time at New College. I was thus able to study without any financial worries. I was also able to contribute toward my up-keep at home, (because my parents were retired and living on father's pension), to pay for all my university expenses, purchase books and engage in many student activities.

Later, through the recommendation of the committee concerned with Education for Ministry, these student attachments were discontinued. Students today are given real insight into the working of various churches, *after* their period of study. They become pastoral assistants generally for eighteen months. The argument is that this allows students to concentrate on their studies while at college. Personally I regret the decision. It was necessary to become very disciplined in regard to time and study in order to be a pastoral assistant while still a student. However, I feel that I and my subsequent ministry benefited enormously by my experiences of being a student pastoral assistant. For me it combined the academic study of theology with the practical task of relating the gospel to the ordinary person. The separation of the two, I believe, has been detrimental to the work of Christ's church and kingdom.

Broughton Place Church

My brother James had been a student assistant in Broughton Place Church in Edinburgh, for a year. I followed him for two years. Broughton Place Church, prior to the union of the churches in 1929, was a Free Church and a former United Presbyterian congregation. It continued to have a UP constitution. The minister was the Rev George Gunn. In my third year I was attached to St Mary's Church, Haddington, where the minister was the Revd James Thomson. It was an ancient historic church and belonged to what was called 'the Auld Kirk'. These two assistantships gave me experience of both the Free Church and Auld Kirk constitutions, for which I was grateful.

I learned much from George Gunn who was an able preacher, scholar and excellent parish minister. He had a large Kirk Session of approximately sixty elders, drawn from all walks of life, representing the law courts, business and various trades. His congregation numbered some 1600 people. The elders had a high regard for their minister. At each monthly meeting, a half hour was set aside for spiritual teaching and instruction. I well remember George Gunn commencing one meeting by saying to his elders that many in their districts would be unable to pray. It was their duty as elders to teach them to pray. He then proceeded to give them practical guidance as to how they helpfully might go about teaching the people in their districts to pray. No elder spoke up or demurred or suggested that this was too difficult. George Gunn always spoke in an authoritative way and his people simply accepted it and loved him. Many of his elders as I later found prayed in the homes when visiting. I was deeply impressed by the Christian witness of these very godly elders and the impact of their praying in the homes of their district. One person told me that they were taught to pray, not through the minister but through listening to their elder praying in their home

George Gunn in explaining my duties as student assistant, said that he anticipated that I preach once a month. After hearing me preach, I was asked to preach twice each month at both a morning and evening service. From this I greatly benefited. Preparation for sermons involved a lot of time and prayer. I wrote out all my sermons, following the advice of one my New Testament professors and pastor at New College, the much loved and respected Professor James S. Stewart. He advised us to do this for at least the first twelve years of our ministries warning us that if we did not we would likely become slack in our preaching and shallow. We would fail to do justice to our preaching of the Word of God and the people would not be properly fed on the Word of God.

I took preaching then and throughout my ministry as a great responsibility before God. Nonetheless I did not find it easy. I was a naturally shy person. Despite my speaking and preaching in student missions, I found it a daunting challenge to preach to a large congregation accustomed to the biblical thoughtful sermons of their own minister. Then, and for a few years afterwards, in my prayer before preaching I would go over in my mind God's call to Moses (Genesis chapter 3). I identified very much with Moses in his fear and hesitation to go in obedience and speak to the people and lead them out of Egypt. I repeated to myself God's call and each of Moses' excuses telling the Lord that he had great difficulty in speaking and asking the Lord to send someone else to do what he required (verse 13). I had not personally wanted to become a minister and throughout the major part of my army career had resisted God's call. I sympathised deeply with Moses. Like Moses, I at length felt compelled to accept God's call as the only way to find peace. I therefore regularly reminded God that he had called me into the ministry and called me to preach. It was his choice not mine, therefore he must help me and speak for me to his people because I could not. Years later, through experience, I could relax and truly enjoy preaching. I hope however that I will never fully escape a certain nervousness, for then I would rely on myself and not on the Lord. It is impossible to preach aright without prayer. Hence, in my early years, in my prayer in the vestry before each service, I recounted Moses' reluctance, God's anger over his excuses and his going forth in obedience. This continued until I followed the beadle (or church officer) into the church. In my prayer in the pulpit I recalled, until the organist ceased playing and I was ready to start the service, verses 1-9 of Joshua chapter 1, concluding with the verse, "Be strong and courageous. Do not be terrified; do not be discouraged, for the Lord your God will be with you wherever you go".

In the summer George Gunn took a month's holiday and said that I was in charge of the congregation. If I did not wish to preach twice a Sunday for a month I was free to make a pulpit exchange with a friend or other minister. As I found the work of preparation for two services each Sunday in the summer rather heavy, I sometimes invited my father to preach. He became very acceptable to the congregation and much loved by some of the elders, who on occasion asked George Gunn to invite him back. I was always amazed that George Gunn was so trusting, when he had such a large congregation and I was only a student. It helped and much encouraged me. My father had a gentle, winsome and very loving way in the pulpit although he was completely frank, never hesitating to challenge people to commit their lives and their all to Christ.

George Gunn said that as an assistant my responsibility was with the youth. He also asked that I visit ten homes each week. Every fortnight he met with me and gave me the next list of twenty homes. He had a most remarkable memory, which he taught himself to have, by memorising in his student days one or two entire columns of the Scotsman! He knew his congregation of some sixteen hundred people. When he gave me each name, he told me who each person was, their faithfulness or otherwise in church and the circumstances of their home. He always told me who in that home were not members of the church and always asked me especially to meet and talk with them. He always seemed to trust me and never asked whether I had done all that he required. I always endeavoured to report back to him and never failed to visit all the homes given to me. It kept me extremely busy. My brother Tom, then a professor at New College, kindly and on numerous occasions loaned me his car otherwise I would have found great difficulty in accomplishing all the visits. At the same time my brother James and I had a small motor bike which I found very useful. Often I arrived home at 10 o'clock in the evening to spend the next two hours studying Hebrew or some other subject.

Throughout my ministry, I always prayed in each home I visited, generally with a short Bible reading. I encouraged my elders to pray in the homes of their districts. Not all elders could, but when they did it was always spiritually very helpful. Elders need to be taught and encouraged to do so.

Pastoral Visitation

Once again, I learned much from my visiting the homes of the congregation. I mention some of the visits. It taught me the need for prayer over every visit.

1 ***Lady with a crippled leg healed through Spiritualism.*** Early in my assistantship I was asked to visit an elderly lady who lived alone in an upstairs tenement flat off Leith Walk, Edinburgh. As I recall it was early in the afternoon and my first visit that day. The lady was very agitated and in the course of my visit told me the course of her agitation. She said that for years she had been crippled in one leg. The doctors had done everything possible for her but she required to wear a calliper. She had a neighbour who was a spiritualist. In the years that followed the war when so many had been killed and people wanted to try and get into touch with their departed loved ones, spiritualism was strong in certain areas and strong in parts of Leith.

For a long time her neighbour kept urging her to accompany her to one of her spiritualist meetings, telling her that if she came she would be healed. Finally she accepted her neighbour's invitation, accompanied her to a spiritualist meeting and was healed. I looked down at her leg. She was not wearing a calliper and it looked completely normal. Clearly she had been healed. She said that occasionally when she was very tired she put on her calliper. However normally she did not require it and did not wear it. She did all her shopping without it. She then asked me, "Have I done right or wrong?" I was somewhat shaken. I did not like to say that I believed that spiritualism was of the devil. After all she had been handicapped and was healed. All I felt able to say was, "You give God the glory and do not go back to a spiritualist meeting." After a reading and prayer I went to the nearest cafe for a cup of coffee to recover from the shock. After I reflected and prayed about the visit I believed that God gave me the right words to say to the lady, on the ground that all healing from whatever source is ultimately of God, even although often the devil steals from God the power to work miracles and heal. God alone has the power to heal.

In my next assignment as student assistant in Haddington I again in my pastoral visitation was asked about spiritualism and answered with more confidence.

*2 **Conversion of an agnostic.*** George Gunn asked me to be sure and speak to one young man of nineteen or twenty whose family came to church but he was an agnostic. When I visited the home the son was present and assured me that he did not believe and was agnostic. I told him that as an agnostic he was really sitting on the fence. He was not prepared to say that he was an atheist and unprepared to accept the reality of God and his claims. I told him that it was impossible to hold to a neutral position, and to sit on the fence as far as God was concerned. God loved him and offered him salvation. He either accepted it or rejected it. He was either on the road to heaven or hell. I deeply regretted the fact that by his claiming to be an agnostic and sitting on the fence, he was content to be on the road to hell!

A short time later an elder came to me with great joy to tell me that the last person in his district who was not a member had decided to join the church. He saw him entering the first communicants' class and asked him what had brought him to church and caused him to change his mind. His reply was that the assistant minister had terrified him! He was the young man whom I had visited. Although I believe that fear of judgement can drive us to God, only the love of God is likely to hold us within the Kingdom.

*3 **Family with two sons.*** Again, George Gunn asked me to be sure and speak to two brothers who were bus drivers and were not church members. The parents were members but rarely came to church. On my first visit to the home, one brother opened the door to my knock but told me that his parents were out. I was not invited in and had no opportunity to talk to the brothers. I called again and this time the mother opened the door and invited me in. She was alone with one of her two sons. I immediately took the opportunity to speak to the son. When I invited him to church he immediately declined, on the ground that all ministers were liars. When I asked why he thought ministers and I were liars he said, "Because you say that there is a God and there is not one". I said that there is certainly a God. I have met him although I cannot prove that to him, in the way that he would like. I said to him, "Suppose that there is someone next door in your kitchen. Suppose that you tell me that, yet, by sitting here you cannot prove it. Suppose therefore I call you a liar because you cannot prove it, just as you call me and ministers liars, because we cannot prove as you would like, that we have spoken to God. What would you say?" He said, "I would take you into the kitchen so that you can see and speak to the person yourself". I replied, "I cannot prove to you the presence of God. I can tell you how you can meet him yourself, how you can speak to him and hear him speak to you. The real question is do you want to meet with God? Are you prepared to meet him?"

The man had nothing further to say and the mother, by way of answer said, "What terrible sons I have". I said, "Do you expect it to be otherwise when you do not give them a godly example. You rarely come to church to worship God although you are a member of the church". Because I felt that I had said enough, I asked whether I had their permission to read a passage of scripture and pray. At that the mother became very agitated, she stood and began to fiddle with things on the mantle-piece. She did not know what to say, so I asked again whether they were willing for me to read a passage from the Bible and pray. At that, the son said, "She is your sheep. You carry on!" He departed next door into the kitchen but left the door open so that he could hear. I asked the mother to sit down and I read and prayed. A few years later, when I was in my first parish in Livingston, George Gunn invited me to have coffee with him. He recalled my visit to that home because I told him about it. He told me that although the sons still did not come to church, both parents attended church diligently twice a Sunday and were among his most faithful attenders at worship. I felt encouraged.

4 A widow lady. In visits I very often read from the *Daily Light.* It contains morning and evening Bible readings. When I intimated what I was about to read, people would not feel that I had chosen that particular reading for them. Sometimes, because of the circumstances of the home and what was said, I did choose a passage that I felt was appropriate. I was particularly grateful on one occasion when visiting a single middle aged lady who lived alone. She told me that she had a bad leg and as a result was unable to go to church. Later in the conversation, forgetting about the mention of a bad leg, she told me of a wonderful holiday that she had had in England. I listened to her and as I recall did not respond to her non-attendance at church apart from expressing sympathy for the difficulty concerning her leg. Before leaving I said, "I will read from the *Daily Light* and then pray". It was my first visit for the day and I did not know the particular reading for the day. It commenced with a quotation from Daniel 5:27, "Thou art weighed in the balances, and art found wanting". The woman trembled all over. She felt considerably shaken and so was I. I said, "We have listened to words of judgement. Now we will listen to the reading for the evening. They speak of God's mercy and forgiveness."

Meeting Excuses

In the course of visiting one inevitably begins to learn how to respond to the things which are said and to the many excuses which people give for their non-attendance at church. I discovered that it was helpful very often to treat these excuses in the light hearted way that they were offered and not take them seriously. I believed that it was helpful to have a sense of humour. A frequent excuse that was given was, "I do not go to Church because those who go are hypocrites." On one occasion when a man said this as an excuse for his not coming to church, I replied, "Well, there is room for one more!" The man promptly burst out laughing and said that I was quite right!

On another occasion a man said to me, "I am not good enough to come to church". I said, "If you are good enough or feel that you are, please do not come to church. The church is not for good people. It is for bad people, so if you are one of them, it is time that you came!" He was most taken aback!

Work with Church Young People

I enjoyed my time with the young people. They were a fine group, aged between 16 or 17 and 25 years. Some were students. Others were teachers, were employed in a bank or some other firm. None were married. I met with them regularly in their weekly meetings. I asked for permission to arrange an occasional special weekend retreat. This was new to them. They were uncertain about what form this should take. Some were doubtful about a Christian programme with an invited speaker. In their uncertainty they left the planning and arranging of these retreats to me. Our first retreat was in Newbattle Abbey and thereafter in North Berwick where we were allowed to use the holiday house of Barnardo's Home for girls. I arranged for a guest speaker and ensured that we had each day, worship and some form of Christian meeting. We had plenty of time for recreation and fun. These retreats were much enjoyed. George Gunn intimated to the Kirk Session that they were an important landmark in the church's youth work.

In our first retreat, three people were converted, Betty Wilson and Dorothy Wallace, who were both school teachers and Mabel Isdaile, who worked in the bank. In speaking to them shortly afterwards Dorothy Wallace said that she had read the whole of the New Testament in a week.

I was concerned that in order to grow in their faith they should learn to pray openly together. I therefore invited them to the weekly prayer meeting attended by 25 and more persons. One regular attender, Maggie, a member of the Woman's Guild, was a simple soul, with little education. She was a very joyful, bright Christian. Her prayers were simple and down to earth. The new converts told me that listening to Maggie they felt they also could pray in company with others.

Two of them, Betty Wilson and Dorothy Wallace went to the mission field. Betty Wilson served for one tour under the Jewish Mission Committee in Egypt. Dorothy Wallace served for over 40 years in North India and for several years was head mistress of the girls' school in Darjeeling. Dorothy and I continue to exchange Christmas cards. For others, these retreats helped to deepen their faith and created a wonderful sense of Christian community.

Helping a New Church

In the years following the war there came about in Scotland a great movement of the population. Large new housing schemes were built and the Church of Scotland started a large programme of building new churches in these new housing areas. Creating a new church congregation was always a challenge. George Gunn intimated to the congregation that whereas they had been given a Church building through the generosity of their forebears, the Kirk Session in thankfulness to God had agreed to be responsible for one new housing area in Scotland, visiting the families who had moved into the area, intimating the plans to create a new church and inviting people to come to it. One Sunday following this intimation he came to the Youth Fellowship intimating that he would like to make an intimation. He said that at the end of the meeting he would be sitting at the table and asked that members of the fellowship would kindly give him their names and the evenings and dates when they would visit this new area. In his authoritative way, he never suggested or created the idea that some would not be free or willing to share in the visitation. To my surprise, all as far as I was aware, intimated their willingness to visit and intimated the days and times when they were free. George Gunn was a gifted leader whom I greatly admired and from whom I learned much.

Importance of thanksgiving

One further thing both interested and helped me. George Gunn was always a very cheerful person. He believed strongly in the importance of praise and thanksgiving to God. Faith is primarily thanksgiving. He therefore encouraged his congregation to sing joyfully. At each service of Holy Communion I was asked to sit next to him at the Lord's Table and listened to his very loud and joyful singing. He was however the only person whom I have met who despite his joyful singing seemed to be totally tone deaf! He sang every hymn on two notes! Such was the man and the respect and love which his congregation had for him I never heard anyone complain about his singing.

I learned very much from George Gunn and benefited from his ministry. Later, when I was minister in Livingston Parish, I asked him for his year's programme for Kirk Session instruction. This he kindly gave me, and following his example I used it in my first parish. Soon I created my own programme. Throughout my ministry in three separate churches, I persuaded my elders to agree to our setting aside half an hour, at each Kirk Session meeting. This we used for instruction or discussion on spiritual matters. Sometimes it took the form of Bible study. In Earlston we studied the Pastoral Epistles. We dealt with topics such as prayer, the need for daily Bible reading, the meaning of Baptism, Holy Communion, the Church as the Body of Christ. Sometimes we discussed a spiritual or theological Report sent down from the General Assembly. I always found this immensely helpful. The elders themselves enjoyed it. Some said that it was the best part of our Kirk Session meetings. Our setting aside of half an hour kept us disciplined in our discussions of other matters. The teaching and spiritual discussions helped to set the tone of our meetings and I believe often controlled the contribution of some of the less spiritual elders generally inherited from previous ministries.

St Mary's Church, Haddington

My work as student assistant in St Mary's was quite different. Again I admired the minister, James Thomson. He was a very good and able preacher and he and his wife were very kind to me, often inviting me to lunch after the morning service. Occasionally I was invited to the home of Mr and Mrs Jenkins. He was a godly elder, lay reader and farmer. On other Sundays and fairly frequently I lunched in the George Hotel. Once again I was invited to preach on a monthly basis in St Mary's. This gave me the experience of preaching to a large congregation in one of the ancient historic churches of Scotland. John Knox had preached there prior to and after the Reformation in 1560. During the period of my attachment the parish church occupied the nave of the original church which had been built after the pattern of St Giles, in Edinburgh, although I was told that it was slightly shorter in length. The rest of the church was a ruin but a few years later was entirely restored. Today it is enjoyed not simply by the congregation but much enjoyed by musicians and choirs because of the acoustics. However the maintenance of the fabric for such a large building imposes quite a financial burden.

The church, in addition to the morning and evening service each Sunday, had three afternoon services, one in the church for children and parents, one in the cottage hospital and a country service in an old building attached or adjacent to a farm. The minister, student assistant and Mr Jenkins, a farmer and lay preacher, conducted these services on a rota basis so that we each in turn preached in all three places.

The Revd James Thompson

Mr Thompson although a kind man, and very able preacher, was a shy man and I think found pastoral visiting difficult. I had to ask him for the names and addresses to visit. The recommendation of the Church's Ministry Committee was that student assistants, with their need to concentrate on their studies, should limit their activities in the parish to which they were attached, to one afternoon and one evening a week. I enjoyed visiting and in both my attachments did more than that, working either two afternoons and one evening or one afternoon and two evenings a week, in addition to preaching. I visited a considerable number of homes in both parishes. Reading a portion of Scripture and praying in each home, I found, not only helped those I was visiting, but strengthened my faith.

*1 **Meeting a widower.*** One morning during the morning service I noticed a visitor wearing a bow tie. At lunch in the George Hotel that day, I noticed the same gentleman, distinguishable by his bow tie, sitting at another table. He caught my eye and asked if I would join him for coffee in the lounge. He commenced by telling me that he did not agree with my sermon that day. It was an interesting and helpful start to our conversation. When I asked him what particularly he disagreed with he replied that I had said a number of things, which I had not actually said and yet, which to me, were biblical. Clearly God had been speaking to him. When I pressed him he confessed that he could not accept the message of the cross and Christ dying for us and for our salvation. He told me that he was a wealthy man. He was a director of two factories in England and had married into a landed family in Scotland. He had planned to retire early, to sit back and enjoy life. Suddenly however everything had changed. His wife suddenly died and the bottom had dropped out of his life.

I felt extremely sorry for him. I spoke of Jesus Christ, of his incredible love giving himself and his all for us and for our eternal salvation. I told him that only in and through the surrender of ourselves to Christ could we find the peace that God lovingly wants to give us. I told him that we are all in God's hands and although many things happen which we find hard and difficult, that ultimately he overrules everything for the good of those who love him. I gave him advice which I often have since pondered. I encouraged him to pray and say to God in prayer that, although he had loved his wife and had not wanted her to die, yet, because God in his love had called her away and in a way in which he could not understand and found difficult to accept, he should say "Thank you" to God. I told him that when he could say "Thank you" to God, he would find peace and begin to receive real comfort from God. I took that to my own heart when my wife died and believe the advice that I gave that day was from God. I was conducting the country service that Sunday and invited him to join me which he did. We kept in touch over a long period and later when I was studying in Basle he sent me a copy of Chaucer's *Canterbury Tales* in gratitude for my help to him.

2 Elizabeth Hamilton. Another person whom I met during lunch in the George Hotel was a lady who also had attended the morning service in church. Her name was Elizabeth Hamilton. She was a single lady, aged about 50 and came from a large farming family. She was highly qualified in a number of subjects, a lecturer in the Domestic Science College, in Atholl Crescent (now St Margaret's University) and during the war had been in charge of the NAAFI (Navy, Army, Air Force Institute) in Scotland. She told me that she had quarrelled with her minister and left the church. She had also quarrelled with her family, resigned her job and was at a loose end unable to settle. Her doctor had advised her to buy a new car to give her a new interest. She found his advice inadequate and had turned to other religions to discover what they had to offer. She was attracted to Christian Science.

I thought a lot about her situation. I prayed for her and wrote her a long letter of approximately 12 pages. I told her that her real problem was that she was a sinner and would not acknowledge it. She had sinned in quarrelling with her minister and the members of her family. That is why the bottom had dropped out of her life and why she was so restless and discontented. She was running away from God. She was attracted to Christian Science simply because Christian Science did not accept or recognise sin, her sin. She must accept the reality of sin and that she was a sinner. She must ask and receive God's forgiveness, apologise to her minister and the members of her family and be reconciled to them. It was the only way to find peace.

She wrote me back a very angry letter saying who was I to tell her that she was a sinner. I replied in a longer letter of some 14 pages saying that it was not I but God who said that she was a sinner. Christ's death on the cross was God's pronouncement that all without exception had sinned. For her to acknowledge that Christ had died for her, was to acknowledge that she had sinned and before God she was a sinner. Before the cross, however, we not only hear God's verdict on our lives that we have sinned. We hear that God in love has forgiven us and welcomes each of us as his dear child. Through that letter she was transformed and converted. We corresponded for a long while. Some years later when I was parish minister in Livingston she telephoned me to ask for my permission to publish these two letters at her expense. They had so helped her she thought that they would help others. I was moved at her humility. Her desire to publish the letters indicated how she had grown spiritually, for the letters would reveal publicly how she had sinned in her quarrelling. They were not complimentary to her. I felt at the time that the letters were personal and private to her so said that I did not wish them to be published. Later, I felt that I was probably wrong and that their publication might have helped others.

3 *A bereaved couple.* One home I visited was that of a retired farmer and his wife. They had only one son who was killed in the war. He had been in the RAF and was killed when flying over what was called the 'hump' between Burma and China. He had been about two years ahead of me at the Royal High School in Edinburgh, which I had attended. I knew of him and remembered him although I did not actually know him. The couple told me that as an only son they planned that he should take over the farm. His death devastated them. They told me that they still, in 1952, wept every day. I felt very sorry for them. Their situation challenged me as a Christian and as a minister. What was I to say to them in their desolation? It helped to drive home to me the words of Jesus, "Where your treasure is, there will your heart be". Their sorrow was very real. Hope, comfort and the love which they so much needed, could only be found in Christ.

4 *A troubled family.* In another home, the father was director of two bread factories. His wife, in welcoming me into their home, said that theirs was a very unhappy home. When I asked the reason she said that they had only one son. The father wanted him to take over after him the management of the two factories. The son however was not interested and wanted to be a veterinary surgeon. I felt compelled to say that it was important that each person should be free, where possible, to choose their own career. The parents should not dictate to their offspring. Only if they were free would they continue to respect and love their parents. I do not know what ultimately happened and what career the son followed.

5 ***Marriage tension.*** In visiting one of the homes in the Council Estate, the wife told me that theirs was not a happy home. The husband was out when I called. There was tension between the husband and wife and I could sense the unhappiness. She told me that she could never forgive her husband for what he had done. I told her that we must forgive one another as the only way to peace and happiness. I said that it was not natural for us to be able to forgive. Forgiveness was a gift which we must ask to receive from God. I told her however that we are all sinners in need of God's forgiveness for our sins. Only as we asked God to forgive us for what we had done, could we receive the gift to forgive others. She was very appreciative and before I left the parish she thanked me for what I had done for the happiness of their home. I felt much encouraged. In the ministry I have found over the years the hardest part of my pastoral ministry concerned my seeking to help people whose marriages were strained or on the rocks. Over the years I have had many failures and also many successes, if I may be allowed to use that word, when it is only God who can heal a broken marriage. The successes, which sometimes were few and far between helped me to persevere in this form of ministry. The encouragement which I received in that pastoral visit early in my ministry encouraged me greatly in the years ahead.

Homes of the Poor

There were at that time many wealthy families in Haddington. Several had worked in India and overseas, were comfortably off and had retired to Haddington. At the same time there were many poor families who lived in a large housing estate situated east of the river Tyne across from the church. In several households, sadly, the man had been severely wounded in the war. He was unable to work and consequently the family was poor. The contrast between the rich and the poor in Haddington was quite marked. I felt that, generally, the poorer homes were the happiest.

Bible Class and Youth Work in St Mary's

In St Mary's Haddington, as in Broughton Place Church I was given the responsibility of caring for the young people. This involved each Sunday endeavouring to teach a Bible class of 27 boys and girls of about 15-17 years. I also ran a club for these Bible Class youngsters on a Wednesday evening in the Church Hall. I found the teaching of the Bible class a tremendous challenge. They were not easy to teach, nor easy to control. It was hard to keep their attention and to keep them interested. I felt concerned that they should really come to know the Lord as their loving Saviour. I felt keenly my own inadequacy and agonised in prayer over them.

In the club I was single handed and on my own. They had so much energy that I always started with a game of indoor hockey, which we played for half an hour. It helped to take away some of their energy. I felt that unless I tired them I could not control them! After hockey I organised between the two rooms a table tennis tournament in the one room and some other form of activity in the other. We had some very memorable evenings.

One day I remained a little longer than usual supervising the table tennis tournament and suddenly became aware that everything seemed unusually quiet next door. When I entered the larger hall I was greeted with an interesting sight. The hall was a former Free Church which many years before had united with St Mary's. It had a small gallery where the church officer stored the chairs when they were not in use. Some of the boys had gone up into the gallery and dropped down a large number of chairs which were caught by other boys below. With these chairs they had formed a pyramid, or pillar which reached practically to the ceiling. It was well done and I was quite amused. At the end of the evening I asked the boys to dismantle it and take the chairs back up to the gallery. I explained that they had managed to do it by working as a team. The church officer was one man. By his attempting to dismantle the chairs single handed some would inevitably fall and could be damaged. The boys refused to dismantle the chairs despite my repeated request. At that I said in a commanding voice, "This is the end of the club. Outside! All of you!" They were startled and waited for me until I had come out and locked the door. I said again, "This is the end of the club". They replied, "Alright, we will not come to the Bible class!" I turned and spoke to each one in turn and said, "You will go home tonight and say to the Lord, 'Lord I am no longer going to go to the Bible class and listen to what you want to say, because I cannot get my own way at the Wednesday club.'" I said that to each boy and girl in turn. Each one replied and said, "I can't do that!" I looked at them, unlocked the hall door and said, "Alright, go in and dismantle the chairs and put them back in the gallery". They all went in like sheep and dismantled and put away the chairs. They bore no hard feelings. They were a likeable set of rogues. I was conscious from experience in the army days that a leader must always be in control.

The halls were some distance from the church. No other organisation or group used the halls on a Wednesday evening. Hence the custom was that I would collect the key from the church officer and would myself open the halls for the youth club. The young people were generally standing up against the wall of the passage leading to the halls, when I arrived. On one memorable night as I greeted them I felt that there was something of a strange atmosphere. As I put the key into the lock I noticed the tip of a rocket protruding from a boy's jersey. At once I remembered that it was the 5th of November, bonfire night, when it is customary to let off fireworks! I have always felt that I never wished to suppress enthusiasm. I have tried simply to guide or redirect it. When the young people had entered the hall I locked the door, because I did not want any elder or other person to visit us. I told the young people that I was aware that they had brought fire-works along with them. I stood them up in a row at one end of the hall and said, "We will set off two rockets at a time". We laid two rockets on the floor, lit them and watched them hit the wall opposite. As they ricocheted back toward us, we all jumped together. Mercifully no one was hurt or killed!

Soon, because this was not exciting enough, some of the boys wanted to light a banger and throw it at the feet of the girls. I immediately said, "No! Enough is enough!" A boy who already had a banger in his hand, looked at me and drew out a match to light it. I promptly picked him up and sat him on the floor. He jumped up and grabbed me, so I again sat him on the floor. At this three boys went for me. I had been taught a fair amount of unarmed combat in the army. I had always served as a combatant in what medically was a first class unit. The university at that time ran a three year course with a diploma in Physical Education. I twice completed the three year course, so I was reasonably fit. Of the three boys one was over six feet two or three inches. He was taller than me. I promptly turned him over, sat on his chest, locked the other two one under each arm and said, "You will jolly well know who is boss here! You will learn to obey and do what you are told".

The boys and indeed the whole group were quite subdued. Probably for the boys to be wrestled to the floor and subdued so easily was a bit humiliating, in front of the girls, for it was a mixed club. Needless to say they were quite obedient after that! There were no hard feelings. They as usual bought me some chips after the meeting was over and accompanied me to the Edinburgh bus. Edinburgh where I stayed with my parents was some 17 miles distant from Haddington. Looking back, I am thankful to God that no one was hurt or injured that night. I think with mature reflection I was crazy to have allowed them to light fireworks inside a building. It was however fun and I enjoyed it, although I could not today do what I did then and seek to impose discipline in the way that I did.

The young people of the Bible class, were an energetic and wild lot but loveable. I never spoke to their parents or any one about their poor behaviour. We seemed to accept each other as friends. I often felt inadequate in what I was asked to do and inadequate in setting them a Christian example or teaching them about the love and salvation of Christ. In the mercies of God two of the boys entered the ministry of the Church of Scotland. Ian Maxton had come to faith as a boy through the help of Malcolm Ritchie, who had been a previous student assistant. Jim Punton after serving as a parish minister became the first Director of Frontier Youth Trust in Scotland and then Director of Frontier Youth Trust for the UK.[4]

One day, during the period when I was a minister in Aberdeen, I was reminded of my former Bible Class and Youth Club in Haddington. The Aberdeen Presbytery had arranged to hold a special conference on the subject of the Gospel and young people, to take place in one of the halls of Beechgrove Church. The guest speaker was the Revd James Punton. I did not at first pay attention to the name of the guest speaker and the name did not register with me when Sangster, the minister of Beechgrove and I were asked to meet the speaker and bring him into the Presbytery meeting. When a car drew up at the door of the church and a bearded figure got out, at first I did not recognise him. When Sangster welcomed him and asked if he had met David Torrance, Jim smiled and said, "Yes! He is my old Bible class teacher". Memories came flooding back. After he had hung up his coat I said, "Jim, you were not only in the Bible class. You were also in the Wednesday club". He laughed and said, "Yes! I was". After the meeting I teased Jim and said, "Was it because you saw a church club run so badly that you decided to become professional and come and teach us how a club ought to be run?" He simply laughed.

A further reference to the Bible class and Wednesday club came much later when I was minister in my last parish of Earlston. When the elders welcomed me as their minister, one elder, James Thomson, a farmer, smiled and said "You were an assistant in St Mary's Haddington. Later when visiting in his home, he again said, "You were an assistant in St Mary's Haddington. My uncle who was an elder in St Mary's when you were there would like to meet you and so would another uncle who was an elder in the West Church in Haddington".

I asked him what he knew about me and about my assistantship in St Mary's. When I referred to the incident of the fireworks in the church hall, he told me that he knew the story of that night. I was astonished and asked him how he knew. I was aware that his father had a farm near Longniddry, and that as a boy he had attended Knox Academy in

4 Frontier Youth Trust was at that time a daughter organization of the Scripture Union. It is evangelical and runs Christian out-door adventure camps for youth.

Haddington, but he had not been in St Mary's Bible class or the club. I said that I had never told a mortal soul about what happened that night. He laughed and said but the boys told what happened. That story went through the whole of Knox Academy and through the whole of East Lothian. He said, "They all respected you!"

United Christian Witness

During my period at New College, and in addition to my other activities, I joined the United Christian Witness Movement, although I was not able to attend regularly. It was an evangelical organisation based in Glasgow and founded by two Glasgow ministers, the Revd Tom Allan, minister of North Kelvinside and the Revd Kenneth Turnbull, a minister in Partick. The movement grew largely out of those who had participated in sea-side or other missions. The basis of membership consisted of two simple rules, clearly drawn up by two ex-service men! Tom had served in the RAF and Ken in the army. The rules were – members must go wherever asked and be prepared to speak whenever asked.

The custom when I attended was a Bible study in the church hall of Ken Turnbull's church in Partick, followed by tea in the church hall. We then met for an open air meeting. These were the days when literally hundreds of people would gather in the open air. It was not uncommon for Tom Allan to speak to a thousand people so gathered. Tom was an honours English graduate. He had a marvellous gift of language and the remarkable gift to be able to speak both to those in church and those on the street who had never entered through a church door. He had a rich sense of humour. To be suddenly called in an open air meeting before literally hundreds of people, to engage in a conversation with Tom as leader and to answer questions about the Christian faith is an experience I will never forget. The open air services were then followed by a large evangelistic meeting in the church hall.

Tom was a most gifted evangelist. He made a deep impression on me. I learned a lot from him. He over-worked in the cause of Christ, was a heavy smoker, before the dangers of smoking were known, and sadly died in his late forties. He made a deep impact on many of the younger ministers as well as being instrumental in many coming to faith in Christ. Apart from Captain Steven Anderson, who came to faith through the Revd D.P. Thomson, Scotland sadly has never in the work of evangelism replaced either DP or Tom Allan. They were both outstanding and dedicated servants of Christ.

Chapter 6

Call to Evangelism: Tell Scotland

Over the autumn term of 1954, having on Professor Burleigh's advice limited the scope of my thesis, I submitted to Professor James McEwen a preliminary outline of 40 pages of my thesis.

In early January I received a telephone call from D.P. Thompson, asking me if I would join him in the work of evangelism that same week. When I informed him that I was involved in my doctoral studies, he explained to me the situation in which he was placed, and assured me that if I agreed to help him I would have plenty of time to continue my studies!

Tell Scotland and the All Scotland Crusade

Tell Scotland was an umbrella movement which brought together under its auspices all the evangelical movements that had emerged since the war, chiefly under the leadership of Tom Allan, minister of North Kelvinside Church, Glasgow and D.P. Thompson, the full time evangelist of the Church of Scotland. The General Assembly of the Church of Scotland under the recommendation of Tell Scotland, in 1954, asked the evangelist Dr Billy Graham from the U.S.A. to lead an all-Scotland Crusade, which he did in the spring of 1955. DP was involved in the preparations for the Crusade for the East of Scotland, hence his invitation to me to assist him. Tom Allan led the preparations in the West of Scotland. I accepted DP's invitation, believing that this was God's call.

The suggestion that I would be able, while working with Tell Scotland, to continue my doctoral studies, was far from the truth. I was unable to resume work on my projected thesis. In working with Tell Scotland, I never worked harder in all my life. I enjoyed the work and was very happy. However great my inadequacies and failures, I was now certain that God had called me not to an academic but a parish ministry.

My experience in evangelism, I believe, was a marvellous preparation for the ministry in the parish. I could wish that every minister could engage in mission and evangelism before entering on the ministry of the parish.

Other churches, like the United Free, Congregational, Episcopal and Baptist Churches united with the Church of Scotland under the umbrella of Tell Scotland, although it was financed largely by the Church of Scotland, which was by far the largest denomination. My salary of £300 a year was paid by the Home Mission of the Church of Scotland, under whom I was employed.

In 1955 and for the period leading up to and including the All Scotland Crusade under Billy Graham, Tell Scotland was allowed the use of the YMCA rooms in South St Andrews Street in Edinburgh. This was their headquarters and office.

Mission to Central Edinburgh

On my first morning in the Tell Scotland Office, DP told me that agreement had been reached to lead a mission to Central Edinburgh in preparation for the Billy Graham Crusade that would start in the spring. When I asked him who would lead the mission, he said, "You will!" So I was plunged into what has remained the busiest part of my ministry.

People throughout the churches in Edinburgh had been invited to help. Each morning a small team of volunteers reported at the Tell Scotland Office at 7am. I met them and arranged that they go out and visit the cleaners and those opening the shops, business premises and offices in Princes Street, George Street and Queen Street. This they did systematically going from one place to the next. They took with them literature intimating the coming All Scotland Crusade and invited those whom they met to come to the Crusade meetings.

On one occasion DP offered to give me a morning off and he himself would come in at 7am in order to direct the team of volunteer visitors. Actually his idea of a morning off was that I come at approx. 8.30am, not 7am, in order to take over the rest of the programme for the day, which started at 9 o'clock! I do not remember if the invitation to take a morning off was repeated!

On that particular morning I arrived in the office in good time to find DP in a mood of mild shock. First he told me that I had not informed him which shops and office premises had already been visited so that DP was unable to tell the team where to go that morning. Accordingly he simply thanked them and sent them away. However he asked one to remain and kindly sweep and tidy the office. When he was finished DP asked him what he did in life. The man, Mr Maxwell, told him that he was a QC and lecturer in Law in the university. DP was a bit stunned that he had asked a QC to sweep out the office! I was highly amused. Mr Maxwell was an elder in St George's West Church and gave us immense help. He joined me later that summer as part of a mission team in West Sutherland. Later in a programme on the BBC he testified as to what the work of Tell Scotland had meant to him and how it drew him out from being an academic recluse into active evangelism, mentioning what it meant for him to visit the cleaners in the shops and offices in the early morning.

At 8.30am until 9am I hastily breakfasted in a nearby cafe, or restaurant. At 9am I met with another team of volunteers and we visited the shops, offices and business premises along Princes Street, George Street and Queen Street. I would endeavour to cover at least five premises in a morning and the corresponding number in the afternoon. I would ask the director of the shop or office if I could address the staff for 15 or 20 minutes intimating the Crusade meetings. This allowed me to give a short Gospel address. Occasionally DP visited along with me and spoke. Amazingly we were never turned away. Our request was never refused. In some of the large shops like Jenner's in Princes Street, or some of the large Insurance firms in St Andrew's Square and George Street, if the director allowed all his staff to listen to what we had come to say, then the shop or business would require temporarily to close. I was therefore invited to call on three consecutive days and I would be allowed to speak to a different third of the staff.

Although the Crusade was held for over six weeks in Glasgow, it was arranged on one occasion for Billy Graham to hold a Crusade meeting in Edinburgh, in the Hearts football ground at Tynecastle. I always took the opportunity when speaking at a meeting of shop and office staff, of asking the director, who was generally at the meeting, if he would allow his staff to have a special afternoon off work, so that they could go to the Crusade meeting at Tynecastle. Remarkably, and certainly under the hand of God, many directors did.

In Queen Street there were, and possibly still are, a remarkable number of lawyers' offices. Visiting one after another I found that the atmosphere of the staff in one differed remarkably from that of another. In some the reception was relaxed and friendly and in others it was stiff and formal. Everything seemed to depend on the top management. In one, the senior director, Mr Fairweather was an elder in the church. He was very friendly, and invited me to sit with him in his office. He asked about the coming All Scotland Crusade and what preparations were being made – and being made in Edinburgh. His friendly, kindly manner seemed to influence the entire staff.

In another lawyers' office I visited in Queen Street, the general atmosphere was entirely different. When I asked to be allowed to speak to the senior director, I was greeted with silence and a nervous smile. The staff appeared to be a bit nervous. One went up the stairs to convey my request to the senior director. I was immediately asked for my reason in asking to speak with him. When I told the member of staff and my request was conveyed to the director, I was told that I could meet him that afternoon at two o'clock. I arrived at the appointed time and was shown upstairs. The director's room was large and carpeted and, as far as I can remember, bereft of additional furniture. The director sat behind his desk at the far end to the door. His secretary was sitting with him. As I was entering the door and before I was fully entered he said in a loud voice, as he if he was addressing some person at the bar, intending to intimidate him, "I understand that you want me to give permission to the staff to have an afternoon off to attend a meeting by Billy Graham. Is that correct?"

I suppose that there is that in me which objects to being spoken to in that way. So I walked up leisurely and stood in front of his table, looked at him and said in a natural voice, "Yes! That is correct". The man was a bit nonplussed by my attitude and refusal to be intimidated, and seemed at first at a loss as to what to say. His secretary shot a quick glance at me, smiled and looked down. She was clearly interested in our conversation and interested in my meeting with her boss. After a momentary pause he said that the staff would not want to go the Crusade meetings. I asked that he should give them the opportunity of attending the Crusade meeting at Hearts Football Stadium, in Edinburgh by giving his staff an afternoon off work. I suggested that he would be surprised by the willingness of his staff to attend the Crusade meeting if he gave them the opportunity. Surprisingly, he agreed that anyone who wished to go to the Edinburgh afternoon meeting was free to go. I felt the hand of God at work because he did not appear sympathetic. His whole manner seemed to affect his staff, whom I found subdued but friendly toward me. The contrast between the spirit in these two offices could not have been more different.

In making my request to a bank manager on Princes Street, it was clear that he was uncertain as to whether to grant my request. He called his assistant manager and asked his advice. He was an elder in North Morningside Church and clearly interested in news about the Crusade. He recommended that permission be given for me to speak to the staff. Reluctantly the manager agreed but said that I was free to come and speak after the bank had closed, the following day! When I arrived I discovered that the entire staff was there. The manager had also come and was standing at the back. After the meeting he spoke to me. He told me that he was relieved that his staff had stayed after the closure of the bank. He said that he had deliberately arranged that time for me to come and speak to the staff believing that no one would stay. His conscience had deeply troubled him, because of his attitude and his arranging that I speak after the bank had closed. He told me that as a result he had not slept well that night. I told him that I had prayed about the meeting and that God was concerned for his staff. It gave me an opportunity to share the Gospel with him and the nature and meaning of commitment to Christ.

Looking back, it was perhaps a bold step on my part to ask the various directors to give their staff an afternoon off work, in order to allow them to attend the Crusade rally at Tynecastle! Nonetheless I do not remember any case where my request was rejected. The directors and managers whom I met were remarkably supportive. It was the hand of God. Whether of course employees actually went to the Crusade or simply welcomed the opportunity of an afternoon off I do not know! I believe, judging from the numbers who actually attended that the majority of those invited went.

The office of Imperial Typewriters was situated on George Street. The director I found very welcoming and friendly. He did not have a large staff but was interested to hear about the coming Crusade. He kindly asked if he could invite me to a Rotary lunch the following day in the North British hotel. I accepted his kind invitation. I enjoyed the lunch and speaking to those whom I met. For me the highlight of the occasion was a speech given by a lawyer in presenting Lord Shawcross, QC, with a gift.

Why he was given a gift, I do not remember. What I have remembered was the lawyer's speech which was humorous. He said that Lord Shawcross had been a brilliant student and from the start of his career had manifested a keen and sharp mind. He illustrated this by saying that as a young lawyer on the completion of his studies he started work in a lawyers' office in Edinburgh. Shortly after commencing work, he left his office to have a haircut. On his return the director summoned him to his office and said, "Young man where have you been?" Shawcross said he had gone out to have a haircut. The director said, "What, in office hours?" Shawcross replied, "My hair grew in office hours". The director said, "It did not all grow in office hours". Shawcross replied, "I did not get all of it cut off!"

In addition to my speaking in shops and business premises I also, and generally alone, but occasionally accompanied by one or two others, visited and spoke in every public house in Rose St. In those days before the development of many modern shops, the lane was largely reserved for pedestrians only, and there were numerous pubs in the lane. I also visited all the pubs around the West End of Princes Street, together with all the pubs between there and Tollcross including the surrounding area. I was never refused the opportunity to speak in a pub, when I requested it.

Occasionally the manager would say, "You are not going to ask them to stop drinking?" I assured them that I wished to speak about the Crusade and leave a short message about Christ. I was always courteously received. Although I always asked that the staff should continue in their serving of drinks, I do not think that they ever did while I was speaking. People in the various pubs always listened very attentively. These visits gave rise to many serious conversations about the Christian faith. I always wore in my visitations a clerical collar. I found men again and again willing and wanting to talk about the Christian faith. Many had a bad conscience about their drinking habits and the depriving of their families of the full benefit of their wages. (I always found men who drank were kinder and easier to talk to than those who gambled. I have always found gamblers harder to talk to about Christ). I felt these visits to pubs were very worthwhile by the opportunities given to share the Gospel.

Problems in Working Life

It was my custom to slip out each day for lunch. The time which I had was limited and it was too far to go home so I lunched in a restaurant nearby. Here I met a young man a little younger than myself. We introduced ourselves to each other and formed a friendship. I told him who I was and what I was doing. He told me that he was a chartered accountant working in an accountant's office. We met regularly for lunch and I talked to him many times about the Christian faith.

After a few weeks he said to me, "Since meeting you and becoming a Christian, life has become very difficult". I asked him why. He said that as a CA (Chartered Accountant) he was asked in the firm in which he worked to do things which were wrong. He said that he was only a junior. He was not a director. He said, "If I do not do these things, I will be sacked. What am I to do?"

It is a problem which I have often met in the ministry. Men have from time to time said the same to me. I have often wondered if many men and women do not come to church because they cannot conscientiously square what they are doing at work with what they hear in church. I have always felt that it was too easy for me who am financially secure with my salary from the church, simply to say, "You must refuse to do what is wrong whatever the cost to you and your family". What I have said, and said on that occasion, to the CA whom I had come to meet and befriend was: "Pray and lay the whole matter before God. Ask God to show you what to do. Ask God to make you willing to do what God wants and ask for the courage and strength to do it."

Preparing for Billy Graham

In the Tell Scotland office the only other full time person was Miss Joan Murdoch. She was DP's secretary. She was a very committed Christian, always calm, cheerful and unflappable, which was necessary for anyone working close to DP! She had a lovely temperament. Later she married and she and her husband worked as missionaries in West Africa.

In addition to organising and running the mission to central Edinburgh I assisted DP in his work of preparation for the Crusade and with planning and organizing Billy Graham's coming to speak at Tynecastle, together with the many preparation and training sessions for those who would serve as counsellors at the Crusade meetings. In addition, DP had many speaking engagements while planning future forms of Christian outreach following the All Scotland Crusade. He also at this time wrote some of his smaller booklets, including one which was a handbook for counsellors. These he asked me to proof-read prior to their publication.

DP worked extremely hard. He drove himself to the limit just as he drove others who worked with him. Some of his assistants could not stand the strain of working with him and I believe resigned. I got on extremely well with DP. I found that I had to stand up to him. I listened to what he wanted done and endeavoured to do it my way and not his which I often found to be impossible. He respected me and I think loved me as I respected and loved him. He once said that I was the best personal worker he ever had. Several times he drove himself to exhaustion. Each weekend he travelled to his home in Crieff. This he found necessary in order to relax. His time with his wife Mary, a marvellous woman who understood and loved him, together with the peace and beauty of the highland hills always refreshed him. Joan and I often saw him off at the end of a week when he looked positively ill and exhausted, wondering whether we would see him again. He always returned on the Monday refreshed, renewed and full of energy. DP had a passionate love for Christ and great zeal for Christ's Kingdom.

During the period of the mission to central Edinburgh, preparation was being made to train Christian counsellors to assist in the Crusade meetings. Volunteers were requested, to train twice a week each Monday and Tuesday for 12 weeks. There were a thousand volunteers from the Edinburgh churches. (Sadly, that would not happen today!) These meetings lasted for two hours. DP himself did the teaching with occasional help from other experienced ministers. The result was that I returned home tired after 10 o'clock at night although I required to be back in the office at 7am because of the mission to the centre of the city. It was tiring but I greatly enjoyed the work. In addition to these counsellors approximately two thirds of the ministers in Edinburgh offered to assist as counsellors in the Crusade. At that time there were about 250 charges in Edinburgh Presbytery.

At the end of the period of training DP announced that he and I together would meet and interview every volunteer, selecting those who we felt should go forward as counsellors. We graded those selected into one of two categories A and B. Over 600 were selected. Those listed in A category were prepared and happy to share the faith and pray with those who wish to commit their lives to Christ. Those in B category would assist them. DP and a professor in the Congregational Church and a former colleague of DP's in mission, interviewed each minister in turn, who came not simply from the Church of Scotland but from other churches and missions in Edinburgh. They likewise were graded. After these interviews DP handed me the cards recording the name of each counsellor, with their grading, sex, approximate age and employment. They came from all walks of life. Some were highly educated, professional people; some were not and held quite humble jobs.

For the duration of the All Scotland Crusade which lasted six weeks it was arranged to relay each Crusade meeting in Glasgow to eleven or twelve selected churches and halls across Edinburgh. In handing me the bundle of cards concerning each counsellor, DP told me to sort out who would serve in each centre. He said, "Remember that the various centres vary in size. For example, West St George's Church is much larger than the Methodist Church in St Nicholas Square. Divide the number of counsellors in proportion to the size of the centre. Do not put all the professionals in one centre and the working class counsellors in another. Make sure that in each centre there is an even proportion of professionals and working people. Do not put all the men in one centre and the women in another. In each centre make sure there is a balance between younger and older counsellors and a balance between counsellors in categories A and B. Put everything in the post today so that everyone will in the morning know to what centre they are allocated. All the counsellors will meet in the Hall of St George's West Church, and if I remember correctly, he said, they will meet tomorrow night! DP allocated the ministers to the various centres.

I was appalled by what DP had asked me to do and the time frame in which he asked me to do it. I received the cards and walked disconsolately towards our Tell Scotland office in South St Andrews Street. I found what DP was asking me difficult, and beyond my capability. By the grace of

God I met a friend from student days, Peter Morrison. Peter was a lawyer. (He became for several years Procurator Fiscal for East Lothian and then when his wife Mary became ordained and was called to a church in Edinburgh, he resigned and became Deputy Procurator Fiscal for Edinburgh.)

Peter greeted me and said, "You are looking downcast, David." I told him my problem. At once Peter brightened. His mind worked in ways which mine did not. He said, "Give me the cards, a room and a heater and leave me alone for two hours". I was immensely relieved and said, "I will give you anything you want if you will do this". Peter did a superb job. He accomplished everything in accord with what DP asked. I thanked him and received the allocated cards. My meeting with Peter and his timely help was the hand of God. I gave the listed cards to Joan who kindly typed them. Each centre was on a different page with the list of names of counsellors assigned to that centre. It was too late to put them in the post as DP had asked so I took the lists with me to the meeting in St George's West Church.

The counsellors had assembled and DP and I were walking up the stairs when DP said, "David, did you put all the information in the post. Does everyone have the required information?" I said, "No DP!" DP turned to me at once with deep concern. I said, "DP this is what will happen. I have here on separate pages the name of each Relay Centre, with the names of the counsellors attached to each Centre. After you have opened the meeting with prayer I will give you one page at a time. You can read the name of the Centre and the names of the counsellors assigned to that centre. You can then ask them to depart and meet in a place (hall or church) which I had named on the sheet, in order to meet with the leaders of their centre." DP looked at me quite humbly. He patted me on the shoulder and said, "David, I know that my orders are quite impossible!"

At DP's request I was allocated to South Leith Church, a large centre. There were over 3,000 communicant members belonging to South Leith Church. I understand that it had the largest congregation in Scotland. Ken Turnbull was the leader, and came over from Glasgow for the occasion. I was asked to lead and guide the counsellors. A considerable number of people gathered each night of the Crusade. After welcoming them, Ken opened each meeting with prayer. At the end of the Crusade meeting in Glasgow, when Billy Graham called the people to come forward and commit their lives to Christ, and as they sung the familiar hymn, "Just as I am", Ken called the people in South Leith to come forward. Quite a considerable number of people came forward each night. My task was to arrange that each person coming forward was met and welcomed by one of the counsellors. Those whom the counsellors found difficult to counsel they passed over to me or to Ken Turnbull.

On one of the first nights, one of the counsellors, a church elder, beckoned for me to come and take over. A man and a woman had been walking down Leith Walk. They had no prior intention of coming to the Crusade meeting. However because the church door that they were passing was open and they saw people going in, they came in. After hearing Billy Graham they felt convicted and answered the invitation to come forward. Both were married although not to each other. Both had been deserted by their marriage partner. They met and had become friends. Here they were, moved by the Holy Spirit and feeling convicted. What were they to do?

The people whom we met for counselling came from all walks of life. Their experiences were different. They each needed Christ who alone could answer their problems and deepest needs.

I found the six weeks of Crusade meetings exciting, deeply moving and enriching to my own faith, as I saw and witnessed many lives spiritually changed. Occasionally I journeyed through to Glasgow to hear Billy Graham. I met and prayed with some of the Billy Graham team which was a help and inspiration to me. Billy Graham and his team had a profound impact on very many people in Scotland. Although some who professed a commitment to Christ backslid, countless others were completely changed. Many entered the ministry, became leaders in their church or offered themselves as missionaries overseas. Two thousand people in Edinburgh and district went forward during Crusade meetings, most in one of the Relay Centres in Edinburgh. The cards of all those who went forward were sent to the Tell Scotland office in Edinburgh and were given to me. It was my responsibility along with Joan Murdoch, to forward these cards to the minister or congregation which the convert had mentioned and was written on the card by their counsellor. At the end of the summer DP asked me personally to visit about 90 people who had gone forward and who it appeared were not linked up with a church. It became very clear to me that those who came from, or were linked to, an evangelical church which understood the message of the Crusade, grew spiritually and advanced in the Christian Faith. Many became Christian leaders and served the church in different ways. Others who came from churches who apparently did not agree with the message of the Crusade and who appeared not to understand what had happened to the converts, sadly, and all too often, backslid. Everything seemed to depend on the receiving church.

The Army

Billy Graham also made a remarkable impact on the military. He spoke to soldiers at a meeting in Redford Barracks in Edinburgh. Several were converted and some were able to come and assist us later on in mission. Billy Graham with his black and white presentation of the Gospel appealed to men, perhaps particularly to officers in the regular army. They themselves were direct and straightforward in speech and in their approach to life.

Major Heron-Watson. On one of my visits to the Crusade Meeting in Glasgow, I travelled on the train with Major Heron-Watson. He had retired from the army and was governor of Saughton prison in Edinburgh. On the return journey he told me that he had answered the call to go forward after the meeting. He said that he was already a Christian but Billy Graham had said come forward if you want to give your life to Christ or rededicate your life tonight. He said, "I went forward. I did not wait to be counselled because I was already Christian. I went forward (and he thumped his knee with great vigour) because it was a matter of discipline!" He accompanied us to take part in the mission to Sutherland, in the summer of 1955.

Colonel Henderson. Following Billy Graham's meeting in Tynecastle I was sitting in the office the following morning. As I checked the cards of all who had gone forward, I came across the name of a Colonel Henderson of the Royal Scots regiment. Many years before in December 1942, I had joined the Royal Scots. I sat with the card in my hand wondering if I had ever come across an officer called Henderson. My idle thoughts were interrupted by a knock on the door. When I opened the door, I came face to face with Colonel Henderson. I welcomed him in and asked him to take a seat. I asked what I could do for him. I will never forget our conversation which followed. He said, "I attended the meeting in Tynecastle". I asked whether he found the meeting helpful. He said, "Yes! Why have I reached the age of fifty, and no minister, apart from Billy Graham, has ever told me what to do?" I replied, "I am sure that many a minister has told you what to do and either you have not listened or you have not done what he said." He replied, "Nonsense! He is the only one. He said, 'Come out and receive Christ', so I went out and I did!" I had nothing to say to that. I could only thank God. Colonel Henderson went right on in the Christian Faith. Later on he helped us in mission. I liked him and came to know him well.

Other army officers. I liked the army men. I felt drawn to them. We seemed to get on and to work well together when they helped us in mission. In addition to Col. Henderson and Major Heron-Watson, whom

I have mentioned, Major Mackay of the India Army and Col. MacKay, commandant of the Royal Scots Depot at Glencorse, near Edinburgh, also responded to Billy Graham's message, and were converted. Later, the four mentioned came to help us in mission. Col. MacKay was basically a shy man. He told me that, like so many other army officers, he had no small talk. After retiring from the army he entered the ministry of the Church of Scotland. Later I became friends with a major from the Black Watch who was converted. He also went on and entered the ministry of the Church of Scotland.

Following the All Scotland Crusade, follow-up meetings were held in Edinburgh each week throughout the month of May. DP led these meetings. He was the chief speaker although the Revd Leonard Small (later Moderator of the General Assembly) also spoke. Possibly others helped; I do not remember. About 800 people attended these meetings.

Thereafter DP asked me to help organise and arrange three residential conferences on three separate consecutive weekends, one in Dalkeith, one in Prestonpans and one in Penicuik. Between 700 and 800 hundred new converts attended one or more of these residential weekend conferences.

These conferences provided opportunities for Bible studies, teaching sessions and sharing together in the matters of the Christian faith. In each of the three centres we encouraged those attending to engage in street evangelism on the ground that our own faith grows when we actively witness to Christ and seek to share the faith with others. I myself led small teams visiting and speaking in the various public houses.

A Church Elder

At Penicuik I spoke to a man who was an elder in St George's West Church, Edinburgh. He was a fine man. He told me that he had gone forward after one of the Crusade meetings. He had endeavoured to do all that Billy Graham asked. He prayed, he asked God for forgiveness, he invited Christ into his life, but he said, "I never seem to get there". After listening to him speak, I initially startled him by saying, "What you have to do is to learn to do nothing!" I told him that in coming to earth, living, dying on the cross, and rising again, Christ had done everything for his salvation. Christ had forgiven and redeemed him. Christ had given him new and eternal life. There was absolutely nothing that he could do but thank the Lord and to go on and on and on thanking the Lord". Suddenly, his face relaxed. He smiled and I think even laughed as the truth about Christ broke home to him. He suddenly felt the burden and worry about his own salvation lifted. He felt free and free to become interested and concerned about the salvation of other people.

I have reflected on that man's concern and what I believe God led me to say to him. Sadly I believe the vast amount of our preaching as ministers is concerned with telling people what to do. We urge them to pray, to read their Bibles, to repent of their sins, to obey God and live lives that are worthy of Christ. However right that may be, we are throwing people back on themselves rather than upon Christ. The religion which we encourage is often a subtle form of works. Everything depends on what they and we do! People become frustrated. There is no joy in their religion. We are not really preaching a Gospel of grace. Often people know what they ought to do but do not have the power to do it and so all too often, they give up and drift away from the church. Our great need is to proclaim Christ and the finished work of Christ: to encourage people to focus their minds and eyes on Christ and to go on and on giving thanks to God, praising him and in thanksgiving living out the new life which Christ has lived out vicariously for each of us. We receive what God in his love has given us as we give thanks.

Mission to Sutherland

In the summer of 1955 and in order to help build up and establish the faith of those who had committed their lives to Christ during the period of the Crusade, through DP's vision, arrangements were made to take a number of them on a mission to Sutherland. The mission lasted three or possibly four weeks. 84 or 85 people took part. It was a large undertaking. Arrangements had to be made to transport beds, cooking utensils and equipment for those taking part in the mission. DP wrote to a considerable number of firms telling them of our plans for mission and asking if they would transport everything, including people, free of charge. Some firms rejected the request. Others responded helpfully and transport was provided free of charge. Some, but not many, travelled by private car. Major Heron-Watson offered to travel in his own car, accompanied by at least another car taking a certain amount of equipment. He told me how with military precision, he planned the journey. He estimated the distance from Edinburgh to the North of Scotland and the time that it would take to arrive there. He planned with military precision their various stops on the way and how long they would halt at each place, and told me with great gusto, "We arrived exactly on time!"

Sutherland, geographically, is a large county in Scotland. It is twice the size of the county of Fife but, at that time, had only 13,000 inhabitants. Our plan was to visit every home in the entire county. Our plan was a visitation mission. We did not conduct special evangelistic meetings or rallies apart from conducting church services each Sunday during the period of the mission. Village communities were situated on or near the coast. Because people were crofting, the cottages tended always to be separated one from another depending on the size of each croft. The villages were generally called townships. There were comparatively few cottages and crofts inland. Cottages inland were generally those of shepherds. Visiting them often entailed travelling narrow roads and country tracks and walking long distances.

DP because of the geographical size of the county decided, for the purpose of the mission, to divide Sutherland into two. He would with half the team, take charge of the Eastern half of Sutherland. I, with the other half, would be responsible for the Western half. I confess that I was rather glad to operate over 70 miles distant from DP and to be allowed freedom in the conduct of the mission in the West! Although I respected and loved DP, I felt at times that in his all consuming passion for the work, he was a slave driver! Life for me, if not for the others, was more relaxed as we were left to plan our part in Mission.

Throughout the mission I was loaned a Ford shooting brake, that belonged to the church. It was commodious and useful in conveying equipment, but it was an old vehicle. Clearly it had not been loved or properly maintained. The driver's seat, for example, was not anchored to the chassis. I had to pile hymn books around it when travelling to ensure that when the car turned a corner I did not fall over! In those days there was not the legal obligation to have cars examined for road safety!

I and the team with me were responsible for the three parishes of Scourie, Kinlochbervie and Durness in the far North West. Both Scourie and Durness were vacant and had not had a minister for over three years. I and most of my team camped in the empty manse in Scourie. The Church of Scotland had a large store of mattresses and camp beds which were used by its Summer Seaside Mission teams, so we had the use of them. The other, smaller part of my team stayed in a remarkable old historic lodge belonging to the former bishops of Rae, in the parish of Durness. The lodge was built near the shore of an estuary looking across the Cape Wrath Peninsula. DP had asked me to negotiate our use of the lodge for the duration of the mission. He explained that in his impatience and with his driving manner, he often upset people. He asked me therefore to negotiate the loan of the lodge on the grounds that I was more patient with people, placid and did not tend to upset people or get on their wrong side.

We were told that the lodge was haunted on account of a murder that had taken place some years before. We were shown the grave of the murderer which was situated near the lodge, but a little nearer to the sea. The grave was covered by a flat tomb stone. The local people told us that the stone was flat in order to hold the murderer, or his ghost, down! They seemed to feel that it ensured that the murderer would not rise and continue his evil deeds!

None of us on the team encountered the ghost that was reputed to haunt the place.

I occasionally stayed with the team in the lodge in Durness. The lodge had no electricity and at night we relied on candles. I remember on the occasion of my first visit to the lodge, after supper one of the team showed me the way to my room. It was certainly an interesting experience to follow him down a long corridor to my room, in the flickering light of a candle. Although the team shared one or two large rooms together, they reserved a room where I, as leader, could stay alone. It was a remarkable, dignified room panelled with wood which I was told came from a shipwrecked Spanish galleon, which had been part of the Spanish Armada. I was duly told that it was the room which by reputation was haunted! I was interested and amused by the team's choice of room for me. I remember getting into bed in the dark, with the light of a candle, sleeping soundly and awaking to the brilliant light of the sun streaming into the room. I never at that or any other time encountered a ghost.

I preached each Sunday in both Scourie and Durness churches, which were over 27 miles apart. Travelling on the narrow, switch back roads of those days took longer time than we would take today on a more modern road. In addition to the service in Durness Church I took a service each Sunday of our mission at an RAF camp situated in the parish of Durness. These services were always attended by a full complement of RAF personnel. My Ford Home Mission car always refused to start right away after the service. Hence on each occasion the congregation with much hilarity pushed me down the road until the engine started. Indeed after my first service with them, their officer judging that my old and rather sad vehicle would not start at once, said, "Well men, help the chaplain to start his car!" The men were always ready to help.

On one occasion, the local ferry man rowed me across in a rowing boat to the Cape Wrath peninsula to hold a service in the only village or township on the peninsula. It was quite small. The only other person who lived in the peninsula was the Light House keeper, twelve miles away. The Light House which he tended was situated on the northern most tip of Cape Wrath.

The people in all three parishes were kindly and hospitable. They gave us a warm welcome when we visited. They were a religious people who at school had been taught and made to memorise the Shorter Catechism (the well established teaching aide in the Church of Scotland). The two churches when I preached were full with scarcely a spare seat. Every home which I visited with one exception held daily family prayers in the home. The family in that home told me that it had been their custom to have family worship but had given up the practice some time before. Sadly, the custom of holding family prayers is not common today in Scotland.

The people did not necessarily however have a living, dynamic faith. The heavy consumption of alcohol was then, as now, a problem throughout the Highlands, just as it is in the Lowlands and the rest of Scotland. As far as I recall in each home that I visited, a bottle of whisky stood on the mantel piece. I used to look for it when I entered the home. Whisky was considered to be a cure for all and every kind of ailment, toothache, arthritic pain, indigestion, flu or simply depression!

Furthermore, their religion tended too often to be legalistic. The comment of the majority was, I am not worthy to be a communicant member of the church and take communion. That is, although they attended church faithfully very few would participate in the sacrament of Holy Communion. They insisted that they were unworthy. Their consumption of alcohol influenced whether or not they considered themselves worthy to become a communicant member. They were also concerned as to whether their neighbours would consider them worthy. They were generally judged not only by their daily conduct but also about their consumption of alcohol. It seemed that a person had to have one foot in the grave before becoming a communicant member! In the congregation of Scourie at that time, despite a full attendance at church each Sunday, there were only five communicant members. One was the doctor and session clerk who came from Orkney; one an elder, who was old and bed-ridden.

When speaking about the problem with the session clerk in Scourie, he told me of an interesting situation which had arisen some years before when they had a minister. Their organist died and the minister told him that he thought that he should ask a certain man to take his place, because he seemed to be the only man in the parish able to play the organ well. The session clerk told me that he protested on the ground that the man was known to be a heavy drinker. However the minister asked him to be the church organist. On receiving and accepting the invitation, the man immediately gave up his consumption of alcohol and changed his ways.

The average sermon preached at a service of preparation for communion, then, and I believe still is in the Western Isles, concerned with what is called 'the fencing of the table', or 'the evidences of the Christian Faith'. It concentrated on a person's way of life and personal unworthiness.

I tried gently and lovingly to remonstrate with some and suggest that in so emphasising our unworthiness they were really insulting the grace of God! God loves us. His salvation is free. The message of the cross is that God has forgiven us. His gift of salvation is ours for the receiving. All of us are unworthy and all we are required to do in our unworthiness is to thank him for his forgiveness and salvation. Grace means God lovingly freely reaching out to give us what we do not deserve.

Personal Encounters

Again, I had many interesting and stirring conversations. Some were humorous. The only petrol pump in the area was outside the local pub. To obtain petrol it was necessary to enter the pub and ask the bar man to serve you. On my first Saturday evening while preparing my sermon, I suddenly remembered that I required to use the car to travel to the service in Durness and I wondered if I had sufficient petrol. It was about 8.20 in the evening. I knew that the pub and petrol station closed at 8.30 pm. I rushed off, entered the pub and asked the man at the bar if I could have some petrol. As there had not been a resident minister for three years he was not accustomed to the sight of a minister – and in a pub! My presence startled and seemed somewhat to shock him. At first his mind could not register. He had one hand on the pump to pour out the beer and in the other hand he held a glass. I had to repeat my quest for petrol, I think, three times, before he finally registered that I was not asking for a glass of beer but petrol. When he finally registered he said, "Oh! I thought you were . . ." He did not finish the sentence. Clearly he disapproved of a minister entering his pub and asking for a drink. He said, "If you wait outside, I will be there shortly. The pub is about to close."

As I waited outside I heard a man's voice speaking and asking me for help, I believe it was with his car. I think that he mistook me for someone else. I was dressed in a sports jacket although wearing a clerical collar. From the back the man was not able to know that I was a minister. When I turned he was startled and somewhat aghast. He was badly inebriated and embarrassed that he had asked a minister for help, especially in his present state of inebriation. All he could say was "A minister, a minister, a minister!" He repeated this several times and as he did so kept retreating backwards, clearly hoping to disappear round the back of the car and out of sight of the minister. I was amused and laughed and said, "Yes, it is a minister!" I followed him as he retreated, reminded him of the time of the church service the following day and expressed the hope that I would see him there.

On another Saturday evening while I was waiting at about the same time of day, for the barman to serve me some petrol, I stood by the petrol pump with my back to the small car park, looking up the glen, enjoying the magnificent highland scenery. Suddenly I heard a voice saying, "Is the pub closed?" When I turned the gentleman who had spoken was clearly startled and non-plussed at addressing his question to a minister. He recovered and immediately said, "What time is the church service tomorrow?" I laughed and told him and then asked if he knew where the church was. He was a visitor and said that he did not, so I took him across the car park and pointed out to him the church on the other side of the glen. I told him that I would be there, that I was taking the service and would look for him. He did attend the service and greeted me rather shyly.

The following morning was gloriously sunny. I decided that before starting the day's work I would slip down and have a swim in the sea. On the beach I decided to go round behind a rock in order to change into my swimming costume. As I did so I met the same man who also was planning a swim in the sea. He again was startled at my presence but I felt clearly that it was the hand of God. We had a long conversation together. He told me that he had worked for a long time with the Persian Oil Company. However his conscience troubled him in that his firm was taking great wealth out of the country while the local people were so poor. Consequently he resigned from the firm and apparently was wondering what to do next. It gave me the opportunity to speak about Christ and the need to try and discover what God was asking each of us to do. For God has a purpose for each of our lives.

Visiting Estate Owners

There were three large estates in the area. The team and myself having completed a large part of the visitation of the local homes, in the three parishes of Scourie, Kinlochbervie and Durness, I felt that I should call on the owners of each estate and invite them to church. Lord Rootes and his brother were owners of a company manufacturing Hillman cars. Their estate was in the parish of Durness. I visited them first. I drove up to the door of their lodge and knocked at the door. Lord Rootes and his brother were sitting playing bridge with two friends. They gave me a warm and friendly welcome. I told them who I was, what we were doing and invited them to church. To my chagrin when I returned to the car it would not start. The Rootes and their friends heard my vain attempts to start the engine. They opened the door, came out and cheerfully pushed the car down the drive until the engine started. They waved me off. I was very conscious that they were pushing a Ford car when they manufactured Hillman cars.

The largest estate in the area was that owned by the Duke of Westminster. I had heard that he had been divorced, had married again and did not appear to be a churchman. However I felt that I should call and invite him to church. This time in driving up to his lodge I was careful to park the car on a slope so that I would be able to free wheel if there was difficulty in starting the engine. I did not think that it would be appropriate or fitting that the duke and his retainers should push my car to start!

I knocked at the door and stated that I had come to visit, if convenient, the duke and duchess. I was received with some surprise and shown into a comfortably furnished lounge. I never saw the duke or duchess. Whether the duke was present in the Lodge at that time I do not know.

The factor came to see me saying that the duchess, who was in the garden at the back had sent him to enquire the purpose of my visit. I was aware that the factor himself owned an estate and was the third biggest estate owner in the area. He owned the land in and around Kinlochbervie. In addition to managing his own estate he was factor to the larger Westminster estate. I was aware that he had been a major general in the army. He was a likeable and pleasant man and I felt an immediate attraction to him. I told him who I was and that I had called to invite the Duke and Duchess and those with them to church. I told him about Tell Scotland and explained that we had a team visiting the homes of all the people in the area. He asked me if we had visited up Kinlochbervie. I told him that we had and he said, "They are all good Kirk folk up there". I looked at him so he said, "Well, they are all good Kirk folk but me". I asked him what his position was and he told me that he did not often go to church.

I looked at him and said, "You were a soldier". He said, "Correct". I said, "When you were given an order you obeyed". He said, "Correct". I said "If you did not obey an order, your disobedience would be treated as an act of rebellion and you would be court marshalled". He said, "Correct". I said, "Remember on a Sunday morning the King of kings is summoning you into his presence that you might meet him and hear what he has to say to you. If you lie in bed or decide to do something else and do not answer his summons that is an act of rebellion and you will be court marshalled by none other than the King of kings". He looked at me. He had not been accustomed to being spoken to in this way, particularly by a young man and a minister. I felt that I had nothing else to say, so said "Good day" to him. I left not before he said, "I would like to donate toward Tell Scotland!" Several weeks later while on mission back in Edinburgh he sent a lovely letter, enclosing a generous donation to Tell Scotland and the work of mission. He was true to his word and had not forgotten our conversation.

Journey Back

When the mission ended and we cleared the manse, I had the responsibility of ensuring that the team had transport home. I travelled in the Ford shooting brake, loaded with a considerable amount of equipment and with our hymn books piled around the base of my seat to secure it when turning corners. I had to travel north past Kinlochbervie and Durness, taking the road across the North of Scotland toward Bettyhill. DP was waiting in Loyal Lodge, in Strathnaver, for me to convey him south. The road north out of Scourie led up a long and very steep hill. My car would not take it! It did not have sufficient power in its loaded state. I retreated and tried three times to get up the hill but to no avail. Happily I remembered that in my boyhood days I had watched tinkers (as they were known at that time) drive backwards up the Devil's Elbow in Glen Shee, in Perthshire. In those days the Devil's Elbow was very steep and intimidating and a challenge to any car at that time. I felt that if travelling people could drive backwards up the Devil's Elbow then surely I could drive up the hill out of Scourie backwards. I reversed to the bottom, turned around and reversed successfully up and over the top of the hill. I had to adopt the same procedure, I think twice more, on that journey.

I was later than expected in picking up DP. We had no telephone communication between us, or mobile phones in those days and he was wondering what had delayed me. We spent the night in Inverness with a Christian businessman who had already helped us with transport. We arrived safely in Edinburgh the next day.

Mission to Abbeyhill Churches

On our return to Edinburgh DP conferred with six parishes in the Abbey Hill area of Edinburgh. We brought them together in mission, visiting each parish in turn. Each day we invited members of the congregation in whose parish we were working, to come direct from work to the church hall in which we were working. Tea was provided in the church hall by some of the ladies of the congregation. This was followed by Bible study and a period of visitation when we visited the homes of the parish and invited people to come to an evangelistic rally in their parish church at 8.00 pm. Many people from among the six parishes were happy to participate in the visitation of parishes other than their own. Some also from other churches in Edinburgh participated with us and assisted in the work of mission. Along with them were some of the army men whom I mentioned earlier.

After we had completed our mission to the two parishes whose churches were on Easter Road and London Road, we moved on to Holyrood Abbey Parish, moving our headquarters for mission to their church hall. Following the Sutherland mission DP no longer had the services of his secretary, Joan Murdoch. I was his only full time assistant in the work.

Through the day I was normally, or largely, on my own. One morning, shortly before 11 o'clock in the morning, when I was alone in the hall I heard the footsteps of someone behind me. When I turned round I saw Colonel Henderson. He told me that he had retired from the army that summer and purchased a house across the city in Morningside, and had heard that we were engaged on mission. He had come to find out how we organised and ran a mission and to find out what happened in mission. I told him that the only way in which he would discover all that was by himself participating in mission. I told him that during the day I was alone and that at the time that he arrived, I was about to visit one of the local breweries, to ask to speak to the staff and invite them to our evening rallies. I invited him to come with me. I said that I would do the speaking and he could speak to the workers giving to each a small advertisement of our meetings. Before going I asked him what he would recommend that I say to those working in the brewery. He thought for a moment or two and said, "Tell them that they are manufacturing spirits. We come to you with the Holy Spirit!" I was impressed.

He came with me and he and I together visited the six breweries in the area, the printing works and other business premises. Whereas I spoke inviting people to our meetings and endeavoured to give a short message about Christ, he faithfully engaged in conversation with the people whom we met. I think that it greatly helped him on his own Christian journey. I enjoyed his friendship and companionship. He told me that to his great sorrow his wife had left him, while he was still a serving soldier. I think his loneliness prompted him to come to the Billy Graham Crusade meeting in Tynecastle, when he committed his life to Christ.

As I mentioned above, Major MacKay formerly of the Indian Army and Col. MacKay commandant of the Royal Scots Depot at Glencorse also helped us on that mission.

These missions led by DP were an encouragement to the ministers involved and a great stimulus to their congregations. People drew closer together. They shared their Christian experiences and many deeper friendships were formed.

The Next Step

I was required in my contract to give a month's notice to the Home Mission Committee before leaving my employment with Tell Scotland. At the end of September I intimated through DP my intention of resigning and seeking a parish of my own. At this time Mr Brown the minister of South Leith Church, who was the convener of the Home Mission Committee of the Church of Scotland spoke to me and asked if I would become secretary of Tell Scotland. Tom Allan as minister of North Kelvinside in Glasgow, although on invitation he often spoke in different places across Scotland, was unable to devote himself full time to the work of Tell Scotland. DP, as the evangelist of the Church of Scotland, had a roving commission covering the whole of Scotland. He had a heavy programme of work and was growing older. What I was being asked was to endeavour to draw together the work being handled by Tom Allan and DP and carry the work of Tell Scotland forward. I appreciated being asked to become secretary of Tell Scotland but confirmed that my desire was to seek a parish of my own.

I felt that I had been greatly privileged. I felt that my experiences in mission with Tell Scotland and in earlier missions during student days were a marvellous preparation for the pastoral ministry, and often wished that other ministers were privileged to have the same experience in mission. Many lives had been spiritually changed through these missions and I had witnessed the change in many lives, both among those who had committed their lives to Christ and among church folk who participated in mission and whose faith came excitingly alive. Sometimes it was later and sometimes considerably later that one discovered how a particular person first encountered Christ, or what had happened to change their lives.

It was a few years later, when, one day, as parish minister in Livingston, I attended a Tell Scotland meeting in Edinburgh led by DP Thomson. On this occasion I had left the car and travelled through to Edinburgh by bus. After the meeting a minister, John Riddell, who had a church in Jedburgh in the Borders, learning that I did not have my car with me, kindly said that he would drive me home to Livingston. I protested that Livingston was far out of his way. I was living 17 miles to the West of Edinburgh. Jedburgh is some 40 miles south of Edinburgh. Another minister, Bill Thomson overheard our conversation. He laughed and said, "Let John drive you home. He wants to talk to you". So I agreed to John's kind offer.

When we got into the car, he said to me, "I have wanted to speak to you, because you had a deep impact on my life". I was surprised and said, "Are you suggesting that we have met before, because if so, I'm sorry that I do not remember". He said, "Do you remember after the All

Scotland Crusade, a Tell Scotland meeting in West St George's Church in Edinburgh and after the meeting talking over a cup of tea in the hall to a Boys Brigade boy aged 14". I replied, "Yes! I do". He said, "I was that boy. I asked someone afterwards who the minister was who had spoken to me, because no one had ever spoken so frankly or bluntly to me before. That conversation led to my conversion and call to the ministry". I felt humble and was naturally thrilled to hear his story although I could not remember our conversation. I have often found that God will give a small and yet sufficient glimpse to encourage us, of the way that he has graciously used us in his work, over-ruling our inadequacy and blessing our weak efforts to serve him.

Lessons in Preaching

Before entering a parish of my own, God taught me many important lessons in preaching, which I found humbling and never forgot. Before and after joining Tell Scotland I preached almost every Sunday in which I was free to do so. I had given my name to the Church's Ministry Department who enabled me to preach regularly. Accordingly, I preached in a large number of different churches.

On returning from Basle, and before joining Tell Scotland, I was invited that summer at the beginning of July, 1954, to preach in Dunollie Road Church in Oban in Argyllshire. It was a glorious sunny and scorching week-end. I love the hills and the West Highlands. The church informed me that they had arranged that I should stay for the week-end in a hotel. I looked forward to visiting Oban and going off on a seven or eight mile walk, enjoying the sheer beauty of the hills. I went to Oban as a minister in all together the wrong way and in the wrong spirit. I put six sermons in my case, travelled on an early train and reached the hotel in Oban early in the afternoon. I thought that I would quickly select which sermon to preach the following day and go off on my walk. I knelt and prayed and asked God to reveal what he wanted me to say to the congregation next day.

I heard him say, "Preach on the resurrection". I was not troubled because I had preached on the resurrection before. When I looked at my sermons however, I found that I had not brought with me a sermon on the resurrection, so I felt that I must preach one which I had brought. I read through all six but was aware that I could not preach any of them the next day. I knelt and prayed and again heard the Lord say, "Preach on the resurrection". With some agitation I again read through all six sermons and knew that I could not preach any of them that week-end. For the third time I knelt and prayed and this time knew that I could no longer argue with the Lord. He was saying clearer than ever, "Preach on the resurrection".

I was completely frustrated. I knew that I would have to sit on a glorious sunny day and write another sermon. I was upset and frustrated that I would no longer be able to go for the walk that I had so looked forward to doing. In my frustration my mind was a blank. I found that I could not pray properly, no matter how much I tried. For the rest of the afternoon and all evening I sat at a table in my hotel room utterly frustrated. I was totally unable to write a sermon on the resurrection. Nothing would come. At ten o'clock that night, I had one sheet of paper on which I had written one short sentence, of a line and a half. I told the Lord that if he wanted to speak to the congregation he would have to speak to them, because I had nothing to say.

I slept well but in the morning my mind was still a blank. Still nothing would come. As a minister, I always like to arrive at church about half an hour early. I told the Lord once again that if he wanted to speak to the congregation about the resurrection he would have to speak because I had nothing to say. I picked up my sheet of paper with the one sentence written on it and went to church. The Session Clerk, Mr Mowat, had arrived early. When he welcomed me he asked if I would allow him to make the intimations that day. He said that their beloved senior elder had just died and he wanted to break the news to the congregation. Suddenly, I felt the hand of God. The sermon just came. I preached for about twenty minutes. The Lord graciously took over and spoke in spite of my inadequacy and sin. The congregation seemed to have been helped and found the service appropriate.

Six or seven years later my wife and I were on holiday in Oban. I was sitting in my car in Oban waiting for my wife who was shopping, when the Session Clerk, Mr Mowat passed. I recognised him and greeted him. When he turned around he said, "Hello! You are the minister who preached in our church and came all clued up when our senior elder died." I invited him to join me for a cup of coffee. Over coffee I told him the whole story and that I had gone to church that day in a wrong and sinful way, and in a way in which no minister should have gone. It was the Lord in his grace who took over that day. I never forgot the lesson that the Lord taught me that day although I have often had to relearn it. The church is the Lord's church, the people are his people. He wants to speak to them. He alone really knows their needs. As ministers we require to pray, and if necessary to wrestle in prayer, to discover what God wants to say on every occasion. We cannot choose of ourselves what to say no matter how biblical, how appropriate, or how able the sermon that we have written is. If we do, the whole thing is a work of man and not of God. True preaching is where people hear God speaking, not man.

One day when called to preach in a certain church, I preached on the atonement of Christ. I had prayed and worked hard on the sermon. I was conscious of the Spirit of the Lord at the service. An unusual number of people spoke to me about the sermon saying that they had found it helpful. I felt that it was an answer to prayer. At the same time there was that in me that felt pleased that my sermon had gone well. A short time later when invited to preach in another church I decided to preach the same sermon. If it had gone well before I thought surely it would go well again. When I preached I did not feel the same presence of the Holy Spirit. The sermon seemed to fall flat. No one after the service commented. I had not gone with the same preparation and prayer. I had not gone relying on the Lord, praying that he would speak. I had gone relying on my own strength, when I had none. Again, it was a lesson I have never forgotten.

As ministers we are utterly dependent on the Lord to speak and act. Only he can speak his Word and open peoples' minds and hearts. We as ministers are utterly unable to speak and act in our own strength and accomplish anything for the Lord. We are at all times dependent on the Lord asking in prayer that the Lord despite us will speak to his people and transform their lives. Certain words spoken by John the Baptist have gone with me through my ministry. "He must become greater; I must become less" (John 3:30). The greatest temptation of a minister is to try and draw attention to him or herself, when all attention must be upon Jesus Christ, his life, death, resurrection and ascension. A minister's task is to try and preach in such a way that he or she slips into the background, so that people feel that they are alone face to face with God in Jesus Christ. They hear God not man or woman speaking. That can only happen through the miraculous working of the Holy Spirit. For that, minister and people have constantly to pray.

Farewell to Tell Scotland

Through my activities I had become fairly well known. As a result, I had, before leaving Tell Scotland, been approached by vacant churches seeking a new minister. There was one occasion when out of sheer tiredness I left my sermon in the vestry and did not have it with me in the pulpit. When I do not have before me a written sermon, I tend to preach too long. On that occasion I preached for half an hour. Unknown to me the vacancy committee of a large congregation was present. The following day their clerk to the vacancy committee phoned asking if I would be their sole nominee.

I was not familiar with the church and had not applied for my name to be considered. They offered a salary of £750, saying that shortly on their union with a smaller church, the salary would rise to £1,000. It was an unusually high salary for those days, and considerably more than the £300, which I received from the Home Mission Committee. I thanked them but declined their invitation. The following day they phoned again asking if I would reconsider my decision and inviting me to see their church. I again declined. I knew that God at that time did not want me to leave the work of Tell Scotland.

Later, and after intimating my desire to seek a parish, when I was invited on a Monday to be minister of Livingston, two other churches invited me the same week one on the Tuesday and the other on the Wednesday. I had not applied to them. I accepted the invitation from Livingston. It was the first to invite me and I had preached before the congregation. It so happened that although Livingston offered 50 pounds above the minimum salary for ministers, the salary offered was lower than that offered by the other two churches. I was clear that this was God's will. I was inducted and ordained as minister of Livingston on 14th November 1955.

Chapter 7

Livingston 1955-1969: Part 1

Livingston was one charge although there were two churches in the parish. The Kirk of Livingston was situated in Livingston village and St Andrew's, a Church Extension charge, was situated in the village called Livingston Station, about two miles distant. Today it is the Deans District of the New Town of Livingston.

When I accepted the offer of the National Church Extension Committee of the Church of Scotland to be their nominee for the vacant charge of Livingston, I did not at first realise that permission had also been given to the congregation to nominate a minister for the vacancy. This was in order to allow the congregation a choice in who should be their minister. The Kirk of Livingston was an old and established charge which had the right of call. The minister of St Andrew's, as a Church Extension charge, would normally be appointed by the Church Extension Committee. The agreement for the appointment of a new minister was reached because the new Extension Church lay within the parish of Old Livingston.

I later became aware of the fact that inevitably the call by the congregation would be a divided call. Therefore, when the session clerk, Mr James Danskin, telephoned to say that the congregation had voted by majority in my favour and asked whether I would accept the call, I asked whether every elder and office bearer was happy in presenting the call. I said that I would not come if some were against. A few days later he telephoned to say that all the office bearers were unanimous in their wish to call me, and asked if I would now come. I replied that I would wait and see how the congregation responded to the signing of the call, because inevitably when the congregation had voted there was a divided vote.

DP was disturbed when I told him the situation and said that I should not treat a congregation that way. I told him that I had said that I would accept the call if the congregation wanted me but not if they did not want me. Under the circumstances almost two thirds of the congregational roll signed the call. It was and still is the highest percentage that I have known in the signing of a call. I do not know what happened but think that the elders must have said to the congregation, "If you want this minister, you must sign the call!"

I was inducted and ordained as minister of Livingston Parish on 14th November 1955.

Livingston Parish

Because St Andrew's was situated within the parish of the Kirk of Livingston there was only one Kirk Session and one Congregational Board, based on the 'model constitution', which I found a great blessing. Unlike so many other ministers I did not have to deal with two Kirk Sessions and two Congregational Boards. In all other respects there were two congregations. In establishing an evening service early in my ministry these alternated between the two churches. About 30 people attended the evening service regularly, drawn from both sides of the congregations. Beyond that most of the church members chose to attend only one and not the other church.

The country in and around the parish at that time was rural and very attractive. There were a number of farms in the parish. The farmers and farm workers who did attend all attended the services in the Kirk of Livingston. Three of the Kirk Session elders were farmers. The old village itself was small but attractive with an old world air about it. Most who were attached to the Kirk of Livingston came by bus from Seafield, a shale mining village about two miles west of the church and situated on the old Sighthill, Mid Calder, Whitburn road from Edinburgh to Glasgow. Seafield from the point of view of the Presbytery was not situated in Livingston parish but attached to the coal mining parish of Blackburn further west. The men of Seafield were almost all shale miners. I doubt if there were any coal miners living in Seafield. The shale miners prided themselves in not being coal miners so that the village was orientated towards Livingston and most in the village seemed to look on me as their minister.

The great majority of men living in Livingston Station worked in shale mining. The parish, along with Seafield, had about 3,000 inhabitants. In sick visiting and much other visiting I did not distinguish between members and non-church members.

Scottish Shale Oil Industry

It was a remarkable industry in the care and attention given to its employees. Shale miners, because of the way they were treated by management, never lost their self-respect during the period of the General Strike. Since then there had never been another strike. If a miner had a complaint, he took it direct to management, who were prepared to listen.

Livingston Station and Seafield, like other villages were built by the shale industry. Both villages consisted of several houses joined together as miners' rows. Families could stay in them so long as one member worked with shale. When a man died his widow was not asked to leave her house which continued to be maintained on her behalf. The industry also provided community welfare halls in both Livingston Station and Seafield.

One of the very few shale miners who transferred to work in a coal pit, after the shale industry closed did not speak well of the coal industry. There, managers were normally called "Mr" and addressed as "Sir". If a man wanted to speak to the manager he had to stand in a queue outside his office. When he finally did see him, the manager immediately, before the man could speak, swore at him, to make sure that he had the upper hand.

In the Scottish shale industry relationships between the managers and the men were remarkably good. The managers were called by their Christian names. The senior manager of all nine pits, Mr Stein, who held various mining qualifications or degrees, was always called by his Christian name. He stayed in one of two bungalows in Livinston Station. One of his daughters married my predecessor. The deputy manager stayed in the other bungalow. If a man at work became sick, or was suddenly bereaved it was customary for one of the managers to drive him home in his car. When a man died the managers attended his funeral.

Among the activities, or social amenities, which the shale industry sponsored was a Shale Oil Bowling Club. Every year Scottish Oil would play against their Welsh counterparts, who I think were Welsh BP. Members of the team were a mixture of managers, foremen and miners who worked at the shale face. They were selected according to their bowling ability. Each year the Scottish team would travel to Wales to play and the following year the Welsh team would travel to Livingston. Players travelled with their wives, expenses paid, as I understand, by the industry. While the men played, the wives of managers and miners shopped together. Each year when the Welsh team came to Livingston there was a celebration meal in the village welfare hall in Livingston Station. As the local minister I was always invited to the meal in Livingston Station. I used to rejoice to see my session clerk, who as a miner worked at the shale face, sitting side by side with the senior manager at dinner. The session clerk was an exceedingly good player and was chosen entirely on his skill with the game. Two of the men, and members of the church, played bowls for Scotland. Others were taken on trial for Scotland. With the encouragement of the industry and the provision of bowling facilities, some remarkable, national class bowlers, lived in Livingston Station.

The wage of a shale miner was slightly less than that of the coal miner. There were not the same facilities at the pit head. After nationalisation, showers and washing facilities were provided by the coal industry and men came home clean. In the shale industry the men came home dirty and washed and changed at home. The shale miners however always seemed a happier and more contented group of men, and felt they were in a different class from the coal miner - and so they were! Men like their fathers and grandfathers worked their entire lives from boyhood in the shale mines. They married into other shale mining families; the industry almost seemed to be comprised of one very large family. The nature of such a close knit community affected the life of the church and my ministry in Livingston.

The Scottish shale oil industry for financial reasons closed, with all nine pits, in 1960. Many years before, the side products of shale which were considerable, were sold off. At the time it would appear that the industry did not realise their commercial value. If the industry had kept ownership of these side products and developed them, I do not think that they would require to have closed down. The day that they finally closed was a sad day for the parish. I shared with them their concern and sorrow for its closure. Within six months the great majority of those who had been rendered unemployed secured work with the British Motor Corporation (the BMC) which had, with government help, just opened a factory outside Bathgate, manufacturing tractors.

My Call as Minister

When I was nominated by the Ministry Committee as their choice as ministerial candidate for Livingston, I knew almost nothing about the parish. The little I knew did not attract me. I did not really want to go. When a ministerial friend asked me about it, after I told him my situation, I said, "I do not want to go. I have however a feeling at the bottom of my stomach that God wants me to go there!" I accepted the call, persuaded that this was the parish to which God was calling me as a minister.

The church was a humble one. The people in the parish, and I do not like the term, were all working class or from a working class background. Apart from the senior mine manager, the headmaster of the local primary school, a few primary school teachers who had gone to a teacher training college, and a man (Jock Purves) who had gone to a missionary Bible College, I was unaware of anyone who had gone on to advanced education, far less to University. I also at first doubted whether people in the parish had the ability to go on to higher education. How wrong I was proved to be.

Prayer for Love

I have always felt that it is important for a minister to love his people; a church can only grow and prosper in this atmosphere. Love between a minister and his people is not just something which we can produce in ourselves. It is a gift of God's grace. Hence each night I prayed for God to give me the gift to love my people. I did this in each of my three parishes. I did it through many years. Gradually I began to realise that by God's grace I did love the people and that by his grace they began to love me as their minister. There followed 13 and a half very happy years, when I was privileged to see again and again the loving hand of God at work in peoples' lives. In the end, when under pressure from the General Assembly Committee to go as minister to another Church Extension charge, I was heart broken and wept a number of times in leaving the congregation. Several of the office bearers also wept.

I always gave this same advice, to pray for love, to young ministers entering the ministry and also when counselling a couple desiring to be married. To those about to be married, I said, "You love one another and so you wish to be married. However you cannot love each other today as you will in ten or twelve years time after you have come truly to know one another and to discover that you are both dependent on the other. Then you will love one another in a much deeper way. At the same time never take love for granted. True love is a gift from God. Pray every day and ask that you will love each other more and more. Be open in your relationships always forgiving one another and practise your love. When you argue, always be the first to say sorry. Never wait for the other to say sorry first. Always pray together and, together ask God for forgiveness and endeavour to worship God regularly and faithfully at home and in church." I took this advice to myself. My wife and I enjoyed over 50 years of happy companionship and marriage until God called her home in May 2008.

My early years of ministry were not easy. The congregation was a humble one and had many problems.

First Meeting with Session and Board

On the evening of my first Sunday I asked if I could meet the Kirk Session, introduce myself to them and say something of what I understood to be the duties of the eldership. Two weeks later I asked if I could meet the Congregational Board. St Andrew's Livingston Station was a Hall Church, serving on Sundays as a place of worship and throughout the week as a church hall. On Sundays the congregation, sitting on separate seats, faced toward the chancel. For the rest of the week a remarkable steel shutter, unable to be seen by the congregation on a Sunday, was lowered shutting off the chancel. The seats were generally turned around to face the other way or temporally stacked when the hall was used by one of the church organisations.

My first Board meeting was an eventful one. It was scheduled for 7.30pm. I had occasion to call in at the church at 6.30pm. The beadle (or church officer) Geordie White was there. He was also an elder. He was very angry with the session clerk, James Danskin, the Primary School headmaster. I had to attend to other matters before the meeting so did not discover what the problems of dispute were. Anxious to be back in time for the meeting at 7.30pm I recommended that he have time alone with the Lord, pray and commit whatever was troubling him to God.

When I arrived back at 7.30pm I could hear the shouting as I entered through the church gates. When I entered the church, the members of the Board were standing around in a circle. In the centre were the two elders Geordie Whyte and James Danskin shouting at each other. I arrived just in time to see Geordie Whyte whip off his jacket in order physically to assault the session clerk. He was a man of quite powerful build. I immediately pushed my way into the centre, seized both men by the shoulder, one in each hand and pushed them apart. Silence reigned! I think all were ashamed that the new minister had caught them in the midst of a first class row about to descend into fisticuffs. I had no idea how to proceed. However, with silence reigning I said, "We will now start the Board meeting", whereon the session clerk said, "I demand a meeting of the Kirk Session".

We proceeded to the other end of the church for our business. I constituted the meeting of the Board with reading and prayer. No one would say a word, so the meeting took less than half an hour. Before pronouncing the benediction I asked that the elders remain for a special meeting of the Kirk Session. I opened the Kirk Session meeting by reading a passage from the first Epistle of St John with the words, "Little children love one another". After prayer, I asked the session clerk, who had requested the meeting, to say what was on his mind. All I can say is that for the next 20 minutes he blew off! In the course of that twenty minutes I learned a lot about the previous ministry, the animosity that existed within the Kirk Session and congregation and how elders and minister criticised each other behind their backs. Some refused to walk with another on the same pavement and would cross the street to avoid meeting.

I eventually had to interrupt the session clerk, who I thought had said enough. I thanked him for saying what was on his mind. I then asked the beadle to say what was on his mind. To his great credit, he stood and said sorry and asked the session clerk to forgive him. I thanked him and asked the session clerk in the name of the Lord to accept his apology. I then said to the session that as members of the church and family of God we had sinned. We had quarrelled and grieved the Lord. God was very displeased with us. I then said that we must pray and ask God to forgive us as a Kirk Session. In my prayer I deliberately used the pronoun "we", indentifying myself through the Spirit with the elders. I had long pondered the fact that when Daniel, Nehemiah or the prophets prayed for Israel, they identified themselves with Israel in her sin and asked God saying, "Lord forgive us for our idolatry and rebellion", even although they themselves had not sinned in the way that Israel did. I felt that a minister has to identify himself with his people in their weakness and sin. Hence I asked God to forgive us for 'our' quarrelling and for 'our' grieving the Lord.

After prayer, I said that there must be no criticism of another elder, no back biting and no breaking of the confidentiality pertaining to meetings of the Kirk Session. I said that if I ever heard of further criticism by one person against another, I would deal with it very severely. (I had no idea what I would do!) After I pronounced the Benediction, Geordie Whyte asked if I would meet with him and James Danskin in the vestry. I said "good night" to the rest of the elders, who left in subdued silence. When I went through to the vestry both men were weeping! I spoke to them about God's forgiveness and love, and prayed with them. I went home with, what was for me very rare, a headache, wondering to what kind of church I had been called. When I told one minister in the Presbytery (who had officiated at my induction) he simply said, "Well, clearly there is a lot of spirit in Livingston!" It was not the Holy Spirit. Another minister friend said, "You were not taught anything about muscular Christianity at New College!"

My predecessor was a very pleasant man, although his ministry was very different from my own. Sadly, he fell out very badly with the Kirk Session and I was told criticised the elders before the congregation. People took sides. Bill McMartin of Brucefield, Whitburn had been interim moderator in the vacancy in Livingston prior to my induction. When I told him about the Board meeting, he confirmed that the last ministry had not ended happily and that as a result there was "a twist right through the congregation". In the quarrel between Geordie Whyte and James Danskin, the beadle had sided with the minister, while the session clerk was one who had with other elders been criticised publicly by the minister.

Need for Reconciliation and Unity

In actual fact, what had happened that night at the Board meeting was very helpful. The causes of much of the quarrelling and things which can badly hinder the life of a congregation and which could have remained under the surface and hidden, were suddenly brought to light. They could be dealt with openly, scripturally and prayerfully. The quarrels were not directed at the new minister.

In the days that followed I had several conversations with the beadle and session clerk, in church and at home. Both men were deeply troubled and kept wondering what the other thought and whether the other had forgiven. It gave a marvellous opportunity to speak about the love and forgiveness of Christ.

The Kirk Session needed to be increased to cover the visitation of the parish prior to each communion. They urged me to ordain two Board members, John Gibb and John Shields. Both lived in the Old Village of Livingston. Sadly they would not speak to one another. When one came along the other crossed the street to avoid meeting. At the time I refused to ordain them. I said, "I will not ordain anyone to the eldership who was not reconciled and at peace with his neighbour". I also said each year, in each of my three parishes, when the congregation met for its annual general business meeting, to elect members to the Congregational Board, "We should elect to office those who truly love the Lord: who worship regularly in church; who show their desire to serve the Lord by what they are already doing: who are reconciled and at peace with their neighbour and will be welcomed into every home in the parish." I always found that these words were helpful in restraining the possible election to office of the wrong people. It also helped to make clear to elders, office bearers and congregation what was expected of those in office in the church.

I commenced my preaching in Livingston by preaching through the Sermon on the Mount and similar passages, endeavouring to point people to Christ and to what in his love he has done for our salvation and stressing the need to forgive and love one another. The preaching, spiritual discussions in the Kirk Session and my visitation of the congregation at home and in hospital where I always read and prayed, began to have an effect, especially in a close knit community, where what I said in one home was soon communicated to others.

After about eighteen months John Shields, who had a post office shop, in Old Livingston, came to me. He mentioned my preaching and the need for forgiveness and reconciliation with others. He told me that he and John Gibb wished to be reconciled. I spoke to John Gibb and he confirmed his desire for reconciliation. I therefore ordained them both to the eldership. I was moved when, following their ordination they asked if they could share together the same elder's district and therefore travel in the same car. They asked for the country district which was extensive and a car was necessary for visiting. John Gibb had been a farm worker all his life until latterly when he drove a lorry. I gladly agreed to their request.

Visit to a Shale Mine

I wanted to know what I could about the people in the parish, the work of miners, its nature, difficulties and dangers. Therefore, early on in my ministry, I asked along with my brother-in-law Kenneth MacKenzie, if I could visit one of the shale mines near West Calder. It was the largest of their mines and had within the grounds a shale oil refinery. Kenneth and my sister Margaret, missionaries in Africa, were back in Scotland and stayed with me for a few months. The managers welcomed our request. They were very courteous and kind. They told us something about the historical background of the industry. We descended below in the cage and walked or travelled along some of the long tunnels under ground. We were able to see men working at the shale face. Above ground we visited the refinery and were informed how the shale was heated and the oil extracted.

The visit helped me to understand better the men when they talked about their work. The men themselves seemed to be glad of our visit to the mine and interest in their working conditions.

Pastoral Visitation

In my visitations in homes, or when visiting people in hospital, after listening to what they shared of themselves and families, and learning something of their interests and concerns, I always liked to have a short reading from the Bible and prayer. I asked them if I could pray and ask God's blessing on the home. I endeavoured to make the prayers simple and practical. After thanking God for his love and salvation in Christ I prayed for whatever the family had shared, problems at work or concerning the children at school, or their financial worries, concerns to make ends meet financially or the health of a member of the family or relative.

In hospital in my visitations I never distinguished between church members and non-members. I often found them anxious about their illness and worried about an impending operation. I told them that healing comes to us in two ways. It comes to us through doctors and nurses and told them that medicine was a great gift of God. I also told them that health and healing comes to us direct from God in answer to prayer and faith. I asked them if I could pray and ask God for healing for them and when necessary, for a successful operation. I found that this was very much welcomed, even by men who were not members of the church and had made no outward profession of faith.

Need for Prayer

From my earlier days on mission I discovered the need to offer a short prayer before knocking on each door. I discovered that a short prayer before each visit made all the difference in making the visit a pastoral and not simply a social one. I also discovered again and again that it was after the reading and prayer that the real pastoral visit began. It was then that people relaxed and spoke more freely of their concerns and spiritual needs.

I think it took approximately six months for the people of the parish to accept that the minister always read and prayed in visiting them. During that period there were some amusing visits. Visiting a man in hospital he said to me with regard to the previous minister, (he spoke in Scots), "I liked that last man we had. He was a *verra* nice man and *nae* one of yon religious types." I was amused, smiled and said, "Let us hear what God has to say, as I read from the Bible, then I will pray and we will ask God to heal you." On another occasion when visiting a man in hospital he said right away, "I have brought my Bible with me. I knew that you would ask. It is in the locker." I asked, "Are you reading the Bible?" He said, "Oh, I did not think that you would ask that question!"

Soon, people came not simply to accept a reading and prayer but to welcome it. In the months and years that followed I found again and again I was asked especially to visit a particular home in order to pray about some special need that had arisen. I often received invitations to visit from non-church members. On one occasion a man, who was not a member, came to the manse. He was dirty, having come straight from the pit, and had not taken time to wash. He said that there had been an accident in the pit. A man had been killed. The men were all upset, would I come. If I remember aright, we met in a home in Seafield which was not in my parish. A large number of his work-mates were gathered. I did not recognise any church member among them. It was a privilege to be invited to meet with them, to try and impart something of the comfort of God and how we obtain that comfort. I read and prayed with them. They were grateful. Among miners, like fishermen, it is rare ever to discover an atheist. They might drink heavily and gamble, but by the nature of their work, life was precarious. Deep down they believed in God. They often told me that no matter who they were, when the cage in the pit, descending or ascending, stuck, or when they were suddenly faced with danger, they each one prayed. The only two people, husband and wife, whom I met and were natives to the area and claimed to be atheists, were not miners.

A few months after coming to Livingston, an elder who was a farmer said to me, "You are the first minister who has ever entered my home and prayed. However if any minister in the future enters my home and does not pray, I will take exception to it." I have often wished that every minister would read and pray regularly in the homes of their people. When so many people find difficulty in prayer and some do not pray, how can we teach them to pray and commit all that concerns them to God in prayer, unless we as ministers read and pray in their homes? They learn from seeing and hearing us pray.

I am 90 years of age as I write now and have been retired for over twenty years. In my last parish I came to know a farmer, Dod Runciman, from Lauder, which was the neighbouring parish to my own. He is a cousin of a farmer, Dave Runciman who was, until he moved farms, an elder in Earlston. Dod often called at my manse and we would sit chatting on a seat in the garden. We continue to keep in touch. He telephones approximately every two months. He is over 80 years of age and retired. His son runs the farm. In his retirement he visits some of the elderly housebound folk in the area, one of whom is the widow of one of my former elders. I said to Dod, "When you visit her, she would appreciate it if you prayed." He said, "I do! I heard David Torrance praying and I said to myself, 'I can do that', so I do pray when I visit." I felt encouraged. It confirmed what I have always believed that our congregations learn not just from what we say but from actually seeing and listening to what we do.

Spiritual Change

The church treasurer informed me, at the beginning of my ministry, that, financially, the congregation was the poorest giving congregation in the Presbytery. The finances of a congregation have always seemed to me an indication of the congregation's spiritual life. A visiting speaker after meeting the Woman's Guild, said that he found the people, in their response, 'wooden'.

Gradually however things began to change. The elders became united as a Kirk Session. There was a happy spirit in the Congregational Board and people began to respond both to the preaching and the visits with prayer in the home.

Jean Galloway, one of our two organists, said to me one day, after I had been there for a few years, that she had counted the people on Sunday in St Andrew's Church Livingston Station, and that the majority were under 30 years of age. The evening services became well attended, with many younger people coming. A number of young people had been converted. We had two thriving Sunday Schools, Bible Class and Youth Fellowship. There came about a happy atmosphere in the congregation and people felt the change. I was very encouraged when the day came when visitors said to me that they found the congregation welcoming and friendly.

Hospital Visits

In hospital, I cannot recall of any occasion when after asking if I could pray and ask for God's healing, a person refused my request. On the contrary, I often found the most hardened non-church members grateful for a prayer for healing and at the close of the prayer said, "Amen!" On many occasions, in my first two parishes I felt embarrassed when patients from other parishes asked me to pray for them, because their ministers did not. During my first ministry, I do not recall any other minister at that time who regularly prayed with each patient. Frequently I heard a patient in the next bed to one of my members say, "You prayed with her but not with me". I often said, "You are not my sheep. You ask your minister to pray with you". Often the person replied, "My minister will not pray with me". My member would then reply and say, "I promised that you would pray!" I therefore found myself praying with those who did not belong to my parish and felt embarrassed in case their minister came and found me in the act.

At my last ministers' fraternal before leaving Livingston, the chairman of the fraternal turned to me in front of seven or eight others and said, "David, do you not embarrass the patients in Bangour Hospital when you pray with them?" I replied, "No! I have never been aware of anyone being embarrassed apart from me. I am embarrassed when your parish members ask me to pray with them because you do not!"

Shortly before that conversation, I had visited a ward in hospital containing, in the old fashioned style, about 24 beds. Approximately twelve female patients were sitting in their dressing gowns at the far end of the ward. As I entered I heard one say, "Here is my minister. He will pray with us all." When I went forward the lady said, "They all want prayer. I told them that you would pray with us all." I was glad to pray with them but embarrassed in case at that moment their ministers came in and found me praying with their folk. I experienced the same situation when visiting in hospital in Aberdeen, although in Aberdeen some ministers did pray with the sick in hospital.

Spiritual Teaching and Discussion within the Kirk Session

Having learned from George Gunn, the minister of Broughton Place Church in Edinburgh, about the value of setting aside half an hour at each Kirk Session meeting for teaching purposes and spiritual discussion, I commenced using a two-year teaching programme for elders. It was an excellent course published by the St Andrew Press. I deeply regretted when they ceased to publish it. Each elder was given a copy. It proved to be extremely helpful. Some said that they found the half hour the best part of our meetings. The spirit in the Kirk Session changed. They became a united body of men. Each I believe had a sincere and strong faith. They attended church diligently and even on our Friday night services of preparation for Holy Communion, an ancient custom which we preserved, we would have one hundred per cent attendance by elders at church. My wife used to say, "If you never have anyone else at a service you will always preach to your Kirk Session!"

A turning point came in the life of the Kirk Session when at one meeting my session clerk said, "There is not much point in continuing to tell us what to do as elders, when we are not invited into the homes of the people of our districts". I asked, "What do you want me to do?" He said, "Tell the congregation what you have been telling us about the duties of elders." When I asked, "When shall I do it?", he replied. "At Easter when there is a large congregation." I agreed to do so.

I said to the congregation, as the elders requested, that when an elder calls they must not keep him on the doorstep but invite him into their homes as a representative of Christ and the church. I said the elder is interested in your welfare so you can share with him information about yourselves and the family. However I went beyond what the Kirk Session had requested. I said, "I know many of you are worried and anxious about whether you can make ends meet financially. (It was a time of much unemployment with the closing down of the Shale Industry.) Some of you are concerned about your children at school: some of you are worried about illness in the family or among your friends and relatives". I said, "When the elder is in your home, take the opportunity and ask the elder to lead in prayer along the lines of your anxieties and concerns!"

When I went home for lunch I said to my wife that I wondered what the elders would say to me. Undoubtedly it was a bit of a bombshell. No elder resigned. The elders told me that it transformed the whole situation. Thereafter it became customary always to invite the elder into the home. Some, but I do not think many elders, were courageous enough to pray in the homes of their district. There was however some interesting feedback. In visiting one couple, the man said to me, "The elder visited us and prayed in our home. I have known John Dunleavy (the elder in question) for years. We work together at the shale face in the pit. We take it for granted that when the minister comes in he prays, but my wife and I think the world of John for he came in and prayed in our home".

It so happened that immediately following that visit, I crossed the street and met John. He said, "I will have to resign as an elder. I have prayed in a couple of homes and it's like sweating blood". I said, "John, I have just visited one of those homes. It's the man you work with in the pit. He said that he takes it for granted that the minister should pray, but he and his wife think the world of you for praying in their home. So John, I think you will have to continue as an elder." He did and some years later took his turn in conducting an early morning service in Church.

A very fine Christian couple (Mr & Mrs Rose) retired to Livingston Station. He had been a lay missionary in one of the shale industry villages. He told me when I happened to visit a short time later that they had a visit from their elder. When the elder knocked he immediately said, "Come in". The elder came in and feeling a little nervous said almost right away, "It is not so easy for an elder as it is for the minister, to pray". Mr Rose said with a great twinkle in his eye, "I was determined not to let the elder off, so I said to him, "Before you leave this home you can lead us in saying together the Lord's Prayer". I was amused. The elder in question was one whom I thought would of all the elders find praying in the home difficult. The saying of the Lord's Prayer certainly changed the nature of the elder's visit.

Having intimated from the pulpit that members should invite their elder to pray when visiting, for the next two years, we could not get one person to join the Kirk Session, no matter how we tried. Yet we needed to enlarge the Kirk Session. Some, who clearly were committed Christians and gave considerable time to the work of the church, said to me that they were willing to do whatever was asked of them in the church, but they would not be an elder, and pray in a home. I therefore said to the Kirk Session one day, "I am sorry. I have dished the Kirk Session in this parish. Everyone refuses to join us. Will you please each one pray every day until we obtain new elders." My treasurer said, "Well, we have tried every other method". Three months later six excellent men agreed to join the Kirk Session. I felt that as far as membership of the Kirk Session was concerned, we had crossed over the hurdle.

Sunday Schools

There were two Church Sunday Schools, one in Livingston village and one in Livingston Station. A considerable number of children attended both Sunday Schools. In Livingston Station there were also two other Sunday Schools. One was run by two Faith Mission families who were members of the church. The other was run by the Christian Brethren. They held a separate service of their own each Sunday. The numbers of both Faith Mission and Brethren fellowships were small and I do not think either exceeded ten. The numbers of children in both the church and the other Sunday Schools were large. In my weekly attendance at school to lead the Assemblies, I frequently encouraged children to attend all three Sunday Schools. (The majority of our children did attend all three.) I felt that by attending all three Sunday Schools, which each had a different teaching programme, the children would profit more spiritually than if they attended only one. By attending all, there was, from the point of view of the children, the inducement of three Christmas parties and three summer outings!

All through my ministry in Livingston I met each month with the Sunday School teachers to go over the lessons which they would be teaching the children. I left the presentation of the lessons to them. For some years we were blessed in having five primary school teachers helping in Sunday School. Gradually over the years I was able to teach them a considerable amount of Christian doctrine, which in later years proved to be most helpful in the life of the congregation.

Adult Baptisms

My predecessor and I between us baptised over 300 adults. It is an indication of the spiritual life of the parish as it was. The Scottish Bible Society, which later united with the National Bible Society of Scotland, at that time through a generous grant given many years before, allowed each parish to purchase, every year, up to £200 worth of Bibles at cost price. The purchase of these Bibles was on condition they were sold at the same price, so no profit was made. Many parishes never availed themselves of this offer. I therefore asked some of my neighbouring parishes if I could purchase their quota. I sold several hundreds of Bibles. I felt that when I went to Livingston there was a dearth of Bibles.

The Need to Read God's Word

I stressed very many times from the pulpit and in homes, the necessity of reading God's Word. I used to say that people would never come to know one another and no friendship could be formed unless they spoke to one another. In a friendship between two people both must speak, otherwise the relationship would be one sided and no true friendship could be formed. I said that prayer primarily is where we speak to God. God speaks to us through his Word as we read it or hear it preached. In our relationship with God it was better for God to do the most speaking. I encouraged them, as my parents taught me as a boy, always before reading the Bible to pray and ask God to speak to them in their own life situation.

Later, I asked three women of deep Christian commitment, much loved and respected in the community, to form a small 'Bible Promotion Committee'. These women were very practical in their caring for the needs of others. If someone was bereaved, or a member of the family became suddenly ill, they would immediately visit the home with a bowl of soup and seek to help and comfort. In their visits they encouraged the daily reading of God's Word. Before I left Livingston, one in five and then one in three homes ordered the Scripture Union Daily Reading Notes and one home in seven ordered Holy Tryst, the prayer diary of the Church of Scotland where every aspect of the Church's work was prayed for every month.

Christian Literature

I have always greatly valued the importance of Christian literature both for children and for adults, in evangelism and education. Therefore every year when selecting prizes for the children in Sunday School I always chose Christian books, generally missionary books. I kept a note of the books given to each child and endeavoured over the years never to give the same book to children in the same family. As they grew older I gave to each child a copy of John Bunyan's "Pilgrim's Progress" and, before they left Sunday School, a Bible. I am sure it played an important part in their, and their parents', Christian education. I am always amazed when so many churches give secular books as prizes. It seems an enormous loss of a God-given opportunity to advance the Kingdom of God.

Weekly Bible Study

From the start of my ministry we had a weekly Bible Study. For several months I felt that such was the lack of biblical understanding on the part of those attending, that we could not advance beyond studying some of the stories of the gospel. I remember my discouragement when after turning to the Epistle to the Ephesians and discussing for the first time, "salvation by grace alone", one of my Sunday School teachers said that she had no idea what the Bible study was all about. She did not understand it. She went on and became a very committed Christian and later studied and gained a Diploma in a two-year theological course at New College. Later, she became an elder and valued lay reader within the Presbytery.

Bible Class and Youth Fellowship

My session clerk, Jim Danskin, the headmaster of the Primary School in Livingston Station, told me that I would never be able to form a youth fellowship. He had tried to do so and failed. At the commencement of my ministry there were no young people over the age of 13, or 14 at the most, who were in church or attached to the church. I therefore started with the older Sunday School children who were at school in primary seven and over and formed them into two Bible Classes one in both of our churches. For the first year I taught both Bible Classes myself. As a result, I had two morning services each Sunday, one in each church, two Bible Classes and, having started an evening service, found Sundays a tiring day.

When my sister Margaret came to stay with me, followed shortly afterwards by her husband, Kenneth MacKenzie, I asked her to take the Bible Class in Livingston Village. She was well liked and did a marvellous job. One of her pupils was Sadie Elliot who later became an elder, Presbytery reader and depute head teacher in Bathgate Academy.

Anticipating the time when my sister and her husband would leave I looked around for a suitable leader to take the Bible Class in Livingston Village. There was no obvious person. Therefore I asked Willie Brown, an elder and shale miner in Seafield if he would be willing to meet with me in preparation for his taking over the leadership of the village Bible Class. He was a godly man and a foreman at work with latterly 400 men under him. For six months I met with Willie, one evening each week and went over the biblical material that I recommended that the young people be taught. I was devoting a lot of time to one man. However, I was very much rewarded in doing so. He became a much respected and loved Bible Class leader, elder and later on, church treasurer.

School Assemblies

I was invited every week to take two assemblies in school, one for Primary classes 1 to 3 and the other for the older children in Primary classes 4 to 7. These were years when it was expected of the visiting minister that what was taught was the Christian Faith not other religions, or yet simply morality. Both Danskin and Meiklejohn, who succeeded him when Danskin moved on to become headmaster of Blackburn Primary School, welcomed me to the school and asked me to conduct their school assemblies. Mr Meiklejohn came from Strathnaver in Sutherland and was brought up in the Highland tradition. Although a deeply religious man he never became a communicant member on the grounds that he was unworthy. He and his wife attended church faithfully twice a Sunday. Later on he became clerk to the Congregational Board.

In the Primary assembly I simply told a Bible story and tried to explain its meaning for us today. The following week, in order to revise their memory, I catechised them concerning the story of the previous week and told them another story. I frequently spoke about the importance of prayer, encouraged them to pray every day and tried to teach them how to pray. Often I asked them to pray clause by clause after me.

With the older Primary children I developed a slightly different method. At that time the Scripture Union produced children's Bible Reading Notes. They harmonised and were gathered up in the reading and lesson on the Sunday. I encouraged the children to purchase these Bible Reading Notes and to read the recommended passage every day.

My weekly visits to the school helped me to know the children and helped the children to know me. After the school assemblies I normally chatted for a while with the headmaster or one or more of the teachers.

When I returned to my car each week, because I did not lock it, I found it crammed full of children. I generally had to gently turf two or three out so that I could get into the car. They wanted a lift down the road no matter how short the journey home. Often when they saw me they would walk with me down the road. I was glad that they were not too shy to talk to the minister. They were always lively and fun to be with. I was grateful for these contacts: I believe that it helped many of them to come to church.

Youth Work

The break-through in work among the young people of Bible Class age came about when the evangelist Tom Rees was invited by some within the Presbytery of Edinburgh to hold a series of evangelistic meetings in the Usher Hall in Edinburgh. Jean Galloway and some of my Sunday School teachers organised a bus to convey people to the Usher Hall meetings. 40 young people aged around 14 years went. Twenty responded to the call to go forward and commit their lives to Christ. Their names were forwarded to me, as minister of the parish from which they came. I knew them because they were in my Bible Class. I met each one individually. I asked them about their response at the meeting with Tom Rees and their commitment to Christ. That group stayed within the church. They came into the youth fellowship. Most of them later on joined me in seaside mission work. Some later entered the ministry of the Church of Scotland.

Eastern Star and Freemasons

The only difficulty or opposition throughout my years in Livingston occurred in connection with the Eastern Star and the Freemasons. When I had been in post for two or three weeks, Jim Danskin, the Session Clerk said, "You are conducting a service for the Eastern Star on Sunday afternoon in Church." I said, "No, I am not". He said that the previous minister did and my name was on the posters advertising the service. I told him that the fact that my name was on the Eastern Star notices was not my concern. I had not been approached and asked to take the service. It had been taken for granted that because the previous minister conducted their services the present minister would do likewise.

The Session Clerk was concerned when I said that I would not take the service and communicated the news to the grand Mistress of the Order. She came to see me and to seek to persuade me to take the service. I said that I was ordained in the name of the Trinity and would not take a service that was not in the name of the Father, the Son and the Holy Spirit. After discussion she said, "All right, you can take the service in any way you wish providing you read from St John's Epistle and say, 'To the sacred lady Electra." Apparently there are according to the Eastern Star five sacred ladies as there are five points to their star. It was the year of the lady Electra. I said that I would not and that John in his first Epistle was writing a pastoral letter. It was not devoted to their lady Electra.

I relented, rightly or wrongly, to the extent that I allowed the service to take place on the Sunday afternoon in church because it was already publicly advertised. I said however that I would not take the service. They would require to invite another minister who was sympathetic to the Eastern Star. The Grand Mistress, who was one of my church members 'took the huff' and would not come to church for the next month. However she recovered and came back to church.

I was deeply concerned about the amount of alcohol consumed in the parish and the amount of gambling that took place. From the revenue which the Chancellor of the Exchequer received yearly from the alcohol trade and the number of homes in the country as estimated by government, I could work out approximately the amount of money spent on alcohol by each household. The local pub manager in Livingston Station would not tell me the pub's weekly turnover of money from alcohol, although I asked him. He admitted, however, that on a Friday and Saturday evening, the turnover was over £500. How much it was over he would not say. I calculated that the average household in Livingston spent at least £5 a week on alcohol and together with gambling over £10 a week. That was an enormous sum of money in those days. It was over half the weekly wage of the average miner. Of course, many and probably most of the church households spent nothing like that amount which meant that the non-church households spent much more.

At one of our Kirk Session meetings in Livingston Station (we alternated our place of meeting) I drew the elders' attention to the fact that the Freemasons, for some special occasion, had acquired the use of the community hall in Livingston Station for a weekend and were applying for a licence for the week-end to sell alcohol. I asked the Kirk Session if we should oppose their application for a licence. To my surprise one elder said, "We will support you in opposing every application for a licence in the New Town of Livingston, but hands off the Masons." I was astonished and said, "Am I hearing you aright"? From what you say are you suggesting that there are two sets of standards, one for the church and one for the Masons?" Another elder said, "If you oppose the Masons, your ministry in this parish is finished"!

At this, other elders in support of the minister were aroused and ready to pitch in to those who had spoken against the minister and in defence of Freemasonry. It became immediately clear that four of the elders were Freemasons and the rest were not. I addressed them very frankly. I said that we must be clear that Christ demanded of all of us, a total, unconditional commitment and he demanded of all who served within his Church an unconditional commitment to Christ. It was impossible to be committed to Christ and to be committed to Freemasonry, or anything else. What was called for was a total, unconditional commitment to Christ. I said if any elder or office-bearer was unable to give himself in an unconditional commitment to Christ, he must consider whether he should continue as an office-bearer. They were strong words. I felt that they were necessary. I did not wish to split the Kirk Session and because the application for a licence by the Freemasons was only for a weekend I agreed to drop my opposition to their application on condition that what I said about Christ's demand for unconditional surrender was recorded in our Kirk Session minutes. The Kirk Session agreed. Never again to my knowledge was a Freemason proposed as an elder. The non-Masons were clear that they did not want any other Mason to be an elder. In fairness to the four elders who were Masons, all I can say is that they continued to be supportive of me as minister.

After the meeting, four of my younger office-bearers said that they were being urged to join the Masonic Movement and asked me to read certain literature which they had, surprisingly, been given in order to persuade them to join. The literature which I read claimed that the Masonic Order had and proclaimed a higher form of salvation than did the Church.

Again, shortly after that Kirk Session meeting, the Revd Bill Thomson, minister of Broxburn West Church, a friend and evangelical, spoke to me. He was concerned and upset over a recent funeral which he conducted. At the grave-side he noticed a neighbouring minister dressed in full Masonic robes. This minister asked him not to pronounce the benediction after his part at the grave side but to step back, because he then would take over the rest of the service – this on the grounds that Freemasons proclaim a higher form of salvation than that proclaimed by the church! Bill Thomson had no prior warning about what would happen. I was appalled and sympathised with Bill. I told him about the literature which I had been loaned and read. I immediately on the following Sunday announced that I would gladly conduct, when asked, the funeral of any person in the parish, whether they were church members or non members. I would not, however, take a Masonic funeral nor participate in a Masonic funeral. I was ordained in the name of the Trinity and would only conduct a service in the name of the Trinity and that there was no other higher salvation than that which was in Christ and witnessed to by the Church.

Freemasonry at that time was strong in West Lothian. Bathgate High Church which had some 2,300 church members was generally regarded as a Masonic Church. Its minister was chaplain general for the Masons in Scotland. No one ever again spoke to me or challenged me in regard to Freemasonry. I also was not aware of any funeral ever taking place in the parish which I myself did not conduct (holidays apart).

Pastoral Cases

A great sin and cause of embarrassment and shame was for a drunk and incapable person to be taken home by the minister! Inevitably, in a parish where people imbibed heavily, that took place. One afternoon when driving on my way from the village to Livingston Station I saw a man, Mr McCan, lying on the grass at the side of the road. Thinking that he might have had a heart attack I stopped and jumped out of the car. When I bent over him, it was clear that he had been drinking heavily. When he opened his eyes and saw me he was aghast. All that he could say was, "It's the minister! It's the minister!" I said, "Yes, it is the minister. Come, I will take you home."

This for him was the height of shame and he protested that he would make his own way home. However he could not stand without help and so against his protests I put him in the car. He was an unmarried man and stayed alone in a small prefabricated house next to the church gate. In front of his house was a broad pavement and the local bus stop. When I got him out of the car and was staggering with him arm in arm across the pavement to his house, the bus drew in and a crowd of men got off and saw us. I felt sorry for him and yet was amused. I knew that he would be the butt of many a joke by those who had seen him drunk and arm in arm with the minister. Some months later when visiting on the other side of the village, when I knocked on a door he opened it. As a minister I said quite the wrong thing and felt rebuked afterwards, I said, "Ha! Ha! We have met before!" He took one look at me and vanished without a word. I felt very rebuked. I felt that I should not have said that to him. He happened to be visiting that particular family, who lived in that house, that day.

About three years later, when I returned from holiday I was told that his brother had died after a heart attack and that he himself had had a mild heart attack and would like to speak to me. The two brothers were nominally Roman Catholics. He had moved to a different house and I went to see him. He greeted me warmly and invited me in. I said that

I understood that he wanted to speak to me. He said, "Yes, I wanted to thank you for the time that you helped me and drove me home." I looked at him and said, "I do not think that that is why you wanted to speak to me. I was very sorry to learn that your brother died after a heart attack. I am sorry to hear that you have had a heart attack although I am glad to hear that it is mild: but you are worried. You are worried about what God thinks of you and what will happen to you when you die". He said, "That's it minister. That's it. That is why I asked to speak to you." It was a God-given opportunity to speak to him about Christ and his love and forgiveness and to help him commit his life to Christ.

One lovely summer sunny day my wife and I drove the car to Seafield for their annual Gala day. We parked near a public house with about 8 drunk men standing leaning against the wall of the pub. The window of the car was open. As I switched off the car engine a face looked in and said, "It is a sunny day. There is a row of drunk men standing against the wall of the pub. As minister, what are you going to do about it?" I asked him for his name and address and told him that when he was sober I would visit him". His name was John Smith. I visited him a day or two later. He was unmarried and stayed with his brother. Both were alcoholics. Their home was desperately poor and shabby. The few articles of furniture in the living room were old and there were no carpets on the floor. I had a long talk with him about Jesus Christ, prayed with him, helping him to commit his life to Christ.

Stranraer Mission

I had at that time agreed on request from D.P. Thomson to help in a mission which he was conducting in Stranraer and district in the far south and west of Scotland. I helped DP on two occasions. In order to help strengthen John Smith's faith and commitment to Christ I invited him to come with me on the missions in Stranraer, which he did both times.

On each occasion DP, in inviting my assistance, said that I would have two speaking engagements, between Sunday evening and Tuesday morning. In fact when I arrived on mission it was to discover that on each occasion I was being asked to take part in four speaking occasions! Knowing DP I was not surprised. On the first occasion, I was asked to speak at an evangelistic rally at 8pm on the Sunday evening. After preaching and lunch I drove to Galloway in a rather old car which I had at the time. I arrived at 7.45pm with DP standing looking at his watch on the door step of the church. He said, "David it is a quarter to eight!" I patted him on the shoulder, knowing his concern, smiled and said, "DP, I am quarter of an hour early!"

Christmas Services in the Public Houses

There were two pubs in Livingston, one in the old village and one in Livingston Station. Each Christmas Eve, prior to the 'watch night service', I visited the two pubs and gave a short Christmas message. I was always very well received. I used to ask that they carry on with serving drinks. They never did – as they never did in any of the pubs which I visited during my Tell Scotland days. I found that the men (there were no women in the pubs in those days) always listened with rapt attention. I used to think that they listened with greater attention and silence than the congregation did in church. After giving a Christmas message, I used to spend some considerable time going round and talking to the men. I never drank but I always found that I was well received. Often men opened up and spoke quite freely and many helpful conversations took place about the Christian faith. I felt that men who drank were on the whole gentler and more open than those who gambled.

Death-bed conversions

There were a number of what might be called 'death bed conversions'.

Angus McQueen was 78 years of age, unwell and bed-ridden when I first met him. An elder told me that he was worried because he had never been baptised. I went to see him. He was an able man who had had various good jobs throughout his life but had lost them through his addiction to alcohol. He told me that he was born and grew up on the Island of Skye and had had a religious upbringing. He had left Skye while still a boy and had lived his life outside the church. He told me that his mind was now dwelling on his early religious upbringing and he was recalling things which he had been taught. We talked about Jesus Christ and his salvation and the need to commit our lives to Christ. On his request I baptised him, while he was in bed, together with his wife. I have always found the service for adult baptism moving. When I asked the question, "Do you sincerely repent of your sins?" he said, very emphatically, "Yes, I do". Likewise when I asked, "Do you put your faith in Jesus Christ and trust him as Lord?" After I baptised him, his face was glowing with joy and he said to me, "I believe that it says somewhere that there is great joy in heaven over one sinner who repents". I was moved. Later I baptised a man of 82 years. He was the oldest man that I ever baptised. It was a great joy to see men so advanced in years coming to faith in Christ.

Jim Stewart along with six or seven other retired men went regularly to watch dog racing. They all gambled and drank. When Jim became ill with cancer, I visited him in hospital. He lived for nine months after being diagnosed with having the disease. During that period, although he was not a church member, I endeavoured to visit him each week or oftener. He came to a marvellous faith in Christ and when I visited him in hospital would announce the fact to the nurses, saying how the minister had helped him. When I visited him in his home, where for the most part he was in bed, very often about six of his gambling friends were present. He would announce before them all in my presence, that he had changed and now was a Christian, believing in Christ. I always took the opportunity to speak to all of them about Christ and invited them to join with me as we prayed for Jim. Of the men present two were nominal church members, one of whom became a regular attender at church. The other, Bill, to my knowledge never came to church. When Jim Stewart died a great number of his former friends and work mates attended the funeral, along with those who went with him to the dog racing. At the service I said that Jim Stewart was not a member of the Church and possibly had never in his life attended a service in church. I said that during his last months on earth he had embraced Christ as Saviour and had come to have a living faith in the Lord. For those who loved the Lord, death was the gateway to life and we could therefore give thanks to God that Jim was now risen and rejoicing in Christ.

Bill, who was one of Jim Stewart's friends and a nominal church member but never came, said to me many times, when I encouraged him to commit his life to Christ, "I will come to it in the end"! Some time later I received a telephone call at about 11 o'clock at night saying that Bill was in hospital and dying. I visited him that night. Again I spoke to him about Christ, encouraging him to look up to the Lord and trust him. When I said I will read a portion of Scripture he immediately lit a cigarette, which one could do in hospital in those days. When I said now let us pray, he reached for the newspaper to see the racing results. I had the chilly feeling that as his end drew nearer he seemed to move further away from Christ. It was the last time that I saw him. I felt chilled.

At his and any funeral service that I conducted I always felt that whereas my task as a minister is to try and help the bereaved to receive the comfort of God, I yet must be honest and true to the gospel. Hence I used to say some such words as: "Our faith is centred on Jesus Christ. If we welcome him as our Saviour, death is the gateway to life with Christ in the Kingdom of heaven. If we do not want Christ and that being our choice we choose to live and die without Christ, then death remains as something very dark. God loves us all. In his love he welcomes all of us, no matter who we are, if we come to him. In his love he wants to comfort us and will comfort us if we come to him."

I said some such words as that at Bill's funeral service. I did not say as of Jim Stewart, that he was risen and rejoicing with Christ. I was thereon duly questioned by his friends why I had not said the same at Bill's funeral service as I had said at Jim Stewart's. I was asked, "What has happened to Bill?" I could only reply, "I do not know. The Judge of all the earth will do right."

Baptisms and Marriages

In my visiting, I always had a long chat with parents who asked me to baptise their child and also with couples who wished to marry. The latter normally came to see me in the Manse.

In regard to baptism I never really met with the difficulties that so many evangelical ministers have in refusing to baptise children who were not members. According to our church constitution at the time, in order for a minister to baptise, at least one parent must be a church member or adherent and able to take the baptismal vows. I never quoted the law. When non-members came asking for the baptism of their child I used to say, "God loves your child and I would love to baptise your child, but whether your child is baptised depends on you."

I endeavoured to explain the meaning of the parental vows. Parents must confess their faith in the Lord. They must with God's help teach their child the gospel of Christ and teach their child to pray. They must set their child a Christian example by coming faithfully to church to worship God so that by their teaching, their faith, their example and their prayer their child would grow up to love the Lord. I told them that they were making these vows or promises not to me, not to the church but to the Lord. If they could not take these vows sincerely, then, because they were to God, it was better not to take them. Some parents having understood the meaning and implication of the vows went forward and entered the church. Others held back and said that in the circumstances it was better that they do not take the vows. It was very, very rare that the parents who in the end did not choose to have their child baptised were upset either by the minister or by the church. In Livingston I can only remember one case of an alcoholic couple, who squandered everything on drink, being upset by my declining to baptise their child. They refused to come to church but wanted me to baptise their child in the home. None the less we remained on good terms.

In regard to married couples like other ministers, I not only went over with them the wedding service but endeavoured to explain the meaning of a Christian marriage. A Christian marriage, as distinct from a non-Christian marriage, involves three people not two. It involves man, God and woman. I used to explain that as a minister I could marry them in the eyes of the law but not in the eyes of God. Only God can truly marry and join together a man and woman in marriage, so as to become in the language of the Bible, 'one whole person'. For God to marry them therefore they must themselves pray (and I always asked them to pray together after they left speaking to me) and in prayer to give thanks to God so that they may hold each other as a gift from God. I asked them to commit their lives to Christ, to commit their love to the Lord and ask God to join them together in marriage. I used to say to them that only when you have done that can you sincerely enter in to the marriage service in church and we can say sincerely over them, "Those whom God hath joined, let not man put asunder". I also told them that I was not concerned if they had a tiff. Every couple does. The all important thing is always to forgive each other, and never to end a day without being at peace with each other, with the world and with God. I gave them in writing Ephesians 4 verse 26 and certain other passages.

From time to time I received a comment or letter from a couple about what I had said to them prior to their marriage. I was always encouraged when non-church members told me that following what I said, they prayed for the first time in their lives, and prayed together prior to their wedding. One couple told me it was what I said that had held their marriage together.

Marriage Breakdown

In those days there were few divorces among church members. Throughout my time in Livingston I can only recall two couples whose marriage came apart. I had not married them. There were however some broken marriages among non-church members. I tried in every case to visit the couple concerned even although on occasion I had to cross Scotland to do so. Throughout the whole of my ministry, I found that the hardest part of the ministry was trying to help couples who had separated. The difficulty which I found was hardness of heart. From time to time God graciously rewarded my efforts, but I also had many failures. The successes (if I can call them that because it was always God not me who succeeded in bringing an estranged couple together) always encouraged me to continue to try and help when a marriage had broken down.

Mary was a member of my Bible Class in my early years in Livingston. She married a Catholic, and moved away from Livingston Station. I think she was married by a Catholic priest. Some time later I was told that Mary was back living with her parents in Livingston Station. Her marriage had split up. I went to see her. I learned that she and her husband had been separated for nine months. She told me that she still loved her husband and would like to be reconciled. I went to see her husband who was living with his parents in Bo'ness, several miles away. I wondered about what kind of reception I would receive, knowing that the parents were very committed Roman Catholics. The husband was out. His two parents were in so I told them the purpose of my visit. I wrote a long letter of several pages to Mary's husband, in which I said that God was commanding him to repent and return to his wife who still loved him. I wrote about Christian marriage, commitment to Christ and prayer. I may have written twice, I do not remember.

They came together and a short time later asked me to baptise their child. I hesitated, knowing that they now belonged to the RC Church. His parents were adamant in asking that I baptise their child. They thanked me for the help that I had given and said that their own, or any priest, would not have done what I did. Almost 40 years later my wife and I were invited to a special service in Livingston. Mary was there. Shaking hands she smiled and said, "We are still together". I was grateful for God's grace.

Church Finance

When I became minister of Livingston, the church finances were not in a happy state. Two weeks after my induction, James Barr, the church treasurer said to me, "I want you to know before you go to Presbytery that Livingston Church, in the matter of giving, is at the bottom of the Presbytery. I want you to hear that from us before you hear it from the Presbytery". He also said, "If ever the Presbytery tell us as a church to do something, we do not question it. We do it. We have appeared once at the bar of Presbytery and we have no intention of standing there again".

When I asked him what had happened, he said that my predecessor had shown signs that he was unwilling to submit to the authority of Presbytery. When therefore without consulting Presbytery and receiving Presbytery's permission, he put up blinds in the church, to prevent people looking into the church on a Sunday evening, he was challenged by the Presbytery Clerk as to why he had not asked and received Presbytery permission. Being unable to reply, the minister and Kirk Session had been summoned to stand at the bar of Presbytery. They were rebuked but the church was allowed to keep the blinds.

The Presbytery Clerk was an exceedingly able, knowledgeable, quiet and kindly man but absolutely firm in the need for adhering to church regulations, even in a very small matter like the erecting of blinds over the windows. I was always very grateful to that Presbytery Clerk who I came greatly to respect and was always grateful for the firm stand which under his guidance the Presbytery took on many matters. I often felt that if each Presbytery took its pastoral concerns seriously and courageously exercised, for the welfare of the ministers and congregations under its pastoral care, the powers belonging to it, ministers would be delivered from much stress and strain which so often arises when the Presbytery fails to act decisively.

The fact that financially Livingston congregation was the poorest giving congregation in the Presbytery was not encouraging. Like other Church Extension charges we were instructed to have two finance books or accounts. In the one was recorded monies raised to maintain the church and its ministry and the money which we were encouraged to give and which it was our Christian duty to give to the wider work of the church both at home and abroad. In the other account was the money given each year to Church Extension. The National Church had built St Andrew's Church and we were required to pay back to The National Church Extension Committee one fifth of the cost of building the church. For a church like ours this was not easy.

When as one of two ministerial candidates for the vacancy in Livingston I was interviewed by the committee representing the congregation I was asked two, and only two questions. "Was I married?' My answer was a simple "No!" The second question was, "Will you organise whist drives and dances in order to raise money for the church". To that I also said, "No!" I went on and said, "If you want that kind of minister, I am not your man. You have two candidates: you must choose the other man. If you call me, there will be no whist drives or dances to raise money for the church. The only right way is to give directly to the Lord in thankfulness". They called me.

I appreciate that many people can enjoy sales of work and special social events which are organised to raise money. They enjoy the fun and fellowship in working together and in 'giving in kind'. I have always tried however to insist that the maintenance of the church and its ministry and a congregation's support for the wider work of the church at home and abroad should be by direct giving. Giving from sales of work can contribute to something special concerning the fabric of the church or be donated to some special concern.

About three weeks after my induction I was challenged on the subject by the secretary of the Woman's Guild in a meeting in the church. I was asked to help in organising a whist drive to raise money for the church. I reminded them of what I had said at my interview, prior to my ordination and induction. The lady said, "Mrs Taylor, wife of the minister in Bathgate High Church has whist drives." I said that I am not here to answer to Mrs Taylor but to the Lord. The lady said, "If you don't have whist drives the church finances will drop." I replied, "Let them drop until we learn that the right way is to give to the Lord in the spirit of thankfulness for what he has done for us." This was greeted in subdued silence, particularly in the light of our financial position.

Stewardship

We had no whist drives and dances or other means of raising money, but the finances from the start began to rise and continued to rise year by year. When the Revd James Matheson, from the Highlands of Scotland, returned from a ministry in New Zealand, he became secretary of the National Church Stewardship Committee. He presented a stewardship programme to the General Assembly which the General Assembly accepted and recommended. The programme involved inviting the entire congregation to a meal, paid for out of congregational funds. After the meal the challenge of Christian stewardship would be presented. This necessitated prior to the meal a programme of visitation by members of the congregation who had undergone training in stewardship. For us as a congregation it was quite a challenge. We had no building which could accommodate the whole congregation for a meal. It would necessitate hiring a large marquee and hiring an outside professional caterer, which was costly. For us in our financial situation it was an enormous venture of faith. We prayed much about it, sometimes in fear and trembling because of the risks that we were taking. With encouragement from Jim Matheson we agreed to hold a stewardship campaign as recommended. Some six hundred people attended the meal in the tent. They were church members, church adherents and some others from the parish. Three of our own people spoke. People present were deeply moved. The evening cost the congregation some £600. We cleared all expenses and our givings jumped approximately 20 per cent, and continued to rise year by year.

Within five years we repaid our debt to the National Church Extension Committee, being one of the first Church Extension churches to do so, and in such a short time. Shortly after that the congregation became financially self-supporting and to my joy we became one of 300 churches in the Church of Scotland, out of over 2,000, who exceeded in what they were asked, in their giving to the wider work of the church.

From the beginning I insisted that in our giving to the Lord, we must first give to others and to mission, before we considered spending money on ourselves and on our own property. That again was not easy for the congregation. We were given a new church building which had a host of serious defects. There was no insulation around the windows and doors which were acquiring green mould. The church tower leaked badly when it rained, so that the beadle had not only to place a bucket on the communion table to catch the water when it rained but to place towels on the communion table to deaden the sound of the drips. The path outside required to be tarmaced and later the surrounding wall had to be rebuilt and plastered. Even when the rain poured down into the chancel I insisted, and the congregation accepted, that our priority in giving must be for others and mission. They always did so. And in all this I was ably and loyally supported by our church treasurer.

Arthur Gunn was a New Zealand minister who for a period had a church in Scotland, first in Abbey Church, North Berwick and then in Glasgow. I came to know him well. He said to me, "When you become minister of a parish, look around for the most spiritual and godly person in the congregation and make that person treasurer." I was deeply grateful for that advice and where possible tried to follow it in my parishes.

When James Barr sold his two farms and bought another dairy farm in the parish of East Calder, he resigned as treasurer. Seeking to follow Arthur Gunn's advice, I proposed that we elect as treasurer Willie Brown of Seafield who was already a Bible Class leader and elder. The Kirk Session and Congregational Board agreed. Willie was a great spiritual blessing to the congregation. He was fully committed to the principle that in giving to the Lord we first and foremost give to others and to mission. His spiritual support and support for mission made my task comparatively easy. Sadly, many ministers struggle with a treasurer who is not ruled so much by spiritual principles as the need to conserve the congregation's finances. I have been blessed throughout my ministry with excellent treasurers who supported me spiritually.

Garden Fêtes

Each year a garden fête, in which I had a personal and vested interest, was held in the manse garden. The garden was approximately one acre in size, containing a few trees and bordered by a row of very large lime trees. It was a lovely garden. I enjoyed growing our own vegetables and soft fruit. However, the larger part of the garden for most of the year looked after itself. A week before the garden fête a team of men volunteers came to weed and tidy the garden, hence my vested interest! The fêtes were much enjoyed by the congregation and were an occasion of fun. Apart from the serving of teas a number of events were held including the letting off of balloons filled with helium gas and horse riding in the glebe at the foot of the garden. Such social gatherings brought the two sides of the congregation together.

Chapter 8

Livingston 1955-1969: Part 2

Livingston New Town

In 1960 an announcement was made that the government had agreed to create a New Town of Livingston to accommodate people from Glasgow, where there was a shortage of houses. In the creation of a New Town, the government appointed a corporation consisting of a chairman and, in the case of Livingston I think, six men, and gave them 50 million pounds. They were charged with creating a New Town which, by attracting new industries would, like a business enterprise, become financially viable and ultimately become independent.

The corporation commenced with the appointment of a general manager, architects, planners, engineers etc. who in turn had the responsibility of making the projected New Town a reality. The first three hundred houses to be built were built in Livingston Station. These were to accommodate the staff employed by Livingston Corporation. As a result, I estimated that approximately 30 architects and engineers and planners came to live in near proximity to St Andrew's church. Some of these were committed Christians and gave us enormous help in the church. The church with its growing needs required further hall accommodation. At the rear of the church was a platform, used when the building functioned as a hall. By widening the platform and creating a sliding door to be rolled back on Sundays a smaller and more comfortable hall could be provided for the Woman's Guild and smaller meetings. I explained our needs to the congregation and said in the presence of some of the employees of the Corporation, "We need your help to create a new hall. Will you help us free of charge?" A cheerful group of men gave their services with no cost to the church apart from building materials.

Visitation of New Homes

Not all of the first 300 new houses were required to house people employed by the New Town Corporation. Most were available to anyone who wished to move into the area. Quite a number of people came from Edinburgh, often young parents or young couples seeking to set up their first home. Consequently we now had many people who did not come from a mining background. We organised a team of church visitors to welcome the new arrivals within two days of their arrival. I endeavoured to follow this up with a ministerial visit. Many and varied were the conversations I had while visiting.

One day a young lady stopped me in the street and asked whether she and her husband could come to church and become members. Their decision followed my visit to their home and from what I had said. I find it difficult when visiting door to door always to remember what I have said and had to ask the lady to remind me. She said that her husband had said that they were atheists, they did not believe in God and would not be coming to church. I had asked her husband if he had made a will, which he said that he had. I had asked whether as a sincere atheist he had stated in his will that at his funeral the name of God must not be mentioned, no minister must be invited to be present and no prayer must be offered. On the husband stating that such a clause was not in his will I had said that as a sincere and honest atheist, he must contact his lawyer as soon as possible and have such clauses inserted in his will. The lady told me that after I had left their house they discussed what I had advised. Her husband thought that it was going too far to have such clauses inserted in their will. They would need to think again and consider going to church! She asked if they could come. I said that they would be welcome.

In another home of a young couple, the man said that although his parents went to church in Edinburgh, he was an agnostic and they would not be coming to church. He was not very happy when I said that although he preferred the Greek word 'agnostic', I preferred the Latin word 'ignoramus'! Sometime later I visited them both in the maternity unit in Bangour Hospital, on the occasion of the birth of their first child. The sister said, "You better go down to the labour ward. The husband is pacing up and down. He needs you more than she does." I went down and visited them both in the labour ward.

Ignoring his previous claims to be an agnostic, I talked about Christ and said we would pray and commit everything to the Lord, pray for a safe delivery and pray that mother and baby would be well. I felt at that time they were somewhat comforted. A few years later, when I was a parish minister in Aberdeen, I met his sister who was a missionary home on furlough from Africa. She told me that following the birth of their child they were in church every Sunday. I was much encouraged and glad. Many people have come to Christ at a time of great emotional crisis. Professor Kemp Smith, Professor of Logic and Metaphysics who taught my two brothers in Edinburgh, was converted on the birth of his first child.

Ecumenical Experiment

When the New Town was announced, it was proposed that it should ultimately have one hundred thousand inhabitants. Things began to change. My congregation was the only one in the projected area for the New Town. Apart from Livingston village and Livingston Station the rest of the projected area for the New Town was rural. There were quite a number of farms in the area. The projected area was more than my parish and included a good slice of rural country belonging to Mid Calder parish. Mid Calder parish was included within the presbytery of Edinburgh.

I immediately wondered and hoped that in the creation of the New Town, the different church denominations of Scotland should share their limited resources in building new churches in Livingston. I envisaged one church building in each area of the town in which different services would take place at different times, Presbyterian, Episcopal, Methodist and so forth. Erecting and maintaining one church building would economically be cheaper for each denomination involved. I envisaged the provision of traditional services according to each denomination, but that teaching of children and youth and other church activities all be shared. A united witness on the part of the churches was surely biblical and would be helpful in a society increasingly becoming secular. I shared my thoughts and ideas with John Lusk the minister of Uphall North Church. He was in agreement with me.

I did not, as minister of Livingston, want to put forward the proposal to Presbytery and if Presbytery agreed, to the General Assembly, in case anyone thought that I was wishing to draw attention to my ministry. I therefore asked John if he would propose the motion to Presbytery and offered to second the motion. John agreed. The Presbytery agreed and the proposal was put to the General Assembly. The GA received the proposal with great caution and appointed a committee composed of 12 men, whom one well-known minister called the 'top brass' of the church. They were ministers, lawyers and trustees of the church.

The Church of Scotland would not hastily create an experiment in church unity without, as far as possible, considering all that such an experiment might involve. I was appointed to be a member of that committee. The GA the following year, although reservations were expressed, approved of the experiment in church unity. Because the proposed area for the New Town included areas within the two presbyteries of Edinburgh and Bathgate (as my presbytery at that time was called) a committee comprised of members from the two presbyteries, including the Episcopal Bishop of Edinburgh, and representatives from the Methodist and Congregational churches was created. I was asked to be chairman. I served as chairman for six years until I moved to a parish in Aberdeen. The committee had to wrestle with many problems, such as the erection and design of a new church, the sharing of finance in construction, the future oversight of the ecumenical church, the future finances of the church once an ecumenical congregation was created, the obligation which such a congregation would have to participating denominations in the experiment and so forth.

Craigshill

The Revd James Maitland was appointed as the first Church of Scotland minister in Craigshill, together with an Episcopal and Methodist minister. I forget, but possibly a congregational minister was included in the ministerial team in addition to a deaconess. Craigshill was on the East side of the town and was planned to house ten thousand people. It was there that the first major programme of building took place.

The neighbouring churches were each asked to loan two assessor elders to enable the new church to start. We loaned Malcolm Drummond, a committed Christian and faithful church attender and also John Gibb, who volunteered himself. Malcolm Drummond was the forestry and horticultural chief for the New Town. Shortly after his arrival in Livingston Station we welcomed him as an elder. John Gibb had earlier in his life worked on one or more of the farms in the Craigshill area and was interested in the development of the area. It is a sacrifice for a church to lose for a few years the services of two loyal elders but we were glad to do so in the circumstances.

Officially the whole New Town area was embraced within the church ecumenical experiment. We however were not at first too much affected. The sixties were years when radical liberal winds were blowing through the church. It was the period of 'God is dead' theology and 'the Church must die' theology. In 1963 Bishop John Robinson wrote his well known and disturbing book entitled *Honest to God*. Mercifully, these radical liberal winds did not affect Scotland to the extent that they affected England. Nonetheless some in Scotland were affected.

Jim Maitland, a member of the Iona Community, came from Appin in Argyllshire. In many ways he was conservative but he was also liberal and influenced by these radical winds. He came to Craigshill with a vision quite different from mine. He interpreted the experiment not as an experiment in churches working together, each offering their traditional worship, but as an experiment in worship. Consequently he endeavoured to create a form of worship that was not Presbyterian, Episcopal or Methodist, but one that drew from each of the different forms of worship. Consequently, many who moved to Craigshill were not initially happy. They wanted a form of worship which they recognised and to which they were accustomed. I believe personally it was one of the many reasons why, for a long time, the congregation remained comparatively small given the size of the population of Craigshill.

I think that in time people became accustomed to the offered forms of worship and the congregation became established, although, to my knowledge, it never in my time exceeded that in Livingston Station.

Jim Maitland did not wish to create a Woman's Guild as in the Church of Scotland. He wanted a woman's meeting that he felt would be welcomed by all women in the parish whether they were church members or not. I was told that, as a result of the liberal winds that were blowing, the meetings for women that were created did not include any form of worship or prayer.

Although in the Old Parish of Livingston, as my parish came to be called, we continued in a traditional way, it was agreed that being within the ecumenical experiment, we would all come together in three out of five Holy Week services. I treasured our own services on Thursday with Holy Communion and on Good Friday when some 100 people would attend. I urged the members of my congregation to attend the three ecumenical Holy Week services on Monday, Tuesday and Wednesday. With my elders I confessed that I found them unhelpful. I remember one which focused on "Light". We were shown three or four slides on blindness. We were told to meditate. There was no sermon. Travelling back with three of my people in the car, my session clerk, Alex Marshall, a godly elder said, "We do not enjoy these services. We only go because you tell us to go!" I shared his disquiet.

Some people, as the New Town progressed chose to come to us in order to have a traditional service whose form they recognised.

Youth Work in Craigshill

A full time youth worker was appointed by the Church of Scotland to join the ministerial team at Craigshill. His name was Max. The Youth Committee of the Church of Scotland were concerned to attract young people into the church. They appointed a full time youth leader and trained a number of younger men in youth leadership. Among those whom they trained was Max who was appointed to the New Town of Livingston and a young civil engineer, Gordon Maclean, to work, possibly part time, in Perth. Gordon MacLean later came to work as a civil engineer for Livingston New Town Corporation.

The plan envisaged by the National Youth Committee and by Max was to run open youth clubs in order, hopefully, to attract the youth and particularly the unchurched youth, in a parish. I felt that the Gospel played little or no part in the youth programmes which were arranged. One day I discovered from one of my church members that Max, in order to create youth work in Craigshill had, without consulting me, invited over 20 of my young people to assist him to start up his youth work. I myself ran a youth club in the Hall Church in Livingston Station each Saturday evening, in addition to the Youth Fellowship which met on a Sunday evening. I always closed both the Youth Fellowship and the Youth Club each evening with a short act of worship.

Suddenly I found myself without a youth club or Youth Fellowship. I was chairman of the joint Presbytery Ecumenical Committee. It was firmly agreed that all Christian leaders working in the area should consult together and seek to work together. I had not been consulted. My agreement had not been asked. I wondered if the reason was that my approach to youth work and my theology differed widely from that being advocated by the Livingston Craigshill team and by Max. My Session clerk spoke to me with some concern. He said, "My granddaughter, along with the others, is not going to your Youth Fellowship or youth club. They have joined the youth club in Craigshill. They are receiving no biblical teaching and their club does not close with worship and prayer. What are you going to do about it?" I phoned Jim Maitland and went to talk to him and Max. When I expressed surprise that I had not been consulted nor officially informed about what they had done, they said little other than that they needed a core group of young people in order to start youth work in Craigshill.

Two months later, Jean Galloway, who helped me with the young people in our youth weekends, when we went off to the hills, said, "You have nothing to fear! The last young person is back!" My young people did not enjoy and could not accept the youth programmes organised by Max. The young people returned and their numbers in Old Livingston continued to grow until they became, I believe, the largest Youth Fellowship in the Presbytery. To my knowledge we never again lost a young person who preferred to cross the town to Craigshill.

The Deputy Chief Engineer

Ian Caldwell was assistant chief engineer for the New Town. He and the chief engineer were both highly qualified, extremely able, and well ahead of the team of engineers under them. Ian Caldwell drove himself and could, I believe, do two men's work. Periodically he had a bout of depression, possibly due in part to physical exhaustion. For a long time he insisted that he was an atheist. When he had his periodic bouts of depression he came and sat in the manse always insisting that he was an atheist.

He came one evening in a depressed state the night before I and my wife and family planned to go on holiday. He sat on to one o'clock in the morning, still insisting that he was an atheist. I myself felt tired and exhausted. I said to him, in part because it was late and I did not know how to bring his visit to an end, "Do you know what is wrong with you? You are a proud man! When you are well you will not seek God's help. You are determined that neither God nor man will help you. You will prove to the world that you can do two men's work and you do it well. When you are down and depressed you are still determined that neither God nor man will help you. You are determined to prove that you can pull yourself up by your own unaided efforts. Your problem is pride! You will get nowhere until you learn to bow that proud head of yours and pray and seek God's help and commit your life to Christ". I then prayed and he departed.

Despite my blunt words, which I hope that I managed to speak in love, before he departed, I gave him my holiday address. A few days later I received from him a lovely letter. He said that for the first time in his life he had prayed and as a result his life had changed. It was as if all the birds were singing.

He had a very active mind. He came repeatedly to the manse and borrowed many Christian books and discussed the Christian faith. As a Christian he grew rapidly in the faith. Some months later he and his family moved from Livingston Station to a new house in Craigshill. He came to my next First Communicants Class in the Manse. He told me that he had commenced attending the church service in Craigshill. Although I was not very conscious of receiving support from my colleagues, I felt and suggested, in loyalty to them and our agreement within the Ecumenical Experiment, that he should approach the ministerial team in Craigshill and receive instruction from them. The following week he told me that he had intimated to them that he would continue to worship in Craigshill but continue to go to Old Livingston for his theology! We therefore continued. My preparation classes lasted for twelve weeks. I always insisted that those attending the class must attend church regularly throughout the period of the classes, although of course I encouraged them to continue attending church beyond that. So, he attended the service in Craigshill and I endeavoured to prepare him for church membership and participation in the sacrament of Holy Communion, not in Old Livingston but Craigshill! It was rather an unusual situation!

Shortly after his move to Craigshill, I said that he must encourage his wife to accompany him when he went to Church. He told me that they were worshipping in church together. I then said, "You must teach your son Ian to pray and begin teaching him the Christian faith." He said, "He always prays. You taught him to pray. My wife and I listen to him saying his prayers every night." I said in surprise, "How and when did I teach him to pray?" He said, "You taught him to pray when he was at school in Livingston Station." Their son Ian was 6 years old. He started school in Livingston at the age of five. Half way through the following year, the family moved to Craigshill. I was much encouraged that my efforts to teach the infant classes in school to pray and to pray every night, had been blessed by God. It is marvellous how a very young child can pray and come to faith, as in this boy's case, prior to his mother and father coming to faith.

Work within the Presbytery

In addition to chairing the Livingston Ecumenical Experiment, I was active in Presbytery. I served as convener of the Foreign Mission committee, served and convened the committee on Union and Readjustments, and Parish Superintendence, and acted twice as an interim moderator in a church vacancy, and twice served and convened special commissions in difficult circumstances.

Seven elders of Torphichen Church on one occasion lodged a complaint to Presbytery, complaining that their minister had introduced into morning worship the saying of the Apostles' Creed. I was commissioned by Presbytery to meet with the seven elders. Another minister was asked to accompany me. When I went to meet them I took with me some documents and a few books. With my ministerial colleague (who I do not think spoke throughout the evening) I asked them for the cause of their complaint. They said that their minister, a young man in his first charge who had recently been inducted and ordained, had asked them to say the Apostles' Creed. They refused to do so, saying that they were Protestants and the saying of the Apostles' Creed was a Roman Catholic custom. I asked them where in the service of the RC Mass the Apostles' Creed occurred. One rather bright elder said that it was discussed in the Second Vatican Council, 1963-65. I said that it had no part in the medieval doctrine of the mass and that it had taken many years before the RC Church officially discussed it, as they did in the Second Vatican Council.

The seven elders then changed their complaint. They said that saying the Apostles' Creed was an Episcopal custom and that as Protestants and Presbyterians they would not say it. Having guessed what the elders might say, I told them (a little mischievously) that I had with me four books about the Scottish Covenanters. I reminded them that after Charles the Second became king in 1660, the following year the Presbyterian ministers had been ejected from their pulpits and men of an Episcopal persuasion had been installed. Presbyterian ministers had been compelled with their people to worship in the open air. So began the covenanting period until 1688 when William and Mary were crowned. I said that I would like to read to them a paragraph from a book written by a well-known covenanting minister. In his book, he complained that the Episcopal ministers who had been installed in the place of the Presbyterian ministers would not say the Creed! I said that is interesting! The saying of the Creed was one of the hall-marks of the covenanters! I said, the clock seems to have turned full circle. Now we have elders of an ancient covenanting church refusing to say the Creed on the ground that it is Episcopal.

The seven elders looked at me in astonishment. I said now listen to the order of service that John Calvin instituted in his church in Geneva. I had brought it with me along with John Knox's liturgy. It contains the saying of the creed. Then I said, "Listen to the order of service that John Knox recommended for use in the church in Scotland. It also recommends the saying of the Apostles' Creed." I said that for over 300 years the Apostles' Creed was said throughout the churches in Scotland. I said it largely fell out of use between the years 1880 and 1920 for two entirely different reasons. In the latter part of the nineteenth century sadly there came about on the part of some people doubts about the miracles. The Apostles' Creed mentions the virgin birth and the resurrection of the dead.

The other reason was altogether different and not theological. If the Auld Kirk said and did one thing then the Free Kirk would say and do something different and vice versa. If one church said the Apostles' Creed the other would not, simply in order to be different. These two different reasons came together and over a comparatively short period of time the saying of the Apostles' Creed largely fell out of use. Nonetheless there are some churches, particularly in the Highlands, which have continued to this day to say the Creed. The Reformers introduced the saying of the Apostles' Creed into Scotland at the Reformation in 1560. Services prior to that were in Latin. The Reformers wanted services to be held in the language of the people and wanted the people to understand the Christian Faith. The Apostles' Creed is a summary of the Faith. Hence they introduced it. The Episcopal Church copied the Presbyterian Church and introduced the saying of the creed in 1714.

I suggested to the elders if, before presenting their complaint to Presbytery, they had asked their grandparents, if they had been members of Torphichen Church and were still alive, if they had said the Creed, they would have said, "Yes"! The seven elders said if anyone had explained all this before they would never have complained. The evening ended with good humour and laughter. Peace reigned and the minister continued and had a long and good ministry. His mistake was to reintroduce the saying of the creed without prior explanation and teaching.

Bathgate High Church. The Kirk Session of Bathgate High Church complained to the Presbytery about their minister. I, assisted by another minister, was asked by Presbytery to convene a committee of two, and meet with the minister and Kirk Session in hope of reconciliation. Bathgate High, the largest church in the Presbytery, was considered to be a Masonic Church. John Taylor who was popular and had had a long ministry, was Chaplain General for the Masons of Scotland. His was followed by a short ministry of two years. The present minister, a Mason, had served for less than two years in Bathgate High Church. He was senior chaplain to the Masons of Edinburgh and the Lothians. It was a difficult situation. Reconciliation seemed impossible and as a result, the minister answered the call to serve in another church.

When I was in Stornoway at the invitation of the Home Mission Committee, I received a call from the Presbytery Clerk saying that the Kirk Session of Bathgate High wanted me to be their interim moderator in their vacancy. I was astonished. The Presbytery Clerk was a Freemason although friendly and supportive of me. I was known in that area of being not supportive of the Freemasons. I said to the Clerk, "If they are asking me then they must be scraping the bottom of the barrel!" He assured me that they wanted me and had asked for me to be their interim moderator.

I accepted and we had a happy time together. After two short ministries and being a very large congregation I did not want them to make a mistake in the minister whom they called. I stressed the need for continued prayer throughout the vacancy and asked that we move slowly and carefully. They called the Revd Peter Bisset from Glasgow. I had first met Peter in a student mission in Motherwell many years earlier. He had been deeply influenced by Tom Allan. He and two other ministers conducted regular evangelistic rallies in St George's Tron Church in the centre of Glasgow. He had an excellent ministry in Bathgate. A year later the session clerk phoned to thank me for my guidance during their vacancy and to say how they all were much enjoying the ministry of Peter Bisset.

Wider Activities

Stornoway. In the Highlands and Western Isles of Scotland, many of the small rural communities are pastored by lay missionaries. They are trained and equipped but not to the level of the ordained ministry. Each year, the Home Mission Committee, under whom they were employed, invited those serving in the Western Isles to a week long training course. One year, along with my brother-in-law the Revd Kenneth MacKenzie (at that time teaching in St Colm's College), I was invited to give a week's lectures. Those who attended the course came from crofting and fishing backgrounds or were weavers of the famous Harris Tweed cloth. They were spiritually dedicated and godly men. Their Gaelic singing was inspiring and uplifting. It was a privilege to be with them and speak to them of the things of God. On Sunday morning I shared in a Broadcast service in Stornoway and in the evening preached in the village of Lemreway, a village some seventeen miles south west of Stornoway.

Broadcast services. Shortly after the intimation that the government had agreed to create a New Town in Livingston, I was asked by the BBC that my morning service in Livingston be broadcast. I preached from the Epistle to the Hebrews chapter 11 and verse 10, "He looked for a city which hath foundations, whose builder and maker is God". It seemed to be well received. In Aberdeen I was several times invited by Grampian Radio Station to take, for a week, a ten minute late night service of worship. In my last parish in Earlston I was again asked that my morning service be broadcast.

These services always required considerable preparation. The challenge was to keep within the time limit permitted for a service.

Conferences. I was invited to take part in wider church activities. The Church of Scotland held a conference in Perth following the pattern of the German *Kirkentag*. I was invited to attend.

I was also invited along with others to represent the C of S in two conferences in connection with 'Faith and Order', one in Nottingham and the other in Birmingham.

The World Council of Churches had appointed a commission to study Evangelism. They appointed a Swiss Pentecostal minister, Walter Hollenweger as secretary. The commission met for four years and produced a Report. That report was brought to a conference in Birmingham. I was asked with three other ministers and a lady, the wife of a minister and missionary in Africa, to represent the Church of Scotland at the conference, which had a heavy representation of Anglicans. The Church of Scotland ministers were Colin Day and Jim Maxwell, both of whom were members of the Iona Community and liberal in their theology, Colin more so than Jim. The other two were Ian Doyle and myself. Both of us were conservative in our theology, and evangelical.

Professor Davis, who held a chair of theology in Birmingham was chairman of the conference. Walter Hollenweger was a guest speaker. It was a time when strong liberal winds were blowing through the church, and Professor Davis said that the New Testament taught that Jesus was Lord of the world, not of the church. The church must not be thought of as an army in an alien world or like a ship in a stormy sea. The church must die. He did not mean die and rise to be a new church in Christ. It must simply die and allow Christ to be Lord of his world!

Delegates were all placed in small commissions to consider the Report. I was appointed to one of two theological commissions. There were 15 in our group. Our chairman began by asking each person his opinion of the opening paper. Fourteen said that they agreed with the paper. I alone differed. I felt, theologically, like a fish out of water! To me the New Testament is saying that the Church is the Body of Christ. In no way is the world the Body of Christ. I found it difficult in a theologically alien environment to articulate clearly what I believed.

On our return to Scotland the four of us who were ministers felt that, as we had been asked to represent the Church of Scotland, we should endeavour to create a similar conference in Scotland in Dunblane in order to consider the Report from the WCC. I was hoping that in Scotland there would be a more biblical response to the Report and was concerned that some biblical theologians should be invited to the conference. Colin Day was chairman of our small group and I asked that a special invitation be given to my brother James and to the Revd James Matheson who later became a Moderator of our General Assembly. We planned the conference programme and I suggested that Colin should be left to plan the service of worship on the Sunday morning, a suggestion which I later regretted. Walter Hollenweger was invited as guest speaker.

I attended the conference but returned home late on Saturday night as I wished to preach in my own pulpit the following day. Jim Matheson told me later that he got nothing out of the service of worship. My brother James phoned me after the conference rather disturbed, and feeling that in what he had said to Colin Day he had, in his words, "gone over the top!"

James told me that the service began with the singing of American folk music, not Christian music. This was followed by a reading from the book of Revelation emphasising that the tabernacle of God was with men. That was followed, according to James, by bloodthirsty excerpts from the newspapers, recording thefts, burglaries, rape and murder. The singing of more American folk music followed. There was no sermon. All were told to meditate silently. When the bell rang they went to lunch, being told that no one must speak and they must continue to meditate in silence. Lunch in silent meditation was part of their worship. After lunch when the bell again rang they were permitted to speak. James had been bursting inside. Whenever the bell rang after lunch he immediately said to Colin Day, "Do you know what you have done? You have created a situation where no one could speak but the world, the flesh and the devil and you call that worship!" To James' consternation, I roared with laughter. I said that he had hit the nail on the head. It was for that purpose that I had asked that he be given a special invitation to the conference.

Walter Hollenweger stayed in my manse in Livingston over Sunday night after the conference. The great slogan at that time, repeatedly stated by Walter and others was that "the world sets the agenda". The world must be allowed to set the agenda for every Kirk Session meeting. If we ask the people of the world what they talk about most, they would reply sex, drains, water, sewage and so forth. These must be the subject of our Kirk Session meetings. Likewise they must be the subject of our church services of worship.

Earlier that same Sunday, Walter had been invited to speak by the BBC as part of the Scottish religious programme that day. He said that in a city the size of Perth with 40,000 people there should only be one traditional service each month! The subjects for worship on the other Sundays must be set by the world. He said that it is likewise for Kirk Session meetings. The world sets the agenda. I was horrified and grieved. I did not like to take him to task when I was giving him hospitality in my manse. However before taking him to the airport I asked him about the cross. I said, "The cross was not on the world's agenda. It was on God's agenda."

Boy Scouts

In my earlier years at Livingston there was a Scout troop attached to the church. The Scout troop was led by a single man in his thirties who stayed in Seafield. I immediately asked to join with the boys on their summer camp. My first camp with them was on the shores of Loch Lubnaig at the foot of Ben Ledi, in the Highlands some miles from Callander. I shared with the boys in their various activities. On the Sunday I arranged in agreement with the captain to hold an open air service. I preached on the story of the rich young ruler in the Gospel story. In the story the young ruler found it difficult to allow love for Christ to come before love for money and possessions. I stressed the need to surrender all to Christ.

Alex Brown was a man in his early forties. He worked in an iron foundry in Bathgate. He was not a Scout but came to the Scout camp, as father of one of the Scouts, in order to assist the scoutmaster. His son Alex later became a chief superintendent of police in Edinburgh. Unknown to me at camp, the Lord spoke powerfully to him during the service, as he told me later, and he was converted. He was not a member of the church. Possibly he had not attended church before.

On the Sunday following our Scout camp, he came to church in Livingston Station. He asked the scoutmaster to accompany him and give him the courage to walk through the church door. Soon he became a loyal member of the church and attended twice a Sunday. He frequently discussed with me the sermons that I preached and became the beadle of St Andrew's church for many years. Later, he was elected to be an elder and joined the Kirk Session.

Boys Brigade

A few years later an elder asked me if he could form a company of the Boy's Brigade in Livingston. I agreed, happy to have both a Scout troop and company of the Boys Brigade attached to the church. Both captain and boys attended church regularly. The captain asked if I would lead the Boys' Bible Class each week. Again I happily agreed but soon joined it and the church Bible Class together. In the end the Boys Brigade attracted more boys than did the scouts.

I joined them in some enjoyable camps. On one occasion I remember washing and shaving above the sand dunes in Arbroath, feeling the wind from the sea, at 7.30am and talking to a boy, Alistair Macindoe, aged 14 years. I felt that God was calling him into the ministry and encouraged him to pray and seek God's guidance. On leaving school Alistair studied theology and is a minister of the Gospel. One of the other lads, Johnny Purves also went on, and after studying physics, entered the ministry.

I greatly enjoyed all my contacts with the young people. I found youth work was tiring. It involved an immense amount of time and energy and much prayer, but it was richly rewarding. We always had a good youth attendance at church, which I found encouraging.

Youth Activities

Every year from the start of my ministry in Livingston I took away the young people on a long week-end camp, first the Bible Class and then as they grew older the Youth Fellowship. This was over and above the Scout and Boys Brigade camps, which I attended. We stayed in various Youth Hostels. For the first two or three years we stayed in a hostel about three miles further up from Peebles in the Tweed Valley. At that time I asked Tom Smail, minister in West Calder, to join us with some of his young people. We bathed and swam in the river Tweed and tramped over the lovely Border hills. Thereafter we always went to various places in and around the Trossachs.

I often invited a student or friend to come as a guest to speak to us in our morning or evening worship. We tramped for long miles over the hills. The young people enjoyed it and so did I. To my knowledge we always had from the number of our young people a one hundred per cent attendance at camp. The camps greatly strengthened our Christian fellowship and helped me to know each of the young people. We had much fun together. I always required and received help with transport to and from these camps from members of the congregation.

Seaside Mission

In my last two years in Livingston, I twice conducted a seaside mission in Girvan on the Ayrshire coast along with a team from Livingston. I asked a neighbouring friend, Bill Thomson, minister of Broxburn West to assist in leadership. If I led the afternoon beach service on the sands, Bill then preached at the evening open air meeting. The following day he conducted the afternoon beach service and I preached in the open air. The young people participated in both services. Both Bill and I were then with our young people in charge of a youth service following the open air meeting. The team held organised games with the children each morning after team Bible Study and worship. In those days before people were attracted to spend their money on overseas holidays, the seaside mission services attracted large crowds. I had myself attended seaside mission services for a few days each year for many years and had frequently spoken as a guest speaker. For a long while I did not feel that we had a strong enough group to take responsibility for a mission. I took to Girvan 22 young people. The team, apart from Bill Thomson, came entirely from Livingston. Sharing actively in mission greatly strengthened the faith of the members of the team. Their parents and grandparents were most enthusiastic and each year organised a bus to travel from Livingston to Girvan to attend the afternoon service and open air meeting and see the young folk in action.

Gordon MacLean had come to work as a civil engineer with Livingston New Town Corporation. He along with Max and others had been trained by the Youth Committee of the Church to try and attract young people to church by organising dances and so forth. He had worked as a youth leader for the church in Perth. Also, before coming to Livingston he had felt that God was calling him in to the ministry. He had been advised if he did pursue the ministry to study in Glasgow where he was told that the college staff were more liberal in their theology than the staff in Edinburgh!

I had many discussions with him and told him that the only way to attract young people to church was by challenging them with the gospel. I invited him to join us in seaside mission in Girvan. He was hesitant so I asked him to come as quarter master and take charge of all the equipment that was required. He came and that completely changed him. We admitted him as an elder and he went on to study for the ministry at New College. He told me that at college he was the chief critic of the Youth Committee of the Church. He said that he had tried all their methods and that they had failed. The only way to draw young people into the church was to challenge them with the gospel.

Gordon Maclean, as a civil engineer, latterly took away the young people on church work camps. They did valuable work in a church in Strath Connan in Ross-shire. This again greatly strengthened the fellowship of the young people.

Roman Style Heating

When I first became minister of Livingston, the elders in the Old Kirk often said to me that, according to tradition, there was a tunnel from under the church to a ruined castle half a mile away. I was sceptical because no one could provide any further information about it.

One Saturday evening the beadle coming up the path from the Kirk Yard gate to the church fell into a hole. On examination, we discovered a tunnel which in length measured the breadth of the church. We informed the Ministry of Works who were able to confirm that it was part of a very old heating system patterned after the way that the Romans heated their baths. The tunnel led to an old and ruinous boiler under the present boiler house, which we had not previously known was there. At the entrance to the ruinous boiler room stood two iron doors on a central spindle. These controlled the input of cold air. A ragged stone hole, which had since been sealed, had been punched through a flagstone on the roof of the boiler room to allow the entrance of air which had been heated by the boiler into the church. The hot air blew along a stone channel along the breadth of the church. The tunnel itself was empty apart from fragments of a human skeleton. Someone in the distant past had obviously found the tunnel and a cheap burial site. I gave the bones to the grave digger for burial in another part of the Kirk Yard. The mound on which the church was built had been a place of worship for over a thousand years. The present church had been built about 250 years previously. Why such a heating system was installed is unknown and remains as a matter of interest.

I discovered one day in talking to the beadle in Old Livingston that there was no water in the village church. Consequently he regularly carried water to the church boiler from a tap located outside the Kirk yard gate. I was concerned and consulted with the Kirk Session, whereon it was agreed that the elders would all meet one evening in the Kirk Yard equipped with a spade. We were each allotted a few feet and asked to dig a trench three feet deep in order to lay a water pipe to the church. As I recall we were helped in this with the tunnel which ran up to the church under the present boiler house. We asked a plumber to fit the pipe at either end. It was a happy way to install water in the church and a happy evening.

Water Conduit

The new Livingston Corporation central offices were built opposite the Manse in the old village. Behind and to the north of the Corporation Offices was a large field. The farmer who, like his father before him, had ploughed that field many times said to me one day, that in ploughing the field, his plough had caught a large stone. On unhooking the stone he discovered a tunnel. Wanting to complete his ploughing he simply replaced the stone. He readily gave me permission to investigate the tunnel.

I invited Gordon MacLean to join in my investigation. The day in question was damp and drizzly. However we both had come with spades and wearing gum boots. I was suitably dressed in old clothes. When we had removed the stone and dug round about we discovered a tunnel with stone steps leading down at an angle of 45 degrees. The entrance to the tunnel measured about two feet by two feet. I immediately said that I was going down to investigate. Gordon said firmly that he was not! To enter the tunnel I required to lie flat down on the mud so that I could slither down, head first, about ten steps. The tunnel met at right angles another tunnel, beautifully constructed with a rounded arched stone roof. It measured about four feet by four feet. The floor of the tunnel was covered in two or three inches of water. Turning right I travelled along about 40 or 50 yards. Turning left I could only travel about 15 or 20 yards because of a fall of stone. When I emerged into the open air excited about our find, it was to be met with a shout of laughter from Gordon and the words, "You are the most disreputable-looking minister in West Lothian!" The rain and mud had not enhanced my appearance.

We again contacted the Ministry of Works. They informed us, after they had consulted old maps, that the field in which we were in was the site of the first botanical gardens of Scotland which moved to its present site in Edinburgh around (I think) 1680. In the centre of the original garden there was a large fountain and several tunnels, some almost a mile long, which conveyed water to the fountain and which were used in the watering of the gardens. Later we discovered another tunnel with a flat stone roof, further off from the other tunnel and near to the old ruined castle. Today the field is built over with streets and houses. I am unaware whether the site was specially marked before building took place.

Baillie Institute, Blackburn

I do not like arguments or controversy yet I did on occasion find myself so involved. The Baillie estates lay further west from Livingston, near East Whitburn. The Baillies were a religious family. Lady Baillie gave the community hall to the neighbouring parish of Blackburn, on the condition that no alcohol was consumed on the premises and there should be no gambling. A notice prohibiting the consumption of alcohol was inscribed on the wall. Those appointed to be trustees of the hall were the ministers of Blackburn and Livingston and the headmaster of the school in Blackburn, and their successors in office. In process of time, the three trustees, before I became one of them, found that they had no money to maintain and run the welfare hall. Blackburn was a coal mining parish so the trustees asked the Coal Board to take over the running and the maintenance of the community hall. A committee of local miners was appointed and joined the trustees in the management of the hall. A miner was chosen as chairman. The minister and headmaster in Blackburn rarely attended a meeting. I think that I only saw them once at a meeting. I felt that it was my duty to attend and I attended regularly.

One day the miners intimated that they had agreed among themselves to apply for a licence to sell alcohol in the welfare hall. I immediately pointed out that this was prohibited in terms of the trust and that therefore such an application would be illegal. They said that they were aware of that but nonetheless would still apply for a licence. I asked if they thought that the consumption of alcohol in the community would benefit the homes in Blackburn and would lead to happier families. They all agreed that it would not but still persisted in their resolve to apply for a licence. I asked to be allowed to record my dissent to which they happily agreed.

I was disturbed over the decision to apply for a licence and wondered if anything had been written in to the document of handover of managerial control to the Coal Board permitting the consumption of alcohol. I very much doubted it as such a clause permitting the consumption of alcohol could only be granted by a decision of the High Court. I went to Edinburgh to the office of the lawyers for the Baillie Estates, asking as a trustee if I could see a copy of the document of handover. I was informed that all documents had been passed to the lawyers of the National Coal Board, in Glasgow. When I visited them, told them who I was, the purpose of my visit and the nature of my request, the lawyer with whom I spoke said, "We do not wish to handle this case. It is our bread and butter!" He declined to hand over the relevant papers.

As a trustee I felt that his refusal was illegal but I had no money to pursue the matter in court and had to call a halt to my pursuit of the relevant papers. Since I held the position in virtue of my office as minister of Livingston, I could not resign as a trustee. I could however have it recorded in writing that I would no longer carry out my duties as a trustee. Accordingly at the next meeting of the committee of the welfare institute I intimated that I would cease to come to the meetings of management and would from that date no longer actively function as a trustee. I stated my reasons and asked that what I had intimated be recorded. The miners listened to what I said with some dismay. They said that they accepted my position. They urged me however to continue on in the committee. I said that I could not, because I could not be party to a breach of the deed of trust, according to which there must be no consumption of alcohol in the Baillie institute. The chairman in his endeavour to persuade me to remain said, "We accept and understand that you take the Christian position. But we want you to stay on the committee because when you are here we do not swear and are able to get on with the business. When you are not here we all swear so much that we cannot carry on with the business!" I was amused, but was not sure about the effectiveness of my witness as a minister if my presence simply meant that they did not swear and were therefore able to conduct their business!

About eighteen months later a police inspector arrived at my manse and handed me a summons to appear in court in Linlithgow for breaking the licensing laws, concerning the consumption of alcohol in the Baillie Institute in Blackburn. He told me that the court had granted the licence in the name of the three original trustees, although two I think were probably unaware of an application to the court and I had asked that my objection be recorded! There had been a large police raid on the welfare institute. According to the law concerning licences, the miners were required to form a club, to have a list of members whose names were recorded when they entered and left the club. Only members could buy alcohol. Invited guests I think could not buy alcohol. The names of invited guests require to be recorded. According to the police none of these things were done. The miners were running the welfare as a public house open to the general public.

I told the police inspector my position. He sympathised and said that he was relieved that I personally was not guilty. However he said that I was still summoned to appear in court to answer charges. I contacted my friend Peter Morrison the lawyer. He was then, or shortly would become, Procurator Fiscal for East Lothian. He told me to leave the matter with him. He said that he would write to the miners instructing them to write to the court immediately apologising that in their application for a licence they had mistakenly included the names of the three trustees in their application for a license. If not, he said that he would take them to court for knowingly misleading the court and wrongfully using my name as a trustee. The miners agreed to do so and I was not required to attend court. I was very grateful to Peter, who had helped me in my Tell Scotland days.

Theft of my Car

In 1960 the Church of Scotland held special celebrations on the 400th anniversary of the Reformation in Scotland. There was held a special meeting of the Assembly in the autumn. The Queen that year instead of sending a commissioner to represent her at the Assembly, attended the meetings in person. She was present at the autumn meeting. I took three of my congregation in my car, a black Austin A40, to attend a public meeting in the evening. I parked the car in Edinburgh behind the Usher Hall, at the foot of Castle Terrace.

When I returned there was no car. The car had been stolen and I told the three church members that they would require to return home by bus. I informed the police and my insurance company, General Accident, which at the time was the largest car insurance company in the country. Their headquarters were in Perth. The insurance clerk in Edinburgh told me that they would compensate me on a Tuesday, 28 days after the date when the car was stolen, provided of course that the car was not recovered before then.

My wife found the car on the Thursday prior to when we were due to be compensated by the Insurance Company. The car had been driven by a man from Renfrew. He travelled to Edinburgh for the day. My wife recognised the car by the positioning on the front bumper of a fog lamp, which she had given to me as a present, despite the fact that the number plates had been changed. Her judgement that the car was ours was confirmed by a small, very thin line of grey paint which had been left by another grey car which had scraped it.

The driver meantime had entered some business premises. He was disturbed to discover on his return police and a strange woman standing by his car, and to be told that the car which he had bought and was driving had been stolen. He was innocent, having bought the car from a large car dealer who in turn had bought it in a car auction sale in Glasgow. This we learned later. The police impounded the car, pending a court case which would only take place after they discovered who had stolen it. When I informed the insurance clerk, he laughed and said I would receive no financial compensation. He also cheerfully said that the last stolen car had taken two years to clear the court.

I was not at all happy. The police had asked me the date and place where I had purchased the car. They also asked the name of the garage. They had phoned Birmingham where the car had been manufactured. They told me that the manufacturers placed a secret number on a concealed part of the engine of every car they manufactured. They had asked for the number and where in the engine to look. They said the number proved that the car was mine. Nonetheless they said they would not release the car until they knew everything about what had happened to it. They also said that the finding of it had opened up a new line of investigation and more and more stolen cars were emerging. They said that they would not go to court until their investigations were complete and until then the car was impounded.

My heart sank. I contacted my insurance company again. I said that because my car had been impounded by the police I had for all normal purposes lost my car. I drew the parallel of a ship stuck on the rocks. There may be no damage incurred by the ship. All the world knew it was there. It was not in that sense lost but, until refloated, it was lost to the owners of the firm who owned the ship. It was normal for an insurance company to compensate the firm. I said that there was no difference between a ship stuck on the rocks and my car which, although its whereabouts were known, was impounded by the police and lost to me. Therefore my insurance company should compensate me. They refused.

I contacted the Procurator Fiscal for Edinburgh and asked him if I could borrow the car on condition that I returned the car when required by the court. He was very pleasant. He said that he had the power to lend the car to me as I requested provided that it was exactly the same as it was before being stolen. He said that he had read the police reports and knew all about the case. He knew that everything pointed in my direction and that I was the owner of the car. However because the number plates had been changed and the car was not the same as it was before being stolen, he was not able to loan me the car. He said that, at present, the car was the official property of the court. He then advised me to persuade my insurance company to compensate me on the ground that in Scots law the court would take into consideration the fact that the man from Renfrewshire was innocent and had paid £650 for the car. Yet because his insurance was covering stolen property he would not be compensated and had lost everything. He told me therefore that the court would release the car to me on condition that I paid the man from Renfrewshire half the amount that he had paid for the car, namely £325! It was in my interest therefore to receive full compensation from my insurance company. I thanked the Procurator Fiscal for his advice, perturbed at the thought of being required to buy back my own car!

Once again I contacted my insurance company at its office in Edinburgh. On the morning that I had decided to make the contact, I received two different letters in two different envelopes, one stating that because I had an outstanding insurance claim I had lost all my bonuses. The other stated that they would not compensate me for the car. On entering the insurance office I asked to speak with the manager. He was a very pleasant man but in my judgement made a mistake in coming to the front office and not meeting me privately. There were some seven or eight tables in the room with lady secretaries behind each type writer. All stopped to listen to the conversation between their manager and myself. The manager asked, "What can I do for you?" I looked at him and placed before him the two letters which I had received that morning. I said, "I am told in the one letter that I have lost all my bonuses because I have an outstanding claim. According to the other letter I am told that your company will not compensate me. I received them on the same day, this morning. I know that you will say that one letter was written from one department and the other from another department. It is not good publicity if there is no co-ordination between the departments of your office."

The manager said, "Are you trying to tell me how to run the office?" I smiled and said, "Yes! I guess I am. It helps the reputation of the firm if the different departments co-operate and co-ordinate their work." There was complete silence in the room. I felt sorry for the manager. I had confronted him in front of a number of his staff. He said, "What are you asking?" I said that I wished to be compensated for the loss of my car. I told him that I had spoken to the Procurator Fiscal who said that at present in law the car was not mine but the property of the court. The insurance company were wrong therefore to say that my car had been found. It would become my car only when and if the court decided that it was mine and I could have it. I had lost my car. The 28 days prior to my being compensated for loss had passed. I wanted to be compensated. The manager agreed and said that he would put the offer of compensation in the post but that I would not be satisfied with the amount of compensation that would be offered. I said that it was up to him to ensure that I was satisfied.

On returning home I received a telephone call from the manager. He was extremely apologetic. Although he had promised that I would be compensated, he had spoken to his boss in Perth. His boss had told him not to compensate me but to hand everything over to the law department. If he had simply said that I would not be compensated I would have accepted that. The fact that he said, "Hand everything over to the law department" aroused me and made me determined to press my claim for compensation. I felt that they were trying to browbeat me and I was determined not to be browbeaten. I read and re-read my insurance policy. I read all the small print. All that was said was that I would be compensated if I lost my car and made no mention of how the loss occurred. I had lost my car!

I consulted a ministerial friend who had formerly been an insurance manager. He gave me helpful advice. I wrote a short letter to the boss in Perth. In it I said that at the next meeting of the Presbytery of Bathgate which was on Tuesday in three days' time, I would intimate that I had lost my car through theft and that the General Accident Insurance Company had broken the spirit of the contract with me in refusing to compensate me for my loss. I intimated in my letter that I was sending a copy to my insurance broker in Bathgate who had sold to me their insurance policy, to the General Trustees of the Church of Scotland, to the Session clerk of Livingston, to the clerk of the Congregational Board in Livingston and to the Clerk of Bathgate Presbytery.

I had previously phoned a lawyer and secretary of the Trustees of the C of S saying that I wished to send them a copy of a letter. I said that the issue raised in the letter was not a matter of concern for the Trustees. I simply wished it to be noted by the insurance company that I was sending a copy of my letter to them. I said that my desire in sending them a copy of the letter was that it gave me a bigger drum to beat in the situation where I felt that the insurance company was treating me as 'small fry'! The lawyer laughed and said, "Send the letter and if I can help you I will".

By return of post on the Monday morning I received a letter from the boss in Perth stating that the insurance company would compensate me immediately on a total loss basis. I also received two phone calls to make sure that I really understood that I would be compensated. It would have been extremely difficult for the insurance company to argue against my complaint that they had broken the spirit of the contract. I understood that in the spirit of the contract, I would be compensated in losing my car, no matter how I lost it. They were clearly alarmed at the possibility of the case being made public and the damage to their reputation.

Now I no longer required to travel to Edinburgh seeking compensation. An insurance representative came to the manse. He offered me 560 pounds, the sum that the man in Renfrewshire had paid for the car. Actually he had paid the price for the car as if it had been manufactured in the current year because it was carrying the current year number plates. The car was actually into its second year. However the insurance company was happy with the amount offered. I accepted their offer and asked that the offer be made in writing, plus a cheque. I was anxious to buy another car. This was promised and I received a letter confirming the amount offered but no cheque.

The letter enabled me to purchase another car, this time a Morris 1,000. After about ten days, not wanting the garage from whom I purchased the car to be out of pocket on my behalf, I asked the insurance company for a cheque. After about another ten days I again made my request for a cheque. This time the spokesman for insurance said, "Oh! Have you not received it? I will send it on". After another similar period when I complained that I had not yet received the cheque, I was told, "We did not know to whom to send the cheque!!" I had informed them that the congregation had purchased the car and given it to me. I replied, "After all our many contacts, do you really not know who owns the car? You should send the cheque to me." I told my wife that I did not think that I would receive the cheque until the end of the year because they would like to collect the interest on it. Before Christmas I received the cheque dated the 31st December. Such is the business world!

My ministerial friend and former insurance manager warned me and said that if I ever had another claim, my claim would pass through the firm like a hot potato. The firm would wish to deal with it as soon as possible. About five years later when I was parked at the side of the road chatting with a boy in my Youth Fellowship, the local butcher crossed the street in reverse and hit my car in the rear. The driver apologised and said that clearly he was to blame for the accident. I took him into the manse to comfort him for damaging my car! I telephoned my insurance company and told them what happened. I was told that everything would be paid for by the insurance firm covering the butcher. I remarked that I had only once ever had an insurance claim. The man whom I was speaking with said, "Yes, I know. Your car was stolen!" He told me the make and number of the car, the date in which the car was stolen and the date of compensation. I put down the phone feeling very small and wondering if my name and particulars had been placed on the office wall!

Very shortly after that, a nephew who is a civil engineer and was working in a large engineering firm in Edinburgh said that a lawyer had come into their office that day. The lawyer had said that there had been a change in insurance law. It was necessitated because a Church of Scotland minister's car had been stolen. He mentioned the particulars of the case and said that never before had a person in my circumstances been compensated. My nephew said, "I know that Church of Scotland minister!" I was surprised. I felt that it was only just that I should be compensated as I was.

Court of Enquiry concerning a Licence Application

Shortly after the case concerning my car, I read in the local newspaper an application for an alcohol licence for the projected New Town area of Craigshill. Craigshill at that time was a rural area and not one single new house had been built. I objected to the application. Some time later I received a phone call saying that mine was the only objection, so would I like to withdraw my objection?

I refused, so was told that according to law there had to be a court of enquiry. I was told that the court, by law, had to meet in a suitable place that was nearest to Craigshill. My church hall in Old Livingston was the nearest place, could the court use my church hall? Given the circumstances, I was amused at the request but agreed to it. The chairman of the court, a sheriff, came with the clerk of court. They put two tables together and covered them with a black cloth. The sheriff put on his wig and gown. He sat with the clerk at the top of the table. I sat at one side of the table with a minister whom I had invited for support, but who did not speak in the court. Opposite to me sat four lawyers, headed as I understand by a QC. They were employed by the brewery firm which had applied for the licence. Some twenty or more architects and planners who worked for the New Town Development Corporation sat in the audience. They were involved in the building plans for Craigshill.

After the sheriff had stated the purpose of the enquiry, quoted the application for an alcohol licence and my objection, he invited the QC to speak. He spoke for two hours. I timed him! In those two hours I learned more than I had ever known about the law and alcohol licences. I learned about the projected licensing plans for Craigshill, and that the application for a licence covered a hotel, licensed grocer shops and at least one pub. None of that I knew before. More importantly I discovered from the QC's speech that in 1959 there had been a 'New Towns' Licensing Act'. That

I had not previously known. Just as after the war the government had passed a 'New Towns' Act' authorising the creation and building of New Towns, so in 1959 the government had passed a 'New Towns' Licensing Act', so that there might be a careful planning of licensed premises in a New Town.

After the QC was finished, I was invited to speak. I said that an application for a licence had been made for Craigshill, when no new house had been built and the people who later moved in would be unable to say whether they wished or not to a have a licensed premise in their midst. This was a denial of the rights and freedom of the future inhabitants of Craigshill. I was here to defend the rights and freedom of the people of Scotland. At once I was challenged and accused of wishing to set aside and ignore the New Town's Licensing Act. The lawyers asked that my objection be immediately dismissed. The sheriff asked whether I had read the Act. I confessed that I had not, whereon he asked the clerk to show me a copy of the Act. The proceedings of the court were adjourned for approximately ten minutes until I had read the Act and briefly thought about it.

The sheriff asked me where in the Act was it stated that people had the freedom to object to an application for a licence made in terms of the Act. I acknowledged that it was not mentioned. Once again the lawyers said, and said vigorously, that my objection should be dismissed. I replied that silence in law does not authorise a particular action. The fact that there was no mention in the Act about the people having the right to object, meant that the New Towns Act was by its silence endorsing all previous Acts whereby people had the right to state their wishes.

The lawyers then said that my real purpose in attending the Court of Enquiry was that I was a minister and objected to all licences being granted. I astonished and momentarily silenced them when I replied and said that such was my concern for the freedom of the future inhabitants of Craigshill that if they wanted to have a licensed premise near to them I felt that their wishes must be granted. They must however have the freedom to say 'Yes' or 'No' to the granting of a licence. I was seeking to defend the rights and freedom of the people of Scotland.

The lawyers repeatedly interrupted me when I spoke. I felt all through the debate that they tried to twist what I tried to say and accuse me of believing and saying what was false. They kept clamouring for the sheriff to dismiss my objection. I did not find it easy to speak but stood my ground. After a long and vigorous debate the sheriff drew the proceedings to an end. He said that as a Court of Enquiry they were required to lay the whole proceedings of the Court before the Secretary of State for Scotland.

His was the final decision. He looked at me and said that he did not think that my objection would be upheld. I replied in closing that if this court implied that the Secretary of State was simply a rubber stamp who had to approve of every application that was laid before him, I do not think that he would feel complimented.

After people had moved in to Craigshill and the population had reached almost 10,000, the application for a licence on behalf of the Brewers was again submitted. The minister of Craigshill and his team of colleagues were happy with the application and it was granted. After the next area of the New Town was populated the minister of that area with, I think, the support of their MP objected and the application was refused. I had won my case, by the grace of God. I did not realise it at that time, but the application for a licence for Craigshill was the first to be made after the passing of the 'New Towns Licensing Act'. It was therefore a test case. If I had not objected and won the case, the ball would have been placed at the feet of the brewers and those who wished to increase the consumption of alcohol in Scotland. It was by God's grace that I, knowing little about the subject and with no previous experience, won that case.

Central African Federation

Fairly early in my ministry in Livingston, the British Government planned to bring together in federation (or confederation) the three African countries of Southern Rhodesia (Zimbabwe), Northern Rhodesia (Zambia) and Livingstonia (Malawi). The government's plan was to create a new Dominion in central Africa. Materially there was much to commend the plan. Northern Rhodesia had considerable mineral wealth. The copper industry at that time was booming. Southern Rhodesia with its white farmers was the bread-basket of Central Africa. Livingstonia was a poor country but the creation of a Dominion comprising the three countries would provide much needed employment. The difficulty was that the African Churches and the African populations of all three countries opposed it. The government of the proposed new dominion would be white. Africans wanted their independence and rule by Africans. The Africans were afraid that a Dominion would follow the example of South African in the policy of Apartheid.

We had many missionaries serving in both Livingstonia (which was largely Presbyterian) and also in Northern Rhodesia. The Foreign Mission Committee sent representation to London to meet the Foreign Office, stating the opposition of Africans to the Government plan. The Government would not listen to the voice of the Church and the representative of the Foreign Mission Committee was snubbed. My brother-in-law Kenneth MacKenzie and his wife (my sister Margaret) were missionaries in central Africa, first in Malawi and then in Northern Rhodesia. They were again on furlough and staying with me in the Manse in Livingston. Kenneth was actively trying to waken the Church of Scotland to the situation in Central Africa. He was the driving force in seeking to persuade the Church of Scotland to oppose the government plan. I gladly gave him all the assistance I could.

We approached not only my own Presbytery of Bathgate but a large number of Presbyteries. Many in the Church were concerned with justice, stimulated in their thinking by George MacLeod and the Iona Community. Kenneth and I between us contacted as many ministers as possible who we thought would be sympathetic, asking them to raise the issue in their Presbytery. The issue came to the General Assembly and was vigorously debated. Quite a number of elders at that time had served abroad, some in Africa, as District Commissioners. The General Assembly disapproved of the government plan to unite the three African countries and agreed that we should petition our Government stating the Church's objection. Meanwhile Kenneth and I between us arranged that a letter of objection to the government's plan be sent to every MP and to every peer in the House of Lords.

The Government gave in. They rejected the plan, quoting the objection by the Church of Scotland, and gave the three countries their independence. The whites of Southern Rhodesia thereon seized power under the leadership of Ian Smith and declared their independence from Britain. Armed African resistance arose under the leadership of Robert Mugabe and Joshua Nkomo. When the white government resigned Robert Mugabe became leader and prime minister. He has continued until the present day.

Theological Reading and Study

Although prior to my working with Tell Scotland I had done considerable work toward a doctoral thesis and submitted an outline of 40 pages of my projected thesis, I never returned to complete it. When working in Tell Scotland and then in a parish I never felt that I had the time to devote to it. In Livingston my theological reading became largely, but not entirely, reduced to the reading of theological commentaries to help in my preaching and pastoral work. In this I was stimulated by my studies under Karl Barth. I did however manage one or two theological articles. In Presbytery I became involved in the question of the remarriage of divorced persons and became much involved in two successive meetings of the General Assembly on the Christian understanding of the Sabbath and published an article on the subject in the British Weekly.

It was at this time that I worked on a new translation of Calvin's commentaries on the New Testament, as described in chapter 4. I enjoyed this, though it was demanding. I generally found myself at the end of a day in the parish working from 10.00 pm to one o'clock in the morning. It took a few years and the work was not finally finished until I was in Aberdeen.

Marriage

For my first two years in Livingston I was unmarried. For about eighteen months my sister Margaret, followed shortly after by her husband (Kenneth MacKenzie), stayed with me which was a great joy. They had been missionaries in central Africa but sadly due to Margaret's health it had been necessary for them to return to Scotland. A nephew, David Wallace stayed with me for a short time. After that, I was alone. A very fine member of the church, Mrs Henderson, came in I think twice a week to clean and tidy the Manse.

I never felt lonely while I was working. On a Monday morning, after a full and busy Sunday, when I was tired, then I did feel lonely. I had long wanted to meet the right person and to be married. In my student days I had been friendly with a couple of girls whom I had met through the Christian Union. Both were very committed Christians. I had been engaged for a short period to the second of the two girls. Despite their Christian commitment, God was clearly saying 'no' to my being married to either. The one to whom I had been engaged later married a ministerial friend. I prayed much about it. I did not want to make a mistake and marry the wrong person. I prayed that God would choose the right one and would give me the patience to wait. I did not always find it easy to wait.

In my final year at New College, while walking on my way to a book shop which sold theological books, I prayed and asked God that he would cause me to meet the right person of his choice that same day and as soon as I entered the bookshop! On entering I paused to look at a book on English literature before going on to the rear of the shop where they kept their theological books. As soon as I had paused to look at the book on English literature, I heard my name spoken. I turned and saw a girl in whose conversion I had been instrumental. She had become a very committed Christian and went on to serve the church for many years. When I saw her I wanted to laugh. I knew that God had answered my prayer but knew that I could not possibly marry this person. After greeting her, I hastened out of the shop. I knew that God had heard and answered my prayer. I also knew that because he caused me to meet that particular person he had put me squarely in my place and was saying, "I heard you, but that was not the right way to pray to God. Just be patient. I will answer your prayer at the right time, in my time". Despite the fact that I felt that God had rightly put me in my place, I felt that God and I had a lot of fun together that day. I laughed all the way along the road.

My prayer for a marriage partner was answered four years later. The consultant in the eye department in Bangour General Hospital was a Christian, Tom Alistair Stewart Boyd, known to his friends as TAS Boyd. I had known of him in my student days although he was four or five years older than me. He had studied in Glasgow. As minister of Livingston I had come to know him. He had visited me at the manse. He was responsible for two eye wards in the hospital and whenever I had a patient in one of his wards I generally went into his staff room for a chat. One day I knocked and entered the staff room. TAS was out, but a lady doctor, Elizabeth Barton, was there, who immediately said, "I know you". We had met in 1942 when we first went up to university. We were the same age. We had met through the Christian Union but did not know each other well. I had joined the army, so Elizabeth graduated a long way ahead of me in 1947. We exchanged news as to what the other had being doing since last we had met. Elizabeth, after specialising in obstetrics and midwifery had served as a missionary doctor, first in Damascus and then Nazareth and for the last five years in Bechuanaland (Botswana) in a hospital in Molepolole. Unable to stick to her own field of specialisation she was involved in a lot of general surgery. The hospital had to deal with many eye operations and she therefore wished to gain a further qualification in ophthalmology. She planned to return to Africa but had extended her furlough in order to gain a further qualification in the treatment of eyes. We were glad to meet and chat.

When I continued my hospital visitation I thought no more about our conversation. The following morning being Saturday, I knelt in prayer in my study seeking God's inspiration and help in the preparation of a sermon. I found that I could not pray properly. Every time that I tried to pray, I kept seeing Elizabeth's face. I asked God to remove this face so that I could concentrate on my sermon and discover what God wished to say. I felt very strongly that it was not God's will to remove her face. Accordingly I arose and phoned the hospital and asked the operator for Dr Boyd's office. As a coward, although I liked TAS very much, I did not want to speak to him that day and did not want him to know who was speaking. I tried to disguise my voice and asked if I could speak to

Dr Barton. Happily he did not ask who was speaking but simply passed the phone to Elizabeth. Our conversation was brief. I asked if we could meet on Monday evening after she had finished work. I suggested that we meet, not at the doctors' residence where she was staying, but at a place outside the hospital which was private. Having invited her to meet me, my mind was remarkably clear and I was able to concentrate on the preparation of the sermon.

I had agreed to meet Elizabeth at the top of a farm road leading to the hospital. When I turned my car to drive up the farm road, a bus stopped and a considerable number of women from my parish alighted from the bus. They had come to clean the hospital wards. They were walking up the short-cut to the hospital. I was long accustomed to give people from my parish a lift in my car. On this occasion I didn't. I rushed up the road. When I saw Elizabeth, who was already there, I leaned over to the passenger side of the car, opened the door and said, "Get in quick!" I then rushed off down another road. Elizabeth for years often teased me about our first evening together and the way that I first greeted her. As a bachelor minister I was shy of the people in my parish seeing me date a girl or young woman. As it happened they knew nothing of our clandestine meetings until I announced our engagement to be married.

It was clear that God had brought us together. We became engaged to be married that summer and were married at the end of that year on Hogmanay, 31st December. Elizabeth's mother thought that we should wait until the spring or early summer before being married. I was tired of being alone and chose Hogmanay as the date. There is a tremendous rush of work in a parish in the weeks leading up to and including Christmas. There is a lull after Christmas and over the New Year until work picks up again in January.

We were married in an Anglican Church in Bristol by Elizabeth's mother's minister. We honeymooned, to the laughter of my Kirk Session when they heard, in the Scilly Isles off Cornwall.

Our start to married life was quite eventful. The office-bearers kindly agreed that the kitchen floor, which was concrete, should be covered with a strong thick linoleum tile which was fixed to the floor by a kind of pitch, which required heating. It was arranged that the work should be done when the manse was empty and before I and Elizabeth returned. By way of preparation I removed the kitchen furniture and stacked it in the front hall way. I asked Mrs Henderson, my home help and her husband kindly to replace it after the work on the kitchen floor was completed. When Elizabeth and I arrived early in the evening, I gallantly picked up Elizabeth, and began to carry her up the steps to the manse.

When I opened the door, everything was dark and we fell over the kitchen furniture. The men belonging to the firm who did the work had completed their task but with their heavy machinery had blown the main electric fuse. There was no light in the manse. Because of the situation the furniture was still stacked in the entrance hall. I had hastily to rush out to the village shop and purchase candles. With the light of a fire which I lit in our sitting room and with the light of candles I greeted the church treasurer and elder who came to welcome us home. He and his wife had very kindly purchased a box of groceries, which was very welcome.

I had prior to our marriage accepted an invitation to speak to a meeting of the Woman's Guild in North Berwick. That meeting was the day after our return from honeymoon. I had put my car into a garage for servicing so Elizabeth and I travelled to North Berwick by bus. To our dismay we discovered that there was no return bus to Edinburgh that night. The minister and his wife, Dr Stanley and Margaret Heavenor, kindly gave us hospitality in their manse and we returned to Livingston the next day. It had been a very cold night. Everything was covered with a white frost which did not lift all day. On our return we found that both cold and hot water systems were frozen.

I was well accustomed to the cold water pipes freezing at the back of the manse. Before entering the kitchen, the main water pipe passed, without being lagged, above the back door to a toilet in the rear of the house and that was below the level of the adjacent kirk yard. Each winter the pipe froze two or three times. I was accustomed to the situation. Previously I had always started at the tap to the cistern above the toilet and worked my way up the pipe with a blow torch. No doubt because I had just been married, I started down the pipe and worked my way, unfreezing the water down the pipe towards the cistern. The inevitable happened. Suddenly there was a gush of water. The tap was still frozen and I had to finish the job standing under a fountain of water, until I released the tap and the water was turned off. The floor was composed of solid stone slabs, so no harm was done except that I had to mop up the water and I was thoroughly soaked.

Dealing with frozen hot water pipes is always trickier. I had to proceed cautiously. However I managed it only to hear the sound of flowing water outside. There was a tap outside on the wall which under normal circumstances was used to turn the water off. Why such a tap was ever placed outside and not inside the house always amazed me. Such is the thinking and planning of some planners or plumbers! I discovered that the tap had burst with the frost and could not be used to turn the water off, which was flowing into the garden. I rushed into the house to get a hammer in order to hammer the pipe. As I started I heard a cheerful voice saying, "Are you in trouble?" The man from the garage had arrived returning my car. He kindly helped me to hammer the pipe to stop the flow of water. After that Elizabeth and I just had time to drive down to the community hall in Livingston Station to a welcome home reception by the congregation.

They were very kind and gave us a wedding present of a refrigerator, which we had chosen. We did not mention our troubles in the manse. The next day I called a plumber asking that he install a new tap, this time inside the house, and went off to visit patients in Bangour hospital. Elizabeth met me at the door of the manse on my return. She said, "Come in here into the dining room lounge. Don't go in there", pointing to the sitting room opposite where the door was shut.

She told me the news. The workmen had called with a new water tap. They said that they would require to turn all the water off temporarily. The manse was a very old house with a stone spiral staircase which I had carpeted. A small bedroom with an adjoining dressing room had been turned into a bathroom. The former dressing room housed the hot and cold water cisterns. In there, were the taps to turn off both water systems. My wife showed the workmen where the taps were and where I recommended that the new tap be placed in the kitchen. She left the men to do the work after asking that they leave some water in the bath, in case it was needed before their job was done. She spent the afternoon writing thank-you letters to friends who had been kind and generous in their wedding gifts. The men put their heads round the door announcing that the job was finished. They had turned the water back on and were going.

My wife continued writing until she heard a strange noise. Coming out of the dining room she saw water pouring down the stairs. She rushed upstairs, padded through two inches of water, saw the bathroom flooded and the bath overflowing. She immediately turned off the taps of the bath which had been left on. How plumbers could leave the bathroom, having turned on the two taps, and walk out leaving the taps full on is to me a mystery. I would have thought that even if they had not noticed the taps still on, the sound of flowing water should have drawn their attention.

I entered the sitting room door to see water flowing down the chandelier. Afraid that the ceiling would collapse, I hastily loosened the chandelier with a screw driver to ease the flow of water. I placed a large aluminium bath to catch the water. The water filled the bath twice and six buckets. Mercifully the ceiling did not collapse. A few years before the ceiling did fall down and had mercifully been replaced by hard board. The carpet, a Persian one with a thick pile was thoroughly soaked as were the upper landing and stair carpet. Each day for a week my wife and I carried the Persian carpet out to the drying green in the garden to dry. We shut the door of the sitting room and I told Mrs Henderson not to trouble to clean or dust in there because at present we were not using the room. We did not tell her about all our troubles.

The elders on a Sunday often entered the garden, walked in front of the manse, walked past the drying green up steps into the church yard. I did not want them to see the disaster within, so I closed the curtains of the sitting room windows that faced the drying green. I thought that if the elders and congregation knew all the disasters that had befallen us they might think that their minister having got married had lost the place and could not cope! Marriage had unbalanced him!

At the congregational farewell meeting prior to our departure to Aberdeen I told the congregation the whole story of our adventurous start to married life and the many mishaps which we experienced. I also told them why I did not have the courage at the time to tell them. They laughed and were much amused.

Elizabeth was a wonderful gift of God to me. She was a loving companion, an immense support to me in my ministry. She took a quiet but active role in the work of all three congregations. The congregations and particularly the women in all three of my parishes welcomed her and loved her. I loved her and often told her that I loved her. I will always thank God for her and for God giving me the patience to wait until he provided the right wife.

Our three children, Grace, David and Ruth were born in the Western General Hospital in Edinburgh. My brother Tom baptised Grace and David and my brother James baptised Ruth. Grace and David commenced schooling in the Primary School in Livingston Station.

Bee Keeping

From the start of my ministry I continued to keep bees. However, after our marriage, Elizabeth and I attended a ten week course in bee keeping at Bush House, which belonged to the Agricultural College in Edinburgh. They had two apiaries of 80 and 60 hives respectively and a wonderful research station. I learned a great deal and became more scientific in the keeping of bees. The college prided itself in having a strain of bees which they had bred over a period of 30 years. Although the college was not permitted to sell bees I was able to buy a strong nucleus of the same strain from Dr McHardie, one of the scientists working at the college. As a result I united my colonies and then united them with the newly purchased nucleus by placing the nucleus on the top. Thus I now had a first class queen from which to breed. I built up my stock to four and sometimes six hives.

I encouraged my brother-in-law Dr Bobby Walker, minister of Lesmahagow, to endeavour to do likewise. In anticipation he brought over a hive to my garden in Livingston. About the second week in October, he called to say that he had been able to receive a queen bee that was being replaced by the College. It was in the middle of the afternoon. He said that he had little time because he had a meeting in the evening in Lesmahagow, and asked if I would give him a hand to replace the queen in his hive. He left about 5 o'clock or a little later.

We had been told at college that a colony of bees should be wintered with a supply of between 48 and 52 pounds of honey. Although my bees were now happily established I had not checked their winter storage of honey. I was due to speak to the Woman's Guild in church for the opening of their winter session and annual dedication. The service was due at 7.30pm. I had prepared my address but had not yet chosen the hymns. I always felt that the Lord's work came first and before any other activity or hobby.

I was keen however to settle my bees for the winter. I did not have much time. I rushed over to my hive and took off the lid. My smoker unfortunately went out. Conscious of lack of time I foolishly did not wish to spend time relighting it. I lifted all 22 frames of bees to assess the amount of honey which the bees had. The weather was cold. It was the wrong time of day to look at the bees apart from being the second week in October and the smoker was out! Consequently I received I think some 30 or 40 stings, chiefly around my ankles. Each time a bee stung what hurt me most was my conscience! Every time they stung I felt that I was wrong to put a hobby before the Lord's work. I should be preparing for the service in church.

The bees were in good order and had sufficient honey for the winter. I finished at 7 o'clock. I had no time to remove any of the bee stings. I rushed into the manse, changed my clothes, hastily chose hymns, collected my sermon and started the service in church in time. All seemed to go well but towards the end of the sermon I felt light headed so skipped the last hymn and closed the service with prayer. After shaking hands with the ladies I returned to the manse. When I looked in the mirror it was clear from my face that I had a rash resulting from a general reaction to the bee stings. I lay down and half an hour later felt fine. I was fine the next day. I seemed to have little swelling from the stings and the rash was gone.

Although I seemed to be none the worse because of all the stings, the fact that I had taken a general reaction to them worried me. There were three doctors in the medical practice in Mid Calder, so I consulted them. The first, an older man, whom perhaps wrongly, I tended to feel was a pessimist, said that because I had experienced a general reaction to the stings I would always do so in the future and hence should consider giving up bee keeping. I consulted the second doctor, who said that it was fifty fifty that I would experience another general reaction. Still not happy and unhappy about the thought of giving up bees, I consulted the third doctor. He was younger and himself kept bees. He was much more reassuring. He said that I had simply incurred a lot of stings at one time and should continue to keep bees which I continued to do.

I consulted my brother-in-law who had been a doctor prior to his entering the ministry. He researched the issue and told me that to be immunised against future stings I would require 27 injections! I felt that I might as well simply receive another 27 bee stings and took no further action. The next season however I was very careful to wear the necessary protective clothing against bee stings and attended to the bees in the middle of the day when it was warm.

However, on the day before taking the bees to the heather, along with two friends and their bees, I came home at approximately 10.00pm. I had been re-queening my three hives, which meant that the young queen that I was keeping was at the top of each hive. I rushed down, stripped the hives, replaced the young queens in the bottom brood chamber, locked up and tied each hive for the removal to the heather the next day. In my haste and not troubling adequately to protect myself against stings I received a line of stings right across my tummy. When I changed and scraped off the stings, there was no general reaction and no local swelling. I was relieved and encouraged to think that I had, after all the stings which I had received, developed a measure of immunity. Nonetheless I always after that tended to take an anti-histamine pill the day before handling the bees.

On reflection I have often wondered what part my spiritual and psychological frame of mind at the time contributed to, or gave rise to, my general reaction to the stings. I received an unusual number of stings and yet, as I have said, my conscience stabbed me with every sting and hurt more than the stings!

Transition to Another Parish

Early in 1969 I received a letter from the National Church Extension Committee asking me if I would go to Summerhill Parish, in Aberdeen. Summerhill Church was a Church Extension charge and as such the minister is selected and chosen by the National Committee and not by the congregation, although the congregation was free to reject the Committee's choice. I refused several times. I said that I did not wish to leave Livingston. The Committee continued to press me to consider the situation. Finally we felt that God was calling us to go to Aberdeen and I agreed.

I was desperately sad to leave Livingston. The induction of a minister to a charge seems to take place quite simply. Yet something profound happens. To me to leave a parish to which I was called as a minister was like leaving a marriage partner. To me it was as if I was being divorced. I never found it easy to leave a parish. As I said previously, I wept many times over leaving Livingston. Several elders and members of the congregation also wept when I intimated that I had been called to go to Aberdeen. I found it heart breaking to leave the young people whom I had come to know so well. I loved the congregation and felt that they had come to trust and love Elizabeth and me. On occasion when I had blundered and stepped on someone's toes, I never hesitated to apologise and say I am sorry. They always forgave me and were kind to Elizabeth and me, and always welcoming.

When I first went to Livingston a missionary who had earlier married a teacher from there said that as minister in Livingston I was "in a hole". My dentist in Edinburgh, when he learned that I had gone to Livingston, said that I had gone to a backwater. Other well-meaning friends were surprised and hinted that they thought the same as my dentist. I foolishly thought that the people of the parish, most of whose men were miners, would never be able to attain to higher education. How completely wrong I was! I believe that the Gospel transformed the lives of many and enabled them to exercise gifts they and I never realised that they had. I had been a minister in Livingston for thirteen and a half years.

Apart from Gordon Mclean who had felt the call to ministry, before coming as a civil engineer to work with Livingston New Town Corporation, eight young people from Livingston entered the ministry. Others have since entered the ministry. Three went to the mission-field. Five completed a three-year diploma course in Theology at New College, meeting on Tuesday and Thursday evenings, while others attended part of the course. Two of that number became readers within the Presbytery and later became members of the Kirk Session. Others went on to higher education and entered one of the professions.

We left for Aberdeen deeply thankful to God for his grace and love over-ruling my inadequacy and mistakes as a minister and graciously extending his Kingdom in the way that he did.

Chapter 9

Aberdeen Summerhill: 1969-1977

I did not wish to leave Livingston and the Aberdeen parish of Summerhill did not attract me. Summerhill was a Church Extension Charge serving a new community of approximately 9,000 people. The National Church Extension Committee of the Church of Scotland kept a book recording details of all the Church Extension Charges built since the Second World War. When I was first asked by the Committee to consider moving to Summerhill, I asked to see their book about new charges. What I read disturbed me. A church's finances give an indication of the spiritual life of the church. Summerhill Church with 800 members gave annually £800. Each Church Extension Church was required to repay the National Committee one fifth of the cost of the building up to £20,000. Summerhill's debt to the National Committee was smaller than the other Church Extension Charges in Aberdeen because it had received a special grant toward its building. As a result it owed only £7,000. Yet, its repayments to the National Committee appeared to be static. It was the poorest giving parish in the Presbytery of Aberdeen, while Aberdeen Presbytery was the poorest giving Presbytery in Scotland! It was not encouraging. It was only after considerable pressure from the National Committee urging me to accept the challenge that I finally agreed, believing that God was calling me to what was obviously a difficult situation.

As the nominee of the National Church Extension Committee I preached before the congregation. They had rejected the previous nominee. They agreed to my appointment and I was inducted by the Presbytery of Aberdeen.

The congregation had first been formed about eight years earlier under the ministry of Mr Duff. He and his family had worked very hard and done much for the congregation, administratively, pastorally and financially and their departure was deeply felt. To them is the credit of creating a new congregation and church. Nonetheless the church had many problems.

When I commenced and enquired about the parish I was informed that during the vacancy five members of the Woman's Guild had been picked up for shop lifting and the Clerk to the Congregational Board had been arrested for indecency. I was also informed of certain quarrels that had taken place among office bearers and warned about the dominance of the Boys Brigade. There were two large Sunday Schools of some 200 children each, namely Summerhill and Hazelhead. (Hazelhead was a large district within the parish). Ian Hogg, the superintendent of the Summerhill Sunday School, asked me right away to sack Robert Munro, the captain of the Boys Brigade. This I declined to do.

Kirk Session

I very soon discovered that there were several other difficulties. At my first meeting of the Kirk Session after encouraging the elders to pray regularly for the families and members in their respective districts, I was informed that the elders did not have districts. Some felt that visiting was not part of an elder's duty. I asked that the matter be rectified and arrangements made for each elder to have a district, in accord with Presbyterian practice. I encouraged the elders to take seriously the pastoral oversight of their respective districts and stressed the importance of elders praying regularly for the members in their district.

Following that first meeting of the Kirk Session an elder and the superintendent of Hazelhead Sunday School resigned both as an elder and from the Sunday School. When I visited him and enquired about the reason for his resignation, he replied that it was because I had asked the elders to pray for their districts and he did not pray. When I asked him further about it he said that he never ever prayed! How someone who claimed never to pray could be an elder and was appointed to be superintendent of a large Sunday School, I do not know. The Session clerk told me that a further reason for his resignation was that he was misbehaving with another woman in the Woman's Guild.

Congregational Board

My first meeting with the Congregational Board was also disturbing. When I asked the treasurer to give us a financial report he said that he had never ever given a financial report in seven years! When I asked him simply to put us in the picture about where, as a congregation, we stood financially, he produced a list of unpaid bills some a year old for work which had been carried out! One of the unpaid bills was from the Electricity Board which said that if the bill was not paid within ten days the electricity for the church would be turned off, which meant that there would be neither heat nor light! He also said that the church had no money to pay any of the bills!

Things were in a desperate state. I could only wonder how the Presbytery through its Quinquennial Reports and annual inspection of church records, could allow a church to get into this situation. Why was it not customary for the Congregational Board to receive regular financial reports from the treasurer? Why were the accounts not published and audited annually? Why were they not passed by the Presbytery? Why was there no apparent enquiry about the church's inability to repay the National Church Extension Committee? Also, why had the Presbytery not raised the issue of elders' districts?

Clearly something had to be done immediately. On my second Sunday I intimated from the pulpit that the church was bankrupt! I told them about the financial situation and the danger of the electricity to the church being turned off if payment was not made within ten days. If that took place the church would have neither light nor heat. I asked that the congregation pray about the situation and said that the week ahead should be set aside to receive donations. I arranged for two office-bearers to be available each day throughout the week to receive gifts. The session clerk said to me that it was a terrible slap in the face to the congregation to intimate that we were bankrupt. I said that there had been no alternative. We could not allow the lighting and heating of the church to be turned off. Thankfully, through a week's special donations, we received sufficient donations to pay all our unpaid bills including that of the Electricity Board.

Financially much had to be done in order that the church could function as a normal congregation. I gained the strong impression that my predecessor was accustomed to pay a number of the church bills out of his own personal account. With his departure bills were consequently not paid. As a result of his generosity, people did not really feel the need to give much. Biblical teaching and encouragement was required before the congregational finances began to improve as thankfully they did.

There was also the need to face up to the fact that the congregation owed the National Church Extension Committee £7,000. Thankfully, with improved generosity and special efforts the congregation cleared its debt to the National Church Extension Committee in 1975 and became the first out of six Church Extension Charges in Aberdeen to do so. This was a relief and encouragement to the congregation and also an honour for which the congregation was commended.

Help from outside the Congregation

It was and is customary for new congregations to be assisted by assessor elders from other established churches. I asked the Presbytery for help in this regard. We were blessed to receive George Sinton and Sandy Wood from Gilcomston South Church and Douglas Duncan from St Ninian's Church. George Sinton became Sunday School Superintendent, succeeding Ian Hogg when he resigned. He was assisted by approximately twelve very dedicated Sunday School teachers. For a short period he also became leader of the Bible Class. For most of my ministry the Bible Class was led by the Boys Brigade captain, Robert Munro. Douglas Duncan later succeeded Bob Byth as session clerk, who in turn had succeeded Alex Douglas when he moved to Edinburgh. Miss Nan Brydon, a very fine and godly deaconess resident in the parish, was assistant to the hospital chaplain. I invited her to become an associate of the Kirk Session. Deaconesses, like retired ministers, were not permitted to be elders and my request was at the time an unusual one. The presence of these people greatly strengthened us.

I invited Andrew Smith, who worshipped in Langstane Kirk to come and help us. His son Gordon was at the time a divinity student and, in his training, was attached to Summerhill Church during my first year in the parish. On his joining us, I recommended that Andrew Smith become an elder and asked the Presbytery to commission him as a reader (or lay preacher). He served as 'locum' in the vacancy following my departure to another parish. In addition to his preaching and pastoral concerns, he was a giant in prayer and I owed much to his support and friendship.

Alex Douglas, from Jedburgh, while studying as a student for the ministry, joined Summerhill Church and became an elder. He is presently minister of Blackhall St Columba's Church in Edinburgh.

Various students worshipped with the congregation and at least one helped in Sunday School. Later, when Jack Hossack succeeded Robert Munro as captain of the Boys Brigade he was assisted by two students for the ministry who were members of my former congregation, Johnny Purves and Alan Brown. Another divinity student joined the congregation but was not an office bearer. He went on to teach R.E. All of these people greatly helped us in the work of the congregation.

Summerhill Elders

When I was inducted to Summerhill, there were about 20 elders. Sadly three quarters of them only came to church once a quarter when they were on duty! One elder came twice a year and one once a year. The Session clerk came once a month but on several occasions, when he did come to church, he went out with the Sunday School so that he was not often present for a full service. Most of them seemed to lack any real understanding of what eldership in the church meant. It is extremely difficult for a congregation to function in such a situation.

When a minister is appointed to a new housing area and charged with the responsibility of forming a new congregation it is all too easy to run social events or dances and appoint the organisers of such events as elders without their having any spiritual qualifications for the office. This clearly seemed to have been the case in Summerhill.

Willie MacKay for many years was a field organiser for Stewardship. He covered the whole of the east of Scotland from the Borders to Shetland. He helped me in all three of my parishes. One day in my manse while drinking a cup of coffee, he startled me by asking what I thought was wrong with the Church of Scotland and what was holding the church back from advancing. He then gave his opinion. He said that from his experience, having visited hundreds of churches, if every Kirk Session in Scotland lost half its number of elders then the church would move forward. I have often thought of what he said. I believe his words applied to Summerhill. I liked my elders but I felt sorry for them when I asked them to do that for which they were not spiritually qualified and what they had never anticipated doing when agreeing to become elders.

The first crisis in the Kirk Session came when I asked that as a Session we visit the entire parish. I had asked the two neighbouring Kirk Sessions of St Ninian's and Beechgrove to assist in the visitation of Summerhill Parish. Both had agreed. Several of my elders however resisted the proposal arguing that they did not regard visiting as part of an elder's duty or said that they were unable to visit. The elder who succeeded as Hazelhead Sunday School Superintendent said that the very thought of visiting put up his blood pressure. Our attendances at church were small and I felt that it was imperative that we carry out a parish visitation, so I pressed the Kirk Session for a vote. By a narrow majority the Kirk Session agreed to the proposal. As a result five elders resigned.

The visitation helped the congregation to turn outward from itself and to take its pastoral concern for the parish more seriously. It also helped to create a warm relationship between the office-bearers of the three parishes. However, it did not seem to improve attendances at worship with one notable exception. Following the visitation a young married man, Ian, of about 26 years of age called to speak to me at the vestry hour. He said that someone from the church had called at his door and he asked what it was all about. He told me that the only times in his life when he had been in church was at school services. He did not understand much about the Christian faith. I told him that I had arranged with the minister of St Ninian's Church, the Revd Robin Keltie, for a joint Youth Fellowship week-end conference to take place the following week-end in the Compass Ski Lodge in Glenshee and invited him to come so that he might meet some of the young people of the parish and learn something about the Christian faith. He agreed to come. During the day we tramped over the hills in Glenshee or played games. Each evening we had a Bible study when Robin and I encouraged our young people to pray. When Ian heard young people praying suddenly, to my surprise, Ian prayed. That prayer, quite remarkably, was his conversion. Later when I was leading an open air meeting down town Ian testified to his conversion having taken place when, after hearing others pray, he prayed aloud before others.

The second crisis in the Kirk Session came after I had been some eighteen months as minister in Summerhill. We had agreed at a Kirk Session meeting to admit twelve new communicants by profession of faith the following Sunday. After agreeing, I said to the Kirk Session, "What do you think that these young people will think about our asking them to promise to attend church faithfully and to live the Christian life, when we ourselves do not keep these vows?" With that question there was quite a solemn atmosphere in the Kirk Session! I went on and said, "What will these young people think about a church which asks them to make these promises, and openly elects to office in the church elders who openly do not keep these vows?"

There was an embarrassed silence as every head looked down. I then said that I could look around this Kirk Session and give a complete record of attendance at worship of every office-bearer for the last eighteen months since I became their minister. I told them that I recorded the attendance at worship of each office-bearer every Sunday! With that the session clerk exploded and said, "Is this constitutional?" I replied that it was thoroughly in accord with the Word of God that every shepherd knows his sheep. I said that every one of them had been ordained as a shepherd of the people in their district and asked how they could know their sheep if they did not come to church to find out about how their sheep were progressing! I promptly lost another six elders.

That night was a turning point in the life of the Kirk Session. I am not sure that I would recommend what I said that night to other ministers. It was pretty drastic but I felt desperate. We were a small congregation in the midst of a large parish. We needed as office bearers to be spiritually committed and right with the Lord if as a church we would grow.

I never ever asked an elder to resign. I always attempted to set a high spiritual standard for the eldership. Those who resigned, resigned voluntarily realising that they were unable, or possibly unwilling, to reach up to the spiritual standards that were set. However, I felt the strain of these resignations. I liked the men who resigned personally, although I felt, sadly, that they were not spiritually qualified to be elders. I think that they and the congregation knew it. My wife Elizabeth often said, "This is a strange congregation. Every time that you lose an elder there are more people in church!"

It later became clear that it was wrong that they had become elders. After the second batch of resignations, I happened in Edinburgh to speak to Dr Horace Walker, secretary to the Home Board of the Church of Scotland. He asked about the parish and I told him that another six elders had resigned. He smiled and asked rather humorously what happened. Did I ask them to pray? I told him the circumstances. Knowing about the church, he said, "David, you have not yet got down to Gideon's three hundred". Horace Walker, who as secretary to the Home Board had pressed me to go to Summerhill, was always friendly toward me and very supportive. I found his words at a time when I was feeling the strain very encouraging.

I was also encouraged at that time by one of my elders, George Watt, a policeman and one of the few original elders who worshipped regularly Sunday by Sunday. George, after an evening service of Holy Communion, which for heating purposes we held in the Church hall, suddenly spoke up immediately after the benediction. There were about thirty people present. He said, "On behalf of the Kirk Session and congregation I would like to say thank you to the minister. We believe that he is God's man and that God called him to this parish". Then, after a brief pause, he looked at me and said, "But, you are a hard task master!" I was at the time dumbfounded and speechless. He said it however in a kindly way. As I later thought about it, I felt that he meant it as a compliment and a word of encouragement

Gradually we appointed and ordained some new and very godly elders to the Kirk Session. We were blessed with our assessor elders and others whom I have already mentioned. When I left Aberdeen I felt that the church was blessed with a very fine and faithful Kirk Session and remember thinking that I would love to have been able to take them with me to my next parish in Earlston. When I intimated my leaving, some of them wept. They were a very different Session from the one which I inherited in my induction to Summerhill.

Congregational Roll

It was the custom in Aberdeen when city churches pruned their communicant rolls of non-active members to hand over their certificates of transference to the Church Extension charges, while actively seeking to hold on to their faithful members. Adding their names to the rolls of the new churches gave those who hitherto had been non-active communicant members a new opportunity, if they so chose, to start again in worship and church commitment. A few certainly did. Sadly, the majority did not. Consequently the communicant roll of Summerhill church which I inherited was greatly inflated with non-participants. In 1969 there were 800 people on the roll. As a Kirk Session we wrote a letter to all who had failed to show an interest in the church for three or more years, encouraging them to consider their position and return to church during the following year, They were assured of a warm welcome. The Kirk Session intimated that during that year each home would be visited by an elder and where possible also by the minister. If those concerned still failed to show interest in the church after a year, the Kirk Session would very regretfully remove their names to the Supplementary Roll.

A few did show interest, but at the end of the year the Kirk Session removed to the Supplementary Roll two hundred people who had never once entered the church and a further two hundred who had only been to church on the one occasion when the church was opened. The pruning of the roll resulted in a more realistic membership and greatly encouraged the elders and office-bearers. They knew that henceforth the homes that they visited were interested in supporting the church. Nonetheless we continued to visit the lapsed members along with communicant members at each communion season. As a result one or two did become interested in the church and were transferred back to the communion roll on each occasion of celebrating Holy Communion.

Sunday School

In 1969 and in the years that immediately followed there were approximately 400 Sunday School children divided almost evenly between two Sunday Schools, Summerhill and Hazelhead. Both Sunday Schools had a devoted group of Sunday School teachers. George Sinton proved to be an able and very committed superintendent in Summerhill Sunday School. He was respected and supported by about 12 Sunday School teachers.

In many churches in Aberdeen and Aberdeenshire, it was not the custom for children to attend church even for the first part of the service. Adults felt that church worship was for them and did not wish the distraction of children's noises. I found this astonishing and immediately took steps to alter the situation so that all the children came into worship for the first part of the service and left after the children's address to go to Sunday School. On the ground that the church is the family of God and is for everyone of whatever age, I also encouraged parents to bring their babies and prams to church and to feel free without embarrassment to leave at any point in the service if the child was crying and had had enough. A creche was provided in the church hall for those who wished to use the facility. This in its way was quite a revolution for the congregation. However, it quickly became accepted.

One year we were invited to receive for two months an African minister, who had been moderator of the Presbyterian Church of East Africa. He stayed with us in the manse. In welcoming him I said that so long as he was with us we would take it turn about to conduct worship and to preach. He told me that he had never preached to an all-white congregation. I told him to try and imagine that all the faces were black and to do and say what he would normally do and say in Africa.

On his first Sunday with us when I took the service he insisted in sitting with the Sunday School children. As soon as a hymn was announced he immediately raised his hands and began to clap. All the children joyfully followed his example and that immediately changed the form and atmosphere of our worship. On the following Sunday when it was his turn to preach he took with him into the pulpit an African drum. He said to the congregation that we have an organ and have lovely hymns but do not really sing them joyfully. He said that in most churches in Africa they had no organ only a drum. So in announcing the hymn he asked the organist to play as usual but he would play his drum. This he proceeded to do and it totally changed our worship. I was very indebted to him. He was able to introduce a real sense of joy and freedom into our worship which I, and I don't think any Scots minister, could easily have done. The services were reverent but relaxed and I believe more pleasing to God and helpful to the congregation.

Bible Class and Boys Brigade

During most of my ministry in Summerhill, the only Bible Class for boys was that of the Boys Brigade. The Company was very large and annually gained many cups and awards at both a city and national level. The Bible Class was led by the Boys Brigade captain, Robert Munro. The captain told me that the Boys Brigade, despite their other achievements, had never produced one boy for the church, which I found very disturbing.

Because of the size and popularity of the Boys Brigade and its attraction for boys, the separate church Bible Class which we formed was for a long time composed only of girls, and one boy who had not been drawn into the Boys Brigade. This was run by George Sinton, the Sunday School superintendent.

In order to try and remedy this situation and in order to try and attract the boys to come to church I managed to persuade Robert Munro of the need to have a joint Bible class which would be led by George Sinton. As captain of the Boys Brigade, Robert Munro was not happy with this arrangement but reluctantly agreed. After about a year, or it may have been two years, he intimated that he would no longer support a joint Bible Class under the leadership of George Sinton. He wanted George Sinton dismissed and implied that as an assessor elder his services were no longer required. He intimated his intention of himself resuming leadership of a separate Boys Brigade Bible Class or perhaps himself being leader of a joint Bible Class.

George Sinton was naturally very upset and considered resigning as an assessor elder. All twelve Sunday School teachers immediately said that if George resigned they would all resign from the Summerhill Sunday School as teachers. Clearly it was a most disturbing and serious situation. George Sinton and the Sunday School teachers clearly had my full spiritual support as minister. What was I to do? I wondered if in any way I as minister was the problem as to why the Boys Brigade could not happily be integrated into the real life of the congregation. I wondered therefore whether I should seek another parish and leave so that another minister might solve the problem. However at the suggestion seven of my best and most godly elders said that if I left before solving the problem of the Boys Brigade and its dominance over the life of the church, they would lift their lines of transference and leave Summerhill Church. Their leaving of Summerhill church and the resignation of all the Sunday School teachers would devastate the church and undermine or destroy everything which I had tried to do in Summerhill.

After consultation with the Presbytery Clerk I took the drastic decision to resign as chaplain to the Boys Brigade Company in Summerhill. By its constitution, without a chaplain and affiliation to a church congregation, a Boys Brigade Company ceases to exist. I posted my resignation as chaplain by registered post to Robert Munro, to each of my elders and to the Presbytery. My resignation came as great shock to the Boys Brigade and to many in Presbytery. The BB Company in Summerhill was, I think, the largest company in Aberdeen and the one that captured most cups and prizes both at Aberdeen and national level.

I did not find the members of Presbytery who were sent to meet with me (and I think, with Robert Munro) helpful. To me, they could not grasp the spiritual issues involved and the importance that for the spiritual welfare of Summerhill Church the problems between the church and the BB Company required to be resolved. I had prayed very much about it as had others and stood firm in my resignation.

Robert Munro resigned as captain, which relieved the tension in the church and left the congregation. He joined Mastrick church and took with him a large numbers of the boys. He was welcomed as Boys Brigade captain in that parish. George Sinton continued to be Sunday School superintendent and also Bible Class leader and all the Sunday School teachers happily continued. Two of the original elders resigned and joined Mastrick Church; the rest were very supportive. I found it a very testing period. It emphasised for me the importance of prayer and that every step in the church and every decision require to be taken in prayer.

Jack Hossack became captain of the Boys Brigade, which was now smaller than previously. As I mentioned above, he was assisted by two divinity students who had been members of my previous church in Livingston and had helped me in Summer Missions: Johnny Purves and Alex Brown. Jack was also assisted by Roy Massie who after his conversion became a very committed Christian. He later became captain of the Boys Brigade in Summerhill until he applied to enter the ministry.

Robert Munro was a very able man. He said to me that in a management assessment course in the Gas Board, with which he worked, he was told that his management skills were very good but he was abrasive. Not many Boys Brigade officers were able to work with him. During my time in Summerhill 15 officers were sacked by Robert or resigned, some after a fairly brief period. There was only one, a police officer, Henry who continued to assist him through the years. Robert made strong demands on the other leaders. The boys however respected and looked up to him. He was a remarkable captain and his company year by year captured most cups and prizes both for Aberdeen and all Scotland.

Robert had come to the manse shortly after my induction wishing to assess the new minister. He told me that according to the BB manual a good captain has to stamp his personality on the boys. I replied that it was important in all Christian work that Christ was pre-eminent and that in the church, as minister I must always ask myself "Is Christ pre-eminent or is David Torrance?" I said that likewise he must always ask himself, "In the BB is Christ pre-eminent or is Robert Munro?" The next day, Sunday, just before the morning service in Hazelhead he said to me, "That terrible question, 'Is it Christ or Robert Munro' has not been out of my mind for two minutes." Later, just before the evening service, I met him going into a BB gathering in the church hall. He turned to me and said, "I am like a bear with a sore head, because of that terrible question of yours, 'Is Jesus Christ central or is Robert Munro?'" He said, "You think that it is Robert Munro who is central." I replied,

"All I asked was that both you and I must ask, 'Who is central in the church or Boys Brigade? Is it Jesus Christ?'" I said, "If you have no peace then you must kneel down and say in prayer, 'Lord, not I but Christ.'" At that Robert stormed and said, "The only way that I will get peace is by going back to the religion which I had before!" He turned his back on me, went into the hall and slammed the door so hard I thought that the glass might fall out! The Boys Brigade was meeting in the church hall at the same time as the evening service.

I had often spoken to Robert, seeking to help him, and prayed much for him, wanting the BB company to become integrated into the church and for the boys with their officers to be committed to Christ. In my first year I went on an autumn camp with them but I was unable to succeed in winning over Robert and integrating the company into the church.

They were, as I have said, a very strong company. Their finances were considerably greater than that of the church, although I was unable to persuade Robert to produce a balance sheet of their accounts. They seemed to run in competition with the church and to regard their welfare above that of the church. Spiritually, I did not find their influence helpful. I was sad over what happened at the end and Robert's departure, but felt that if the congregation were to grow and develop spiritually there was no other solution.

Youth

I myself formed and led the Youth Fellowship of young people of 15 years and over. Because of the dominant influence of the Boys Brigade and its hold over the boys of the parish, the Youth Fellowship was primarily composed of girls. However I worked hard in endeavouring to reach the young people of Youth Fellowship age. I began by sending out each year about seventy or eighty postcards personally addressed with a short personal invitation to come to our Bible Class or Youth Fellowship meetings. I did this year by year in each of my three parishes. In all three parishes, the personal invitation resulted in about eight or ten young people responding.

I also with the help of the secretary of Summerhill Academy, who was an elder of Summerhill Church, created a card index of all the young people in the parish between fifteen and eighteen. There were just over three hundred. This enabled me to send out written invitations and fliers to special meetings and events in the church. In addition I received permission from the police to move around the parish intimating through a loud speaker all youth events in the parish. We were not allowed to stop and speak through a loud speaker. We had to keep moving as we spoke but it did enable us to keep the parish informed about all that was happening.

As a result of these efforts I had a Youth Fellowship of approximately 10 or 12 young people meeting regularly on a Sunday and was able with them to look at many Gospel themes and forms of missionary outreach.

Five Australian nurses, staying in a nurses home in the parish, came regularly to our Youth Fellowship meetings and shared in our outings. One day they asked me for my advice concerning their work. They were all trained nurses and had come to Aberdeen to gain a nursing qualification in midwifery. They told me that they did not approve of abortions. What were they to do? They said that if they refused to take part in abortions they could not continue on their course and would not gain their degree or qualification in midwifery. Once they were qualified they could of course decline to conduct or take part in an abortion. What were they to do now? I found their question difficult to answer. I felt that all I could say was for them to lay the whole matter before God and ask his guidance on this issue. I believe that that is what they did. All qualified as mid-wives.

In addition I was able to create a mixed youth club of some twenty four or five young people. We met each Saturday evening in the church hall. After various activities we always ended with a reading from God's Word and prayer. The boys who came were not in the Boys Brigade and were really totally outwith the church. The girls were different. A number of them came to church and one later married the Revd Ian MacLean who later had a long and good ministry in Summerhill.

Perhaps twice a year I had to be really firm with the young folk, particularly with the boys, and lay down the law. One night a boy spilt a cup of tea on the floor. When I asked him to mop it up he refused. At the same time I asked other boys to wash some writing off the wall in the men's lavatory and they refused. With that, all I can say is that I thundered in a loud voice, halted all that was taking place and told them that it was the end of the club unless they did what they were told. They were quite subdued and obediently mopped the floor and washed down the wall. When we gathered for our evening worship I apologised in speaking so strongly to them, whereon one lad said, "You had to, Sir, otherwise we would not respect you!" They taught me a lot and I prayed that I might teach them something of the Gospel.

Because I was desperate to reach the young people for Christ and they seemed to know so very little about the Gospel, in my eight years in Summerhill, in order to arouse their spiritual interest, we held 12 summer missions. Each lasted a fortnight and was led by an outside church team.

In addition we also ran several week-end missions helped by young people, some of whom travelled up from Edinburgh and Glasgow. I was amazed at the Christian commitment of some of these folk who travelled to Aberdeen at their own expense. I was deeply grateful for them and their help. All these missions were directed towards young people. They greatly helped the work both of the Youth Fellowship and the Youth Club.

Meetings with St Ninian's

Summerhill at that time had a close relationship with St Ninian's Church. Their minister, Robin Keltie was a long-standing friend whom I had known since my latter days at school. Both Summerhill's and St Ninian's Youth Fellowships met on various joint occasions, which spiritually was a great help to both. Each year Robin and I organised a joint and memorable week-end camp in either the Compass Ski Centre in Glenshee or Kilravock Christian Centre, near Culloden. Members of the Summerhill youth club also came to these weekend camps. Although we organised various activities and explored the surrounding countryside, we always had morning and evening worship. Evening worship always included Bible study and a time for corporate prayer. Undoubtedly this was new and no doubt strange to some in the youth club who had not grown up in the church but we felt that it was right and helpful. It never deterred young people from joining us. As I mentioned above, one young man was converted during one of these sessions of corporate prayer.

From time to time we arranged joint evening services of worship in Summerhill. Throughout my ministry in all three parishes of which I was minister, I conducted less formal evening services. I never chose the hymns. I asked the congregation to choose them. I never wrote out a sermon or took notes with me, although I certainly prepared for each service. I simply preached through a book of the Bible. At first it was suggested that the congregation from St Ninian's who, as Aberdonians, were accustomed to more formal worship, would find my less formal approach a little difficult and would not respond for example in the choosing of hymns. It immediately became clear that this was not the case. I teased Robin over the fact that his members responded immediately to the choosing of the hymns and responded far more quickly than mine!

My wife and I introduced the providing of tea or coffee after the morning service. Once that became an established practice, we introduced the holding of family meals in the church hall. Our elders suggested that such a practice in Aberdeen would never be supported because people were anxious to get home in order to plan the rest of the day. In actual fact these family meals became very popular. We appointed five teams who were responsible for arranging and providing the meals. We held them five times a year, and during my ministry they became established in the congregation. Many requests were made, especially on the part of pensioners who lived alone that we have them more frequently. Because we did not wish to overtax those who provided the meals, we restricted them to five a year. We invited members of St Ninian's to join us, which enabled members of the two congregations to meet and know each other. Those attending these meals generally numbered over one hundred and fifty, occasionally approaching two hundred and never dropped under one hundred.

In addition, Robin and I arranged an annual conference on a Sunday afternoon between the two Kirk Sessions of Summerhill and St Ninian's. Kirk Sessions always have a lot to learn from each other. These joint meetings brought the elders of the two congregations together and friendships were formed which were spiritually advantageous. However Robin did have a very abrasive elder, a lecturer in physics in the University. He was highly critical of Robin's evangelical ministry and voiced his criticisms at one of our joint sessions. This disturbed me as I did not want his criticisms to rub off on to my elders! However, shortly after that Robin moved from Aberdeen to Dufftown, to the parish of Cabrach and Mortlach in the Presbytery of Moray, and under the new minister in St Ninian's we did not continue our joint Kirk Session meetings. Shortly after Robin Keltie moved to Dufftown, the particular elder who had been so difficult and abrasive had a deep spiritual experience and completely changed. He visited Robin and told him that now he appreciated and agreed with Robin's ministry.

North West Churches

In Aberdeen there seemed to be a gap between the Church Extension charges, which embraced large new housing areas and the older established churches, which tended to cater to middle class congregations. Following a suggestion which I put forward, ten churches, five church extension charges north of the river Dee, and five established churches, agreed to come together monthly holding a joint service or meeting generally with a guest speaker on a Sunday afternoon. The church extension churches were Garthdee, Summerhill, Mastrick, Middlefield and Northfield. The established churches were St Ninian's, Beechgrove, Rubislaw, Queen's Cross and Melville Carden Place.

These monthly meetings were very helpful and particularly encouraging to the Church extension churches which were for the most part struggling with their extended commitments. It brought Christians in the area closer together, ideas and concerns were shared and in some cases members of the established churches were led to assist in such matters as parish visitation.

Summer Missions

The first seaside summer missions of the Church of Scotland took place in 1934. Before World War II, the missions were led by a minister, a divinity student and pianist. Each mission tended to last for a month. After the War, these missions were led by ministers and sometimes divinity students, with a team of mainly, although not entirely, young people. Each of these missions lasted a fortnight.

Although various young people from Aberdeen had taken part in these missions, prior to 1969 no mission team had been recruited from Aberdeen itself. Between 1969 and 1977, Summerhill and St Ninian's churches, not only raised Summer Mission teams from within their congregations but with the addition of young people from the churches of Livingston Old and Abbeygreen, Lesmahagow, raised the largest teams in Scotland. Over sixty took part for the whole two weeks of the missions. Those who came for part of the mission, generally at weekends, raised the numbers to over one hundred.

Both Douglas Duncan, who later became session clerk in Summerhill, following Bob Byth and Sandy Wilson, the session clerk of St Ninian's, came each year. Douglas Duncan was the assistant head teacher of Northfield Academy and Sandy Wilson was a retired headmaster. Ladies from Summerhill generously came and cooked for the teams along with Nora Keltie, Robin's wife and my wife, Elizabeth. Many of the young people taking part went on to serve the church in later years, and some like Roy Massie entered the ministry.

Open Air Services

I raised with the Presbytery the need for the church over the summer months to conduct open air services in order to try and reach with the gospel some of the many people who never come to a church service. The Presbytery agreed to the proposal and asked that I organise these services. This I did for seven years, organising open-air services in Union Street, just inside the gates of the cemetery surrounding St Nicholas Church. These services took place from the first Sunday in June to the last Sunday in August and lasted from 9.30pm to about 10.15pm. Some six or seven ministers in the Presbytery shared in the conduct of these services regularly, supported by young people from Summerhill and St Ninian's.

We always had good attendances. A reporter with the Aberdeen Press and Journal counted over 120 people attending on our first evening. As we became established we sometimes had more people. Although the ministers preached, we always involved our young people, encouraging them to share their faith and commitment to Christ.

We witnessed some moving conversions to Christ. One man over 50 years of age who came from a well known professional family was converted. He was unmarried, was an alcoholic and had drunk a fortune of approx. £50,000! He became a completely changed man. His flat was in a terrible state and my wife cleaned and tidied it, for which he was deeply grateful. Unfortunately his health was so badly damaged by his consumption of alcohol that he required prolonged hospital treatment. I visited him regularly and he died several months later. Another, a young man, who was converted in the open air, went on to university and later to hold an important and influential educational post.

Overseas Mission

Soon after moving to Aberdeen I was appointed to be the Presbytery's representative on the Church of Scotland Foreign Mission Committee, later called the Overseas Council (now World Mission). In order to promote interest and support for the church's work overseas, I organised each year with the help of Robin Keltie a public meeting open to the general public. These were intimated through the churches and were well attended. We invited as guest speakers missionaries who were home on leave. One year one of our speakers was Bishop Lesslie Newbigin from South India. Hearing of our open air services on a Sunday evening he asked the Revd Bill Thomson if he could join us and as well as his other speaking engagements, speak in the open air. This surprised the Presbytery clerk but encouraged us. We felt that it was a witness and challenge to our fellow ministers.

We also organised each year an overseas meeting especially for young people. We contacted the other Youth Fellowships in the Presbytery and for some years gradually increased our attendance until we reached 220 young people. That year I had invited as a speaker a delightful and evangelical African minister from Nigeria. We were also asked that year to receive a small ecumentical team under a former warden of Scottish Churches House in Dunblane. The latter were touring Scotland, endeavouring to create concern for the poor overseas.

Because of the large number of young people attending we had to divide them into two groups in two different rooms while the speakers circulated so that everyone was given the opportunity to hear each speaker. The leader of the visiting team was anxious that his group take over and asked me to dismiss the African minister whom I had invited. I declined. It would have been an act of grave discourtesy. As it happened, the African was the one speaker of the evening who, with his simple evangelical enthusiasm went down well. The young people appreciated what he said and the way that he said it. Unfortunately, the others endeavoured to present their message in an intellectual way that was suitable for thoughtful university students. It was over the heads of many present. When driving home some twelve or thirteen of my own young people, they asked, "What was that meeting all about"? The visiting team, later reporting the results of their Scottish tour, said that they regarded their visit to Aberdeen as the highlight of their tour. I did not attempt to disillusion them. From our point of view, having struggled to build up the attendance at these youth meetings, it was a disaster. In numbers it knocked us back. The following year we dropped to about 150 young people and although numbers crept up over the following years to about 180 we never again reached the same attendance which we had on that eventful night.

Concern for the poor is exceedingly important. We can only rightly present the gospel to others when, in love, we are concerned both for their spiritual and physical welfare, but our message about the poor, which was the concern of that ecumenical team, requires to be presented in an evangelical way in order to be effective, and they seemed unable to do that in a way which could readily be grasped and understood by the young people.

Some Pastoral Cases

In the ministry and through the preaching of and witness to the Word of God people are wonderfully changed and transformed. For some the change is over a prolonged period of time. For others their conversion can happen suddenly. I mention a few.

John. John came from the North East. He was a lawyer and after working further south returned to Aberdeen. In coming to Summerhill Church he told me that he had been an elder in his former church and would like actively to serve the church. Shortly after his arrival in Summerhill he joined the Kirk Session. He found the preaching challenging and disturbing. When I preached the message of the cross and the need for forgiveness and committal to Christ I could sense his opposition. I several times spoke to him about the cross. On occasion he called at the manse. When he did so it was because he was disturbed or angry about what I had preached. He told me that I had no right to single him out, hold him up before the congregation and preach a sermon at him. When he said this, I found that often I could not remember what I had preached on the previous Sunday!

On occasion, we discussed evangelism. We organised a number of missions to the young people in Summerhill. At the same time, before I left Aberdeen, the South American evangelist Luis Palau, had been invited to lead a mission to the city. I was a member of the planning committee. John's response was, "If the C of S is evangelical I am leaving the C of S!" Matters came to a head one night at a Kirk Session meeting. He asked to speak immediately after I had opened the meeting. He spoke and for over 20 minutes 'blew off' about the minister. I thanked him for feeling free to speak his mind. Because I was calm and not angry I thought he was about to cry. He said, "There you are, you do not even get angry". His outburst stunned the rest of the elders. Hence under the circumstances I adjourned the Session. When the other elders had departed I spoke to John and said that I had listened carefully to all that he has said and that his grievance was not really with the minister but with God. John agreed, so I told him that it was time that he made his peace with God.

Before the next Kirk Session meeting, Douglas Duncan phoned to say that he had spoken to several other elders and before we commenced business he would call for the resignation of John from the Kirk Session. John was apprised of the situation and resigned as an elder and member of Summerhill Church. He joined a neighbouring church and later became an elder of that church.

After leaving Summerhill, Robin Keltie told me that one of his elders had partnered with John as a counsellor in the Luis Palau mission that had taken place the following year. I was at that time minister of Earlston. Clearly he was spiritually a changed man. Later I met him in Waverley Station in Edinburgh and then at a meeting of the General Assembly. On both occasions he gave me a warm and friendly greeting, welcoming me as a long lost brother. Sadly he has since died but I rejoice in the wonderful spiritual change that had taken place. He was a good man.

Mrs Fraser. Shortly after my induction in Summerhill I preached a series of sermons on the parables. In preaching on the parable of the Prodigal Son, or what I prefer to call the parable of the Two Sons, I spoke about the younger son. He had rebelled against his father, gone into the far country, did everything wrong but after squandering everything in riotous living was down and out, and decided to return to his father. I endeavoured to dwell on the father's love, his forgiveness and loving welcome of his son on his return. I suggested that the older son, although he stayed at home, worked hard and did all the right things, was at heart just as distant from the father as the younger son in the far country. He did not understand his father's spirit of love and forgiveness and when he witnessed his father's love and forgiveness of the younger son, became angry. I likened the older son to the person who sat each Sunday in the church pew yet never really understood the meaning of God's love and forgiveness: when such a person witnessed it, he or she became angry!

When shaking hands at the door after the service, Mrs Fraser, a lady of sixty, asked to see me. I invited her to go through to the vestry and said I would be with her shortly. One of the last to shake hands, a lady office-bearer and member of the Woman's Guild, was not in the least happy with her minister and expressed her annoyance or anger. She did not seem happy with what I said. I have always found it salutary and humbling to listen to a church member expressing their feelings after a sermon. It can reveal a lot.

When I went through to the vestry Mrs Fraser said that she had been away in the world and done many wrong things. She had come back and asked me, "What does God think of me?" When I said that we had been thinking of the prodigal, she said I am the prodigal. When I asked her what the father did when the prodigal returned home, she burst into tears and said that the father welcomed him. I assured her that the heavenly Father welcomed her and had forgiven her. We prayed and she was movingly converted. I reminded her that there was a large cross on the wall in the church and another on the church outside. I said, "Whenever you see that cross, remember that God is saying, 'I love you and have forgiven you.'" I went home that day with my ears still burning from what one lady had said to me and my heart wonderfully warm because of what the Lord had done for the other lady!

Some two weeks later I spoke to Mrs Fraser and asked her how she was. She told me that she had asked her son-in-law, a joiner, who was not a member of the church to make her a cross and put it above her bed so that she might have a perpetual reminder that God loved her and had forgiven her. She became a member of the church and regular attender at worship and a wonderful witness to Christ.

Mrs Sinclair was a widow when I first met her. Her daughter, who stayed across the city in Torry, phoned one day to tell me that her father had died in Corby in England and her widowed mother had moved back to Scotland and was now a resident in Summerhill parish. I said that I would visit her mother. When I did and invited her mother to church, she replied that it was such a long time since she had last gone to church, she lacked courage. However she assured me that when her sister from

Glasgow, who was a church member, came to Aberdeen in the summer she would go with her to church.

When I returned from holiday that summer Mrs Sinclair was sitting in church with Mrs Fraser. In the providence of God when Mrs Sinclair and her sister did come to church they sat in the same pew as Mrs Fraser. Mrs Fraser welcomed her and through her witness Mrs Sinclair became a Christian. She in turn completely changed and became an outspoken and loving witness to Christ.

An atheist's widow. One summer I was informed that John was unwell. John was a communist and well known as an atheist. Because he lived in the parish I went to see him. When I first met him, he was not a well man and so I visited him many times over the next nine months. After my first visit I said that I would like to read from the Bible and pray. He told me that he did not believe and was an atheist. I told him that I believed and if the parish minister visited him he could 'thole' (put up with) having a reading and prayer! Despite his continued assertion that he did not believe and was an atheist I continued in my many visits to subject him to a reading and prayer! On my last visit, when he was very ill and dying he asked me not to pray in the room with him. I agreed but said that I would continue to remember him in prayer. He said that he knew that, and asked me to pray for him in the room next door!

When he died the superintendent of the crematorium phoned to ask if I would take his service and in the place of the prayer following the committal, have the playing of the Red Flag! The organist, who was a church organist had refused to play it. To the superintendent's chagrin I refused, but said that I would visit the widow.

When I visited the home their one married daughter was present. I discovered that according to the will I was named as the person to conduct the funeral service. Communists and atheists in Aberdeen did not have any form of Christian service at a funeral. On the one hand, therefore, I was touched that after my many visits we had built up a relationship and John had come to accept me as a minister and had named me in his will as the one to conduct his funeral service. On the other hand I was certain that John had endeavoured to get his own back on me. Because I had subjected him to a reading and prayer in my many visits, he would subject me to the playing of the Red Flag, in the middle of his funeral service!

The daughter particularly was anxious to carry out her father's wishes as expressed in the will. In the end, having endeavoured to explain what happened at a Christian funeral service and the meaning of prayer, where we asked God to comfort the loved ones, we came to a compromise. On my suggestion they purchased a record of the Red Flag and played it as the relatives and friends gathered. Thereafter I conducted a Christian service. In the end, I felt that the widow came to a real faith in the Lord. Although over the weeks and months I had established a friendly relationship with John, I do not think that he ever came to faith.

Endangered marriage. James and his wife were members of Summerhill church but very rarely worshipped. He was a postman and 64 years of age when he became attracted or infatuated with a woman in her late forties who was a member of the Close Brethren. On visiting his wife I found her suffering from nervous strain. Not only had her husband left her after 40 years of marriage but shortly before they had received a visit from two women whom James had adulterously fathered during the war. They had managed to trace their father and had wanted to meet him.

This came as a great shock to James' wife who had never known of her husband's adulterous past. When I visited she had consulted her lawyer with a view to a divorce. I urged her to halt the legal process and commit the whole matter in prayer to God. I also told James that what he was doing was wrong and that God was commanding him to repent and return to his wife. I said to both of them that although they had been married for forty years they required to start married life again at the beginning, allowing God to recreate them by his Holy Spirit and allowing God to recreate their marriage and give them his love for one another. I told them that to allow God to do that each must kneel at the foot of the cross and ask God's forgiveness, not for the other's sin but each for their own sin. As God enabled them to die to themselves and to their sins so God would raise them up to a new life united to Christ and to one another. I visited both of them back and forth for about three months. Things did not look hopeful. However when I returned from holiday in the summer, I rejoiced to see them both sitting side by side in church. Thereafter they attended church regularly every Sunday and were the last couple to come and say good-bye to me when I left Aberdeen for my next parish.

I have found broken and strained marriages the most difficult area to deal with in my ministry. I have experienced many disappointments and also have been greatly encouraged in the wonderful way that God has recreated and blessed marriages that were under threat.

Mr and Mrs McEwen. Mr McEwen was a son of the manse and a cousin of the Very Revd Leonard Small. He and his wife were very musical and operated a husband and wife band playing for concerts and other gatherings on Friday and Saturday evenings. They did not often come to church. On returning from holiday I was informed that Mrs McEwen was not well. On going to see her I discovered that she had a slipped disc, had been in bed for over six weeks, flat on her back and was no better. On welcoming me she said that she felt very guilty in not worshipping in church because often they arrived home at 3.00am on a Sunday morning and felt too tired to go to church. Clearly she felt guilty and repeated her sense of guilt several times. Because she was in pain I felt unsure about what to say in regard to her and her husband's non-attendance at church and said nothing. I simply listened and then had a short reading from the Bible and committed her and her husband in prayer to God.

The following Thursday I visited her in Woodend Hospital. She told me that after my visit and prayer in her home she was healed. She got out of bed and was very well all weekend. On the Saturday evening she did not go out with her husband John to play at a concert. However because he came home at a late hour and was tired on the Sunday morning she and her husband did not go to church. On the Monday morning she bent down and as a result her disc was again put out. The doctor said that this time her back was much worse and sent her into hospital. She underwent an x-ray and was examined, as a result of which she was told that she would have traction for several weeks. I arrived in hospital and visited her after her examination and while she was waiting for the staff to return and put her on traction. She told me with floods of tears that she felt very guilty. She had not come to church even after God had healed her.

Again I did not know what to say and how to respond to her sense of guilt but after listening to her said that we would pray and commit her and her health to God. She was in a large ward, with a sub-ward. There were no screens round the bed and we were visible to the other patients in the ward and sub-ward. As we prayed she hung on to me with both hands and with tears streaming down her cheeks. To my shame I felt embarrassed. The following Sunday as I looked down from the pulpit there she was sitting with her husband. Shaking hands at the door I asked her how she was. She said that she was healed. When the medical staff returned with weights to put her on traction, they re-examined her and said that her disc or discs had clicked back into place, so they discharged her. She apparently would not risk not coming to church this time! I rejoiced with her over God's wonderful healing but was tempted to laugh and wish that God would do the same with others in order to persuade them to come back to church!

Healed of cancer. Robin Keltie, minister of St Ninian's Church, and I were near neighbours. Nora Keltie some years earlier was diagnosed with cancer and had a mastectomy. After several years of good health the cancer sadly returned. My wife Elizabeth and I each week prayed with Robin and Nora with the laying on of hands. After a period in hospital she was discharged although she continued to deteriorate in health.

One Sunday after lunch Elizabeth and I visited them and prayed for Nora. Nora was very ill and unconscious. On our return Elizabeth pressed me to do something about it. She said Nora should be in the hospital but suggested that her GP had given up any hope of her recovery. I telephoned and spoke to an elder in Robin's church who was a doctor and medical consultant. He said that Nora was not his patient but he would speak to his colleague, which he did. As a result on Monday Nora was taken in to hospital.

I visited Nora on the Tuesday afternoon and she was deeply unconscious. On the Tuesday evening, after speaking to the Woman's Guild of Summerhill Church, I found Robin sitting and waiting for me. He said that the consultant in the hospital had visited him that evening. He said that the cancer was all over Nora's body and over the brain. He was sorry that there was nothing that he could do and said to Robin that Nora would die within the next two hours. I prayed with Robin and we committed Nora to the Lord. When I arrived home I told Elizabeth the news. She promptly said that we were wrong and had no business giving up on Nora's health. I remonstrated that, as a doctor, no matter how hard she and other doctors had tried, some patients died. She insisted that we had prayed for Nora and we had no right to give up. Consequently at 11pm I went to bed and Elizabeth went up to the hospital and sat and prayed with Nora.

She returned at 7 o'clock in the morning and said that Nora had recovered! She said, "If you do not believe me phone the hospital." I did and received the hospital confirmation. After phoning Robin he asked that I should come with him to the hospital and pray. It was Wednesday. In his emotional state he felt that he would simply weep. I allowed Robin to go ahead of me into the ward. I followed about 10 or 15 minutes later. Nora was sitting up in bed, radiant and chatting. Robin was sitting mesmerised. Robin thanked the consultant for all that he had done. He replied, "Do not thank me, I am only the office boy."

The hospital staff were amazed at Nora's recovery. They discharged her on the Friday. For the next year Nora was remarkably well. She did the house work, spoke at church meetings, drove the car and led a very full life. A year later she suddenly took ill and died. Unknown to us at the time Nora herself had asked the Lord for one more year of life, for the sake of her family. The Lord granted her request. It was a remarkable answer to prayer.

Prayer Support

Prayer always plays an important and essential part in the work of the church and played an important part in my ministry. In addition to some very committed, supportive and praying members of the church, I mention three who were giants in their prayer life and prayed much for the Summerhill minister and parish. One was a retired and housebound fisherman. One was an old lady, Miss Lemon, who in her early days had been a fellow student along with my mother. She was in her nineties, blind and resident in an eventide home. She prayed three times a day for the parish and had a marvellous Christian influence. Her generous financial donation helped toward the running of youth work in the parish. The third was Andrew Smith who prayed for an hour each morning, between six and seven o'clock for both minister and parish. He exercised a marvellous Christian ministry not only in the parish but also throughout Aberdeen. As I went about my work as minister in the parish, I always felt strengthened and upheld in the knowledge that these three were praying.

Every week as I recall some six or eight ministers met on a Wednesday morning for prayer. The ministers were mostly from the Church of Scotland. One was a Pentecostal minister. We prayed for each other's needs and the needs of our parishes.

I thanked God for all of them. I owe more than I can say to their prayers. We were in debt to each other. I also felt strengthened in the knowledge that others in the congregation were praying.

I did not find the work of the ministry easy in Summerhill. Difficulties with regard to the Boys Brigade and the apparent indifference to the Gospel on the part of so many and various difficulties that the church had to face, altered my own prayer life. I had always prayed. In Aberdeen I became more dependent on prayer and my prayer life deepened. I found myself praying for the parish for an hour every morning as well as frequently throughout the day as I went about my work. I experienced great answers to prayer. At times God seemed very close.

School Chaplaincies

There were two separate schools in Summerhill. There was a Primary School and an Academy. I was chaplain to both. In regard to the Primary School I was never invited to take part in a school assembly or other activity. The school however came regularly to church for an end of term church service. I welcomed this as it gave me an opportunity to meet both children and staff.

Summerhill Academy. My chaplaincy to the Academy took a different form. Summerhill Academy was a very different school from Summerhill Primary not simply because the pupils were older but in its ethos, outlook and non-discipline. It was a school where, through the influence of the headmaster, Mr R.F. MacKenzie, a different educational policy was advocated and where discipline was not administered!

RF was always friendly and welcoming to me. He was an avowed atheist and told me so. Many times, after my becoming chaplain, he invited me to have coffee with him in his retiring room and we often discussed issues concerning atheism and discipline.

RF was well known in the teaching world as one who was unorthodox and progressive in his teaching methods. He had authored a number of books and articles which stated his position. He did not believe in discipline. As I have heard him say in school assembly, "We make no rules and regulations in this school. We advise and recommend but allow pupils to use their own judgement and exercise their freedom."

He would say, as he said to me personally, that when first you remove the rules, pupils tend to behave like savages. However they soon realise the futility of such behaviour and learn to settle down and act and behave wisely. Many who were familiar with the school would say that in Summerhill Academy, pupils never did! In many of the senior classes pupils having checked in their attendance absented themselves. Even in the fifth year some teachers would find that out of a class of twenty five or more, only five pupils would attend regularly. Furthermore teachers found it almost impossible to maintain discipline. If a teacher complained to the headmaster about a pupil RF would almost invariably take the side of the pupil arguing that if a teacher was sufficiently inspiring he or she would hold the attention of the class and pupils would wish to behave and learn. Vandalism within the school was rife and teachers found themselves helpless and unable to control it. The expense to the school authorities, resulting from vandalism, could be described as astronomical. Sadly one of the school gangs called 'Gringo' dominated and controlled much that happened, intimidating both pupils who did not belong to the gang and also teachers. It was such that teachers declined to walk down a corridor alone. I think that I was probably the only one who did so and I was never assaulted. As minister of Summerhill Parish and through visitation of families with children at school I was aware of the school situation before accepting the invitation to be school chaplain.

The headmaster invited me, as minister of Summerhill, to teach within the school curriculum, on the grounds that, in his words, nothing was being taught about moral and social behaviour. I accepted. He invited me to teach once, twice or three times each week. I opted to teach twice. He offered me the 1st to 3rd year classes, or the 4th to 6th year. I chose the latter. Accordingly it was arranged that for my first year I would meet each week with one fifth year and one sixth year class. However before my attempt at teaching commenced he informed me that class 4c had rebelled and asked if I would like to teach that class! On my asking why they rebelled he surprised me by saying that it was because they claimed that their form teacher was an atheist. Knowing that RF was a professed atheist I asked whether that was the real reason or whether they rebelled for the sake of rebelling. He agreed that the latter was the likely reason. Certainly they were known to be the worst class in the school and the most difficult.

Probably unwisely I accepted the challenge and said that I would be willing to try but might require at the end of the term to ask for a change. He happily agreed. In accepting the challenge I was aware that I would be on my own and unable to appeal to him or others for help. Form 4c had the reputation of being the worst class in the school. To try and teach them was quite a challenge.

The class involved some 24 or 25 pupils. From the start, apart from one incident, they treated me with greater respect than they seemed to treat other teachers. Unlike other classes they seemed all to attend. For the first two or three sessions two other teachers sat in to see how I coped. They were both complimentary and said that I had nothing to fear. However one day about ten minutes after the start of the class suddenly the door was flung open and a girl flounced in, shutting the door with a bang. She was unusually dressed with multi-coloured stockings. She passed between me and the class, looked at me from head to toes, drew out a chair at the front, turned her back and began a loud conversation with those next to her. At the same time she began to comb her blond hair, eat an apple and spoke in a loud voice. Clearly she was issuing a direct challenge to me as I attempted to teach. The class became very quiet, wondering how I would meet the challenge. I said, "Alison, come out here". She turned her head and said, "I can't" and went on talking in a loud voice to the other pupils. Again I said, "Come out here" and again she repeated, "I can't" and went on talking loudly.

What was I to do? I knew that I was on my own and the class waited in silence. I can only say that for me it was a throwback to army days when I had been taught to drill a squad of soldiers on the far side of the parade ground. In a loud voice that must have echoed through the adjoining class rooms, I said, "Alison, you will come out here". She received the shock of her life and came out. There was a chair beside me and I said in the same loud voice, "Sit down". She sat down and I said, again very loudly, "About turn!" As she turned she faced the wall which was about a foot in front of her. She was now isolated and unable to assess the reaction of the rest of the class. I said that I was appalled at her behaviour and the rude woman that she was likely to become and appalled that I required to speak to her in such a way. I let her sit there for the rest of the period looking at the wall.

The rest of the class was silent and subdued for the rest of the lesson. I myself felt subdued. How in such a situation can one teach RE? I walked out of school feeling quite humble that day. The following year I took a fifth and also a sixth year class. On one occasion the fifth year class did not turn up. It was the only occasion that ever happened to me. As I waited in anticipation that some might turn up, the full time RE teacher for the school came in. In addition to RE he also taught English. His class also did not turn up that day. He had the other fifth year class and came to enquire how I was getting on. I informed him that I simply tried my best. When I put the same question to him he replied that he too tried his best in a very difficult situation. He said however that he had one and only one bright star in the whole school, a pupil in the fifth year. When I enquired about the name, he said, "Alison"! I told him the story of what had happened the previous year. In the light of what he said, perhaps no one had previously taken her heavily to task, and spoken to her in the way that I had. Clearly she had become a changed person. I felt much encouraged.

In the course of my parish visitation I continued to hear the complaints of parents and sometimes witnessed their tears in regard to the school, so much so that I became unwilling to ask parents about their children's school welfare. Then one day I received a telephone call from a parent. She told me that her daughter in, I think, the third year, had refused to go to school one day. After much questioning and pressure her daughter said that in her year there was a rota for girls to have sex with the boys and it was her turn. Hence she refused to go to school that day. I was asked as minister and chaplain what I was going to do about the situation! Another parent approached me at about the same time on a similar issue. Both parents were responsible people. One was a nurse and the other a school teacher. I was also aware that many other things were happening in the school which should never happen and was aware of the apparent unwillingness of anyone in the school staff or the educational authorities to do anything about it.

Feeling the need for action I wrote a public letter to the Secretary of State for Scotland and invited the Revd James Tyrell, minister of the neighbouring parish of Mastrick, to sign it along with me. It was published in the Scotsman and possibly other papers but I do not remember. It was a difficult thing to do while I was still chaplain. In the letter I drew attention to a number of horrendous happenings which needed to be addressed. It caused quite a stir and was mentioned on the radio in the Scottish news.

The Presbytery Clerk of Aberdeen was very annoyed and challenged me in front of the Presbytery Business Committee of which I was a member. I replied that as parish minister of Summerhill I was aware of the thoughts and concerns of my people and would continue to take such action as I felt was in their interests. The Education Committee of Aberdeen at that time was composed I think of 25 members. Five were Conservative. The twenty Labour members were evenly split between the middle of the road Labour and the far left. Officially my letter was dismissed, but I learned privately that it provoked an emergency meeting. As a result the Education Committee drew up a document, prohibiting some 12 or 15 forms of activity and behaviour such as assault against teachers and sexual activity from taking place within school premises. It was a remarkable document in that by listing activities which were being forbidden, it was acknowledging that these activities were happening in Summerhill Academy. The Committee intimated that all present and future teachers must accept and adhere to the document. The headmaster refused to sign it and intimated his refusal publicly.

Shortly after that the father of one of the boys in our Boys Brigade in the church telephoned me to say that his son had been assaulted in a classroom by a member of the Gringo Gang, kicked unconscious and taken to hospital. His son recovered consciousness after twenty minutes and I believe made a good recovery. According to the father, when the headmaster was informed of the incident he asked the class whether or not they should punish the boy who initiated the assault. The class voted not to punish so the boy was told to stay off school for half a day. In other words he was given a holiday! The father was deeply upset. He said that he could not himself speak to the headmaster or he would physically assault him. He said that it was my responsibility as minister and chaplain of the school to take action.

I was again under pressure and felt with the father of the boy that action must be taken. I asked to meet with the principal Secretary for Education for Aberdeen and met with him and with two of his deputies. I invited my ministerial neighbour, James Tyrell, to accompany me although he took no vocal part in our meeting. I laid before them the seriousness of the situation, the fact that serious assaults were taking place, nothing was being done to restrain physical assaults and no disciplinary action was being taken. I reminded them of the gravity of the situation in that they had drawn up the document concerning moral standards to be observed in school which all teachers were required to sign and yet the headmaster had publicly declined to sign it. I informed them that after several years I had not encountered one family in Summerhill Parish which had confidence in or supported the policy of Summerhill Academy. I also said that I was aware that the police could only enter the school on the invitation of the headmaster but was disturbed that he would not issue the invitation even in the case of serious assault. I said that as his superiors, however, the members of the Education Committee had the authority to invite the police to take action on the ground that assault wherever it took place was a crime. It was necessary for them to suspend R.F. MacKenzie!

Their immediate reaction was to affirm that it was difficult or impossible for them to take such action. I knew that there had been two previous occasions in the North East of Scotland where the educational authorities had suspended a head teacher and then were forced to retract the decision as the result of an appeal. I said that Mr MacKenzie was due to retire in eighteen months and suggested that they should retire him forthwith on full pay and with full pension rights. As such he would be unable to take issue with the Education Committee.

I went on and said that if they refused to take such action to rectify and reduce assault, I would invite members of the parish legally to indict the members of the Education Committee in a court of law for endorsement of crime, in that they had it in their power to take action and refused! I also said that I would canvas my parish asking whether they had confidence or no confidence in the Education Committee of Aberdeen. I was confident in what the response of parents in Summerhill would be. When we left the meeting my colleague suggested that I had gone too far but I felt that I had been right to press the Committee for immediate action. Actually, as I learned later, whereas we met the directors at 11am, on that same morning they had received intimation of another assault, which led to a boy having brain damage. In the circumstances, the committee took seriously my threat to encourage legal action against the Committee for endorsement of crime. In accord with my suggestion, the committee suspended the headmaster with full pay and full pension rights.

In that final year of Mr MacKenzie's headship, out of 96 teachers, which included the headmaster, two deputy head teachers and two assistant head teachers, some 25 teachers had asked for a transfer or resigned from teaching at Christmas and another 26 at Easter. Some felt broken in spirit and disillusioned with teaching. Of the remainder some 25 teachers had under two years' teaching experience and were waiting for their parchment qualification and felt unable or unwilling to express their opinion.

For the next year until things settled one of the education deputies acted as an interim headmaster.

Over the next two weeks some five headmasters and deputy headmasters thanked me for what I had done. They said that they were themselves unable to speak up because they were employed by the Education Department and felt encouraged that someone outside the profession was willing to take such an interest and action. In addition, two teachers who lived in the parish but were members of Queen's Cross Church expressed their gratitude and said that they believed that God had brought me to Aberdeen in order that Mr MacKenzie be removed from office. One was a high school teacher in Torry, while his wife taught between Summerhill and another academy. I was encouraged because I had wondered what other teachers might think of what I had done.

Some two years later R.F. Mackenzie had a heart attack and was admitted to hospital. I visited him in hospital. Knowing that he professed to be an atheist I did not pray with him but he received me in a friendly manner. Some years further on after I had left the parish, following my brother Tom's retirement controversy broke out over the appointment of a Roman Catholic to the Chalmers Chair of Theology in New College, Edinburgh. Writing to the Scotsman newspaper, I said that concern should not be over the appointment of a Roman Catholic as such but over the fact that the professor appointed did not represent the mainstream of the Church. To my surprise R.F. MacKenzie wrote to the Scotsman supporting me in what I said. He intimated that I had earlier expressed similar views concerning a possible appointment to an RE post in Summerhill Academy. Despite the fact that I was instrumental in his early retirement he still seemed well disposed toward me which I appreciated.

Revd Edmund Jones

Throughout the period of my concern over Summerhill Academy I found the Revd Edmund Jones, minister of Queen's Cross, very unhelpful. At first I had thought to raise my concerns in the Presbytery in the hope that the Presbytery would be persuaded to take action. Edmund Jones was at that time Convener of the Committee on Public Questions (I cannot remember the exact name of the Committee). I twice approached him and asked if the matter could be raised through his committee. He resolutely declined.

Prior to my going to Aberdeen the Presbytery had endeavoured but failed to indict him for heresy, on the ground that he was quite unorthodox in his beliefs. Shortly after my arrival in Aberdeen at a large Presbytery meeting in a theological debate I happened to say, what I firmly believe, that anyone who does not believe in the resurrection of Jesus Christ from the dead should not be a minister of the gospel. Edmund Jones immediately shouted across the Presbytery, "This is challenging a man's bread and butter!" I think that I should have shouted back, "Make sure that you are earning your bread and butter in an honest way!" I did not. Ever after that Edmund Jones seemed to look on me as an enemy. I do not think that I could say or do anything right in his eyes. At least on one occasion he attacked me publicly in a meeting of the North West Group of ten churches. The chairman however ruled him out of order and my session clerk, Douglas Duncan, in my defence took him heavily to task.

Shortly before leaving Summerhill for my next parish, it was the turn for Summerhill to have a Quinquennial Visitation from the Presbytery. Two or three ministers, knowing that as a church we would shortly have a Quinquennial Visitation, warned me to be on guard because Edmund Jones was wanting to discredit me. I was surprised, and said that had been the case ever since I had said in Presbytery that no one should be a minister who did not believe in the resurrection.

When the Quinquennial Visitation did take place, I and the Kirk Session were asked an unusual number of questions as the Visitation Committee probed the life and health of the congregation. They produced a very fine and encouraging report both about the minister and the congregation. Later the Presbytery Clerk remarked in conversation that I would be very pleased with the report. I said that I was, but nonetheless was surprised, although encouraged that the Committee would seem to have gone out of their way to commend me as minister. The Clerk said that it was necessary because Edmund Jones had written to the Presbytery and lodged an official complaint about me as a minister. In the circumstances the Presbytery had no alternative but to take action and therefore had handed the letter to the Quinquennial Committee which was about to visit Summerhill. They had considered his accusations and responded in my favour. In the end I felt indebted to Edmund in that I left the Presbytery with the unusual privilege of having a recorded commendation of my ministry.

I treasure the friendships formed in Aberdeen and am deeply grateful for the love and support which I received from so many, particularly within the Session. I give thanks to God and continue to pray for the parish.

As I have said, I learned more about prayer during my ministry in Aberdeen and became more dependent on prayer. I prayed more and became more dependent on the prayers of others. I found it a great strength and source of joy.

I felt however that the time had come to move to another parish. I had found the task of tackling the problems, and seeking to establish the congregation on a more biblical and spiritual foundation, exhausting. A minister, who later became Presbytery clerk in Aberdeen, had called at the manse shortly after I had arrived. He said that he had often wondered whether there was a church in Summerhill – its attendances at worship were so small! With its many problems he said, "Make it a short, sharp ministry and leave". I was approaching eight years in Summerhill.

Despite my tiredness and feeling encouraged by what I felt God had done, I felt that Summerhill was a young man's parish. I had regularly been involved in door-to-door visiting not just of members but of people in the parish. This was in addition to the considerable time spent in youth work. During my ministry the size of the parish had grown from around 9,000 to almost 10,000. I felt that the parish could be helpfully served by a younger man. I was now 52 and approaching 53 years of age.

One morning my wife brought me in the study a cup of coffee and a copy of the Scotsman. Looking casually at the Church advertisements I noticed that the parish of Earlston in the Presbytery of Melrose and Peebles was vacant and advertising for a minister. I telephoned the Revd Dick Baigrie, clerk of Melrose and Peebles Presbytery, an old friend from my first Presbytery, and enquired about the parish. The Revd Jack Duncan had recently retired. He telephoned back and said that he had given my name to the vacancy committee. The next day he telephoned to say that St Andrews Leckie Church in Peebles was vacant and was offering a higher salary. He wanted to submit my name to that church. In so far as he had already submitted my name to Earlston Church I did not feel that it was right for him to submit my name to the church in Peebles and asked him not to do so.

I did not give Earlston Church my *curriculum vitae*. I simply wrote a very brief note to say that I would be happy if they chose to consider my name. I told them that I was married with three children and gave the names of two ministerial referees. To my surprise about six weeks later I was invited to preach in Melrose and meet the vacancy committee. As one of six candidates I was chosen as sole nominee and preached before the congregation the following January. I was inducted to Earlston Parish Church the week after Easter.

When I told the session clerk, Douglas Duncan, that I had become sole nominee at Earlston I asked him to break the news to the Kirk Session. In announcing it he said that this was news which he had always dreaded. In announcing it he wept and so did some of the other elders.

One of the elders, Mrs Carnegie was weeping one Sunday after the service. When I asked her why she was weeping she said that it was because I was leaving. She said, "When you first came here and I listened, I kept saying to myself that I have got to leave this church. I cannot stand it. But deep down I knew that what you were saying, or preaching, was the truth. Now that you are leaving I feel sad. We want the same ministry again."

I had become very fond of the people. I felt close to them and appreciated their love for me. As when leaving Livingston, I found it hard to leave the congregation. I felt however that God was calling them and myself and family to something new.

Visit to America

Some two years after moving to Aberdeen I received an invitation to preach in America for a month. The invitation came from The Colonial Church of Edina in Minneapolis. The senior minister the Revd Dr Arthur A. Rouner, Jr. had studied in New College Edinburgh. He wrote and asked Professor James Stewart, professor of New Testament studies in New College, to recommend a Scottish minister who was, in his words, "one of the greatest of the younger preachers in Scotland today". He wished to invite him to conduct the services in Edina for a month while he, Arthur Rouner, was on holiday. I did not feel in the words of Rouner's request, that I was "one of the greatest of the younger preachers in Scotland today". However Professor Stewart kindly recommended me and so I, accompanied by my wife Elizabeth, was invited.

Being in the summer, our children were on holiday from school. We made arrangements that they be looked after in our absence, first by my sister Grace, who was married to the Revd Dr Bobby Walker, minister in Lesmahagow, and then by my wife's mother Mrs Barton. Mrs Barton stayed in the old school house next to our manse in Livingston.

Elizabeth and I took the opportunity before going to Minneapolis, to fly to Calgary, Canada, to visit my wife's brother Dick and his wife Nancy. It was a memorable and happy visit. Because we required first to fly to Winnipeg before flying on to Minneapolis, we visited my father's cousin's widow and her unmarried daughter. Her surname was Brownlie. She and her husband had farmed for many years. Winnipeg airport was built on their farm and we were able to see the farm house and steading at the far end of one of the runways. We received a warm reception from them. I was interested in that despite her living in Canada for approximately sixty years she had not lost her Scottish accent. It was the same with another of my father's cousins who, having farmed in Luss, Loch Lomondside, now farmed in the Rockies in the USA. He also after 40 years had not lost his Scottish accent. I presume that whether we keep or lose our accent has something to do with our musical hearing ability.

The people in Colonial Church Edina were extremely friendly, welcoming and kind. We were given a self catering flat and provided with a car, a 3 litre Ford Rambler. The Sundays when I would conduct and preach were 11th, 18th and 25th July and the 1st of August, 1971. The church was comprised of two thousand members. Situated in a near suburb of Minneapolis they comprised much of the business executive, medical, legal and teaching leadership of the city. There was each Sunday an early service, called a 'Sailors' Service' (for we were near the lakes where many went boating), and then in mid-morning another service. Both were very well attended with few if any spare seats. In addition there were various other services and prayer meetings which we attended and often spoke at. I also conducted a funeral. We were frequently asked to answer many questions over a wide range of subjects.

My wife's niece and husband were at that time studying at the university in St Paul's, Minneapolis and it was joy to be able to visit them and on one occasion to have a lakeside picnic.

We learned much from the visit.

Chapter10

Earlston: 1977-1991

When I was called to Earlston Parish I was astonished that I had not been required to submit a *curriculum vitae*. All I had done was to write a brief letter saying that in the light of my name being submitted to the vacancy committee by the Presbytery clerk I was happy that I be considered as a possible candidate for the vacancy. I stated that I was married with three children and mentioned the names of two ministers who were willing to act as a referee should they wish to know something about me.

It turned out that two members of the vacancy committee had known me previously. One, a teacher in Earlston High School, during her studies in Aberdeen had worshipped under the ministry of Robin Keltie, had shared in our joint youth fellowship activities and been with me on summer missions in Fife. The other, an elder's wife had been a member of Broughton Place Church in Edinburgh where I had assisted for two years in 1950-52. In addition an elder and farmer had been a boy in Knox Academy in Haddington when I was assistant there at St Mary's in 1952-53. He had not been a member of my Bible Class and club because his father farmed near Longniddry. One of his uncles was an elder in St Mary's, and another uncle an elder in the West Church, Haddington where I had often preached. He therefore knew about me and my earlier ministry. Another knew my family and remembered me as a boy and yet another was a god-daughter of one of my aunts. I was surprised and yet encouraged in that knowing so much about me they still wished to call me as their minister.

Manse and Garden

An immediate practical change was the manse and garden, which I and the family thoroughly enjoyed. The manse was an old building. It had central heating down stairs and in one bedroom, which my wife and I used, upstairs. They made alterations to the kitchen and utility room prior to our arrival. In a later ministry they have modernised the kitchen, put central heating throughout all the bedrooms, which our children had found cold, double glazed the windows and made other changes, making it in my judgment one of the best manses in Scotland. There were two attic rooms above the main part of the house which we used only for storage and a third attic above the kitchen which, being a bee keeper, I used as a room in which to extract honey. Coming from our manse in

Aberdeen which was north facing, what immediately appealed was the way in which Earlston manse faced into the sun.

The garden was about one acre, and a large part of it was walled. It contained fruit trees and we grew enough vegetables and fruit to last almost a year. There were five outhouses which had served as carriage house, stable and cow-byre in the days when the minister farmed the glebe, as did my predecessor. Later on I came to a happy arrangement with a retired farmer, Coulson Nicol. In exchange for his parking his car in one of the outhouses he cut the grass in the garden. I also allowed him a large part of the garden for his own use. Unusually for a farmer, he was keen on growing vegetables which he showed successfully in various agricultural and horticultural shows, winning many prizes. He and his wife with her sewing and baking, between them one year won some 56 prizes.

Ministry in Earlston

My time was a very happy one. My predecessor, the Revd John (Jack) Duncan had exercised a very good and evangelical ministry for over 30 years. Unlike my two previous charges in Church Extension, the church was an established one and financially self-supporting. I had none of the problems which I experienced in Aberdeen Summerhill which was a joyful relief. After the stress I felt in Aberdeen it was quite healing. The Border people are friendly and I found myself warmly welcomed by both Kirk Session and congregation.

My ministry however was very different from that of my predecessor. Jack Duncan said to me at the beginning of my ministry in Earlston, "If you want something done, do it yourself." I was appalled to find that he was the roll keeper and personally wrote out the communicant cards and lines of transference. He acted as finance convener and property convener! In my first meeting of the Congregational Board I asked for various conveners and committees to be appointed to be responsible for areas of church work. The office-bearers gladly rose to the new situation and seemed to appreciate the apportioning of responsibility for the work of the church. I kept before me in my ministry 'the priesthood of all believers'. I never succeeded however in helping the ordinary members of the congregation to exercise to the full their God given gifts. That I believe is one of the urgent needs facing every church leader.

Kirk Session

In all three churches where I served, prior to my ministry, the Kirk Sessions had been accustomed to meet only when required. I asked in all three as soon as I was appointed that the Kirk Session meet monthly.

All three churches readily agreed. In Earlston, at my first meeting after the elders agreed to meet monthly, I said, "Thank you gentleman. I now intimate that I hate long meetings. We will begin each meeting sharp at 7pm and end sharp at 9pm. I give you warning that if we do not finish our business by 9pm I will lay it on the table and take it up at the next meeting. At 9pm we will have a spiritual discussion or Bible study and end sharp at 9.30pm. I think the elders liked having a disciplined timetable and ending each meeting at precisely 9.30pm. In practice we quite often finished our business before 9pm and so had a little longer for our discussion.

Following a practice which I developed years before, I endeavoured to have an office-bearers retreat at least once a year. At first I held it for elders and wives but soon extended it to all in Session and Board along with their marriage partner: sometimes over a week-end but more generally over a Sunday afternoon and evening. We used a number of retreat centres situated away from Earlston. These I found very valuable. They helped to create a spirit of 'togetherness'. Above all it enabled us to have some serious spiritual talks and discussion. Whenever possible I invited a guest speaker.

Worship and Preaching

I always wrote out my morning sermons although I did not always adhere strictly to them. I felt careful preparation was necessary. In my student days Professor James Stewart had advised us strongly that for the first twelve years of ministry we should write out our sermons in full, otherwise we would develop bad habits. I felt his advice was helpful and necessary and continued the practice throughout my ministry. However, I never wrote out my evening sermon. The service was more relaxed. I allowed the congregation to choose the hymns, which was a practice I started in Aberdeen. People mentioned the sick and loved ones for whom they wanted prayer and we prayed for each one. The sermon was a Bible exposition when we worked our way through various books of the Bible. I invited questions after the sermon. Sometimes there were many questions, for example when we studied the book of Revelation. For a long while we had, in Earlston, quite a steady attendance of 30 to 40 people. After we moved to the church hall in order to allow work to proceed with the boiler, attendances dwindled. However I loved the evening service and continued with them all my ministry in all three churches until I retired.

Sundays when we had the sacrament of holy communion were heavy. We celebrated the sacrament at the morning service at 11.00am and in the afternoon at 3.00pm. This was followed by a communion service in the church hall for the disabled. Generally some ten or twelve people attended in wheel chairs plus their relatives. Then we had our evening service.

On Sundays I conducted an afternoon service in the small village of Redpath about one and half or two miles south of Earlston. We met in the village hall. Here we also had a small but active Sunday School. For a short period I also conducted an afternoon service in the community hall in Mellerstain. When one family with about four children moved from the district these services were not sustained, although I continued to visit those homes which were connected to Earlston Church. Mellerstain house, the home of Lord Binning and now the Earl of Haddington, was in Smailholm parish.

Ministry with the Elderly

After my arrival in Earlston I started a monthly service on a weekday in Hanover Close, sheltered housing in the centre of Earlston, and celebrated communion with the residents. Most came and came regularly.

Many Border folk, farmers, farm workers and others retired to Earlston. I did not like the idea that because a person had become frail and house-bound they no longer felt that they belonged to the worshipping community. Hence at each communion season I took the sacrament to them in their homes. Because several retired people lived close together, two, three or four would meet together in one home for holy communion. This I found was much appreciated. It became for some the first occasion when they actually visited their neighbour and often firm friendships developed. At each communion season I held the sacrament in some 16 to 20 homes. Several people who through their working life had tended to fall away from the church and been placed on the Supplementary Roll became very interested, shared in these services and insisted in giving financially to the church.

I calculated that with the services in the homes and in the sheltered housing, some 50 people received the sacrament at each communion season, who would not otherwise have done so. It helped the elderly and house-bound to feel that they were remembered, visited and included within the church. As a result I was not aware in my ministry of any complaints from the older people that they were neglected or not visited. These visits took place over the two weeks following the service of holy communion in church.

Elizabeth helped in the 'Meals on Wheels Scheme' where meals were delivered to the house-bound. About two dozen people in Earlston received meals under this scheme and my wife was responsible for one day a week. I used to help her in the delivery of these meals as it gave me a fresh and continued contact with some of the elderly.

Communicants' Classes

In Livingston my First Communicants classes where people were prepared to come to their first communion service and enter the church by profession of faith, lasted six weeks. In Aberdeen and in Earlston I extended the length of these classes to last 12 weeks and insisted that during the period of the class, they attend church regularly. Sadly like many ministers I still found that many after attending church regularly for a period fell away to infrequent attendance at worship. Some however became faithful and some found their faith during the course of these classes, which was a great joy. In order to ensure that everyone attended all the classes I frequently ran the same class twice in a week in order to meet the needs of their work situations. With elderly or retired folk who might be shy to attend a class with people of a much younger age group I was willing to teach them on their own. This happened in Livingston and also in Earlston, where one retired lady came to a very warm and living faith, being converted in the course of the class.

Ministerial Visits

Ministers, with the many pressures of parish work and the need to visit the sick in hospital and the bereaved, often struggle to visit the normal homes within a congregation. I did. Therefore in Aberdeen and again in Earlston I deliberately asked the Kirk Session to leave one elder's district vacant which I visited. At the following communion I asked another elder to visit the vacant district and I visited his. By working my way through the districts in this way I was able to visit the whole congregation every two to three years. With the other demands of the parish I needed this pressure in order to visit the whole congregation on a regular basis.

In Earlston there was a fairly large country district of twenty five to thirty homes. Previously this was a postal district where the invitation to Holy Communion was sent by post. I did not like the idea and hesitated to ask any elder to undertake an area extending from fairly near Lauder to Newtown, Galashiels and beyond. For the most part the people in the country district were farmers or farm workers. I therefore intimated that I would take over the visiting of the country district as well. This, with a vacant district in Earlston meant that at each communion season I had approximately fifty homes to visit. The visitation took three weeks and frequently I struggled, concerned that each home be visited prior to communion. Frequently I asked my wife Elizabeth to help, which she gladly did. Elizabeth did not enjoy public speaking but always enjoyed meeting with and talking to people. She was happy to visit and the people always seemed happy to welcome her and never complained that it was the minister's wife and not the minister who visited. She was an enormous help to me in the ministry.

Sunday School and Bible Class

When I went to Earlston the Sunday School had approx. 120 children staffed by a fine group of Sunday School teachers. One, Elizabeth Bruce, later on accepted a post with the Sunday School Union. Margaret Agnew, a friend and fellow high school teacher of Elizabeth Bruce later accepted a senior teaching post nearer her parents in the North of England. Regrettably, the Sunday School, in line with the trend of other churches, with the sporting activities taking place on a Sunday dropped in numbers. When I left Earlston the Sunday School had dropped to about 50 children.

I myself taught the Bible Class of some 12 young people in 1st to 3rd year in High School. I much enjoyed teaching the young people. After six or seven years, attendance at the Bible Class halved every other Sunday with the start of junior sports on a Sunday. Like other ministers I was very concerned about the situation but felt that there was little or nothing that we could do about it. On one occasion I met with parents and consulted them about their preference whether to continue to conduct Sunday School and Bible Class on a Sunday or on another day. The unanimous decision was to continue on Sundays despite the competition with junior sports.

School Chaplaincy

Earlston had both a primary and a senior secondary school taking in children from the parishes of Earlston, Legerwood, Lauder, Channel Kirk, New Town St Boswells and Melrose. At first, both schools were under the one headmaster, Mr Reid. I was invited to be chaplain of both. In regard to the Senior School I was never invited into the classroom but held end of term services each year, which took place in the church. It was always a challenge to speak to young people from Primary One to sixth year Secondary. After about two years the schools were divided under separate headships and I found the services easier. The Primary School services were held in the school.

For the first two or possibly three years the Primary School headmaster was a devout Roman Catholic. He welcomed me and I was invited to their weekly Assembly meetings of worship. He asked if I would lead them week about with himself. In practice I was asked to lead about 75 percent of the meetings.

When he moved on to a senior post in the South West of Scotland a very pleasant, friendly man succeeded him who was an agnostic or atheist. Under him, the weekly school assemblies with a Christian input ceased. He was keen nonetheless that I should still visit the school. Having enquired if I played the game of chess and discovered that I did, he asked if I would tutor the children. The game of chess was encouraged in the Border schools on the ground that it taught the children to concentrate. Each year they held a Border competition in Galashiels. Hence for a number of years I visited the school each week tutoring the game of chess. I enjoyed it. It gave me a chance to get to know the children and for them to know me. I took the opportunity to invite them to a children's club which I ran in the church and several came. In the inter-schools competition each school was invited to field a team of four. Twice we came second and on one occasion a pupil from Earlston won the individual cup for the Border Region.

Youth Fellowship

I myself led the Youth Fellowship. They were young people who had moved on from the Bible Class and comprised school pupils in fourth to sixth year. Numbers generally remained about 8 or 9. Quite often we met in the home of Miss Ann Hughson, a retired French and German teacher. Ann as a pianist and organist helped enormously. Meeting in her home allowed our meetings to have a very informal and friendly atmosphere. I endeavoured to take the young people away for one or two long weekends every year. In the Borders we were fortunate in that there were a number of outdoor centres which formally were country schools. They were situated in hilly country and were wonderfully situated for allowing outdoor walks as well as indoor facilities for talks and Bible studies. My wife Elizabeth came with me and along with Ann Hughson looked after the catering.

Latterly, when I was asked to become chaplain to Dingleton Hospital and was required to conduct a morning service in the hospital before returning to the service in Earlston, I invited a trainee doctor and his wife, Dr and Mrs Isbister, to take over the leadership of the Youth Fellowship. They were a very fine Christian couple but my personal regret was that with their leadership, I inevitably did not have quite the same intimate contact and influence with the young people, although I was still involved.

Hospital and Nursing Home Visitation

The age of residents in Summerhill parish, a fairly new Church Extension parish of some nine thousand people, tended (when I went there) to be on the youngish side. For example the secretary of the Woman's Guild was 19 years old! I wondered if it was a record in the Church of Scotland. I had a card index of some 300 young people aged 16 to 18. There were for the size of population far fewer retired people. The situation was such that generally there were not more than five or six people in hospital and I was able to visit them comfortably in one afternoon.

In Earlston, in a long established community with a parish population of approximately 2,200 people, the situation was very different. Every week there were about 12 or 14 people in hospital, and about 12 long-term residents in nursing homes. With those who were sick, in a nursing home or elderly I did not differentiate between those who were church members and those who simply resided in the community and had no Church membership.

For a long while I endeavoured to visit all in hospital or nursing homes every week. For my first years in Earlston, these visits stretched from beyond Greenlaw in Berwickshire, to Kelso, Melrose, Galashiels and the Peel Hospital, a few miles west of Galashiels. Latterly I visited those in hospitals every week and those in nursing homes every fortnight. I continued the practice which I adopted from the start of my ministry of praying and when possible reading a portion of Scripture with each patient. In Earlston although I always prayed I did not always read a Scripture passage because of time and the desire to visit all the sick. I found patients, even non-church members, always welcoming and appreciative. I was often surprised at the frequency in which non-church men, who otherwise showed no interest in the church, would say "Amen" at the end of the prayer.

Hospital Chaplaincy

For the last seven years of my ministry I was chaplain to Dingleton Hospital. I had previously visited the Hospital on a regular basis and the then chaplain the Revd Bobby Henderson, minister in Melrose, often told me that I was the only one, or one of very few ministers, who ever visited it. It was a psychiatric hospital of some 350 beds. There were three distinct sets of wards, those caring for people with nervous breakdowns or long-term nervous disorders, geriatric wards (where people had mental health problems) and wards for those with learning disabilities. When Bobby Henderson moved away to another parish, there was for some six months a vacancy in the hospital chaplaincy. I had no desire to become a hospital chaplain but the convener of the relevant Presbytery committee urged me to accept as no one else in the Presbytery had volunteered and I was one of the few ministers who was not in a linked charge. After some thought and prayer I accepted.

It was an unusual hospital, different I think from any other. The manager over a cup of tea explained how the hospital was managed. Each week the staff, involving consultants, doctors, nurses, cooks etc. met to determine the general running of the hospital. When vacancies occurred, the names of applicants were displayed on the hospital notice board, and any or all invited to comment. As chaplain I was invited to take part. I was informed that all staff could speak and make proposals; decisions would be made even on matters which were clearly in the chaplain's department. I was also informed that I could speak and make proposals on any and every matter even concerning medical work or catering! It was an interesting and radical change from any other situation which I had known. I found it challenging and helpful.

Doctors and nurses did not wear uniforms, as they believed this would be less threatening to patients. Until I came to know who the staff were, I found this difficult when entering a ward. I soon decided that the staff, whether doctors or nurses, could generally be distinguished because they were the most scruffily dressed!

It took me about a year really to settle down and feel at home in the work. I visited the hospital for two full afternoons each week and held a morning service on Sundays. I endeavored to visit every ward and if possible have a brief word with every patient. In addition to the Sunday services I held two weekly services, one in a geriatric ward. There were 8 or 9 geriatric wards graded on their level of mental capacity.

One of the wards, in which I held a weekly service, was occupied by patients who were least disabled. The other was occupied by patients who were the second most severely disabled. In the latter ward, it was not possible to hold a normal conversation with the patients. However the ward sister was very concerned that I should hold services in her ward and was always very welcoming. She often said that it was possible to tell the difference among patients in the ward for half an hour after each service. Another senior member of staff told me that that was high praise. Certainly although unable to speak normally or converse, many of the patients responded to the music and one particularly had a remarkable singing voice and kept the tune although unable to articulate the words.

In order to help the singing I obtained permission to buy on behalf of the hospital a number of tape recordings of hymns sung by a well-known choir of one of the English cathedrals. These I regularly used and found very helpful. I also used these tapes when taking my turn along with our ministers in the Presbytery to conduct worship in some of the nursing homes. It greatly helped the worship. Patients were encouraged to sing without embarrassment along with the cathedral choir.

I came to enjoy the pastoral work in Dingleton although I frequently returned from my afternoon visits physically exhausted. Each patient was different. Listening to them and seeking to help them I found tiring. I believe however that quite a number of the patients were helped, particularly those who had had a break-down, suffered from nervous tension or who came to the Sunday services. I received over the years more letters of gratitude and appreciation from ex-patients in Dingleton than I did from members of the parish.

I found my contact and conversation with hospital staff members valuable. There was a weekly prayer meeting for the staff. Four or five nurses generally attended and also, quite often one of the four consultant doctors, a lady called 'Rathie'. Being a part-time chaplain however my time was limited.

One unexpected but welcome fact was that I received £2,000 pounds per year for my chaplaincy work. All my ministry Elizabeth and I struggled to live within my income. We only did so with the help of Elizabeth's many medical locums. With the remuneration for the hospital work our financial situation eased considerably.

Visit to Africa

I served on the Church of Scotland Foreign Mission Committee (later called Overseas Council) for approximately 21 years. All three of the Presbyteries to which I belonged, Livingston, Aberdeen and Melrose and Peebles, each in turn asked me to represent them on the Overseas Council. In addition I was also appointed for a few years by the General Assembly on the recommendation of the Overseas Council. In these years I served for eleven years on the Executive Committee, for three years as convener of the Overseas Bursary Committee and for eight years as convener of the personnel committee.

At first the personnel committee of which I was convener was responsible only for the selection and appointment of missionaries. Soon this committee was expanded and became responsible for selection, appointment and training of new missionaries, pastoral oversight while missionaries were overseas together with pastoral oversight and housing of those who returned from overseas because of age and retirement. In those days we had several hundred missionaries. I received their regular prayer letters and much enjoyed my contact with them.

In 1980 I was invited to visit pastorally our missionaries in Livingstonia and Kenya in Africa. I was accompanied by the Revd Ian Moir a former missionary in South Africa, who was working in the Church Offices under the auspices of the Overseas Council. He had visited Africa a number of times and was well acquainted with our work there.

Beginning in Blantyre in Malawi we visited each of our mission stations. I preached in a large church in Blantyre, which had a large congregation, and then in a mission station. The Revd Howard Taylor was minister and a close friend. Officially the mission station could accommodate five hundred people. It was so packed that I wondered at first how I could enter the building. It was surrounded by people outside, listening in at the open windows.

The joy and spiritual enthusiasm of the people, with whom we had many conversations, was most inspiring.

We visted the hospital at Mulanje and the theological college, where I was invited to speak and had interesting theological discussions with some of the staff. We then visited Ekwendeni, where I was invited to speak in the school and also at our mission station in Livingstonia.

Thereafter I travelled alone to Kenya. This gave me the opportunity of visiting and seeing for myself a very poor district, or shanty town, in Nairobi, where we had been asked to provide missionary support. I enjoyed visiting the hospital in Chogoria and Dr Geoff Irvine and his wife. Geoff was a friend from student days, with whom my brother James and I with others had shared many camping and climbing holidays in Scotland.

In all the mission stations that were visited I had long conversations with each of our missionaries. I listened to what they said, and endeavoured to encourage them in their work, assuring them of our prayers.

On my last night in Nairobi, before flying home I foolishly ate a fresh fruit salad with ice cream as a result of which I returned to Scotland with an upset stomach.

I was very grateful to the Overseas Council for the privilege of visiting Africa and our mission stations and being able to meet and talk with our missionaries on the field.

Bible Exhibition

During my ministry in Earlston, the Revd Bruce Gordon, the Episcopal minister in Duns, arranged to have in Duns a 'Bible Comes Alive Exhibition'. Bruce was a very active and evangelical minister. The exhibition, which was a large one, lasted a week. I had earlier seen it in Aberdeen. They exhibited a model of the temple and its furniture and in their other exhibits and talks helped to bring to life many Bible stories. With several hundred people visiting over the week, and wanting my elders to attend, I promptly offered the services of my Kirk Sessions as stewards! I did not consult the elders prior to my offering their services but they very happily responded and I think all took part. They told me that they greatly enjoyed it.

Crusade Meetings

In 1989 Dr Billy Graham held a series of Crusade meetings in England which were relayed by satellite to various places in Scotland. Some months prior I received a telephone call from a member of the Bible College in Berwick asking if I would support satellite services in Kelso and serve on a committee of management. The cost of such an enterprise was estimated to be £8,000. I replied that I would gladly support the venture but confessed my lack of faith in the Borders being able to raise the required amount of money.

In the event I was happily proved wrong and I felt rebuked over my lack of faith. We received £12,000, which was the largest amount raised for any satellite meeting in Scotland. As a result we not only covered all our own expenses but were able to give money to other centres which were short. In 1990 when Billy Graham came to Scotland on the invitation of the ex-moderators of the Church of Scotland, led and encouraged by my brother Tom, we again had meetings in Kelso. I again, eager for my own elders to benefit from these evangelistic meetings and in order to persuade them to attend, volunteered their services as stewards. Again, they all happily agreed. No one demurred when I informed them that I had volunteered their services. Instead they told me that they enjoyed them and were sorry when they were over.

We encouraged our people to attend when Billy Graham spoke in Murrayfield rugby stadium and ran buses to convey people to the meetings both in Kelso and in Edinburgh, Murrayfield.

In preparation for the meeting in Murrayfield and the meetings that took place earlier in Kelso a number of preparation meetings for counsellors were held. A number of ministers were selected to lead these preparation meetings, following the special course prepared by the Billy Graham Crusade Team. I was invited to lead the preparation classes over a few weeks both in Galashiels and in North Berwick. About 90 people took part in North Berwick meeting in Abbey Church. It helped me to meet and to come to know quite a number of people in North Berwick before retiring here, although as a result of my years in Summer Mission in North Berwick I had already met many of them.

Quite a number of people from Earlston attended the Billy Graham meetings in Kelso and also the one in Murrayfield. To my knowledge only two went forward by way of making a commitment to Christ, namely a young woman, Mrs Edwards and her son Christopher. I had previously had considerable contact with her, and with her husband and son. The husband, after divorcing his alcoholic wife many years before, had gained through the decision of the courts custody of his son. Having done so, he invited a young woman to help in the home. I visited the home many times and held a first communicants' class in their home. The couple decided to marry and I felt all three came to faith in Christ. At Murrayfield, as soon as Billy Graham made the invitation to accept Christ, Christopher, without looking to his friend who was with him, rushed forward followed by his adopted mother. I was delighted for them. Mr Edwards, after giving considerable service to the church, later became an elder.

Summer Mission

Robin Keltie moved from St Ninian's, Aberdeen to Mortlach parish in Dufftown about a year before I left Aberdeen. Having led summer missions along with Robin, I then led for two years a summer mission team to Dufftown, the first when I was still minister in Aberdeen and the second when I was minister in Earlston. To my great regret and sorrow Robin, who had been deeply influenced by the charismatic movement particularly after his wife Nora's death, left the Church of Scotland and accompanied by his new wife Helen Linton became leader of a Fellowship Church in Kingussie.

Thereafter, for the next three or four years I partnered with the Revd Willie Frame, minister of Garthdee, Aberdeen, whom I had known since my Tell Scotland days. Along with Willie I led a summer mission to Port Seton, East Lothian. Here we were based in a large caravan park in the centre of which was a wooden church built around 1930 when the caravan park opened. It was a unique situation. The teams conducted Sunday worship and held children's services for six weeks every summer. The church was really the centre of the holiday community. Families, chiefly from Glasgow, came for many years because of the services provided by the church. The whole camp was later bought over by a holiday firm. Sadly the church was demolished and the six weeks of summer missions ceased. The caravan park was redeveloped; sports and recreational facilities were erected making it in the words of the manager a 'money spinner'.

For the next eight years, along with another friend the Revd Ray Sawers, I led a summer mission in North Berwick. Ray had previously led a mission to North Berwick for I think 18 years. Each centre in which summer missions took place was different. North Berwick was very different from Leven and Burntisland in Fife or from Girvan in Ayrshire where we had large gatherings of teenagers. In North Berwick, we had large gatherings of children both in our beach services and games and in Tantallon Caravan Park where we were always welcomed. Open air services were important along with evening prayers in the church which were open to all who wished to attend. Although some came with me on summer mission from Earlston and were greatly helped in their Christian faith and life, I never had the same numbers accompanying me in mission which I had in Livingston or yet in Aberdeen.

Preaching

Preaching and pastoral visitation lie at the centre of parish ministry. I have always enjoyed both and have always struggled against other pressures to give them priority in my ministry.

The greatest event in the history of the world is the coming into this world of God the Creator of heaven and earth, his taking our flesh and blood in order through Jesus' life, death, resurrection and ascension, to redeem us and redeem the whole of creation. This is what as ministers we are called to proclaim. We are called to trumpet forth both in preaching and teaching the mighty acts of God, in church and in the homes of our people.

Always the challenge in preaching and teaching is to help our people come face to face with God in Jesus Christ. As my former teacher at New College said, "Resist all temptations to dilute your Gospel. Your task is not to send people away from church saying, 'That was a lovely sermon' or 'What an eloquent appeal!' The one question is: did they, or did they not, meet God today?"[1] I have always found the hardest thing in the ministry is to preach in such a way that as minister I slip into the background or out of sight, and people are brought face to face with the Lord. If that does not happen, and it can only happen in the context of prayer, then our preaching is not truly of the Lord. When people are brought face to face with God, when they hear the Lord speaking things happen and lives are changed. By the grace of God, when I have witnessed that happening I have felt quite humble and known that it is not because of me.

The same I believe is true of pastoral visitation. It is a great privilege to meet with people of all walks of life and to be invited into their homes. Much of a minister's conversation with his people is social as he shares in the joys and needs of each family. Nonetheless I have always felt the need to pray however briefly before each visit, even while waiting on the doorstep for the door to open, so that the visit might be spiritually blessed and Christ be glorified. I have also endeavored, before leaving that home, in however a humble a way, to direct their thoughts to Christ. I personally have found that even those outside the church who do not otherwise

1 James S. Stewart, *Heralds of God*, Hodder and Stoughton, London, p. 31.

show any interest in the things of God have welcomed the suggestion of asking in prayer for God's blessing on the home and family. In my experience it is very, very rare for a person at home or in hospital to ask me not to pray. Very often it is after prayer that the real pastoral visit takes place and people open up spiritually and sometimes are converted.

Many people in our congregations and communities do not know how to pray or find prayer difficult. As Dr George Gunn taught me at Broughton Place Church, minister and elders need to teach our people to pray. How better can we teach them than actually praying with them in their homes or in hospital?

People Converted

One of the greatest joys of the ministry is to witness lives being changed by the Holy Spirit and people coming to faith in Christ or to witness the deepening of their Christian understanding and life. I have been privileged in each of my parishes to have this joy. I mention only a few.

Miss Ann Hughson. Ann was head of French and German in Earlston High School. She was a member of the church but did not attend frequently. I visited her shortly after my arrival in Earlston. We had a friendly but very frank conversation. I enquired about her personal faith, her prayer life and whether she read the Bible. It was one of those kinds of visit which I have thought to be a make or break situation. Either she would be helped in her faith and enter more deeply into the life of the church or possibly be put off! Ann was much moved by the visit and became a most diligent member of the church and strong supporter of her minister and the work of the church. She soon became the church organist and agreed after some hesitation to become an elder. It was an office which she served with great diligence. She was deeply interested in the young people and gave considerable help with the Youth Fellowship, which often met in her home. She came with my wife on our week end youth fellowship camps. I greatly appreciated her help.

Mrs Muriel Ross and her husband were retired and living in Hanover Close, a sheltered home for retired people in Earlston. Her husband was not a well man and I visited them many times, although they were not members of the church and had never professed faith in Christ. After he died I invited Muriel to become a member of the church. Because it can be difficult for a retired person to join in a communicant's class with young people I held a special series for her alone in the Manse. She was converted during the course of the class, came to faith in the Lord and has continued in the inner fellowship of the church in Bible study and prayer since. We continue to exchange Christmas cards.

Mary. As a committed Christian, Mary sadly suffered from frequent bouts of depression. The doctor despaired of helping her and felt that all he could do was prescribe anti-depressant pills. For a long while I did not know how best to help her. In her continued bouts of depression she often spoke about her attraction for another Christian lady. One day I asked her whether hers was a lesbian attraction. She said it was. I did not comment. I did not say it was wrong. Clearly she was troubled by the way she felt. I kept in regular touch with her. Gradually she opened up and spoke of her past. She said that, although her father clearly loved her, he always said, even when she was a mature woman, "Because you have done this, I will need to do it again". He did not believe that she could do a thing properly or well. He never affirmed her, or said, "Well done", or "I am proud of you". As a result her self esteem was nil or minus.

When she was able to talk about it and lay it all before God and when she discovered how she was loved and valued by the Lord, a precious member of his family and a princess, she blossomed. Her bouts of depression disappeared and also to my knowledge her lesbian orientation. She visited my wife and I a few days before her death from cancer. She died in peace and was much missed by her friends.

Stroma Lauder was converted as a girl at high school through the Scripture Union and under the influence of her teacher, Elizabeth Bruce. She was in the Youth Fellowship and studied to be a doctor. As a student she joined Holyrood Abbey Church, Edinburgh. She married a Church of Scotland divinity student and with her husband, served 21 years as a missionary with the OMF. They are now living back in the UK. He is a lecturer in All Nations Missionary College, London. We keep regularly in touch.

Graham Austin worked as a storeman with a firm in Earlston. He and his younger brother were both converted as teenagers. Graham was converted through a Christian film, and his brother Peter in the manse through my son David. They came from a large family, where some of the family drank alcohol rather heavily. On several occasions we invited Graham to stay with us in the manse over New Year to escape the atmosphere and effects of alcohol in his home. My wife and I encouraged him to study at the Bible College in Glasgow, which he did, resigning his job as a storeman with a local firm. After working with youth in church work in Sheffield, then as an assistant in Newbattle Parish, Church of Scotland, Graham proceeded to study for the ministry at New College,

Edinburgh. He had left school at fifteen without any qualifications. Through the influence of the gospel he developed and matured and finally graduated with an honours degree in theology. He has been a parish minister for several years exercising a good evangelical ministry.

Jimmy and Jane Maclean were in the Youth Fellowship. They married after Jimmy graduated. He rose very rapidly to become senior agricultural adviser in Scotland and for a number of years has worked as an agricultural finance adviser with the Royal Bank of Scotland. It has been a joy to see their growth in Christian maturity. In our weekly Bible Studies and prayer meetings we moved around three homes. Their's was one in which we often met. I ordained him as one of our younger elders. He and Jane, as lay people, have exercised and continue to exercise a marvelous ministry in the church.

People in Dingleton Hospital

I received many letters of appreciation and thanks from people who had been patients in the hospital.

A nursing sister. In the long-term psychiatric ward I met a nursing sister. Her marriage had come apart and she had had a nervous breakdown. I visited and prayed with her many times, endeavouring to help her trust in the Lord. She was always friendly and seemed to welcome my visits. For a long time however I felt that little progress was being made, then one week I discovered that she had tried to commit suicide by jumping out of a third story window. It left her crippled.

As I talked to her I felt led to ask if she had had a happy childhood. She did not. She did not know who her mother and father were and was not allowed to ask. Her grandparents brought her up. Her grandfather was a very stern man who seemed to lack any spirit of love or kindness. His form of discipline or punishment was to lock her in the coal house. To be locked in a dark coal house as a little girl seemed a terrible and cruel form of punishment. I could only listen to her story. Clearly her upbringing deeply affected her life. Although she had done well in her profession she was not emotionally adjusted and when her marriage came apart she emotionally collapsed. It was helpful simply to allow her to talk and then in prayer to commit her past and all that concerned her to the Lord.

I felt that contact helped me in my pastoral work and thereafter I asked many people both in hospital and in the congregation and parish whether they had a happy childhood. Having had myself a very happy childhood, I previously had imagined that other people had also. How wrong I was! I became astonished how often I was told by people whom

I would not otherwise have thought, that they had a very unhappy or broken childhood. I felt that God had directed me to ask this question and believe it is a very valuable one to ask in pastoral work.

A woman who did not want to live. One day in the common-room occupied by patients with an acute breakdown I sat down on a settee with a woman in her mid-thirties. She was looking at family photographs of her son and daughter aged approximately 12 and 14 and of her husband, whom she assured me that she loved very much. When I asked why she was in hospital, she told me that she did not want to live. She was terrified to be alone because she would harm herself; hence the doctors advised a period of hospitalisation. When I asked her if she had had a happy childhood she said, "No!" Her parents were alcoholic and divorced when she was five. Her mother thereon married an alcoholic who physically and sexually abused her.

It was painful listening to her story. I asked if she could forgive her parents and she said, "Never!" I asked whether she saw any connection between her inability to forgive her parents and her lack of desire to live. She replied, "No! And no doctor has ever raised the issue or suggested that there was a relationship." I told her that I thought there was a very real relationship. She had been deeply sinned against and hurt. Nonetheless God loved her and offered his complete forgiveness for everything that she might have done and offered her new, abundant life. To receive his gift of forgiveness she had to allow God to give her the grace to forgive her parents. None of us in our own strength can forgive the hurts that we have received. She of herself could not forgive the hurts that she had received. All that she could do was to pray and ask God to give her the gift of grace to forgive her parents. I assured her that the day that she did that would be the day that she began to be healed. She agreed that I should pray with her and ask God to give her the grace to forgive. Although I think she was only a nominal member of a church, the result was dramatic and the hospital discharged her within the week.

A girl of 18. I learned a lot through my pastoral visits in Dingleton. I asked a girl of eighteen years why she had been taking drugs. Her immediate reply was that she had done it to attract the attention of her parents, who she felt did not really love her. In such cases one can only listen as a minister and try to help the person to lay everything before God, asking where necessary for the gift to forgive and the gift to love, assuring them of God's love.

A case of deliverance. One day, when visiting in Dingleton, I had a very startling meeting with a man of about 40 years of age and physically well built. He told me that he was troubled by a ghost which appeared to him every night. He was terrified, and because in terror he would shout out he had to sleep in a different room from his wife. He told me that the ghost was his mother and that he wanted a minister to stand over him and deliver him. I felt prompted to ask whether he had being playing with a Ouija board. He said that he had and that it was evil and he would never do it again. He again asked that I stand over him and deliver him. I told him that I could not deliver him but the Lord could. He told me that he could not go to church. If he tried he would be physically prevented and if he held a Bible it would physically jump out of his hand. It sounded bizarre. I told him to hold my hand and I would pray.

As soon as I mentioned the name of the Lord it was as if both of us experienced a powerful electric shock. His hand shot out of mine, and he looked at me in terror with perspiration pouring down his face. He said, "I told you I cannot pray". I said that we would try again and pray. This time I gripped him with both hands, asking the Lord to deliver him and send the ghost to its own place. (I did not like to ask the Lord to send the ghost to hell because he said that the ghost was his mother.) He seemed quite calm after prayer.

The incident disturbed me. No doctor was present at the time so I told a staff nurse, a man. He thanked me and said that they would give him a strong sleeping pill that night! I later phoned Rathy, the Christian consultant and told her about the man. To my surprise and disappointment, she said that the man was suffering from some ailment the name of which meant nothing to me. She said that in his condition even prayer would not get through to him!

A few days later when I was in the ward I hunted for him and could not find him. When I asked where he was the staff nurse, to whom I had previously spoken, said that he was better. He said, "Whatever you said to him helped him so we discharged him". Interestingly the chaplain of the Borders General Hospital had a similar case at that time and we shared our experiences. In such cases I liked to contact the minister of the parish in which the patient resided and ask him or her to visit the person and provide further spiritual help.

Holidays

For a long period in the ministry we could not afford an expensive holiday. In the early years we holidayed in the summer, either in our caravan (a converted bus) or in a chalet in North Berwick. Later in Aberdeen we bought a second-hand camping trailer. It was commodious allowing my wife and me to sleep in the inner tent and the three children in the extended tent. We purchased a zip-on extension tent in which we sat and had our meals. Quite frequently we asked a vacant parish if, in exchange for my taking the church services for a month, we could camp free of charge in their manse. This was always welcomed and with our camping equipment we camped in the manse and not outside in our tent. We holidayed in Cromarty in the Black Isle, in Leven, Fife and in Kintyre and twice on the island of Lismore off Oban. Later we bought a second-hand caravan, and enjoyed holidays in various places in England, including Cirencester, the Cotswolds, the Peak District and Yorkshire Dales.

For seven years Elizabeth served as medical locum in Arisaig. At the end of the month I joined her and the children and camping trailer, and holidayed nearby on the shores of Loch Morar.

After I became chaplain at Dingleton Hospital and received an annual income of £2,000 things improved. Things further improved when Margaret Thatcher became Prime Minister and introduced a new law allowing a person who had reached 65 years to draw their pension while still continuing to work. This allowed us for the first time to holiday abroad, which we did in the Greek Islands of Rhodes, Patmos, Corfu, and Crete. In Corfu and Crete Grace, Peter and their children joined us, which was fun. In addition we had, along with Grace and Peter, several short winter holidays in November at Killiecrankie, staying in an Episcopal Church holiday home.

Bees

We moved from Aberdeen in April. I brought down the bees separately on our trailer. Having set out the hives (the number varied between four and six) I put the empty boxes at the back door of the manse. On, I think, the second day, which was very warm and sunny, Peter Davidson, a retired minister staying in Earlston, called at the back door to express his welcome. While talking to him I noticed that a swarm of bees seemed to be settling in one of my empty hives. I rushed to collect my jacket and was dismayed to find that the bees had flown. Unable to see them I enquired at the butcher shop, which was crowded at the time, if anyone had seen a swarm of bees. I was informed that there was a swarm up the lane at the side. There they settled in the hedge in a small garden belonging to a retired gentleman, who did not want them. I happily collected them and that evening ran them into a hive. So it became known that the new minister kept bees! It caused considerable interest in the parish. Twice that summer when visiting I was told that the husband was in the back garden running in a swarm of bees. I asked to watch the operation and then visited the home. I believe in its way it helped in my ministry.

In the years that followed, I was asked many times to remove a swarm in places where they were not welcomed.

Health Centre

During my ministry in Earlston, Dr John Burns, a young man, was the local doctor. When I arrived in Earlston the doctor's health clinic was situated in a council house in Summerfield Road. He was naturally very keen to have a purpose-built health clinic. Plans were made and I received a request that the clinic be built in the glebe. Half a hectare of land was requested. Because it clearly was in the interest of the community to have such a clinic, I readily agreed. Then began protracted negotiations with Borders Health Council. Having asked for half a hectare of land, they submitted architectural plans embracing well over one acre on the north side of the glebe and reaching from the garden to Kidd Gate, a quiet road running parallel to the main north/south road, the A8. The proposed entrance to the Health Centre was through the gate of the manse garden. I objected to the plans, pointing out that the request was for half a hectare of land not for an acre and a half. The director for road transport said that they would not receive permission to open a new entrance from Earlston High Street to the proposed new Health Centre.

Thereon we received new architectural plans covering approximately the same area of land, with the proposed entrance to the Health Centre replacing the main entrance to the glebe. I again objected, on the ground that, whereas the glebe had a gate into the field on the south side, this was the only gate suitable for a combine harvester if ever there was a desire to plough and cultivate the field, and use the field for other than for grazing cattle. Feeling frustrated over the way that the planners for the Health Board were treating the Church of Scotland, I contacted the General Trustees and one of the surveyors, and we pegged out half an hectare of land adjoining Kidd Gate and said that was the area of land originally requested. It was thereon up to the planners to accept it or reject it. The Health Centre and car park were duly built.

The negotiations ended on what was for me an amusing note. The erection and maintenance of a fence separating the Health Centre car park and the glebe was the responsibility of the Health Board. In the agreement we required the erection of a fence with pig netting, because in the spring sheep and lambs customarily grazed in the field. Thereafter bullocks normally were grazed. In the erection of the fence, the pig netting was put on the wrong side of the posts which held it up. The farmer, Dave Runciman, who rented the glebe drew my attention to this. When I contacted the Planners for the Health Board, one met me with the words,

"The church is complaining again!" With some amusement I pointed out the church had no complaints. I was simply drawing his attention to the fact that when a bullock leaned against the fence and scratched itself the only thing to support the weight of the bullock was the staples on the wrong side. They would soon break down the fence and walk around the Health Centre car park! The planner was rather silent and made immediate plans for the fence to be taken down and erected properly.

The South Glebe

The church had two glebe fields, divided by a disused railway embankment. The one on the north of the railway bank was five acres and the one on the south side was a little under one and a quarter acres. The South Glebe had no water for grazing animals. It adjoined a nine acre field with a substantial stream flowing through it. The customary entrance to the nine acre field was through the south glebe. Mr Dave Runciman, an elder and farmer, for many years rented both glebes and ran the south glebe and his own nine acre field together. When he sold his two farms and purchased a farm near Greenlaw, he sold the nine acre field for building. Thereafter began a series of events.

Having paid £40,000 per acre to Mr Runciman, the building firm offered the church £5,000 for the South Glebe, which had one and a quarter acres. I declined the offer, so they offered, I think, £6,000 for the glebe. I again declined the offer. Thereafter, the building firm acted as if they owned the glebe. They took down the fence between the glebe and the adjoining field which they had purchased. They brought their earth moving machinery through the South Glebe and dumped a huge heap of top soil on the glebe. I telephoned the General Trustees of the Church of Scotland several times who said that they were in touch with the building firm's lawyers, who assured them that all was in order!

One day, a short time later I went down to inspect what was happening to the South Glebe. To my astonishment, the building firm had removed the top soil and in order to accommodate their sewerage pipes, had cut a trench twenty two feet wide, in the glebe and down the whole length of the boundary fence! The town sewerage works lay to the west of the South Glebe so that the glebe lay between the sewerage works and the new building site. The church had not been informed nor had permission been requested nor given for the pipes to pass through the glebe. I was astonished and contacted the building firm's managing director. He came to the manse. When I explained my concern and about the whole way that his firm had dealt with and treated the church, he said, in a rather high handed way, that they should never have had any dealings with the church. I promptly said, "Agreed! You remove your sewerage pipes from the glebe, and let us have no dealings with one another!"

He was nonplussed at that, and silent. I pressed the matter and repeated what I said. I also said that I was aware that if he removed his pipes from the glebe and put them on the other side of the fence, he would be unable to build two houses, for main sewerage pipes cannot be made to run under houses. I proceeded to point out a number of difficulties which were facing his firm. Access to the sewerage works, if not through the glebe would require to go through the town's football grounds and it was very doubtful if that permission would be granted. Electric cables crossed the sewerage works to pylons which formerly stood on the present building site. The building firm required a small portion of land in order to erect an electric pylon, from which the electric cables would be buried. Building regulations forbade their crossing over the building site. If the building firm had requested in a gentlemanly way the church could have made available a small triangular piece of land on the south part of the glebe, that would suit the purpose. However I was very happy on his suggestion that the building firm have no further dealings with the church. The director, who clearly was not happy, still tried to keep a brave face and said that the firm owned the railway embankment and had acquired building permission.

Earlier the church, on my recommendation, had offered Borders Regional Council £3,000 for the embankment. However the church was forestalled by the building firm which offered £14,000. I now replied by asking, how would the firm obtain access for building on the railway embankment? I assured him that the church, which owned the ground on the north and south sides, would not grant the firm permission for access and that the owner of the small piece of land on the east had obtained planning permission and almost certainly would not, or could not grant permission for access to the embankment. I looked at the director and said, "All these were the firm's problems. You said that you wanted no further dealings with the church, and with that I am perfectly happy!"

The director left in silence. He was clearly an unhappy man. I am not a business man. I do not enjoy such negotiations but I hate seeing the church walked over and being taken advantage of. The next day I received a phone call from the chairman of the firm's directors. He was straightaway very apologetic. He acknowledged that the firm had treated the church badly. He was very sorry and asked if the managing director could come and see me. I was happy to agree. When he arrived he was a humbler man. He asked if, without any money changing hands, I would agree to give to the firm the small portion of land which I had indicated, both for access to the sewerage works on the part of the building firm, and for the erection of an electric pylon. If I so agreed, the firm would give the church the railway embankment without cost. I agreed and we shook hands on it. I thereon phoned the General Trustees and spoke to the lawyer concerned. He told me that this was not the way that they were accustomed to handle business deals but said that I had done well! We had parted with a small portion of land that in itself had little value and gained the railway embankment of over an acre, thereby joining both the north and south glebes.

One matter continued to trouble me. According to Scots law if the church chose to build on the south glebe, the cost of acquiring access from the south glebe to the neighbouring site, no matter how short the distance, was one quarter of the cost of the land. That is to say, if for building purposes, the glebe was valued at £40,000, the cost of access would be £10,000. However that problem was solved shortly afterwards. When planners for the sewerage works asked if the church would give permission for a new road to be built to the sewerage works through the glebe, I readily agreed, arranging that the new road be on the south, inside the glebe and that the boundary fence be placed about six or nine feet south of the road. With that arrangement the road belonged to the church, but was built and maintained by the Council who had permission to travel over the top of it. I telephoned the General Trustees who were very happy about our agreement. Their lawyers covered the necessary formalities.

Fabric: Church Hall, Manse and Church

Before I retired, the congregation carried out considerable fabric alterations and improvements.

There were two halls situated in the main street in the centre of Earlston and some distance from the church. The larger of the two halls was a former Free Church and the smaller one, adjacent to it and physically a separate building was the hall of the former Free Church. The hall of the Established Kirk, before it was united to the Free Church in Earlston, was situated at the other end of the village to the church and near the manse. Although, I understand, it was a very good building it had been sold prior to my ministry. The larger of the two existing halls had many problems including the need for a new roof. This we sold to Mr and Mrs Grierson, the residents of the old Free Church manse, who, in exchange, sold us their garage which adjoined the smaller of the two halls. This enabled us, mostly through using a considerable amount of voluntary labour, to modernize the existing hall and kitchen and create a very comfortable lounge, equipped with a small kitchen for the use of the Guild, Kirk Session and smaller meetings. Latterly we used it for our evening services.

We produced plans, which were carried through, to enlarge the church vestibule and create on entering the church an attractive 'welcome centre' that was carpeted, together with a modern kitchen and toilets, which the church had hitherto lacked. Previously the church had only one toilet situated in the vestry which was not convenient or suitable for visitors or members of the congregation. We invited the firm, Rogers, which had built the church 100 years previously, to carry out the alterations and improvements. They did a very fine job, removing carved wooden paneling and replacing it in new positions, so that for a visitor it was hard to see what had actually been done. We installed loud speakers in the entrance room and also in the kitchen, which served as a crèche, so that parents and others in these places could hear the service. At the same time the church was entirely redecorated and the heating improved.

The Presbytery had welcomed our plans for the church but approved them on condition that we first reroofed the manse, which badly needed attention.

In a remarkable and miraculous way, after the congregation approved that we go forward and carry out all that was planned both for the manse and the church, we received some very generous grants, one of approx. £60,000 in the will of a former resident who had left the parish about 40 years previously. As a result, after the manse had been reroofed and when the church was reopened and dedicated in November 1991, everything had been paid for. We were deeply grateful to God and to the generosity of those who gave. It was a marvelous answer to prayer.

Through the generosity of an elder and farmer, Mr Dave Runciman, a car park was created next to the church to allow cars on such occasions as weddings or funerals to park. The path, now widened to allow the passage of a car, was also lit when it was dark.

I did not look forward to retiring. I hated the thought. However the church was shortly to celebrate the hundredth anniversary of the present building. It was, I understand, the third church which had been built on the site since the Reformation, the first church going back possibly to Celtic times. I felt that with the celebration the church should engage on a new programme of mission and outreach. This should mean long term planning and because I was now 67 and a half years of age, I thought that it was right to retire and allow a younger minister to take over. I retired on 30th November 1991.

Chapter 11

Retirement

I retired on 31st November 1991. The pressure of church work prior to that date had meant that I was unable to attend to the personal matters of our removal from the manse until then. I gave half of my library of books, together with my bookcases to my son David, a minister in East Lothian. My wife and I finally moved on 3rd February 1992 to our present home in North Berwick, East Lothian.

On my first attendance in the meeting of the Presbytery of Lothian, I was asked to be interim moderator and locum of Chalmers Memorial Church, Cockenzie and Port Seton. I asked the Revd Ray Sawers to share the duties of locum minister with me. Between us we visited a large number of the congregation in addition to attending to funerals and marriages, until the congregation called a minister.

Abbey Church, North Berwick

The Revd Milton Cashman, minister of Abbey Church linked with Dirleton, asked Elizabeth and me to join Abbey Church, which we were glad to do. I had known Milton when he was an elder of a church in Galashiels, in my former Presbytery and had been his theological tutor when he trained as a reader in the Church. Abbey Kirk Session then invited me to become assistant minister to Milton, a role I held for six years until Milton retired. During this period, I preached regularly in both Abbey and Dirleton churches, visited a considerable number of people and conducted several marriages and funerals.

I preached in several other churches throughout the Presbytery and acted as interim moderator and locum in the parishes of St Clement's and St Ninian's in Musselburgh and locum in the parishes of Borthwick, linked with Cranstoun, Crichton and Ford. On Milton Cashman's retirement, I shared the locum ministry with Ray Sawers in the parishes of Dirleton and Abbey, North Berwick.

University Church Chairs

In the early 1990s, I was appointed to serve on the General Assembly committee for the appointment of university professors to church chairs. This continued for six years. Twenty four people serve annually on this committee, six for each of our four colleges in Edinburgh, Glasgow, St Andrews and Aberdeen. Each of the four universities appoints six representatives to sit alongside the church representatives. I was one of the six church representatives for St Andrews, and participated in the appointment of professors to the chairs of Theology and Old Testament.

For the chair of Theology, five candidates were short listed, representing very different theological perspectives. Each of the church representatives undertook to read four articles published by each candidate. We met and discussed together some days prior to meeting in St Andrews on the day of selection.

The committee met in St Andrews at 9am. The selection process required each candidate to give a public lecture and answer questions from anyone in the audience. The twelve university and church representatives then met each candidate in turn, followed by discussion together in private. At 8.30pm the decision was reached to appoint the Revd Dr Trevor Hart, then a lecturer in theology in Aberdeen.

In the case of the Old Testament chair, two candidates were short-listed; Christopher Seitz, a professor from Yale University, and a Roman Catholic priest from Germany. Again, as church representatives we undertook to read four articles published by each candidate, and discussed together prior to our meeting for the appointment. The Roman Catholic priest was extremely liberal in his theology, while Christopher Seitz was more conservative. At that time, there were some in the university Theological Faculty who seemed to be cautious or even afraid of a conservative theologian. Finally, shortly before 9pm, after a long discussion, the unusual agreement was reached to appoint both men. The priest did not stay in St Andrews very long, I believe less than two years. Christopher Seitz, although he stayed much longer, has since returned to the USA.

I found the experience tiring, although I was glad to help ensure that conservative, biblical theology would be taught to those studying in the Faculty of Divinity in St Andrews.

The Committee on Social Responsibility

For eight years, I served on the Church of Scotland Board of Social Responsibility (now named Crossreach). On three different occasions, I was a member of a commission concerned with aspects of medical ethics; namely transplants, embryos and artificial insemination, and the occult. I endeavoured to persuade the committee to study the subject of Law, and was invited three times to submit a short paper on the subject. My concern was, and still is, that laws in the UK prior to and including the period of World War II were based or guided by Judaic/Christian ethics. There was moral authority behind them. Since the war, our laws have endeavoured to reflect the will of the people and are therefore based on the whims of a particular generation. The result is that laws vary from one generation to another and lack any real moral authority. Consequently, there is no longer the respect for law today, as formerly. While the committee agreed the subject was important they did not feel sufficiently competent to tackle the subject. To this end, a series of public lectures was arranged, and the lectures published.

Travel and Writing

Grace Communion International is a remarkable church which in the last twenty years has undergone a spiritual and theological revolution, greater I believe that any church since the Reformation. Formerly, the church was unorthodox. Today it is evangelical, theologically orthodox and strenuously engages in theological education by extension. For this purpose, they have interviewed and recorded video conversations with more than thirty theologians. In 2010, I was invited to travel to California, USA to record four half-hour interviews which can be accessed on the web.

Publications. Since retiring I have co-authored three books, *Passion for Christ, Israel God's Servant*, and also *Embracing Truth*; and edited *God, Family and Sexuality*. The earlier book which I edited, *The Witness of the Jews to God*, has been republished.

Having presented talks at several theological conferences arranged by my nephew Dr Robert Walker, a number of my articles have been published, while two more are due to be published in a book later this year.

I have also been persuaded to have a website which a friend helped to create, in order to publish some of my sermons.

Visits Overseas. I first visited Israel along with some other ministers in 1981. In August 1994, Elizabeth and I worked at the Garden Tomb in Jerusalem for the month. I acted as a tour guide and Elizabeth worked in the shop. Thereafter, we led three tours to the Promised Land.

My elder daughter Grace and husband Peter relocated to the eastern USA for work in 1994. On five occasions, Elizabeth and I were able to visit them and their two daughters. After three years back in Scotland, the family then moved to New Zealand, firstly to Auckland and then to Wellington. Through their kindness and generosity I have now visited New Zealand six times during the southern hemisphere summer.

In 2012, Grace and I flew to Chengdu in China where I was born. We visited the church building where my father preached and my family were baptised. It had been closed by the Communists, but reopened in 1989 and a sizable congregation of approximately a thousand people worship there every Sunday. Although the family house has been replaced by a kindergarten school, I found it very moving to visit the site and recall stories my parents told of the riots and killing of missionaries which took place whilst my family lived there. We also had the joy of visiting the steep mountain villages where my father worked as a pioneer missionary among the Xiang tribes.

Last Words

Elizabeth. After over fifty years of happy married life, Elizabeth was called home to be with the Lord on the 3rd May 2008. She had been unwell for some time and I am deeply grateful to God that I was given the strength to care for her. Although we were always close, this time brought us even closer together. Elizabeth was a wonderful gift from God.

I never thought that I could cope in life without Elizabeth. However, God's grace, strength and comfort have sustained me over these last few years.

Prayer and healing. I have been interested in kingdom healing my entire ministry and have witnessed some great answers to prayer. In recent years I have read considerably on the subject and belong to a group who meet each week to pray for the sick. I have a list of people for whom I pray each evening and have been greatly encouraged by answered prayer.

Conclusion. Whereas I had been reluctant to become a minister, I found the work of ministry so fulfilling that I was reluctant to retire. However, I have found these years to be among the best in my life. I am deeply grateful to God for the gift of good health and for all that he has taught me and continues to teach. I have underlined in my Bible, verses 12-15 of Psalm 92, "The righteous will flourish like a palm tree . . . They will still bear fruit in old age, they will stay fresh and green, proclaiming, 'The Lord is upright.'" I pray that I may continue to witness to Christ until I am called home to be with the Lord.

Appendix 1

Reflections on Ministry

I believe that there is no greater calling and no calling which is more satisfying and fulfilling than that of the Christian Ministry. It is an immense privilege to be called by God to preach the "the unsearchable riches of Christ" (Ephesians 3:8) and to seek to make Christ and his salvation known to our fellow men and women and to boys and girls.

In my retirement, looking back on my ministry, I am conscious of my own inadequacy and many failures and yet am grateful that despite my failings God has so often helped and blessed the people to whom I was called to minister. In what follows I am not saying what I have done or achieved but rather what I had hoped to do and what I believe to be important and essential in ministry.

The Minister's Life

It is imperative for every minister to know the Lord personally and intimately and to have experienced the power of God's grace in his own life and in the lives of others. As ministers we are called to live close to the Lord day by day. For this to take place we need with prayer to read the Bible every day, not as a normal book but as the place where we encounter the Lord. If we read the Bible as a normal book it will fall flat on us. If we read it simply as a book about God it will still fall flat on us. If we pray every time that we open the Scriptures and ask that the Lord will come afresh and speak to us and transform our lives, making us day by day more like Christ, then the Bible comes alive. We will hear God himself speaking in Christ, we ourselves will be strengthened, empowered and enabled by his Holy Spirit to discern his will for us and for our people.

I was taught from an early age to read the complete Bible every year. I have done that for many years. Now that I am retired I read it through three or four times each year. In the beginning God spoke and through his Word created the world out of nothing. His Word today is life and light and power. The prophets were told to eat the Word (the scroll). We require to so read and meditate on Scripture that it enters into our very being and continually transforms our lives and recreates us. In receiving the Word that is God we receive and actually share in the life of God. Only so can we live and serve the Lord as he requires.

God calls us to pray. Prayer is the very breath of the Christian life. It is vitally important for the ministry. We read in Acts 6:4 that the Apostles said, "We will give ourselves continually to prayer, and to the ministry of the Word". Prayer belonged to the heart of their ministry as it belonged to the ministry of Jesus Christ. The men and women who have accomplished most in the ministry are the men and women who each day have spent time, often hours each day, in prayer to God. The effectiveness of our ministry is dependent on prayer. One of the reasons why so little seems to be accomplished today and churches are growing smaller and fewer and fewer young people are coming to church, is that ministers and people spend so little time with God in prayer. Jesus said, "If you shall ask any thing in my name, I will do it" (John 14:14). "Hitherto you have asked nothing in my name; ask, and you shall receive, that your joy may be full" (John 16: 24). "Ask and you will receive."

The Gospel that is Preached

The gospel is Christ, the one who was born at Bethlehem, died, rose again, ascended and now reigns. Jesus Christ was a man. He is also God. As Paul says in Colossians 1:19 and 2:9, in him, in Christ the man, dwells all the fullness of God. This is breath taking! Our earthly minds can scarcely grasp that God who created this vast universe and created each one of us, became a man like us, and lived on this earth: that he came alongside of us, identified himself with each of us in our weakness and frailty, took upon himself all our sins and his own condemnation on our sins and died for us that through his resurrection and ascension we might receive a new life and be made heirs of his everlasting kingdom. We are called to proclaim the holiness of God, his hatred and condemnation of sin, and his love and mercy in Christ forgiving us our sin and giving us new life in his family and kingdom.

Unlike a former generation, ministers today preach little about the holiness of God and his judgement on sin. We today do not call people to repent as we ought, as our forefathers did, as John the Baptist and the apostles did and as Jesus himself did. Far too often there is something lacking in our proclamation of the gospel and people are not stirred as they should be. Too often we are tempted to speak about love apart from the holiness and judgement of God, to speak about love apart from God's love as revealed in Christ's death and resurrection. Too often we are simply proclaiming a form of human love.

It is at the cross that we see true love in its reality and depth. There we see the holiness of God, his judgement on sin and his love. There we see the full outpouring of God's love, where God gives himself for us in Christ. The fact that Jesus died for us proclaims the holiness of God. It proclaims God's verdict that we are sinners, proclaims God's judgement on our sin and, above all, it proclaims God's love. It proclaims his forgiveness and salvation. The cross proclaims his mercy and love. It is in the light of the cross and of Christ's life, death, and resurrection that we rightly understand the meaning and wonder of God's love.

In preaching, it is important always to emphasise that God the Father and God the Son are one. As we see the Son we see the Father (John 14:9). The

Father and the Son are one in all that they do. As Jesus loves us and willed our salvation so the Father loves us and willed our salvation. It is wrong to preach Christ as if he in some way is separate from the Father, as if our salvation was the work of Christ and not the work of the Father. In the Gospels, Jesus repeatedly stressed that he and the Father are one, that what the Father does the Son does and what the Son does the Father does. Paul says that he is "an apostle of Christ Jesus by the command of God our Saviour and of Christ Jesus our hope" (1 Timothy 1:1). God the Father, together with the Son, is the author of our salvation. God was in Christ reconciling the world to himself (2 Corinthians 5:19). Unless we emphasise the oneness of the Father and Son in the Holy Spirit, our people will lack the assurance and security of salvation that God wants us to have.

If today there is little mention in preaching about the holiness of God and his judgement on sin with the need for repentance, there is often little mention of the resurrection and what that means for our daily living. How often do we today hear or preach a sermon announcing that we "have been raised with Christ" and are called to live today in the power and certainty of Christ's victory over sin and the world?

Likewise today there is little preaching about the ascension. Often Ascension Sunday is commemorated simply by singing the odd ascension hymn! I can recall only once ever hearing a sermon on the ascension, either on holiday or since retiring over 23 years ago! Yet without the ascension of Christ our salvation has not been completed. The preaching of the ascension is essential if our people would understand the wonder and joy of Christ's salvation and be empowered to live a life of victory in Christ.

The Gospel is Christ

The gospel is not the good news about Christ, nor yet about God and about what God in Christ has done for us and our salvation. The gospel is Christ, God in Christ, together with all that God has done for us and our salvation in Christ. What Christ has done, is doing today and will do cannot be separated from his person. Far too often as ministers we have been content to speak about Christ and about the things of God and have not actually presented Christ to our people as someone who has died, is alive and whom we are called to meet and encounter personally today. The great challenge to a minister after every service of worship is to ask, "Have the people met with, and encountered God today in Jesus Christ, or, have they simply heard a man speaking?"

Many church people and many young people despite their attendances at church, Sunday School or Bible Class, have never been brought face to face with God in Christ. They have never personally encountered Christ and do not know him as their personal Saviour. As Professor J.S. Stewart and other great evangelical preachers have said, as preachers we should "preach for a verdict". Lives should continually be changed. We need to reconsider the need to give to people after every service, no matter how we do it, the opportunity to respond to Christ.

The gospel is Christ, clothed in his saving work and teaching, offering himself to us for our salvation. Christ, in his earthly life, lived out vicariously for us a new and perfect life of obedience to God. When therefore we pray we are called thankfully to receive Christ and in him to receive a new and perfect life, the life that he has lived out vicariously for each one of us. His saving work is not separate from his person and in receiving the new life that he gives us, we receive him.

One of the disastrous things today is to encourage people to pray and ask God to help them in the way that they live, or to help them in what they are doing! If we simply ask God to help us, then we are seeking to remain in control, or in charge of our lives – we are acting as the master of our lives and our destiny! We are really asking God to be our servant! That spiritually is an unhelpful and disastrous situation! Every time that we come to God in prayer he seeks continually to renew us by giving us a totally new life, the life that he himself lived out for us, and to become the Lord and Master of our lives and all that concerns us. We are asked in prayer continually to receive that new life in Christ, and to receive Christ as Lord and Master.

As ministers we are often failing to teach this to our people and to teach them always to surrender themselves to God and to seek and receive joyfully and thankfully God's gift of new life each time that they come to him. As a result, people in our churches often become discouraged. Many feel that they have tried hard to live the Christian life. They have tried in their own strength, asking God's help, to obey him and do what he wants. Yet they feel defeated. Some even become doubtful or sceptical about the Christian faith and give up. It is desperately sad. God has done everything for our salvation, everything that we may live a full and abundant life (John 10:10). On the cross, Christ raised a triumphant shout. He said "It is finished" (John 19:30). All that we are asked to do is joyfully, thankfully to receive Christ, his new life and salvation.

If we were faithful in confronting people with the person of Christ and proclaiming his finished work for our salvation there would be far greater joy in our churches. Our people would feel assured of salvation and be more ready to take the Gospel to others.

Evangelism

Professor James Denney once said that all our evangelists should be theologians and all our theologians, evangelists. Every minister should by his calling be an ambassador for Christ, an evangelist. When I was a student at New College, the whole college once a year embarked on mission, preaching in churches and in the open air, visiting people in their homes and in speaking to them on the streets. Some of our professors came with us and led us in mission. Sadly, and to the loss of the church, that is no longer done. Ministers enter on their ministry with no experience of evangelism, and some even oppose it!

I feel that I was very privileged in this respect. After being discharged from the army, I took part in missions every year until I was called to my first parish. I participated in children's missions, and in parish missions. I visited numerous public houses, and endeavoured to take the gospel to people many of whom would never otherwise have heard it. I was never refused permission to speak in a public house, when I asked, although I did not drink, and I had many helpful and sometimes lengthy conversations with men. It was a marvellous experience.

As I have said in my memoirs, one summer every Sunday evening another student (Malcolm Ritchie) and I preached at the foot of the Mound in Edinburgh. It was a marvellous place to learn to preach in the open air. We had to be simple, direct and challenging in what we said. On most Sundays, we would be heckled by someone in the crowd, and we had to learn to give a quick, and if possible, effective reply. Our experience in street work often helped us in our replies.

Then in 1955 as I have said, I served full time in evangelism under the banner of Tell Scotland, and was employed by the Home Mission of the Church of Scotland. I found my experiences in mission enormously helpful in parish ministry. I am deeply grateful for all that I learned. I wish every minister had the opportunity to engage in mission prior to his or her entry to ordained ministry.

Christian Education

The contribution of parents cannot be overemphasised. My parents prayed for me, as they did for each of their six children, before I was born. In prayer they dedicated each of us to God, asking that we would be set apart for Christ and his ministry. It was after I had accepted the call to the ministry that I came to realise that this is what my parents had prayed. I am deeply grateful to God for calling me into the ministry, despite my years of resistance to his call when I was in the army. I have no doubt however that my parents' prayers had a profound effect on my life and on my call to ministry. I am deeply grateful to them.

The importance of this was confirmed for me when I was a part-time chaplain, for seven years, in Dingleton Psychiatric Hospital in Melrose, in the Borders. I often talked to members of the staff in regard to some of the psychiatric problems with which they were confronted. They told me again and again that they regarded the first months and years of a person's life as very important in seeking to understand some of the problems which a person faced in later years. They said that if a child was not wanted when in the womb, along with the life style of the parents, it could have a traumatic effect on that child's later life. They stressed the importance of talking, and expressing love to a child in the womb, and in the very early years of a child's life. As Christians, my parents did this, prayed, and set us as children a wonderful example.

It is profoundly important that all parents pray for their children from the beginning of their lives, starting when they are in the womb. It is also important even at this pre-birth stage to talk to their children about the Lord. I stressed this when I met with parents prior to their child's baptism. I assured them that if they prayed with their children and talked to them about the Lord, thanking him for his love and salvation, every day from the day that they were born, and preferably before, their children would have an awareness of God before they were eighteen months old. A child's awareness of God can be very real and very wonderful. That awareness is all important for their coming to a saving faith in God as they grow up.

I endeavoured always to stress the importance of teaching their children about Christ and the importance of teaching them to pray. In this it is important and necessary for parents and children each to pray, to thank God, to ask God for forgiveness and to pray for others. I said to parents, that whereas it was important to teach children to ask God for forgiveness, it is very important for parents, in front of their children, to ask God for forgiveness, and also to ask their children for their forgiveness when as parents they have acted wrongly or spoken unhelpfully. I personally did this as a father. I found it humbling but necessary. I always found that when I did this, it increased my authority and the respect of the children. When a father and mother are prepared, when necessary, in family prayers, to apologise to their children, and ask God to forgive them, then children know that the parents are acting under a higher authority and that when they ask their children to do something they do so because it is right in the eyes of God. They are not simply being asked to do something because it is right in the eyes of the parents. It is right in the eyes of God.

As ministers we need to take time to meet with, and talk helpfully to parents in the congregation about their God-given responsibilities.

Sunday School

Sadly all our churches today are seeing a dramatic drop in the numbers of children attending Sunday School. This underlines the importance of taking more seriously than we, as ministers, often do, what is done and taught in our Sunday Schools.

I found it extremely helpful over many years to meet regularly once a month with my Sunday School teachers. I often said to the teachers, as did John Calvin, that Christian education involved two things, namely the introducing of a person to Jesus Christ, and teaching about Christ. If all that we did was to introduce a person to Christ, then our evangelism is too shallow. If all that we did was to teach about Christ, then we as a church have failed. Christian education must always seek to introduce a person to Christ and teach about Christ.

With this in mind, I went over with the teachers, each month, the lessons for the next month. I was concerned with the spiritual and theological meaning and interpretation of each biblical passage being taught and the lessons to draw. I left to them the actual presentation of the lessons, especially because many were trained school teachers, able to present a lesson better than I could. I found that this was always much appreciated.

My meeting with them in this way, kept me in touch with all that was taking place in Sunday School. It helped me to know the teachers more intimately and I found that the teachers themselves grew spiritually in their own faith and Christian commitment. Once again, I stressed the importance of prayer. I encouraged the teachers to help the children to pray and to encourage the children to pray openly as a class. If a child learns the importance of prayer and learns to pray openly with others, it strengthens their faith and he or she will find it easier to pray openly with others as an adult.

Bible Class

The spiritual foundation is laid in the early years of a person's life. I believe, therefore that no matter how demanding and time consuming it can be, it is helpful that the minister, as a teaching elder, leads the Bible Class. I did this in my first and third parish. In my second, in Summerhill, Aberdeen I had an excellent associate elder, George Sinton. He was an elder with the Revd Willie Still in Gilcomston South Church. He acted as Sunday School superintendent and Bible Class leader.

In Livingston, I taught both a junior and senior Bible Class. One year I set four of the boys, who were in the Boys Brigade, an examination on Christian Doctrine at diploma level. They did extremely well. Two went on into the ministry. One became a school teacher and session clerk of a neighbouring church. The fourth became a civil engineer and moved away. I have lost touch with him.

Youth Fellowship

Today, comparatively few young people attend church or are members of our churches. It has been suggested that the average age in our congregations is over 60 years. All my ministry people have said to me that it is difficult or impossible to attract the young. In Livingston and Summerhill, both Church Extension Charges, I literally had to start from scratch in attracting the youth. Summerhill Parish when I first went, seemed especially, to be a spiritual desert!

I found the task of attracting the young difficult, and demanding. I did not feel that I had any particular gifts for it. I never felt that I was gifted in speaking to young people, as others are. Nonetheless I have been much encouraged in seeing God working among the young people in each of my parishes.

It is all important for the minister to seek to meet with his or her young people regularly and to try and know them. In my ministry I almost always led a Bible Class, Youth Fellowship and youth club.

I regularly took the young people away for various week-ends, staying in youth hostels, and, in Earlston, in outdoor centres. We tramped many miles over the hills, swam in a loch or river, or did other activities. It brought me very close to the young people. I talked to them, listened to their chatter and they talked to me. It brought us close together. Always my desire was that the young people would come to a personal faith in Christ as their Saviour and Lord.

Where possible they shared with me in evangelistic outreach. Speaking and testifying about their own faith and challenging others to commit themselves to Christ, helped considerably to establish them in the Christian faith. It was a great joy to see some enter the ministry, go overseas as missionaries or simply take an active part in the church at home.

Street Missions and Open Air Meetings

Participation in these helped my young people to grow and mature in their faith.

Captain Stephen Anderson led one of our two-week missions in Summerhill. When he led a mission to those living or working in the centre of Aberdeen, I took my young people to participate in his mission, and accompanied them in street evangelism in the centre of Aberdeen.

In regard to the Presbytery open air meetings, which I organised for seven years and which took place late on a Sunday evening from the beginning of June to the end of August, I always encouraged the young people to take part, and many did. Although a minister always preached, the young people led the singing, answered questions about their Christian faith or gave their personal testimony. Their participation, I believe, helped them to appreciate that we are all called to witness to Christ and helped them to grow stronger in their own faith. We always had a good crowd of some 120 to 150 people, although most were in some ways under the influence of alcohol, such is Aberdeen! There were a few notable conversions.

Congregational Meals

Eating together helps to create fellowship.

In Aberdeen, my wife and I suggested that as a congregation we should have tea or coffee after each morning service. It soon became a regular and much appreciated part of our church life. Thereon we proposed having from time to time a family meal after the morning service. This also soon became a regular and much welcomed event, particularly by elderly people who lived alone.

For some years therefore we organised five family lunches each year, and appointed five different teams to organise and cook the lunches. One of the team was composed of elders and another the young people of the Youth fellowship, who entered the task with great enthusiasm. On these occasions, because of our partnership with St Ninian's Church, we invited members of their congregation to join us. Numbers attending never dropped below one hundred and generally numbered between 150 and 200. It greatly helped the fellowship within the congregation, and helped members of the two churches to meet and become friendly with each other.

Pastoral Visitation

I have sometimes listened to ministers, particularly those working in large new areas, say that visitation is not possible with all the other things that a minister is required to do. This always disturbed me. I believe that preaching "the unsearchable riches of Christ" and pastoral visitation belong to the heart of ministry. Our regular contact and conversation with our people greatly help us in our preaching. Nonetheless I shared with other ministers the difficult challenge of finding time to visit every home, in addition to the visiting of the sick and elderly, and the many other things that we are called to do.

As I said earlier, to endeavour to meet the challenge in Summerhill and Earlston, I deliberately arranged that one elder's district be kept vacant. With Holy Communion being celebrated four times a year (although I arranged more informal celebrations of the sacrament), I visited the vacant district. At the next Communion season I asked another elder to visit that district and I visited his or hers. This enabled me to visit the whole congregation over a period of approximately three years.

In Earlston I also visited a large country district. Altogether this invlved about fifty homes (in addition to sick visiting). It took me three weeks, when other things (including Presbytery Committee meetings) had temporarily to be dropped.

On several occasions when I felt hard pressed I asked my wife Elizabeth to help me. The people enjoyed her visits and I never heard anyone complain that it was the minister's wife and not the minister who visited! On one occasion fellow ministers, at a conference, criticised me for my temporarily dropping attendance at committee meetings, in order to visit, and said that I was breaking my ordination vows in which I had promised to take my full part in the work of the Church. I replied that I was ordained as minister and pastor of my parish and felt that was my first priority. I have often felt that as ministers we can excuse ourselves from doing the most important part of ministry to our people by becoming over-engaged, and too busy with attendance at committees.

Holy Communion

The celebration of the sacrament is important in the life of any congregation. Christ has given it to us as a special way in which we can meet with him.

Throughout my ministry, in addition to our celebration in church, I took the sacrament of Holy Communion to the elderly in their homes, when they were not well or housebound. I did this in all three parishes. In Summerhill there were comparatively few elderly people, in Livingston and particularly in Earlston, there was always quite a large number of retired people. In Livingston, most had worked in shale mining. In Earlston, some had worked in the local timber firm or in an office or factory. Many were retired farmers or farm workers who on retirement had moved into the village. I arranged that those living close together should as far as possible meet in a nearby home. When I asked an elderly person if I could invite their elderly neighbours to meet along with them in order to celebrate Communion, my request was never refused. People gladly responded and came in their household slippers. As a result some met neighbours who previously they scarcely knew and many friendships resulted. I encouraged lapsed members to these home services and found that several who had lapsed became, in their retirement, very interested in the church and without my asking contributed financially, regularly and generously to the church. In Livingston, I took Holy Communion in 6 to 10 homes each quarter. It naturally varied year by year. In Earlston I conducted a Communion Service, generally in 17 to 20 homes, and never to less than 15. This enabled me to meet four times a year with 40 to 50 house-bound people. I enjoyed meeting them and as a result they felt that they still belonged to the church and were not neglected. In Earlston it took me two weeks to visit these homes with the sacrament.

Hospitals and Nursing Homes

Visiting the sick is an important part of any ministry. In my parishes, the numbers of required visits each week varied.

In Livingston, I had, between hospitals and nursing homes approximately 16 or 17 visits each week. In Summerhill, because the age of people in the parish was on the young side, I often had only five or six. In Earlston I regularly had approximately 27, and for a few years visited them every week. Later in Earlston I visited those in hospital every week and those in nursing homes every fortnight. Those in nursing homes generally numbered about 12. In all three parishes I endeavoured never to distinguish between those who were members of the church and those who were not. If they resided in the parish I was glad to visit them, and was aware by their response of how much it was appreciated. I was disturbed when Bobby Henderson, minister in Melrose and chaplain of Dingleton Psychiatric Hospital, often said to me, that, with rare exceptions, I was the only minister apart from himself who visited psychiatric patients. Other ministers avoided visiting them.

When Bobby Henderson moved to another parish, I was asked by Presbytery, on the ground that no minister had offered or agreed, to become chaplain. I was minister of a single parish and if I did not accept the post of chaplaincy would be dropped. Reluctantly I agreed. I did not feel qualified for such an appointment. It took me approximately a year, visiting the hospital on two long afternoons each week, before I began to become accustomed to the task. It was at that time a 350 bed hospital, with three distinct parts, the psychiatric, the geriatric and the mentally handicapped. I visited each ward and endeavoured where and when possible to talk briefly to each patient. I held two services in wards each week and one on a Sunday morning. I often found it tiring and exhausting. Patients who had suffered a nervous breakdown often required time for the chaplain to listen and whenever possible to pray with them. I found it however immensely rewarding and found patients often very appreciative. I received more letters of thanks and appreciation from patients who had been helped and discharged, than I did from members of any of my congregations.

Reading and Prayer

I always regarded reading a portion of Scripture and prayer an essential part of a minister's visit. I very often used the reading from the Daily Light which had the advantage on many occasions of my reading the meditation for the day and not choosing a particular passage, which I thought appropriate for that home. Nonetheless because of the sheer numbers of homes or sick people to visit I sometimes omitted the reading and simply prayed. I always however endeavoured to direct their attention to Christ. Ministers have said to me that they prayed when they felt that the occasion required it, or when there was a special need. I always did. Having asked if I could pray and ask God's blessing on the home, or ask for God's guidance or healing for a family member, depending on the particular needs of the home, I do not think that my request was ever refused. Accordingly I have prayed in the homes of ardent atheists. There are few people who, when sick or worried, refuse the offer on the part of the minister to ask God's blessing! In hospital prior to an operation I have often heard men who never came near the church, say "Amen!" at the end of the prayer. On numerous occasions people, church members and non-church members have expressed gratitude. Some have said that their healing was a result of the prayer.

I always felt disturbed when other ministers visiting people in hospital never prayed. I frequently found both in the home and in hospital that it was after prayer that a person opened up and spoke of some special need or concern, and the real pastoral visit began. People, in my experience, greatly appreciated the minister praying with them or with the family.

A further important reason for the minister praying when he visits, is because many people do not know how to pray. It is through hearing the minister, or elder, praying along the lines of a family's needs that many people learn to pray and are encouraged to begin to pray. People have spoken appreciatively to me about this.

The Minister's Prayer Life

Prayer has always played an important part in my life. I have always prayed. Prayer is a vital part of any ministry.

I found it important in each of my parishes to pray, for without prayer and our continued prayerful reliance on the triune God of love to accomplish what we cannot do, we can accomplish little or nothing in ministry. One of the greatest needs to day, when our church is facing so many problems, being invaded by the world and declining in membership, is a prayerful ministry . . . yet not simply a prayerful ministry: we have to encourage our people to pray. If our churches did as we read Jesus' first followers did, as recorded in the Book of Acts, great things would be happening. God would be glorified in Christ.

No matter how long we have lived as Christians and served the Lord, there is always so much more to learn about prayer and the powerful way that God acts through prayer. In Aberdeen, where I found the work of ministry hard going, I began to pray for an hour a day before breakfast and found it both helpful and essential. I was also very conscious of the prayers of others, particularly of a retired house bound fisherman, an elderly blind lady in an eventide home, who prayed for the parish three times a day and an elder and hairdresser who prayed for me and for the parish, each morning for an hour before breakfast. I told the people from the pulpit that I was praying for them and asked for their prayers that God would bless and build up his Church. I am glad to say that many did pray.

I found it necessary and helpful in each of my parishes to pray every day that I would love the people to whom God had called me to minister. I prayed for Christ's love so long as I was minister of that congregation. We are all weak and sinful. We can all, minister and people, say and do things which can trouble or upset others. We need to be understanding and patient with one another, to ask one another for forgiveness, when perhaps quite unwittingly, we have upset someone. For this we need the love and humility of Christ. On occasion, when I discovered that someone was disturbed or upset by what I have said or done, I never hesitated to visit and speak to that person and apologise.

I always found my people ready to forgive me. Almost invariably they graciously replied that he or she was to blame, not the minister. I soon discovered if a congregation knows that their minister loves them they will always forgive him/her. As the apostle Peter said, "Love each other deeply, because love covers over a multitude of sins (1 Peter 4:8). We need minister and congregation to pray that we will grow in the love of Christ.

Having prayed day by day that I would love my congregation, I found it very hard to leave a congregation and move on to another parish. God had created a bond of love. The service of ordination and induction, no matter how seemingly simple, had become under God a marriage between a minister and his people.

I also found it helpful to pray before every meeting of the Kirk Session and Congregational Board and also before every visit. I found that often the briefest of prayers while knocking at a door and waiting on the door step greatly helped the nature of the pastoral visit.

James said in his Epistle (5:16), "Pray for each other".

Marriages

Ministers are given a great opportunity to speak about Christian marriage when a couple come asking to be married in church. Many years ago, the St Andrew Press published a little book, *Christian Marriage*. I have long been disappointed that that booklet is out of print. The opening sentence in the booklet was, "A Christian marriage is between man, God and woman, three people not two." I always endeavoured to explain that there is a form of marriage, open to anyone throughout the world; and this involves two people, a man and a woman. A Christian marriage is different. It is 'in the Lord' and involves three people. It is a marriage in which God is the builder and maker (Psalm 127:1). I used to say that whereas I, as a minister of the Church of Scotland, could marry them in the eyes of the law, I could not marry them in the eyes of God. That is something that only God can do. If they wanted God to marry them and to have the security of knowing that God was the Lord of their marriage, then it was necessary for them both to pray and commit their lives to the Lord, to commit to God their love for one another and to ask God to marry them. I asked them to do that after leaving me and when they were alone together. I said that in so far as they had done that before we met together in Church, then we could say with meaning after they had publicly taken their vows, "Those whom God had joined together, let not man put asunder."

I encouraged them always to give to God the foremost place in their lives and in their marriage and to seek day by day to pray, give thanks to God, to read the Bible together and together to seek God's blessing on their lives and marriage. I always recommended them to read certain portions of Scripture prior to their marriage and always throughout their marriage to keep before them Paul's words in Ephesians chapter 4:26, "Do not let the sun go down while you are still angry".

Every couple will from time to time have a tiff or worse a quarrel. I said never be the last to say "sorry!", and always pray together and together ask

God's forgiveness, for your own part in the quarrel, not for the other's part. I was always encouraged when a couple told me later that they had prayed together before their marriage and committed themselves and their marriage to the Lord. Sometimes, non-church members who to me seemed the most unlikely to do so, told me that following my advice they had prayed. Sometimes years later, I was told or received a letter that said prayer had saved their marriage.

Sadly today almost fifty per cent of marriages come apart. In the early days of my ministry, I rarely saw this within the membership of the church. Later on members' marriages came apart, then elders, and today sadly broken marriages occur all too frequently in the ordained ministry. Throughout my ministry I always tried to visit both parties to the marriage, and endeavoured to persuade them to be reconciled with each other. Quite often I visited one of the parties who had moved away to the other side of Scotland. I found that other ministers, even evangelicals, were unwilling to help in these circumstances so I myself visited the one who had gone to stay in their parish. I pointed out the need for both parties to kneel at the foot of the cross and each to ask God for forgiveness for their sins and for their responsibility for the break down, and thereby through the Holy Spirit to rise up as one new person in Christ. On occasion, it might mean starting married life again from the beginning. I found this the most difficult area of ministry. I experienced many failures but God always graciously encouraged me to continue by allowing me to see occasions when a couple came together, sometimes after weeks or months of separation.

I believe that the failure of so many marriages within the Church is because of our failure as ministers to teach that God calls for us to surrender our entire lives to him and to receive a totally new life, the life which Christ has lived vicariously for each of us. For far too many members, and sadly for many ministers, their Christian lives seem to be compartmentalised. Intellectually they believe in God. They worship and seek to serve him, but their physical and sexual lives do not seem to be committed to God. They do not pray about their physical and sexual emotions and they are not truly committed to God. For far too long as ministers we have failed to speak and teach about marriage and the part that our God-given sexual emotions rightly play. Our sexual emotions are God-given and holy and need always to be so regarded. As Billy Graham has said, "Sex can bring heaven into the marriage and into the home or it can bring hell."

I will not here speak about divorce and the remarriage of divorced persons having written about it in the book *God, Family and Sexuality*.[1]

The Priesthood of Christ

As the Bible so strongly affirms, Christ is our great high priest. He alone has made atonement for our sins and reconciled us to God. He alone is the

1 Ed. D.W. Torrance, Handsel Press 1997 p. 108.

mediator between us and God. Only in a secondary sense is a person a priest, and only in Christ, by sharing through the Holy Spirit in Christ's priesthood.

As Christ alone is priest so there is only one ministry, Christ's ministry. Our ministry is and can only ever be a sharing through the Holy Spirit in Christ's ministry. There is not a multiple number of ministries in the Church. There are many who are called to share in Christ's ministry, but always it is his ministry. We often forget that! We often think and plan and act as if it is we who are ministers and that the work and development of the Church depends on us! I am sure that this is a common cause of what is called "ministers' burn out". We fail far too often to discover through prayer what God is seeking to do and is doing and therefore fail to engage with him in what he is doing.

God has come in the man Christ Jesus and lived a vicarious human life for us. He alone in a perfect and holy way responded to the Father on our behalf, in love, in worship, in obedience in the service of the Kingdom. We can only rightly respond in love, worship obedience and service, as we are clothed with Christ and through the Holy Spirit share in his response to the Father. We are called to be united with Christ through the Spirit and to share in his ministry.

The Priesthood of all Believers

The apostle Peter (1 Peter 2:9) writing to the Church said, "You are a chosen people, a royal priesthood". I have tried to keep these words before me throughout my ministry. Christ is our great high priest. He alone is priest. There is only one ministry, Christ's ministry, yet all of us are called through the Holy Spirit to share in his ministry, his priesthood.

This means that the ministry can never rightly be a 'one man show', as sadly can be all too common in the Church, where everything depends on the one set apart as minister. A minister once said to me on my entering a new parish, "If you want something done, do it yourself!" I have always believed that in the Presbyterian Church the minister and elders are called to serve as a team. I believe not only that the elders should share responsibility for the administrative affairs of the church but also share in the spiritual oversight and the pastoring of the congregation. I have in my ministry tried to train and educate the elders in this direction, encouraging them where possible to pray in the homes and in helping people in their faith. I feel I have had very modest success. In Livingston I was blessed in having Jock Purves a former missionary in India and then lay missionary in the Shetlands. I made him an elder and asked the Presbytery to commission him as a reader. Not only did he preach when I was on holiday or at special services but he regularly shared with me in the conducting of funerals. His help was much appreciated both by me and the congregation.

Before I left Livingston, we had in the summer months three morning services, one in Livingston Village, and one in St Andrews, Livingston Station plus an evening service. Two elders on occasion took a service and preached in the morning. Some years later, and long after I had left, I learned that when a vacancy occurred, seven of the elders whom I had endeavoured to train volunteered to conduct and preach in turn at one of the morning services. I was greatly encouraged. In Summerhill, I invited Andrew Smith, a very godly hairdresser, to be an elder and asked the Presbytery to commission him as a reader. He in turn preached in my absence and took funeral services. Aberdeen Presbytery when I was a member and before it was split in two was one of the largest presbyteries in Scotland. They had within the Presbytery only two readers. At the last Quinquennial to Summerhill parish before I left, the Quinquennial Committee expressed surprise that we had five in training to be readers. I left Aberdeen before they were commissioned. I felt that it was spiritually helpful to have a team who were able and equipped to conduct worship. Other elders however in each of my parishes found it difficult to pray publicly or conduct worship. Earlston Parish today is blessed with quite a few who are so equipped and able to give a real spiritual lead.

The apostle Peter said of the church to which he was writing, "You are a kingdom of priests". Everyone in whom God lives in Christ through the Holy Spirit has been given the gifts of God, in all their manifold fullness. Everyone is called of God to exercise their gifts and through the Holy Spirit to share in the ministry of Christ. I believe one of the great needs today is the enabling of all the members of the Church to exercise their God-given gifts. For me it has been a joy to witness some ordinary and humble members of my congregations exercise some of their gifts.

God, in the course of my ministry, called seventeen people to be ministers. Three more were commissioned as readers, or lay preachers, five as overseas missionaries. Five completed a three year course in theology in New College, with others attending particular course lectures. Others have held positions of Christian leadership.

The majority in my ministry, however, have not exercised all the gifts that God has given them. I have not known what to do and how to help them. In this, sadly, I feel I have failed. My continued prayer is that the Holy Spirit will come afresh upon them and his whole Church, to renew and equip every member to use their God-given gifts and live to the glory of God.

Appendix 2

The National Bible Society[1]

Shortly after I was inducted as minister of Livingston Parish I was invited to be a director of the National Bible Society of Scotland. With my father's long association with the Bible Society in China and my own concern to see the Bible made available, as far as possible, to the nations of the world, I gladly accepted the invitation and continued to be a director for a number of years until I moved to Aberdeen.

There were approximately 60 directors drawn from various parts of Scotland and an Executive Committee of some ten or twelve directors who planned and ordered the business.

The layout of the agenda and minutes for the meetings of the directors when presented seemed straightforward. They were of a similar pattern to those of the Foreign Mission Committee of the Church of Scotland, of which I later became a member. Nonetheless, for a long time I found it difficult to understand the business and the decisions being taken by the directorate, who simply endorsed, or rubber stamped, the recommendations made by the Executive Committee and presented by the general secretary. At first, I accepted the situation and assumed that it was because I had very much more to learn.

Mr Ian Morrison was at that time superintendent of the Bible Society Office in Malaya with, I think, about 12 of a staff. I was deeply impressed by his work and had occasion to use a video film which he produced about the Gospel among the Murut people of Borneo. It was an exciting story of the marvellous power of the Word of God, when translated into the language of a wild, warlike indigenous people, and their spiritual transformation. Largely because of the work of the Bible Society as portrayed in that film and what Ian Morrison was doing, I held Ian Morrison in high regard. However to my surprise and dismay not long after I was appointed to the Board, the directors endeavoured to sack him, despite the fact that he had given over 30 years excellent service in the work of the Bible Society.

The decision to dismiss Ian Morrison was promptly challenged by the Council of Churches in Malaya. I think the chairman of the Council was the Revd Mr Fleming, who later became a reader and lecturer in theology and missions in St Mary's College, St Andrews University. The Malayan Council of Churches represented all the mainstream churches in Malaya. They wrote to the National Bible Society supporting Ian Morrison and saying that if the Bible Society dismissed him, they would discontinue all contact with the National Bible Society of Scotland.

1 Now called the Scottish Bible Society.

Accordingly the Board of Directors rescinded their decision to dismiss Ian Morrison and he continued as superintendent in Malaya.

Although a director and attending the various meetings when these matters came before us, I did not at that time take an active part in the decisions taken, feeling that I did not have sufficient knowledge. Nonetheless the whole matter disturbed me. I was relieved that Ian Morrison, whom I respected, was still the Society's agent in Malaya.

Sometime later the general secretary of the Bible Society resigned and moved to Australia. The Revd Hamish Alexander, a missionary in Malawi, was appointed the new general secretary and Ian Morrison returned to the UK. Ian was for a short time employed in the Bible Society central office in St Andrew's Square, Edinburgh. Ian was perhaps the ablest person employed by the Bible Society and one of the most, if not the most, hard working and efficient of the Bible Society staff. Ian would start work in the office at 8 o'clock and attend to his mail before the rest of the staff arrived to start work at 9 o'clock.

That summer, following Ian's arrival back in the UK, I was disturbed to learn at a meeting of the Board that the accounts of the Bible Society did not pass the annual audit! I have never enjoyed matters of finance and accounts. I have always been glad to leave such matters to accountants and those who enjoy working with finance. However, with others, I was much disturbed to be told that the accounts of the Bible Society had failed an audit. I did not know why and was glad when some months later they passed. As I learned later, it was through Ian and his hard work that they passed the audit. Ian told me that there were hundreds of Bibles, that should have gone to Malaya, rotting in the basement, and which required to be destroyed. These Ian attended to, barrowing out several tons. Not content with estimating the number of Bibles in a room, he meticulously counted each one. It was as a result of his efforts, not those of the secretary or accountant, that the finances were put in order and the books were audited.

In the months that followed there was a considerable reorganisation of the work of the Society in Scotland. A new general manager was appointed in addition to the accountant. Scotland was divided into five regions and five different people were appointed to each region. It was his or her responsibility to promote the work of the society in their region and to seek financial support for the Society. Ian Morrison was put in charge of the Western region which embraced Clydesdale and Ayrshire and possibly Argyllshire. He told me later that he requested to work for the Society as far away as possible from their headquarters in Edinburgh. With his hard work and attention to detail, his colleagues in the head office found him hard to work with and Ian recognised that.

Difficulties soon emerged under the new general manager. He was an experienced Christian businessman and his appointment to the Bible Society was his first experience of working in a Christian organisation or society. He, perhaps understandably, tried to implement the method of employment used in secular business. He wanted each employee to clock in and clock out at a definite time each day, and a record kept of what was done each day and the time taken to accomplish a particular piece of work. If for example one of the five regional officers gave hospitality to a guest speaker, and conveyed the speaker to a railway station or airport, he required that the exact time spent in the giving of hospitality be recorded, along with the time taken to convey the speaker, and the time when the officer returned to work.

Ian Morrison refused to comply and in so doing voiced the thoughts or complaints of his colleagues. The Executive immediately, with the support of the general manager, sought the approval of the Board of Directors to dismiss Ian on the ground of insubordination and refusing to obey instructions.

I received through the post the intimation of Ian Morrison's proposed dismissal a few days before a meeting of the Board of Directors, which on that occasion was held in Perth, where our chairman was a Church of Scotland parish minister. I, along with the other directors, was given no reason for Ian's proposed dismissal other than a brief statement that he was a difficult employee of the Society. This was in spite of the fact that Ian did more than any of his colleagues to publicise the work of the Society, worked harder and brought in more money to the Society than did the other regional representatives. Prior to the meeting I spoke to the chairman and secretary and said that I was unable to endorse Ian's dismissal, because I had no intimate knowledge of the circumstances which gave rise to such a proposal. Both chairman and secretary were disturbed by my refusal to endorse Ian's proposed dismissal and said that they required the approval of the directors.

I insisted that because Ian's livelihood and reputation was at stake, and I did not have the information to make a responsible judgement I could not endorse their proposal. In the meeting that followed the secretary spoke at length saying that for years Ian had proven himself to be a difficult person, insubordinate to management. He laid on the table two very thick folders, said that the information concerning Ian was all there and any director was entitled to read the two folders. Thereon it was agreed that Ian be dismissed forthwith. Only I and another director, the Revd John Stevenson, who at that time was a Church of Scotland minister in Leven, Fife, objected. His dismissal meant that he lost his pension!

I promptly contacted the office in St Andrew's Square and took up the challenge of reading the two very large folders. I was the only director to do so. Over the next two or three days, and spending several hours each day, I read through the entire minutes, covering thirty years, of the Malaya agency. I also read through every letter over a period of thirty years, which was sent from the office in Edinburgh to the agency in Malaya, and every letter sent from the Malaya agency to the Office in Edinburgh.

As I read many things became clear, things which had long puzzled me. I discovered the sad fact that, shortly before my appointment to be a director, £20,000 of Bible Society money had been stolen or gone missing. The general manager had confessed to stealing £10,000 and had been sentenced to 18 months in prison. £10,000, however, had never been accounted for. I presume, but do not know, that the general manager, although confessing to the stealing of £10,000, was actually responsible for the loss to the Society of £20,000.

In the early or mid-fifties that was a very large sum of money and hugely embarrassing to a Christian charity like the Bible Society which relied on the generosity of Christian supporters. It was also very embarrassing for the general secretary, who was in charge of the central office and whose room was next door to that of the general manager. As Ian Morrison told me afterwards, in the course of the trial of the general manager it had become clear that the manager over a period had been giving substantial Christmas presents to the general secretary, such as a refrigerator or washing machine. These presents, and the friendship that followed, prevented the secretary seeing what was actually happening in the office next to his.

From my reading, and subsequent conversations with Ian Morrison, I learned that the general manager, in order to carry out his embezzlement, had forged the signature of Ian Morrison, presumably because Ian was in Malaya and not in the UK. As a result, when the short-fall in the finances was first discovered suspicion fell on Ian and he was challenged or accused. Ian immediately went very meticulously through all the accounts of the Malayan agency. Having ascertained that all his accounts were in order, he then, in order to satisfy others, and in order to clear his name, called in an outside agency. He asked them to go through all the finances and audit the accounts. This they did. They were in order. Ian then informed the general secretary, suggesting that responsibility for the shortfall in the finances lay with the management in Edinburgh. It was then discovered that the general manager was guilty. Sadly, this led to an unhappy relationship between Ian, who had been falsely accused, and the general secretary, who was no doubt sensitive to his own shortcomings in failing to notice the terrible things that had being happening under his administration.

Following the court case and imprisonment of the general manager, the secretary with the support of the directors wished to employ at considerable cost an outside agency to travel to Malaya and Borneo and film the exciting work taking place among some of the indigenous peoples, to which I have already referred. Ian, who was a competent photographer, objected because of cost and chose to produce and edit the film himself. The general secretary, and from his letters it is apparent, was angry and accused Ian of not submitting to the decisions of the directors. This was the cause of the abortive attempt to dismiss Ian to which I have already referred, but did not at the time understand. In my opinion, Ian had acted in the best interests of the Society, and was totally innocent of the accusations made against him

I also discovered from my reading that the Executive had attempted to sweep under the carpet the acutely embarrassing fact that £10,000 was missing from the Society's funds, and had never been accounted for. To accomplish this, there were created two sets of minutes! One was for decisions taken by the Executive. The other was for the proceedings of the Board, who were not presented with all the information and were called simply to endorse the decisions of the Executive. I believe that most of the directors were not aware of the loss to the Society of such a vast sum. There was a clear lack of transparency in the working of the Society. I discovered why hitherto I had been unable to understand, or follow the proceedings of the Society.

I further discovered that the amount of money spent in the UK was over 45% of the total monies received so that only a little over half the monies was sent overseas. In fairness to the Society, it is difficult to decide whether money spent on Bibles for overseas that were published in the UK should be credited as home or overseas expenditure. Still I was disturbed at the finances of the Society and what, to me, was an imbalance of home as against overseas expenditure.

Also at that time, I was disturbed by the fact that the full time staff field agents of the Society, whether working overseas or in Scotland, were not permitted to attend the meetings of the directors, were not permitted to state their views, despite the fact that they knew more about the needs of the society than the directors, and were not permitted to share in discussion prior to decision making.

I wrote out my assessment of the events which led up to the present situation and to the dismissal of Ian Morrison. I gave what I wrote to the secretary, and to agents in the office and the home field. At the next meeting I intimated to the Board of Directors what I had discovered and presented certain proposals. I spoke at some length, although tried in the circumstances to be brief. I was greeted with a measure of stunned silence. I made the following statement and presented the following proposals.

I stated that from the minutes and letters which I had read, Ian Morrison was in my opinion totally innocent of all the accusations that had been laid against him. He had proved to be a most dedicated, competent and able servant of the Society.

I said that his dismissal was wrong.

The loss of his pension was wrong and unjust.

I stated the loss of £20,000 pounds which the Society had incurred and that £10,000 had never been accounted for. (I think many or most of the directors at the time had not been aware of this)

I stated that there had been an attempt to sweep the loss of £10,000, which had not been accounted for, under the carpet and to try and conceal the loss by creating two sets of minutes, thereby failing to give the Board much necessary information that was required to make decisions.

I stated that as a Christian society there must be complete transparency in the handling of all monies, that the directors required to receive the fullest possible information on all matters, and that whereas the minutes of the Executive were a guide to directors, there should henceforth be only one minute of all decisions taken.

I proposed that all field agents should be invited where possible to attend all the meetings of the Board of Directors, on the ground that they knew far more of the needs of the Society than did the directors. I proposed that they be encouraged to speak and enter into discussion over all matters that were before the Board, although possibly the decisions should be taken only by the directors. I raised the whole issue of the Society's finances and my concern that there was a serious imbalance of the money allocated to home expenditure compared with what was being sent overseas. I strongly recommended that the Society employ a competent outside agency to advise the Board on such matters.

I had throughout this period only one supporter in John Stevenson, although he did not, as far as I can remember, speak in the meeting. I felt very much that mine was a lone voice.

The chairman, the secretary, the treasurer and general manager were kindly and well-meaning Christian people. Hamish Alexander, although I liked him and he always remained, even after all these events had passed, friendly toward me, was not in my opinion an efficient secretary and organiser and not one who could competently tackle and clear up the mess which he inherited. Unfortunately when the general secretary resigned and handed over to Hamish, he briefed Hamish (and I believe the chairman) about past happenings in the Society and wrongfully accused Ian of being a difficult person, who in his opinion should not continue to be employed by the Society. I doubt whether Hamish, or the chairman of the Society, ever read the past minutes and letters in the files which Hamish laid before the Board. Both I believe had been influenced by the opinions of the previous general secretary. That coloured their opinion of Ian and led to the proposal to dismiss him.

Following my contribution, the Board, on the recommendation of the Executive, was adamant that it had made the correct decision in dismissing Ian. I was unable to persuade them otherwise. I was equally unable to persuade the Board to give to Ian his well earned pension, which I found unjust.

I was also dismayed that no one in the Society was concerned to help Ian in his situation. In my concern I approached Dr Horace Walker, the secretary of the Home Board of the Church of Scotland. Horace had always been friendly to me. We had lunch together. I shared with Horace my interpretation of the unhappy events in the Bible Society leading to Ian Morrison's dismissal after over 30 years of service. I asked if the church could help. Horace rightly said that he did not wish to become involved in the affairs of the Society but was willing to accept my opinion of Ian and my suggestion that he was an extremely competent organiser and photographer. As a result Horace persuaded the Home Board to appoint Ian as Head of the Department of Visual Aids of the Church of Scotland. Ian much enjoyed the post and held it for five years until his retirement.

Because I felt that mine was a lone voice among the directors and I felt that I had become, unwillingly, a disturbing presence in the Board and because controversy disturbs me, I took the opportunity in accepting the call to a parish in Aberdeen to resign as a director of the Society. I felt that some of the senior members of the Board were relieved.

Ian now had a salary and work security. Nonetheless, I was still concerned over the Society's failure to give him a pension, and later on I tried again, with my brother-in-law Bobby Walker. We stressed that it was a matter of Christian justice and in our opinion we could not expect God truly to bless the work of the Society unless justice was done. However we failed to persuade the new Secretary to reconsider the case.

When Mrs Morrison died Ian, who had been deeply grateful to me for my support, asked me to take her funeral service. Some time later Ian, being not well, moved into sheltered housing near Lanark, run by a Christian charity. He was well looked after and was happy when I visited him. It was while he was in sheltered housing that his youngest son, a colonel in the army, persuaded the National Bible Society to rectify the past, and award his father a pension.

A few months after I had moved to Aberdeen the Bible Society agent responsible for the work of the Society in the north east of Scotland called at my manse. He told me, with some enthusiasm, that all my proposals and recommendations to the Board of Directors, concerning the scrapping of two sets of minutes, transparency, the invitation to all field staff to attend and contribute to Board meetings, the invitation to an outside body to examine and make recommendations concerning the finances and work of the society, had been approved, carried through and implemented. He personally thanked me on behalf of himself and fellow field staff for my recommendations and speaking up on their behalf, allowing them to contribute toward decision making. I was surprised at the news but encouraged.

What I have recorded was a sad episode in the history of the National Bible Society. It came about by one man's sin, that for too long was undetected. The event is now long past. The Bible Society today is in a healthy state. It is doing excellent work helping, with other national Bible Societies to provide Bibles in many countries. It deserves our whole hearted support.

Appendix 3

Israel

Both my father and mother, despite being missionaries in China, were always deeply interested in God's purposes for the Jewish people and believed that the day would come when God would restore his people to the Promised Land. Through them I also became deeply interested. My mother, despite knowing that God was calling her to be a missionary in China, during her days in college, tithed her income for mission work to the Jews. Father, over the years, was friends and kept in touch with the Revd Dr David W. Torrance and his son Dr Herbert Torrance who were medical missionaries in Tiberias. They were related and Father visited Herbert and the hospital in Tiberias on his final return to Scotland from China. I have known of the work in Tiberias all my life and the work that was being done both among Jews and Arabs.

My brother Tom published an article entitled "Salvation is of the Jews", in the Evangelical Quarterly 22 (1950) which I found helpful and which deepened my own understanding.

In 1969, I wrote an article entitled, "The Witness of the Jews to God", which was published in *Renewal* by the editor the Revd Tom Smail. Through that article I came to correspond with and meet Mrs Yohanna Ruth-Dobschiner (Hansie Douglas). She was a remarkable Christian Jewess who miraculously survived the Holocaust as told in her book *Selected to Live*. Hansie was married and lived in Glasgow. She was a godly woman of prayer whom God used to bring a remarkable number of Jews to faith in Jesus Christ.

VIA SUCOT

Following my meeting with Hansie and some discussion, Hansie organised a series of conferences for the next few years. She formed a small committee which came to include, apart from myself, the Revd Alistair Lamont, the Revd Howard Taylor, the Revd Kenneth Johnstone and a lawyer from Helensburgh. Alistair Lamont was the Convener of the commission appointed under the Overseas Council to study and report on both Israel and anti-Semitism.

The first two conferences were held in a hotel in Largs, in the West of Scotland. Interest increased and attendances grew so that for the next, I think, three years, the conferences were held in Crieff Hydro, and rose to 300. Alistair Lamont, Howard Taylor and myself became regular speakers and some of our addresses were published in booklet form by the Revd Jock Stein of the Handsel Press.

Under Hansie's guidance we named the organisation sponsoring these conferences VIA SUCOT, that is *Victory, Israel is Alive*, and *Sucot* the Hebrew word for covering.

People (including Jewish people) were converted and many became more deeply interested in and supportive of Israel and what God is doing through Israel for the redemption of the world. Gradually the organisation of these conferences became too much for Hansie who had carried the burden of organisation and regretfully the conferences at Crieff ceased. It was followed by a final smaller conference in Carberry Conference Centre in East Lothian.

During these conferences, money was raised through SUCOT to purchase an ambulance for medical work in Israel.

Hansie has passed on to be with the Lord. The work of Sucot however continues with a monthly breakfast and prayer meeting in Glasgow under the Revd Tom Houston, who for a period served as the Church of Scotland minister in St Andrews Church, Jerusalem.

The Church of Scotland

My brother Tom and I discussed many times the Church of Scotland's work in Israel and the Church's commission to witness to the Jewish people. We discussed what to say in the General Assembly concerning Israel and we both spoke many times on the subject.

In 1977 my brother Tom, when he was moderator of the General Assembly of the Church of Scotland, was invited to visit Israel by the President of Israel, who as a scientist, knew Tom through the International Academy of Science. Tom was welcomed in Israel on the ground that he represented the only country in Europe which had not persecuted the Jews.

On his return he submitted a report of that visit to the Overseas Council and moved in the General Assembly that the Overseas Council should consider the implications of Christian/Jewish Dialogue. In response the Overseas Council appointed a group consisting of the Revd Professor J.K.S. Reid, the Revd Professor George W. Anderson and the Revd Dr George F. Knight with Tom as chairman. They produced a report entitled, "Christian/ Jewish Dialogue: Report of the Overseas Council of the Church of Scotland". At its meeting on 18th March, 1980, the Overseas Council agreed to make the report available to commissioners of the General Assembly meeting in May 1980. That report was published in the book *The Witness of the Jews to God.*[1]

Also on Tom's recommendation the General Assembly in 1980 declared that it "would welcome the appointment of a scholar to participate in Christian/Jewish Dialogue in Israel" and approved "the policy of working

1 *The Witness of the Jews to God,* ed. D.W. Torrance, Handsel Press, 1982, appendix A (2) page 139f.

for reconciliation and understanding between Christian and Jew, and of opposing all forms of anti-Semitism".

Sadly, the decision to appoint a scholar was never implemented. After advertising for the post there was only one applicant, an Anglican from Oxford. That application was declined on the ground that in order to strengthen relations between the Church of Scotland and Jews, it was desirable that a member of the C. of S. be appointed. The secretary, the Revd Tom Kiltie asked if I would be willing to accept the appointment. Although I was deeply interested and supportive I declined on family grounds. There were no other applicants. Later, because of a change of position towards Israel on the part of the Overseas Council, no further action was taken.

In 1981, the following deliverance was moved by Tom and approved by the General Assembly: "Instruct the Overseas Council to initiate Christian Jewish consultations between the Church of Scotland and our Jewish brethren; and urge the World Alliance of Reformed Churches to prosecute Christian/ Jewish dialogue at a world level."

The first part of this decision was implemented in the initiating of dialogue with Orthodox Jews in Glasgow. This dialogue continued for ten years until it came to an unhappy ending which I will mention later.

The second part of the 1981 Deliverance was fulfilled in passing on the General Assembly's request to the World Alliance of Reformed Churches. In response to that request the Alliance set up the following committee of 8 people:

Dr Ellen Flesseman-van Leer, the Netherlands
Dr Lukas Visher, Bern, Switzerland
The Revd D.W. Torrance, Scotland
Dr C.S. Song
Professor Sigbert Axelson, Sweden
Professor Kenneth E. Bailey, Beirut, Lebanon
Mr Bertolan Tamas, Budapest, Hungary
Revd Dr Alan P.F. Sell, Switzerland

This conference took place in Switzerland. Dr Alan Sell, secretary to the Department of Theology of the World Alliance of Reformed Churches, chaired the committee. They met and produced a report in 1985 concerning those aspects of historical Reformed Theology which are pertinent to the relations of the Reformed Churches and the Jewish people. The report was entitled "Reformed Theology and the Jewish people", edited by Dr Sell.

Very surprisingly, despite urging from me, the Overseas Council never to my knowledge informed the General Assembly that their request to the World Alliance of Reformed Churches was adopted in so far as they created a small theological working group and produced a report. To my knowledge, that report was never mentioned nor brought before the General Assembly, an indication of a changing outlook towards Israel and the Jewish people on the part of the Council.

I personally do not believe that we can go back to the kind of evangelism of Jewish people that as a church we conducted over many years prior to World War II. Even so, I believe that we are commissioned as a Church to witness to Christ first to the Jewish people and then to the world.

In 1982, Tom brought to the notice of the General Assembly some quite obscene publications against Jews and Christians circulating in Scotland as a result of which the General Assembly agreed that a dossier on anti-Semitism be established in the Church Offices at 121 George Street, Edinburgh for consultation by members in the Kirk concerned in combating anti-Semitism. I was asked to assemble this material and handed over to the Middle East Committee of the Overseas Council a large collection, which included copies of the abominable Nazi cartoons by J. Streicher. A small amount of money was also set aside for the purpose and the Revd Tom Kiltie bought some books which could help people wanting to combat anti-Semitism.

Sadly, Tom Kiltie became ill and on health grounds retired as secretary to the Middle East Committee, and David Lyon, general secretary of the Overseas Council also retired. Subsequently, a very fine library concerning the Church and Jewish Missions, that was housed in the secretary's room, was given to the National Library of Scotland and the dossier on anti-Semitism, with the books purchased by Tom Kiltie, was lost or possibly given to the National Library. A change of approach and attitude to Israel and the Jewish people had begun.

Prayer and the Overseas Council

I believe a spiritual change came over the Overseas Council. For many years the Overseas Council, formerly the Foreign Mission Committee of the church could be regarded as the spiritual wing of the church. As a member of the Council (formerly Foreign Mission Committee) for twenty years, a member of the Executive Committee for eleven years and convener of the Personnel Committee (responsible for the appointment and pastoral care of missionaries) for eight years, I personally witnessed that change.

Around 1985 or 1986 (I do not remember the exact date) the Executive Committee, because of their concern for lack of finance, decided to hold a moratorium for one year and for one year to appoint no new missionaries. It was a time when we had over sixty vacancies, some of an urgent nature. I moved that before each meeting of the full Overseas Council, we should have half an hour of prayer. With my motion the room immediately disrupted in chaos. One well known minister turned to me and said, "What do you think of those of us who do not believe in this kind of thing?" The secretary, David Lyon quietened the meeting saying that he would attend to the issue.

Along with our minutes for the next full meeting of the Council, there was a brief statement saying that the chapel in 121 George Street, Edinburgh would be open for half an hour before the meeting for "quiet and reflection"! There was no mention of "prayer"! About five people turned up and with the second meeting the matter collapsed. Determined to pursue the matter fuller, when it was my turn as convener of the Personnel Committee to report to the Council, which at the time had over 100 members, I said, "We have taken the decision because of lack of money to appoint no new missionaries for a year, at a time when there are over 60 overseas vacancies. I would like to draw your attention to a minute of the Foreign Mission Committee meeting in Edinburgh in 1899 (or 1898?). According to that minute the Committee was so concerned because of lack of money and lack of candidates that they adjourned for two hours and spent two hours in prayer. I would also draw to your attention the minute at the end of that year, according to which it is stated that the year closed with all the money and all the candidates required. Can I ask what we learn from that minute?" There was considerable silence. No one spoke, and then we moved on to the next item of business!

The General Assembly of 1982, in addition to instructing that a dossier concerning anti-Semitism be created to guide the church, instructed the Overseas Council in co-operation with the Church and Nation Committee to "look into the forms anti-Semitism is taking in British society and the world". A group was appointed to undertake this study. This group embraced those involved in the Christian/Jewish Consultation group along with others. The Revd Alistair Lamont was appointed chairman. After an interim statement to the General Assembly in 1983 they produced for the General Assembly in 1985 a report entitled "Anti-Semitism in the World Today". I do not know whether that report in any way influenced the church or the Board itself in its future thinking.

In regard to the General Assembly of 1981 and the instruction to the Overseas Council to consult with representatives of the Jewish Community in Scotland, regular meetings took place for ten years. Unlike England where Orthodox and Reformed Jews seem to be fairly evenly divided, in Scotland the Orthodox predominate. There is only one Reformed synagogue in Scotland. Although at first it was suggested that meetings might take place four times a year, they were held monthly, with the Orthodox in Glasgow. On one occasion the rabbi of the Reformed synagogue met with the Church of Scotland representatives in Edinburgh. Two chairmen were appointed who chaired the meetings in Glasgow on successive months. These were Dr Henry Tankel, a consultant surgeon and chairman of the Jewish Welfare Council, and the Revd Alistair Lamont, chairman of the Israel Committee of the Church of Scotland. Tom Kiltie of the C. of S. was secretary.

A wide range of subjects was discussed with complete frankness and with growing mutual understanding, which led to the production of "The

Common Statement" (1985), which was presented to both communities. The following is what was discussed in the Dialogue Conversations:

Understanding Initial Conversations
a) Jewish Prayer
b) What constitutes being a Jew?
c) The organisation of the Glasgow Jewish Community
d) How does Halacha develop

Common Statement etc
a) Reports to the General Assemby
b) Comments on the Report – Henry Tankel
c) Reports on Holocaust Conference 14th February 1985
d) Dr Samai Davidson (Holocaust survivor)

Anti-Semitism
a) Anti-Semitism today - Walter Sneader 28-4-83
b) Anti-Semitism – a Christian viewpoint – David W. Torrance 5-10-83

Ethics
a) Jewish Medical Ethics – Henry Tankel 25-10-84
b) Comments on Human Transplants - Henry Tankel

Atonement
a) A Jewish View on Atonement - Henry Tankel 23-6-86
b) A Christian View of Atonement - James B. Walker 4-9-86

Law
a) A Christian Viewpoint - David W. Torrance 18-11-86
b) Jewish Law in the State of Israel – Daniel B. Sinclair 18-11-86

Political
a) The Zionist Cause – Henry Tankel
b) The Refugee Problem – Henry Tankel
c) End the Ecumenical Dialogue? – Henry Tankel 31-1-11

Theology
a) Covenant and Law - James B. Walker - May 1984
b) *Eretz Israel*: A Christian Perspective – Alistair G. Hunter -32-4-87
c) A Christian View of Jesus – David W. Torrance
d) A Jewish View of Jesus – Alexander Broadie
e) What do Christians Hope for? – Alistair Lamont
f) What do Jews Hope for? – Alexander Broadie
g) People, Land and Covenant – David W. Torrance
h) The Jewish Concept of Mission – Alexander Broadie
i) Faith and Land – Daniel B. Sinclair
j) Jesus and the Torah of the Kingdom – Alistair Lamont

General

a) Arthur with Grief – Arthur Shenkin
b) A Story – Kay Ramsay – 1990
c) The Pharisees – Stefan Relf
d) The Pharisees – Alexander Broadie
e) Religious Education in a Secular Society Margaret Allen & Diana Wolfson 12-11-87
f) Jewish Family Life: Patterns and Challenges – Kenneth Collins
g) Family Life: The Christian View – Anna Blair 9-2-88
h) The Trial and Death of Jesus – Henry Tankel February 1989
i) What we have Learned – David Lyon

In theological issues such as God's covenant with Israel and the atonement, despite our differences there was at times remarkable common ground and a shared faith. To my regret, the subjects discussed and the papers delivered were never printed and never came before the Overseas Council. Hence although those participating in dialogue grew in understanding, the dialogue and what was learned by participants had little or no effect on other members of the Overseas Council.

Following the General Assembly's instruction in 1981 and in order to assist the Church and its representatives in dialogue, the Overseas Council appointed a committee to consider relevant issues. Alistair Lamont was appointed chairman and Tom Kiltie the secretary. The committee, after long discussions came to remarkable agreement on several crucial theological issues and in 1985 produced the report, entitled "Christians and Jews Today". This came before the Overseas Council and was presented to the General Assembly of the Church of Scotland that year.

The report was sent out to all Presbyteries with a questionnaire. Twenty-one of the forty-six presbyteries replied. Fifteen generally welcomed the Report. Two made no comments. One stated it was too academic, and two were highly critical.

Messianic Congregations in Israel

Tom, Howard Taylor and I at different times spoke in the General Assembly asking that the Overseas Council should produce a report on Messianic congregations in Israel. After the matter was brushed aside by the Overseas Council agreement was finally reached and the Revd Paraic Reamonn (then minister of Cockburnspath, linked with Innerwick and Oldhamstocks) was asked to convene a sub-committee to produce the report. It is a sad indictment that after the long years in which the C of S had worked among Jewish people and in Israel, the committee appointed had no idea where to begin their investigation. I was approached and supplied considerable information and put the committee in touch with Dr Arthur

Glasser, dean of the Faculty of Mission in Fuller Seminary, Pasadena, LA, California. The latter was very helpful and a report was produced.

For a long period there were no Messianic congregations in Israel. By 1973 there were five. At the time that the report was produced there were probably about 30 congregations and fellowships. Today they number over 100 and continue to grow. The Report was presented to the General Assembly, but beyond that, without encouragement from the Overseas Council, it had little or no influence.

Arab Christian Conference

The Revd Alistair Hulbert, with encouragement and approval of the Board, arranged an Arab Christian conference in Dunblane, 8-12 June, 1987. Six Arab pastors were invited. They were chiefly Melkite or Greek Catholic (owing allegiance to the Pope), Syrian and (I think) Arab Episcopal. It would have been helpful to have had present representatives of the Orthodox and Coptic Churches which are more representative and have a different attitude to the Old Testament. (A Greek Catholic bishop in Jerusalem was arrested for gun-running!)

The Jewish members who participated in dialogue were concerned about the growing critical attitude of members of the Board and asked me to go on their behalf, offering to pay my expenses for the conference. I had not intended going and said to Mrs Judith Tankel, who was then chair of the Jewish Welfare Council that I was a Christian, they were Jews and consequently we were not in agreement. She replied that they knew that but looked on me as a friend, wanted me to go on their behalf and reiterated that they wished to pay my expenses in going to the conference. I agreed in the end to attend the conference but declined their kind offer to pay my expenses. I said that I could only represent myself. I found the conference difficult. There was a group of women, including the wife of the assistant secretary of the Board, Robin Ross, who were pacifist (almost militantly so and intolerant of any view other than their own!), unsympathetic to Israel, and strongly pro-Palestinian.

The six Arab pastors each said that they would never read the Old Testament in church while four said they would never read the Old Testament even in private. Elias Chacour, author of *Blood Brothers,* said that he personally would read parts of the Old Testament for devotional purposes but there was need for great discrimination in the use of the Old Testament. I challenged him in private and said that without the Old Testament we could not understand Paul who made liberal use of the Old Testament. Also we could not understand Jesus Christ who frequently quoted the Old Testament. I said that as a result the gospel which he endeavoured to proclaim was reduced to the Sermon on the Mount, and most of that was in the Old Testament.

I reported my assessment of the conference to the Jewish representatives in dialogue and they thanked me. Some time later Elizabeth and I were invited to a civic reception given by Glasgow Council to the Jewish Community, who had invited as a guest speaker their Chief Rabbi from London. The Jews intimated a recent publication of the history and establishment of a Jewish Community in Scotland. In presenting it to the Glasgow Council they intimated that they also wanted to give a copy of the book to a friend. To my surprise they kindly gave me a copy. Inside the book was an envelope with a cheque, which amounted to the amount of my expenses in attending the conference in Dunblane! There was no note with the cheque and no mention of why they had given it to me. I did not feel free to mention this to my colleagues in the Church of Scotland.

The Five Groups

Shortly following the appointment of a new general secretary of the Overseas Council, five groups were created to consider different issues concerning Israel and anti-Semitism. The Revd David Lyon, the former secretary of the Overseas Council was appointed as secretary of all five groups. Sadly, Tom Kiltie, the assistant general secretary of the Overseas Council, had not been well and was forced to take early retirement. He had been very sympathetic to Israel. His absence was a loss.

The suggested topics for the five groups were –

Supersessionism
Mission
The Holocaust
The Land
God in History

I was appointed to the group to consider 'The Land of Israel'. I believe at least one representative of the Glasgow Jewish Representative Council was appointed to each group. I certainly found that those who were in the group considering 'Land' differed theologically, so that it was difficult to come to any kind of agreement. I was invited to present a paper on 'Land' as a basis for discussion. After presenting it, I was immediately challenged by the Revd Alistair Hulbert who said that I had rubbished the issue! When I replied with a quotation from the Old Testament, he immediately said that through his friendships with the Palestinians he had given up reading the Old Testament. He did not read it! It is difficult to have a meaningful discussion, far less come to a common theological agreement in such a group.

The group on 'anti-Semitism' did make considerable progress and were drawing near to their report when suddenly without explanation, prior warning, or consultation with the Jewish members involved, all five groups were suddenly cancelled. No explanation was given. Whether this was a decision by the Executive of the Overseas Council I do not know. I rather think that it was a decision by the secretary who did not seem sympathetic to the views concerning Israel that had previously been expressed. The sudden cancellation of all the groups greatly upset the Very Revd Robert Craig, who was a member of the group considering 'Anti-Semitism'. He expressed his disquiet in the General Assembly, asking me to support him. It was to no avail.

The End of Jewish/Christian Dialogue

The growing feelings of support for Palestinians and the feeling that they were suffering as a result of unjust Jewish actions began to undermine the Board's attitude to Israel, which in turn began to affect our relationships with the Jewish community in Scotland. On 25th February, 1991 Dr Henry Tankel, Vice-President of the Jewish Council in Glasgow and Joint Chairman of the Jewish/Christian Consultation Group, wrote to the Revd J.L. Weatherhead, principal clerk to the General Assembly of the Church of Scotland. In his letter he wrote,

> It therefore came as shock to find in 'Openline' of January 1991 which bills itself as 'A forum of News from around the World' and is published by the Department of World Mission and Unity, an article entitled 'Elegy for a Woman of Constant Sorrow'. This article does not miss a single opportunity to question the legitimacy of the State of Israel. Britain is accused of violating the League of Nations Covenant by promoting a Jewish National Home, the United Nations is accused of exceeding its legal powers in voting to partition Palestine, and so on, although both these accusations are false. Another statement carries the implication that a young man has been unjustly treated in receiving a prison sentence for putting a bomb in a Jewish restaurant presumably in order to kill or maim innocent civilians.
>
> Furthermore, it is symptomatic of a changing attitude to our dialogue of which you have become aware. You therefore leave us with no alternative but to suspend our joint consultations in protest while we await a satisfactory response to this letter. In suspending these consultations, we wish to place clearly on record that we have no quarrel with the Church of Scotland as such, or with its members, only with the action of the Department of World Mission and Unity. We also wish to reiterate our respect and admiration for the members of the original Joint Consultation who are still with us, whose company we have enjoyed and whose friendship we value greatly. We would be happy to continue our dialogue in the future, provided we could be assured that its original basis would be maintained.

Sadly, dialogue with our Jewish brethren ceased. Difficulties have remained and continue to this day between those representing the Church of Scotland and the Jewish Community.

Christian Aid: the Palestinians

Another issue which deeply troubled the Jewish Community at this time was the attitude of Christian Aid. The general secretary of the Board of World Mission was also chairman of the Middle East Committee of Christian Aid.

Christian Aid produced a four-page leaflet entitled "The Palestinians in the Occupied Territories of the West Bank and Gaza". Some of us felt that it was strongly politically motivated and in what it said presented an unbalanced and factually inaccurate picture. Both Henry Tankel and I wrote letters of concern, which were published. In addition I spoke to the general secretary in his office pointing out I believe six inaccuracies and exaggerations. He listened and seemed unable to contradict anything which I said. His only comment was that what was stated "is an exaggeration, but we wished to make a point"! I was disturbed and shocked by his reply and unwillingness to rescind anything. I said that exaggeration is a lie and has no place in anything that the church or a Christian organisation does. At that I left. The Board continued for several years to use the publication and include it in church book stalls.

The Arab Episcopal Church

With the encouragement of his boss, Robin Ross, as assistant secretary and secretary for the Middle East, arranged a partnership between the Church of Scotland and the Arab Episcopal Church with its headquarters in Jerusalem, arguing that it was 'a bridgehead' between Christians, Arabs and Jews. This disturbed my brother and me and both of us protested. Tom wrote a letter to the Board saying that it had acted in an uneven-handed way, bypassing the Christian Jewish congregations and allying itself with the Arab Episcopal Church that refuses to acknowledge the Old Testament as Holy Scripture and is bent on what it calls 'the Palestinianisation of Jesus'. How could their action be a 'bridgehead' when Christian Jews were not being contacted nor consulted?

Undoubtedly, our alliance with the Arab Episcopal Church, which some have claimed to be the most politically-minded of all Middle East Churches, has deeply influenced the thinking and attitude in many in our committees and church. It has helped many within the church to understand the issues confronting Israel and the Palestinians as solely political, arguing that what we are concerned with is 'justice'. Theological considerations have no weight.

Gulf War 1991

During the Gulf War and the threat against Israel, the Board temporarily but for some months closed the hospice in Jerusalem and withdrew our staff. An Arab was given custody of the key of the hospice.

I was deeply concerned about the closure, because in the Arab/Jewish War in an earlier period, when the Hospital was closed Jewish squatters moved in to the Hospital and Dr Bernard Walker who had been appointed to succeed Dr Herbert Torrance, had much difficulty in regaining full possession of our buildings. The Board withdrew our staff, fearing for their safety.

Although I understood the Board's decision, I was concerned about the witness of the Church of Scotland to Israelis in a time of uncertainty and possible danger. I was also concerned about our keeping possession of the buildings and not losing them to possible squatters. Accordingly I wrote to the Board and said that if they would supply a temporary locum for my parish of Earlston, I would gladly go to Tiberias to take charge until the war ended. My offer was not accepted.

I later listened to a recorded statement of an Israeli Messianic Jew living in Israel who criticised the Church of Scotland as a Christian Church for running away and failing to present a Christian witness in the face of danger. I felt our Church once again was not prioritising our Christian witness in Israel and the winning of Jews for Christ.

Lausanne Consultation on Jewish Evangelism (LCJE)

As a member of LCJE I was invited as a guest speaker to the International Conference of LCJE in All Nations College, London in 1992. Some 160 people attended the conference from different countries but chiefly from the USA and Israel. Approximately half those attending were Jewish. I was also invited to speak at subsequent regional (European) conferences at Amsterdam, Holland, 2-4 March 1987, and Copenhagen, (Denmark), 29 Sept-1 Oct 1988. Despite the growing lack of sympathy for Israel and lack of interest and support for Jewish mission, I was, following my request, given expenses from the Board of World Mission and Unity, to attend these conferences. I was not however invited to report to the Board or its Middle East Committee and felt a considerable lack of interest on the part of the secretary and the Board and a distinct lack of concern for evangelism.

A Nazi Cartoon

In August 1992, a Nazi cartoon, drawn by Julius Streicher and published in the Nazi paper *Der Sturmer*, of a Jew and some bedraggled peasants was printed in the Life and Work magazine of the church. When my attention was drawn to it, having earlier compiled a dossier of anti-Semitic literature for the church's guidance, I recognised it as a Nazi cartoon and was shocked and scandalized over its publication. I phoned the church offices and made my views clear. The immediate response was a refusal on the part of the general secretary and others to accept that it was a Nazi cartoon, saying that they acquired it from a Christian pack published by the church in Bolivia and were simply stressing the need for justice for the poor.

The Jewish community in Glasgow was deeply distressed and correspondence took place between them and the secretary of the Overseas Council. The latter, and also Christian Aid, were unwilling to acknowledge that it was anti-Semitic, although the following year Christian Aid altered the cartoon by withdrawing the face of a Jew. The Council secretary, in a letter dated 23rd October 1992, expressed regret over any offence given and made a "promise to take steps to ensure that any future use of the cartoon or others on the same topic will remove any possible grounds for complaint on the grounds of an implied anti-Semitism"! The Jewish Community felt that there was a lack of awareness of the sensitivities of Jewish people on the part of the Board of World Mission and Unity (formerly Overseas Council) and felt unable to accept the apology or responses given.

In order to try and persuade the Board about the origins of the cartoon, I asked the Board to consult the dossier on anti-Semitism, which contained a copy of "Der Sturmer" and of the same Nazi cartoon. I did not realise at that time the Board no longer possessed that dossier!

Tom wrote to the Board, to Life and Work and also to the Scotsman Newspaper. I also wrote to the Scotsman newspaper. We both asked the Board to withdraw the cartoon and publicly apologise for using it.

Both I and my brother-in-law Dr Bobby Walker raised the matter publicly in our respective Presbyteries of Melrose and Peebles, and Edinburgh, calling on the Board to withdraw the cartoon and to apologise for its use. As a result, in a letter addressed to Mr E.J. Borowski, hon. secretary of the Glasgow Jewish Representative Council, the Revd Margaret R. Forrester, Convener of the Board of World Mission and Unity, wrote:

> 1 "We apologise for having used the cartoon which has now been permanently withdrawn.
>
> 2 "We are distressed by the hurt that has been caused. For us this has been a learning experience and we see the need for healing.
>
> 3 "Representatives of our Executive would be happy to meet with representatives of yours as soon as possible.
>
> We look forward to your response in the hope that friendly relationships may be restored".

A meeting between representatives of the Jewish Community and the Executive of the Board took place on 1st December 1992. Members of the Executive, although they had been forced to withdraw the cartoon and apologise, were slow and unwilling to acknowledge that it was a Nazi cartoon drawn by Julius Streicher and published in "Der Sturmer". It was a difficult meeting. The Jewish representatives brought a copy of "Der Sturmer" containing the cartoon demonstrating that it was a Nazi invention, to the Board's embarrassment and humiliation.

Sadly, the attitude of the Board did great damage and undermined the good will built up between the Jewish community and the church. The Jewish representatives felt, throughout the whole episode, that the church had been unwilling and slow to listen and lacked sensitivity to Jewish feelings.

Tiberias and Messianic Jews

For many years, commencing in the year 1840 when the Church agreed to work among Jews in Budapest, Hungary, and up to World War II, the Church of Scotland had the largest missionary outreach to the Jews of any church or mission. Sadly today, despite having a church in Jerusalem and a church in Tiberias, and a school in Tabeetha, Jaffa, the Church of Scotland does little or nothing to take the gospel to the Jews. It has not manifested any real concern about Jews in Israel coming to faith in Christ or the rise of Messianic congregations in Israel. Although the Revd Paul Re'emi (a Jewish believer, converted through the ministry of our minister in Jerusalem, the Revd Gardner Scot) and his wife Clarla started a Messianic Fellowship in Tiberias when Paul was the Church of Scotland minister there, the Overseas Council and its representatives have taken little or no interest in that community.

There are today two Messianic Fellowships or churches in Tiberias. The larger is Peniel, under the Pastor Daniel Ya'hav. Several hundred are members. The smaller is Morning Star with its Jewish pastor, the Revd Claude Ezagouri. Their membership is a little over 100. For many years both fellowships worshipped in the open air, although Peniel was allowed to worship in an Arab church several miles away when it was raining. Both now own their own buildings in which to worship.

Prior to that, for I believe over two years the Overseas Council debated whether to allow Morning Star to worship in our church in Tiberias. Because they could not come to a decision, I arranged with my brother-in-law Bobby Walker that he move publicly in the Presbytery of Edinburgh calling on the Israel Committee of the C. of S. to invite the Morning Star congregation to worship in our church In Tiberias. I moved in the Presbytery of Melrose and Peebles, of which I was a member, that the Presbytery do the same. Because both Presbyteries called publicly on the Committee with the same request, Morning Star was given permission by the Board to worship in the C. of S. church in Tiberias. I expressed the opinion that the Overseas Council, to my knowledge, had never acted with such hesitation, or lack of sympathy and understanding, toward any other overseas church.

The history of Morning Star's relationship with the minister in Tiberias however was not a happy one. Their presence and use of the church seem to be tolerated but not welcomed and not encouraged. On a number of occasions Claude Ezagouri was rebuked by the minister about the behaviour of children, noise and the apparent inconvenience of their presence.

Because probably all the pogroms of Eastern Europe took place on the occasion of Christian holidays such as Christmas, Good Friday, Easter and Pentecost and were carried out under the sign of the cross, Jewish believers in their evangelism do not exhibit the cross, although they proclaim the message of the cross. Accordingly in their services and in their efforts to attract non-believing Jews, the Morning Star congregation took down the cross, which hung on the wall of the church, replacing it when the service was over. Also in order to accommodate the number of Jews attending their services they temporarily removed the communion table. Matters came to a head when, on one occasion they forgot to put back the cross and also the communion table. Thereon the minister screwed the cross into the wall so that Morning Star could no longer take it down for their services. He also summoned Claude Ezagouri and said that Morning Star was being given a month's notice to leave the building. Claude contacted me because as a congregation at that time they had nowhere else to go. I contacted the secretary of the Board of World Mission and Unity, the Revd Dr Kenneth Ross and informed him of the situation. As a result Morning Star was allowed to continue using our building.

At a later stage Claude Ezagouri contacted me having heard that the Church of Scotland was advertising the sale of the church building, although he had not been officially informed and at the time the congregation had nowhere else to worship. I again contacted the Secretary of the Board, Kenneth Ross. He arranged that I meet with him along with the Convener of the Board and Mr Walter Dunlop, Associate Secretary, Israel/Palestine and Local Supported Partnerships. I expressed to them my grave disquiet about the action of the minister in Tiberias over the years, in that he seemed to wish to deny the use of our building in Tiberias to the Morning Star. I went on and stated a number of things. Our attitude as a church toward Jewish Christians differed from our attitude to all other Christians in the Third World. We were doing nothing to take the gospel to the Jewish people, which I linked to the near collapse of overseas missions on the part of the Church of Scotland. They informed me that at the time we had only 15 people serving overseas, whereas formerly we had several hundred. I suggested that the collapse was a sign that as a Church we were out of step with God!

We met in September and I said that in the previous General Assembly, the Convener commenced his report to the General Assembly with our concern that the gospel was for the poor. This had been the hallmark in the reports of successive conveners, for the last ten to fifteen years. Yet, despite this we concentrated in Israel to building a five-star holiday hotel for the wealthy! On their remonstrating that the aim of the hotel was reconciliation between Jews and Arabs. I replied that 40 per cent of the population in Israel, namely Arabs, were below the poverty line, and could not afford to stay in the hotel! I suggested that single Messianic congregations in Israel were doing more towards reconciliation in that Arabs were worshipping with Jews in probably the majority of Messianic congregations in Israel. They listened and were gracious to me but I think our conversation accomplished nothing beyond Morning Star being given permission to continue to use our building until such a time that it was sold. They said that they planned to build a new church and after it was built the congregation would be allowed to use it. They had no plans apparently or suggestions of what Morning Star should do between selling the church building and building a new one.

For a number of years, with the emphasis on the issue of human rights for the Palestinians, there has been a lack of understanding and sympathy for Israel. There has been a lack of concern in taking the gospel to the Jewish people, and a lack of understanding in how best to witness to Christ before Jews, who in their long history had suffered under Christian anti-Semitism. Today Morning Star has acquired their own premises in which to worship and to engage in outreach among the young, in which they have been very active.

Tiberias Hotel

In 1979 I received a letter from Fuller Seminary in Pasadena, Los Angeles, asking if the Seminary could co-operate with the C of S in Israel. They explained that the Church of Scotland was the only Reformed presence in Israel, hence their request to work with us. Fuller is the largest Protestant Theological Seminary in the USA and over the years has trained a number of Messianic pastors, several of whom work in Israel. Over the next ten years I received three (or possibly four) such requests. To me the request was exciting. The C of S hospital in Tiberias, after closing as a hospital, had become a hospice for visitors to Israel and for others in Israel who chose to holiday there. I welcomed the thought of turning our hospice into a Bible College for Jews, Arabs, and American and Scottish students. I believed that it would be marvellous to give our candidates for the ministry in Scotland the opportunity to study for a period in Israel.

On each occasion the Committee declined the invitation to work with Fuller on the ground that the C of S does not work with colleges! The Committee of the Overseas Council (later Board of World Mission) did not inform the General Assembly about their decision, even when instructed to do so.

In my judgement we lost a wonderful opportunity to help forward the gospel in Israel, to strengthen ecumenical relationships and to help our own Church.

Because the Overseas Council declined the invitation, following the year 1979, Fuller Seminary gave money to help create the Bible College in Bethlehem for Arabs, and for Jews they founded the theological journal *Mishkan*, which is published in Jerusalem. For the first few years I was a consultant editor.

When it became necessary to upgrade the Hospice in Tiberias, the Revd Ian Paton, who had been appointed to be minister in St Andrews, Jerusalem, was asked in 1997 to conduct a feasibility study about the future use of our Hospice in Tiberias. In so doing, he asked me what Fuller Seminary's present position was. When I told him that I did not know he said that the committee commissioned me to find out. I contacted Fuller Seminary and spoke to Dr Arthur Glasser, who had retired as dean of the Faculty of Mission but was still professor in charge of Judaic studies. I told him that I was commissioned to enquire whether Fuller Seminary was still interested in co-operating with the Church of Scotland and whether they would be interested in helping to support a theological/Bible college in Tiberias for Jewish and Arab students, along with Scottish and American students. He was cautious in his first response and asked me what was the theological position of the Church of Scotland! I could only reply that there were in the Church of Scotland people of various theological perspectives. However he told me that he would take the matter to their Senate Meeting and that they would give the matter serious consideration.

In the meantime, knowing that Fuller, in the creation of a college, would wish plans to be carried out on an academic level and would not wish simply to co-operate with a committee, I took the initiative and contacted St Mary's College, St Andrews, believing that they would be the most helpful and theologically conservative of our four colleges in Scotland. I explained our contact with Fuller Seminary and my own vision of a college in Tiberias and asked whether they would be willing to co-operate with Fuller in creating such a theological/Bible College in Tiberias. I suggested that if the proposal materialised, it would be necessary, in order to maintain academic standards, that one or two members of St Mary's staff, should be prepared to stay in Tiberias for six months or a year at a time.

I was listened to with sympathy and interest. I was later informed that the Senate of St Mary's were happy to agree to the proposal in principle. After three months, I received word from Fuller Seminary that regretfully they were not in a position financially at this juncture to engage on the project. There had been a collapse in the Asian economy. Approximately two thirds of their students were from Asia and as a result had lost their scholarships and financial support. In the circumstances Fuller Seminary generously agreed to underwrite them all financially and therefore were not able at that time to undertake any further financial commitments. I informed St Mary's College and was told that they were still happy in principle to proceed with the proposal. However, the proposal was not followed up and the Board decided to create instead a five-star hotel. The argument for this decision was that the Church of Scotland was in a unique position to create a place where Jews and Arabs could come together in a relaxed way and that the hotel would become a centre for reconciliation between Jews and Arabs.

I found the decision of the Board very disappointing. I believe that the Church is not in a position to run hotels! I believe that our earlier refusal to co-operate with Fuller Seminary when they were in a position and willing to do so was a tragic error of judgement. It would have been a glorious opportunity to advance the cause of Christ among Jews and Arabs.

Jewish Mission Funds

For years the Jewish Missionary secretary, Mr Macana, used to boast that the Jewish Mission Committee never asked for money. This was because members of the church, in their interest in Jewish missions, gave generously and the committee received many legacies. After, I think, 1960, the work of all overseas Missions, which included Jewish Mission work, was handled by the Foreign Mission Committee, later known as the Overseas Council and then the Board of World Mission and Unity. The work of overseas mission was redefined and I believe the assets of all overseas work was controlled by the Board.

On a number of occasions I asked the Board, and also asked within the meetings of the General Assembly, what had happened to monies which has been especially designated for Jewish Missions. This was for some time, brushed aside until finally I assured the General Assembly that in asking the question, I was seeking a moratorium on any past expenditure of Jewish Mission funds. I was not raising the issue of possible, unthinking mistaken misuse of Jewish funds. I received support within the General Assembly from the Church Treasurer, Mr Donald F Ross. I found Mr Ross very helpful. After some research it was reported that there was £778,328, of which £350,245 was restricted for work with orphans, education, Mission to Jews in Holland, etc. That which was not restricted was at the disposal of the Board, who I believe put it toward the creation of the hotel in Tiberias. I did not pursue the matter further, which would have been very difficult. Personally, I have wondered if some of the Jewish Mission funds, despite their original designation by the donors, and because the church no longer engaged on Jewish Mission work, was unthinkingly absorbed into other overseas mission work.

The collapse of Jewish Mission work on the part of the Church of Scotland, should be, I believe, a matter of deep concern. I believe it has led to the collapse, very nearly, of all our church's overseas mission work. We are commanded by God to take the gospel to the Jew first and then to the Gentiles – on the ground that when the Jews come to faith in Christ there will be a forward advance in world mission (Romans 15:11). As a church we have stressed political considerations and seem largely to have lost the vision of seeking to make disciples of all nations and to evangelise the whole world.